50+ Real W[illegible] Applications of Blockchain

Blockchain fundamentals, consensus mechanisms, smart contracts, Web 3, dApps, IPFS, scaling solutions, NFTs, Metaverse, and more

Aman Gupta

Roohi Bansal, PhD

About the authors

Aman Gupta graduated from Indian Institute of Technology (IIT) in the field of UX Design and holds an MBA degree in marketing. Among many of the things he loves - Blockchain tops the list! He strongly believes that we are standing on the brink of a massive technology disruption with Blockchain leading the way. So you better be on this boat!

Roohi Bansal holds PhD in Biotechnology and has taught more than 11000 students. She has authored 2 other books and various scientific papers. Her love for technology inspired her to learn about Blockchain technology and how it works in the real world. She is always motivated to simplify technical terms in a very simple and easy to understand language.

No previous knowledge or background in computer science, mathematics, programming, or cryptography is required. Throughout the book, technical terms, concepts, and jargons are explained in a simple way using graphics, analogies, and metaphors so that anyone can understand them easily.

Some say Blockchain is just a hype while others say it is the most important invention since the internet. After reading this book, you will be in a better state to decide whether Blockchain is a hype or a revolution?

Follow us on Medium for more information on Blockchain Technology: *https://medium.com/@techskillbrew*

You can also write us on techskillbrew@gmail.com for any queries.

Contents

Section 1: Blockchain Basics

Section 8: Tokenization and Blockchain

Section 9: Non-Fungible Tokens or NFTs

Section 1
Blockchain Basics

Chapter 1: Introduction to the Blockchain

We, as individuals and businesses, interact with a lot of other businesses and service providers online and offline on a daily basis. We buy clothes online, import medicines from different parts of the world, and use remote financial and banking services. In such a scenario, where everything is available at your fingertips except the trust for the other party, how do you validate the authenticity of the clothes that you got online, or how do you know that the medicines you imported are genuine and not some cheap counterfeit or how do you know that your financial and personal data is safe and is not getting misused by some hacker sitting in some part of the world. There has always been a dire need for a system that can assure us that whatever we are buying is authentic; whatever data we are sharing is safe and secure. There has always been a need for a system that is reliable and robust so that trust is no longer a barrier for businesses and individuals to get things done.

The solution to all of these pain points lies in **Blockchain Technology**. You might be familiar with cryptocurrencies like Bitcoin, Ether, Ripple, etc., and Blockchain is the technology that powers them all. *(Fig 1-1)*.

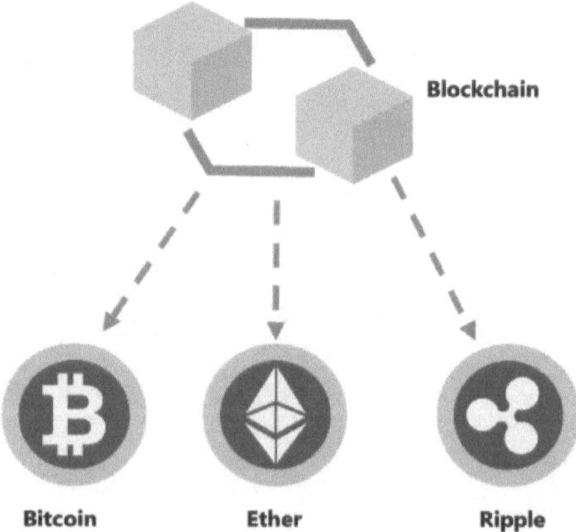

Fig 1-1: Cryptocurrencies are powered by Blockchain technology

Blockchain has gained a lot of popularity recently. It has been claimed to be a game-changer and has been even referred to as the internet of value by many industry experts. The invention of Blockchain technology can be compared to the invention of the wheel, motor, and internet, that changed the world. It has been predicted that Blockchain technology will rule the next decade.

1.1. What is Blockchain?

Blockchain is a tamper-proof distributed digital ledger. This digital ledger is safe, secure, transparent, and decentralized, which simply means that it is not controlled by a single authority *(Fig 1-2)*. It is like a ledger that a bank uses to keep track of all customer transactions. However, in a bank, the ledger is controlled by the bank, and only the bank can see the transactions. Whereas in Blockchain, there is no central authority, and the ledger runs on multiple computers and doesn't require any single person to authenticate or settle transactions.

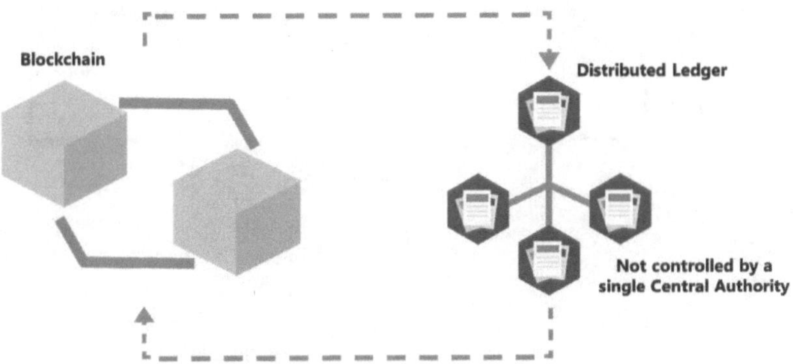

Fig 1-2: Blockchain is a distributed digital ledger

Let's try to understand how Blockchain works through a real-life analogy. For this analogy, we are going to take the example of Google Sheets on Google Drive. While Google Sheets is not technically a Blockchain, it's a pretty accurate analogy to how Blockchain works.

- When someone creates a spreadsheet on Google Drive, they can share it with multiple people *(Fig 1-3)*. In our analogy, this spreadsheet can be compared to a Blockchain.

- The spreadsheet is generally shared over a large network of computers when shared with multiple people. The computers having a copy of the spreadsheet are referred to as **nodes** in the Blockchain world.
- Every node on the network has access to the same spreadsheet. Whenever someone edits or modifies the spreadsheet, it gets updated automatically on every computer on the network. Thus, the spreadsheet is updated in real-time, and a single version of the spreadsheet is always visible to everyone on the network.

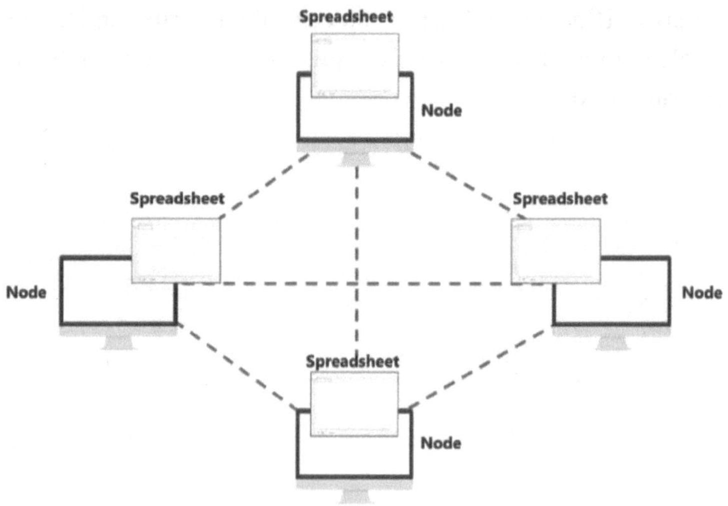

Fig 1-3: A spreadsheet is shared with multiple computers on the network

On the contrary, if you put data on an Excel sheet on your computer, it is just one file that has to be shared with other people on the network by emailing them. If one makes some modifications in the Excel sheet, the modified file has to be saved and emailed to other recipients. Sometimes, many versions of a single Excel sheet are created, and it is quite possible to lose track of the most recent versions of the document and wind up updating old versions of the Excel sheet.

Also, when the records or files are present on one central computer, they can easily be **hacked and manipulated**.

On Blockchain, like Google Sheets, there will be multiple copies of the digital document, and each node/user on the network will have a copy and access to the same exact document. Therefore, it is not possible to tamper with them. Additionally, before any change can be made in the documents, the majority of the users have to agree to it. It puts the control in the hands of all the users instead of one central database that can be changed anytime by anyone with proper access.

Also, Blockchain technology is secured through cryptography, thus making it nearly impossible for hackers to hack it and tamper with the data inside it.

1.2. Properties of Blockchain

There are certain features and properties of Blockchain that makes it suitable for such a wide array of industries:

1.2.1. Decentralized

Decentralization is one of the most critical components of Blockchain. It has even been viewed as a revolutionary technology that will decentralize the web. Decentralization refers to the transfer of control from a centralized entity (individual, organization, or group) to a distributed network *(Fig 1-4)*.

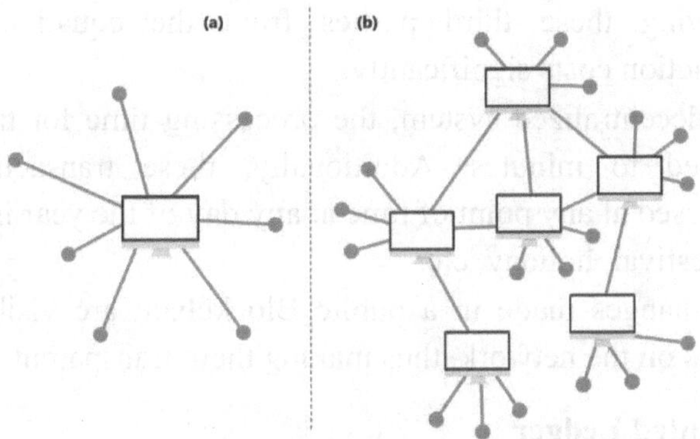

Fig 1-4: (a) Centralized and (b) Decentralized network

Decentralization gives you the power to store your valuable assets like your data, money, and documents in a network that can then be easily accessed from anywhere in the world over the internet. Through this decentralized technology, a user has direct control over his asset via his private key.

A user can also easily transfer his asset to anyone at any point of time from anywhere in the world. This feature of decentralization eliminates the need to rely on any third party or middlemen for these transactions. Thus, cutting down the high transaction fees charged by third-party service providers. For instance, when you transfer a sum of money to your friend, you have to rely on a bank to perform this task. But with Blockchain, you can do these transactions without the involvement of any third party.

The main rationale behind this concept is to place your trust in the network rather than in a single centralized body like a bank or a government.

The benefits of a decentralized system are as follows:

- A decentralized system shifts the power back to the users as they are the ones controlling all of their data and transactions.
- A decentralized system is complicated to hack and is not prone to failure. As there is no central point in such a system, it can better survive a malicious cyberattack and accidental failures.
- As the data doesn't reside with a third party, this eliminates the possibility of data tampering and misuse of the data. Further removing these third parties from the equation lowers the transaction costs significantly.
- In a decentralized system, the processing time for transactions is reduced to minutes. Additionally, these transactions can be processed at any point of time at any day of the year irrespective of any festival, holiday, etc.
- The changes made in a public Blockchain are visible to all the parties on the network, thus making them transparent.

1.2.2. Distributed Ledger

Distributed Ledger is the second critical feature that makes a Blockchain so powerful and effective. The word distributed ledger is composed of two terms - Distributed and Ledger. Ledger, as the name suggests, is the record of all transactions, and distributed means that the ledger is shared with every node on the same network. The distributed ledger contains the record of each and every transaction that took place over the network.

And every node of the network has access to a copy of this updated ledger *(Fig 1-5)*. Any updates or changes in the ledger are reflected in almost real-time in all the copies of the ledger across the network.

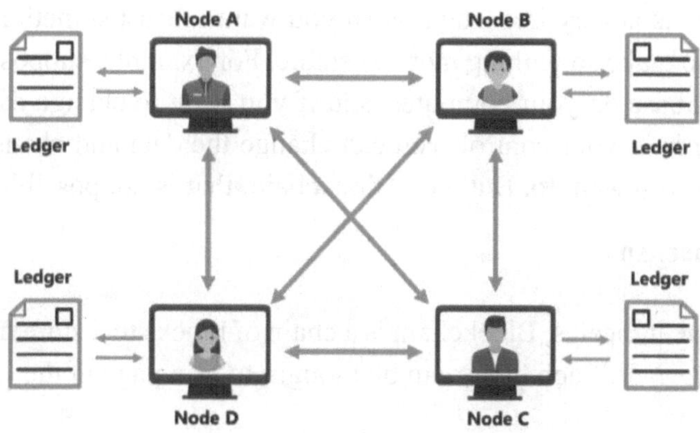

Fig 1-5: Distributed ledger

Some of the key advantages of such a distributed system for the stakeholders involved are as follows:

- A distributed system makes it easier to track the movement of goods as the same ledger is shared across all the users on the network. This is one of the main reasons why many big companies have started integrating Blockchain Technology into their supply chain.

- All the transactions are recorded on one single ledger, making it easier to manage, view, refer to, and verify the transactions. In simple terms, it reduces the complexity involved in managing multiple ledgers.

1.2.3. Immutability

Immutability is another critical component of Blockchain. Immutability means something that can't be changed or altered. Once the data has been recorded inside a Blockchain, it becomes nearly impossible to change it, thus making it tamper-proof and immutable. To better understand the concept of immutability, let us take the example of an email. Once you share a document in an email with a group of your friends, you can not take it back. The only way to do this is to ask all of your friends to delete that email which is quite difficult. This is exactly how immutability works in the Blockchain network. This is very important when you want to trust something or when you want to make something more trustable. For example, suppose you have built a database on your computer, and if you want to change data because everything is in your control, you can change the data and change the data in any way you want to. But with Blockchain, that is not possible.

1.2.4. Consensus

As the name indicates, Blockchain is a chain of blocks that store transactions or data *(Fig 1-6)*. Each block can be thought of as a page in the ledger.

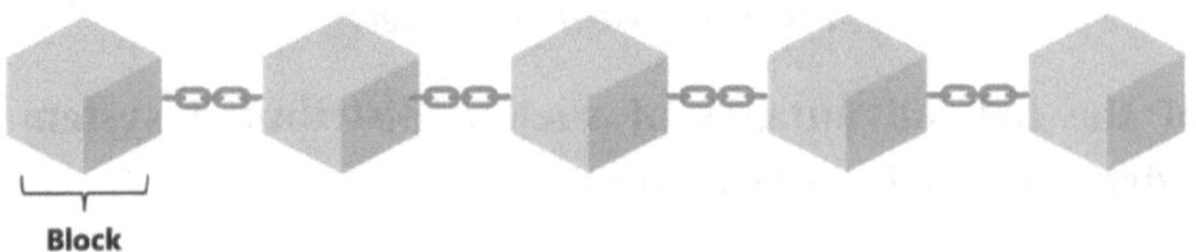

Fig 1-6: Chronologically linked blocks in Blockchain

A new block is created after a certain number of transactions containing all the relevant information. The block is then sent to each node which verifies the block. And once the verification is done, the block gets added to the Blockchain *(Fig 1-7)*. This verification and validation of blocks by the participating nodes is called consensus.

Without consent from the majority of nodes, any transaction block can not be added to the ledger. And once the transaction block gets added to the ledger, any user on the network won't be able to edit or delete it.

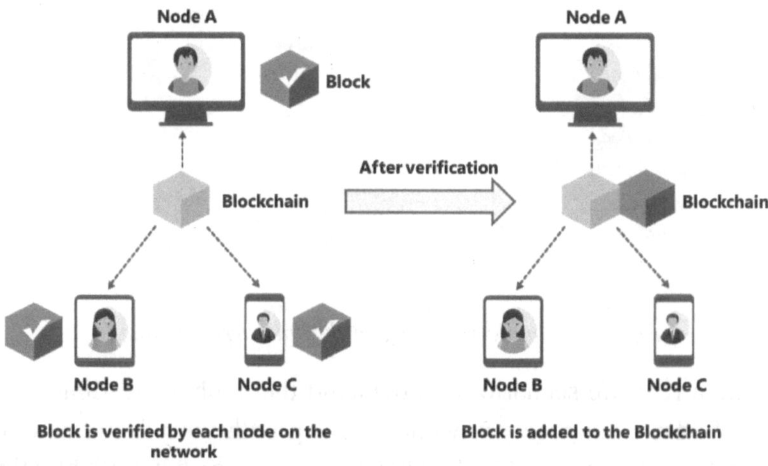

Fig 1-7: Block is added to the Blockchain only after getting verified by each node

1.2.5. Solution for Double Spending Problem

Before understanding how Blockchain solves the problem of double-spending, let us first understand what double-spending actually means. Double spending is simply the risk that a user may spend the same currency units twice. Double spending is a potential loophole specifically applicable to digital currencies. Suppose you go to a cafe and order coffee worth $5. You pay in cash. The service provider at the cafe confirms that you have paid, and you receive your coffee in exchange for the money. Now, is it possible to spend the same $5 somewhere else to make another purchase? The answer is NO. The double-spending problem never arises in physical currency. But unlike physical currencies, a digital currency consists of digital information which can be reproduced or duplicated easily. In the case of digital currency, a currency holder can make a copy of the digital token *(Fig 1-8)*. He will now have two copies of the same token. He can send one token to a merchant while keeping the original token with himself. Thus, spending digital currency twice by its owner.

Double-spending was one of the very serious concerns with Bitcoin initially because there was no central authority to verify that a token is spent only once.

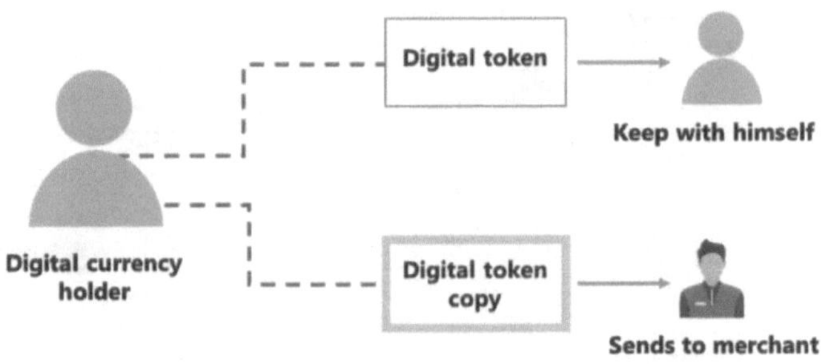

Fig 1-8: Double-spending of digital currency/token

Let's take a real-life scenario to understand the double-spending of digital currency better - Suppose you went on a trip with your friend and clicked his photo on your mobile. He asked you to share his picture with him through WhatsApp. You shared his picture on his demand, but now there are two copies of the same picture - one is with him, and one is with you. This is a classic example of understanding the issue of double-spending. In traditional online transactions, banks are the centralized authorities that ensure no double-spending.

Blockchain, being decentralized, found a solution for double-spending through the consensus mechanism. The consensus mechanism requires users to vote on valid transactions, and only then these transactions get appended to the latest block.

For better understanding, let's take an example - there are three persons Phil, Lyra, and Matt. Lyra has 1 Bitcoin with her. Lyra sends that Bitcoin to Phil. Simultaneously, Lyra does another transaction and sends the same Bitcoin to Matt as well. The second transaction will be rejected by the participating nodes on Blockchain *(Fig 1-9)*. Every transaction before getting committed to the Blockchain is verified against the ledger records by the nodes. So in the first case, when Lyra sends money to Phil, the transaction will be validated against the ledger, which will show that Lyra has one Bitcoin with her, which means that she can transfer her one Bitcoin to Phil. Thus, making it a valid transaction. But in the second transaction, which Lyra does to Matt when the transaction is validated against the ledger, it gets rejected as there is no Bitcoin left with Lyra, so she can't make any transaction with Matt.

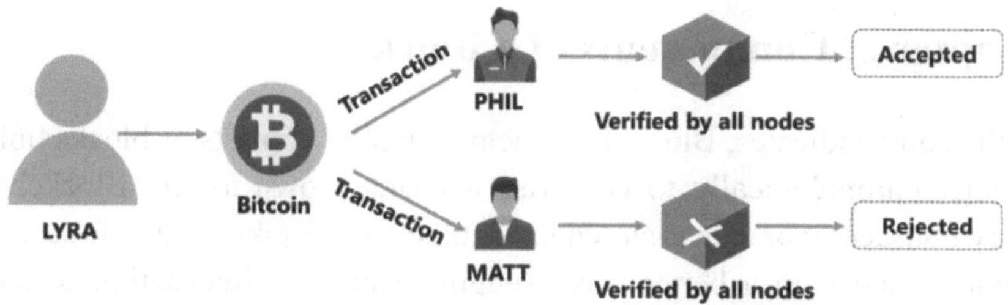

Fig 1-9: How Blockchain handles the double-spending problem

Thus, mitigating the problem of double-spending.

Chapter 2: Components of a Block

As the name indicates, Blockchain metaphorically consists of blocks linked together chronologically to comprise a chain known as the Blockchain. Every transaction or data is stored in the block. Let's take a real-life scenario to understand it in a better way. Suppose I make a transaction of some amount in Steve's account. There has to be a place where this transaction information will be stored. This place is called a block in the blockchain. A block records some or all of the most recent transactions that have not yet entered any prior blocks. Each time a block is 'completed,' it becomes part of the past and gives way to the next block in the Blockchain. A completed block is thus a permanent record of transactions, which, once written, cannot be altered or removed.

2.1. Block time

The average time it takes for the Blockchain network to generate a new block of transactions and add it to the Blockchain is called block time. Some Blockchains create a new block as frequently as every five seconds, and some may even take a few minutes. For instance, the block time for Ethereum Blockchain is between 14 and 15 seconds, while the block time for bitcoin Blockchain is around 10 minutes. In cryptocurrency, a shorter block time means faster transactions.

2.2. Elements of a block

The first block in the Blockchain is known as the **genesis block**, as it is the block from where the chain originates *(Fig 2-1)*.

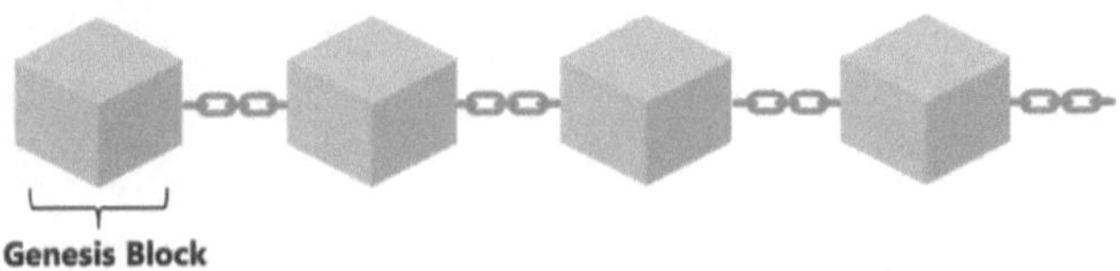

Fig 2-1: Genesis block in the Blockchain

Each block has five elements.

2.2.1. Data and transactions

The first element is data and transactions. Let's come to our example. The amount associated with that transaction and all the other related information, like sender information, receiver information, etc., will be stored in the block. The data contained in each block depends on the type of Blockchain. For example, the food supply Blockchain will have information on all the processes involved in that specific food supply chain.

2.2.2. Hash

Each block also includes a Hash- a unique identifier for the block and all of its contents. To better understand, you can assume a hash to be equivalent to a fingerprint. It is always unique, and no two blocks can have the same hash, just like in the case of fingerprints. As soon as a block is created, its hash gets generated simultaneously *(Fig 2-2)*. Tampering with a block changes its hash. Simply put, if fingerprints or hash of the block change, it indicates that the block has been tampered with and is no longer the same block. So hash can be a very powerful tool to detect any changes made in the block.

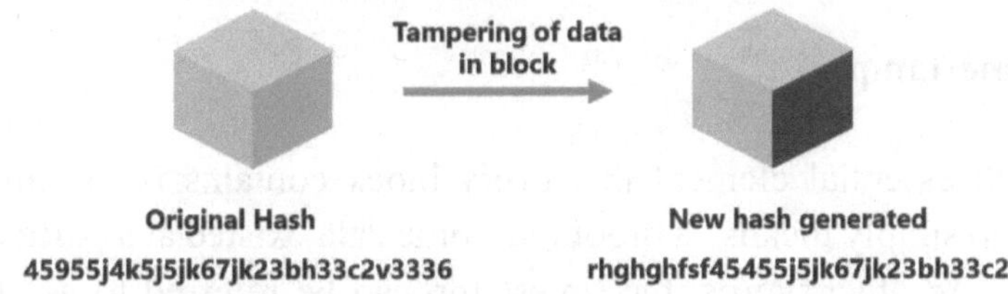

Fig 2-2: Tampering with block changes its hash

2.2.3. Hash of the previous block

Another important element that every block contains is the hash of the previous block. This piece of information is what links one block to another and makes the whole network safe and secure. In *Fig 2-3*, block 4 contains the hash of block 3, block 3 contains the hash of block 2, and so on. As discussed earlier, any change in the data of a block leads to a change in its hash. In the given figure, when we change the data in block 2, the hash of block 2 gets changed as well, which makes the whole Blockchain unstable.

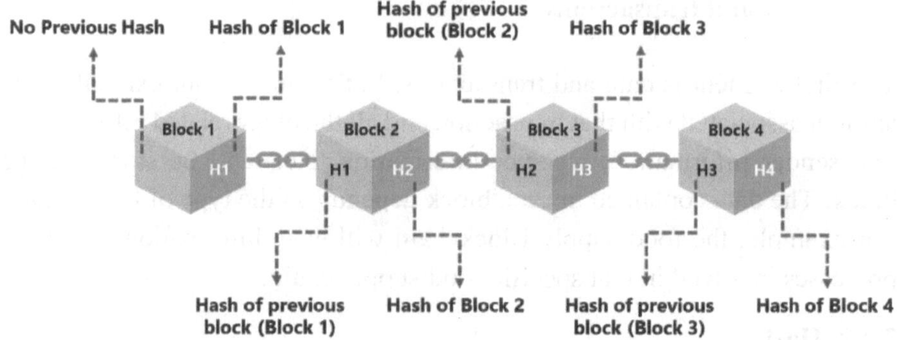

Fig 2-3: Hash of the previous block links the block to another block in the Blockchain

This happens because each block contains a hash of the previous block. When block 2 is tampered with, the old hash becomes invalid, and a new hash is generated for the block. This affects all the subsequent blocks in the chain and thus making all of them invalid. This unique property of the Blockchain makes it transparent and secure, as in any case of data tampering whole network gets to know which block got compromised in the Blockchain.

2.2.4. Timestamp

The fourth essential element that every block contains is the timestamp. Timestamp simply means "a proof that some data existed at a particular date and time." In other words, the timestamp can be referred to as "Proof of existence." Any digital data can be timestamped. The hash of the block containing data and transactions is timestamped and is then published on the network. By doing so, it is ensured that the transactions have existed at this point in time *(Fig 2-4)*. Implementing a timestamp on the block also makes the block impossible to be repeated in the future since, in addition to the time, the date of creation of the block is also stored. Therefore, there is no possibility that any block in the future can be assigned a repeated hash that was given to any of the previous blocks a week, six months, or a year ago.

Moreover, Blockchain-based timestamping is an entirely secure way of tracking the creation and modification time of a document. It is secure enough that even the owner of a document does not have the power to change any data once a document has been recorded on the Blockchain.

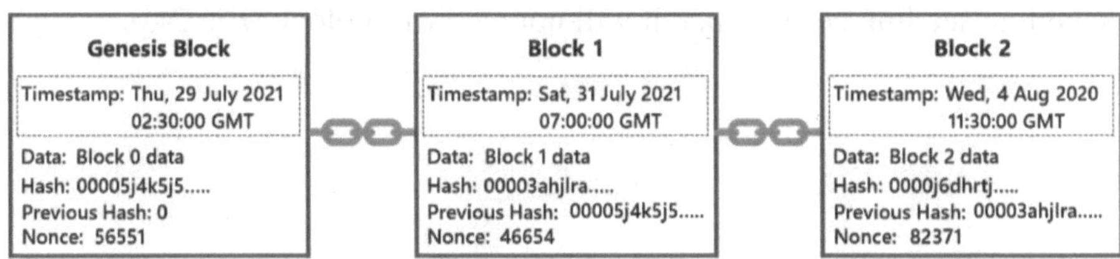

Fig 2-4: Timestamp, along with other information of blocks in the Blockchain

2.2.5. Nonce

The fifth element of a block is the Nonce. The nonce is an abbreviation for "number only used once." A nonce is an integer number that, along with the block number, data, and previous hash, serves as an input for the hashing algorithm to calculate the valid hash for the block. A valid hash for the block is a hash that meets a certain difficulty, i.e., contains a number of predefined zeros at the beginning of the hash. Let's take the example of the Anders Brownworth Hash Program to understand how nonce value is used to generate a valid hash (https://andersbrownworth.com/blockchain/block).

In this case, the **valid** cryptographic hash contains 4 leading zeros *(Fig 2-5)*.

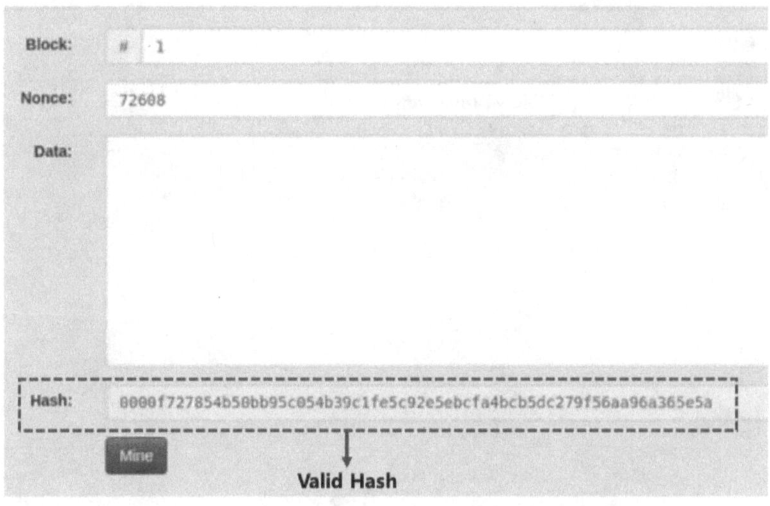

Fig 2-5: Valid cryptographic hash contains 4 leading O's

If any change is made in the data, the hashing algorithm generates a completely different hash for the block. If the newly generated hash does not have four leading zeroes, then it will not be a valid block *(Fig 2-6)*.

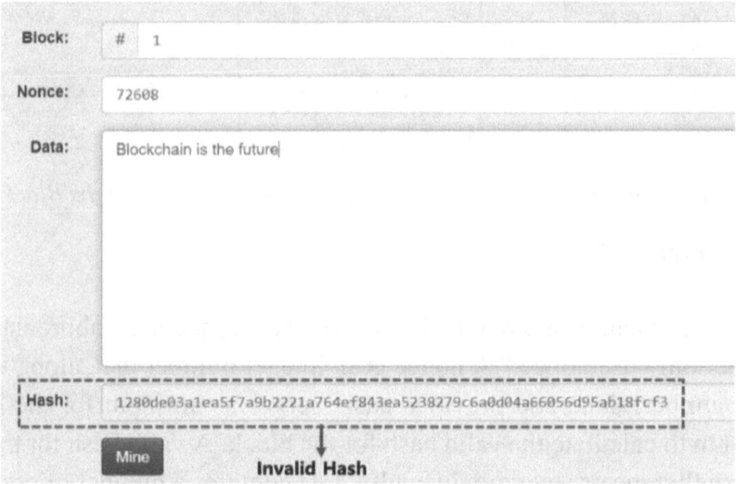

Fig 2-6: Invalid hash if it does not contain leading O's

The block is made valid by the field called a nonce, which is not predetermined. Every time a new nonce is selected for the same block, the resulting hash will be a different value *(Fig 2-7)*.

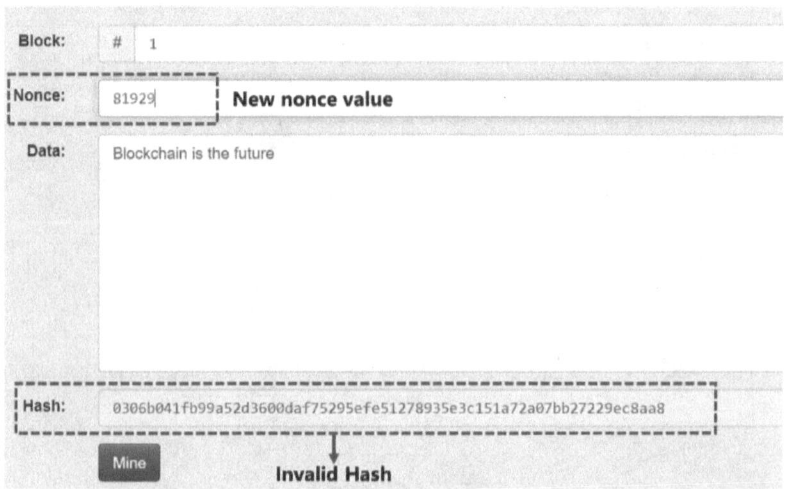

Fig 2-7: New nonce value results in a different hash of the same block

A nonce is basically a random number; it is important to find a nonce value as it helps to generate a valid hash containing leading O's to make the specific block valid. One way to obtain a nonce value is by changing the nonce manually. Thus, it may take several iterations until the desired hash with leading O's is generated. The other way is to click the mine button as shown in *Fig 2-8*, it will give a unique nonce that corresponds to a hash with leading O's to make a valid block. Once the block becomes valid, it becomes a part of the Blockchain, and new blocks are added to this block.

Fig 2-8: Mining gives a unique nonce that corresponds to a valid hash to make a valid block

Since the nonce value can only be used once, it plays an important role to keep the Blockchain immutable. Suppose the data is changed on Block 2, because of which the hash changes as data is used to calculate the hash. Also, Block 2 becomes invalid because its hash no longer has four leading 0's. Block 3's hash changes because Block 2's hash was used to calculate Block 3's hash. Also, Block 3 becomes invalid because its hash no longer has four leading 0's *(Fig 2-9)*. The same is the case with other blocks in the Blockchain. The only way to mutate Block 2 is to mine the block again to find a valid hash with four leading 0's and then mine all the blocks after to find their valid hash because all the blocks are linked together with the hash of the previous block.

Since new blocks are always being added, it's nearly impossible to mutate the Blockchain.

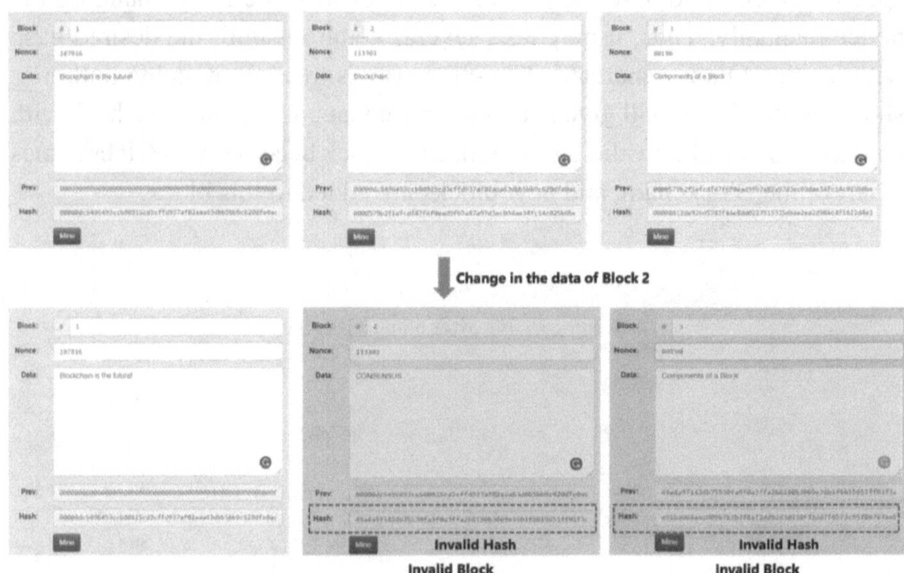

Fig 2-9: Change in the data of Block 2 makes other blocks invalid in the Blockchain

Chapter 3: Hash functions in Blockchain

To understand Blockchain, it is crucial to have a fair idea of what Hash functions are and how they work to make the whole Blockchain safe & secure.

Hash functions are one of the most extensively used cryptographic algorithms that generate a fixed-length output for any input data, irrespective of its size and length. The input data can be a word, a sentence, a longer text, or an entire file. The fixed-length output generated for the input data is called a hash *(Fig 3-1)*. Many types of cryptographic hash functions/ algorithms are available, like MD5, BLAKE2, SHA-1, SHA-256, etc. Secure Hashing Algorithm 256, commonly referred to as SHA-256, is one of the most famous cryptographic hash functions used extensively in Blockchain technology. It was developed by the National Security Agency (NSA) in 2001.

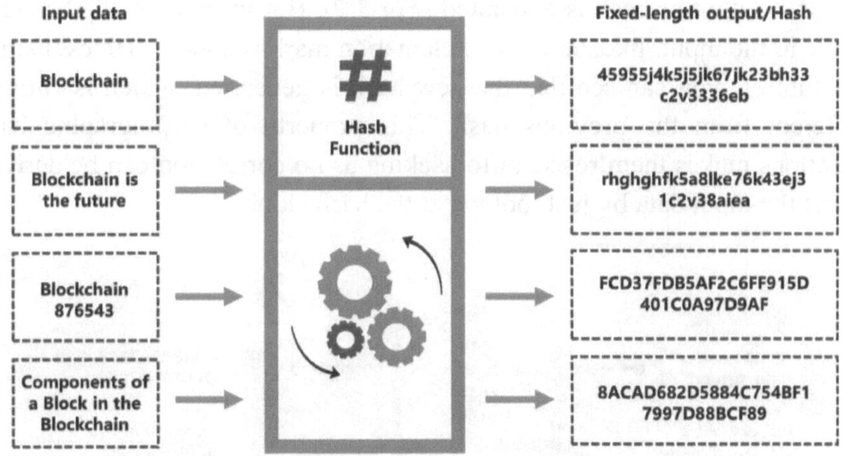

Fig 3-1: Hash or fixed-length output for any input data

When we pass a certain message through the hash algorithm, it generates a hash against this input. Regardless of the size of the letters or numbers you input, the hash algorithm always generates a fixed-length output. The fixed-length output can vary like 32-bit, 64-bit, 128-bit, or 256-bit depending on the hash algorithm being used. For instance, SHA-256 generates a hash value of 256 bits, equivalent to the size of 64 characters.

Using a fixed-length output increases security since anyone trying to decrypt the hash won't be able to tell how long or short the input is simply by looking at the length of the output. The only method to determine the original string from its hash is by using "**brute-force**." Brute-force basically means that one has to take random inputs, hash them and compare them with the target hash. For instance, if the SHA-256 hash algorithm is used, a brute-force attack would need to make 2^{256} attempts to generate the initial data.

Now, let's discuss the important properties of a cryptographic hash function used in the Blockchain:

3.1. Avalanche Effect

One of the unique properties of a cryptographic hash function is that even a small change in the input value brings about a drastic change in its output value. This is referred to as the Avalanche Effect. For instance, when the first input, 'Blockchain is the future,' is passed through the hash function, a specific output or hash is generated *(Fig 3-2)*. But when a small change is made to the input, like, an extra exclamation mark is added- 'Blockchain is the future!' you can see that the new hash is generated, which is entirely different from the previous hash. This property of cryptographic hash functions makes them resistant to hacking as no correlation can be derived about the input data by just looking at the hash alone.

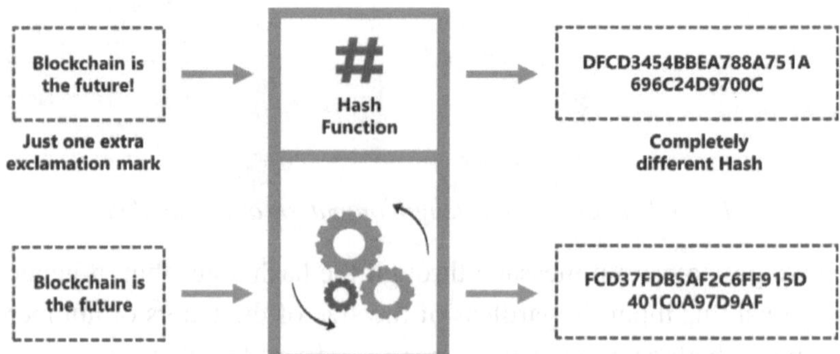

Fig 3-2: Different hash is generated when a small change is made in input data

3.2. Computationally Efficient

One of the other crucial properties of a cryptographic hash function used in the Blockchain is its quick computation. The hash function requires computers on the Blockchain network to perform certain complex mathematical tasks to generate a hash from the input data. So when we say that the hash function should be computationally efficient, it simply means that the computers should be able to finish the required mathematical task in a short time to generate a hash.

3.3. Deterministic

A cryptographic hash function used in the Blockchain must be deterministic. In simple words, a hash function is said to be deterministic if it generates the same hash whenever the same input is passed through it. No matter how many times we pass an input ‘ Blockchain is the future’ through the hash function, it should always generate the same exact output or hash every single time.

If different outputs are generated by a hash function for the same input, the hash function will become useless, and it would be impossible to verify a specific input.

3.4. Pre-Image Resistance

The input for a cryptographic hash function can be any kind of data. This data can be a number, a word, a sentence, a passcode, a song, a book, or a complete movie. But the hash generated for any kind of input data by the Hashing algorithm will be an alphanumeric code and that too of a fixed length.

It is very crucial for a cryptographic hash function to be Pre-image resistant. Pre-image resistance means that the output generated by a cryptographic hash function must not reveal any information about the input data. For example, in *Fig 3-3*, when an input X is passed through the Hash function, the hash generated is represented as H(X). Pre-image resistance simply means that even if you know H(X), it must be infeasible for you to determine the corresponding input X.

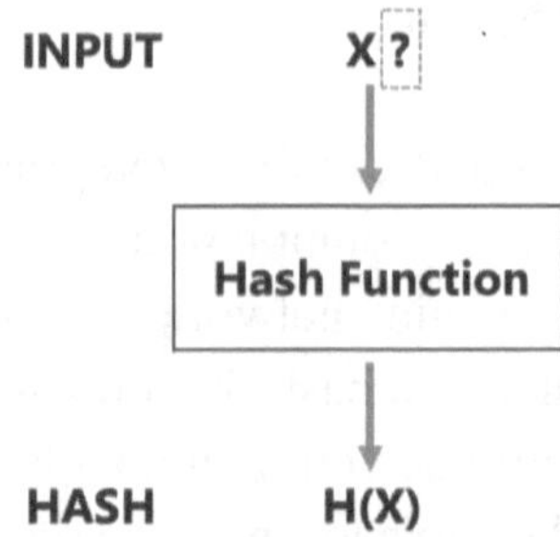

Fig 3-3: Pre-image resistant hash function

3.5. Collision Resistant

Collision resistance is another important property of a cryptographic hash function. Being collision-resistant simply means that it should be highly improbable to generate the same output or hash for two different inputs *(Fig 3-4)*.

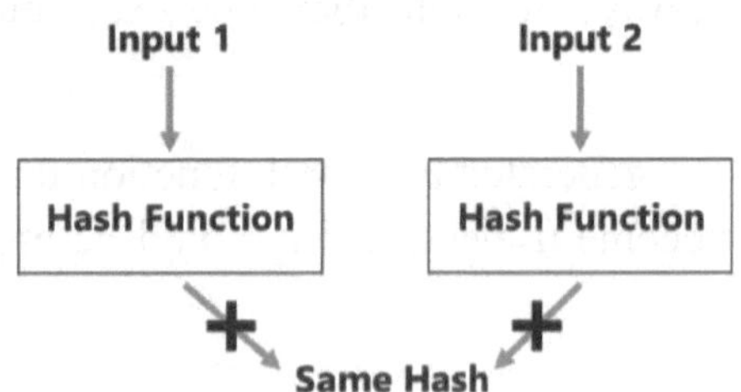

Fig 3-4: Collision-resistant hash function

As discussed earlier, the input for a hash function can be of any type, size, and length. Therefore, there are infinite possibilities for the data input that can be fed into a hash function. But the corresponding hash or output generated will have a fixed length. This means that there will be a finite number of outputs that can be generated using the hash algorithm. If inputs can be infinite and outputs are finite in number, it is quite possible that more than one input can produce the same output.

So the goal of being collision-resistant is to make the probability of finding any two such inputs which share the same output negligible. So if a hashing function is collision-resistant, this possibility won't pose any security risk to the data.

3.6. One-way functions

Hash functions are generally referred to as one-way functions because they are not reversible. While a hash function is a cryptographic function, it's not encryption. Encryption works by encrypting the relevant data with an encryption algorithm and an encryption key. This results in a ciphertext that can only be viewed in its original form if decrypted with the correct key *(Fig 3-5)*. A hash function, in contrast to encryption, works as a one-way function; in simple words, if you have a hash, you can not decrypt it to find the corresponding input. So in a real-life scenario, even if a hacker gets access to a hash output, it is completely useless as he can't decrypt it to get the input.

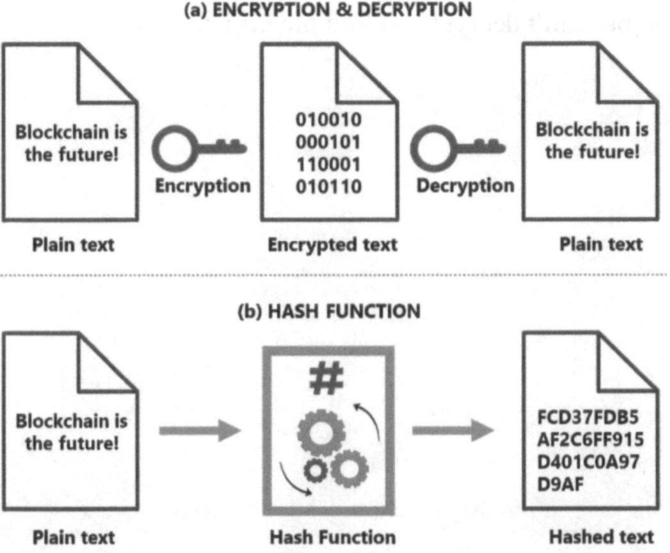

Fig 3-5: One-way Hash Functions

Therefore, cryptography used in Blockchain requires one-way hash functions, making it safe, secure, and reliable. Though hash functions can be used to track and validate the input data, they can't be used to decrypt and reach the input data.

To help you understand it in a better way, let us take an example - Suppose Mr. A holds the land entitlement of a piece of land. That information is stored with the relevant Government Authority in their database. This land record data is now given a unique hash using a hash function. As the record is a centralized record, it can be tampered with, and changes can be made in the records by some corrupt officials because of their personal gains. Assume that some corrupt official tampers the data and changes the land area Mr. A owns. In this case, when the altered land record data will be passed through the hash function, the hash generated would be different from the previous one. Thus, indicating that the land data has been tampered with. So this is how a hash can be used to track and validate the data.

On the other hand, it is not possible to decrypt this hash by anyone and find out that it represents land record data for the land owned by Mr. A. Therefore, we can say that a hash can be used to track and validate the information but can't decrypt and find the original data.

Chapter 4: Types of Blockchain

There are different types of Blockchains that are being used currently. Learning the basics of these Blockchains will give you a clear understanding of the type of Blockchain you can use for your business or for starting a new project.

4.1. Public Blockchain

Public Blockchain, as the name suggests, is public. A public blockchain is completely decentralized and does not have a single entity that controls the network. In this type of Blockchain, anyone with an internet connection can join the network and participate in reading, writing, or auditing within the Blockchain. Hence anyone can review anything at a given point of time on a public blockchain. Simply put, anyone can use public blockchain from anywhere to input data and transactions and review them as long as they are connected to the network.

Public blockchain can also be called **Permissionless Blockchain** because it allows any user to create a personal address and join the blockchain network, i.e., their device/computer can become a 'node' of the network. Also, the public blockchains do not restrict the rights of the nodes on the Blockchain network.

Another critical point to remember is that these types of Blockchain are more transparent and secure than permissioned blockchains because there are many nodes to validate transactions. Thus, it would be difficult for bad actors to collude on the network. Also, it is not possible to modify or alter the data once it has been validated on the Blockchain.

(i) To be part of a public blockchain, one needs to download the code without needing any permission from anyone and start running a public node on their local device. Once this is done, he can then validate transactions in the network, thus participating in the consensus process – the process for determining what blocks can be added to the Blockchain.

(ii) Anyone in the world can send transactions through the network and can expect them to be included in the Blockchain if they are valid.

(iii) In a public blockchain, anyone in the world can access and read Blockchain transactions using a block explorer, which is a program or a website that allows a user to search and navigate the blocks of a Blockchain, their contents, and relevant details.

(iv) Speed of transactions in the public blockchain is slower than in the case of private blockchain.

Examples: To date, public blockchains are primarily used for exchanging and mining cryptocurrency. A few examples of cryptocurrency public blockchain platforms include Bitcoin, Ethereum, Litecoin, etc. Ethereum is the most popular public blockchain at present.

Limitations: One may face some challenges while using a public blockchain. For instance,

(i) Difficult Fraud Tracking: The transactions on the public blockchain can be done anonymously or pseudo anonymously and are not tied directly to the real identity of the user. These transactions are linked to an account address comprised solely of numbers and letters. With no real-world identity attached to this address, it is impossible to track the transaction's originator. It raises a very critical concern, what if activities like fraud, hacking, or money laundering take place in this type of Blockchain. How will the guilty party or person be tracked and punished?

(ii) Lack of governance and regulations: The public blockchain being completely open and decentralized makes it susceptible to a lack of proper regulation and governance by an authorized body. Thus, there is no safe upgrade path for any protocols, and there is no one who can be held responsible for setting and maintaining the network standards. It is definitely good to keep the development of Blockchain technology as decentralized as possible; however, we still need some organization that can look after its features, upgrades, and code of conduct. For instance, if a developer designs a new standard or protocol but gets busy and forgets to respond, then the progress on that protocol halts regardless of how valuable that protocol is for everybody. You cannot hold anyone responsible for maintaining the network standard, thus making the entire system dicey and skeptical. Therefore there is a need for leadership that needs to look after all these aspects. Additionally, the public blockchains are not suitable for use in any internal system and for projects that have strict criteria to follow.

(iii) Slow speed and massive consumption of energy: Another critical area of concern while using public blockchain technology is its speed and the energy it consumes. Public blockchains are slow because it takes time for the network to reach a consensus. For instance, public blockchains like bitcoin manage to process seven transactions per second compared to Visa, which can do 1700 transactions per second. Also, public blockchains like Bitcoin rely on a consensus mechanism- Proof of Work to validate transactions and add new blocks of transactions to the network. In this process, a lot of energy gets consumed while solving complex mathematical problems to validate the transactions and create a block. As per the studies published in June 2017, each bitcoin transaction consumes 80,000 times more electricity than a Visa credit card transaction. But various other consensus mechanisms have been proposed, like Proof of Stake, which uses far less electricity.

4.2. Private Blockchain

The second type of blockchain is Private Blockchain, where the network participants have control over who can join the network and who can participate in the consensus process. This is in contrast to public blockchain which is open for anyone to participate in the network. Access controls in the network will vary for every participant, and the Regulatory Authority or central organization would decide on various activities inside the network starting from joining the network until executing any of the functionalities in this closed network. In this platform, the digital identities of the participants need to be managed and monitored by the Regulatory Authority. Therefore, it is not necessarily decentralized even among its members but is a centralized system that uses distributed ledger technology.

However, private blockchain offers several advantages over public blockchain:

(i) In the case of the public blockchain, the credentials of nodes are not known; therefore, nobody can decipher who these validators are, which increases the risk of malicious activities. But in the case of a private blockchain, the credentials of participating nodes are present on the blockchain; therefore, it is much easier to track where the fraud happened.

(ii) Additionally, since private blockchains are generally smaller than public blockchains and have far fewer participants, therefore it takes less time for the network to reach a consensus. As a result, more transactions can take place. Private blockchains can process thousands of transactions per second. Also, they take up a lot less energy and power to validate transactions. On the contrary public blockchain networks, which usually have thousands of computers to verify transactions, consume tons of energy.

(iii) Private blockchain provides exciting opportunities for businesses to leverage trustless and transparent activities for internal and business-to-business use cases. For instance, banks and financial institutions can use private blockchain as they are regulated entities that cannot operate over open protocols or public blockchain without performing due diligence of the parties involved in the transaction. Additionally, with the advent of smart contracts, this technology could eventually replace many centralized businesses.

Limitations: There are certain challenges associated with the private blockchain. For instance,

(i) Centralization of private blockchain is one of its biggest disadvantages. Blockchain was built to avoid centralization, and private blockchain inherently becomes centralized due to its private network.

(ii) The second disadvantage of using private blockchain is trust. The credibility of a private blockchain network relies on the credibility of the authorized nodes. They need to be trustworthy as they are verifying and validating transactions.

(iii) Security is another concern while using a private blockchain. With fewer nodes, it is easier for malicious hackers to gain control of the network. Thus, compared to the public blockchain, a private blockchain is far more at risk of being hacked or having data manipulated.

4.3. Consortium or Federated Blockchain

The third type of blockchain is consortium blockchain that tries to remove the sole autonomy which gets vested in just one entity as in private blockchain. In the case of consortium blockchain, unlike private blockchain, more than one entity is present on the network. Since there is no single authority governing the control, it maintains decentralized nature. There will be a group of companies or representative individuals making decisions in the best interest of the whole network. Such groups are called consortiums or federations; that's why this blockchain got its name consortium or federated blockchain *(Fig 4-1)*.

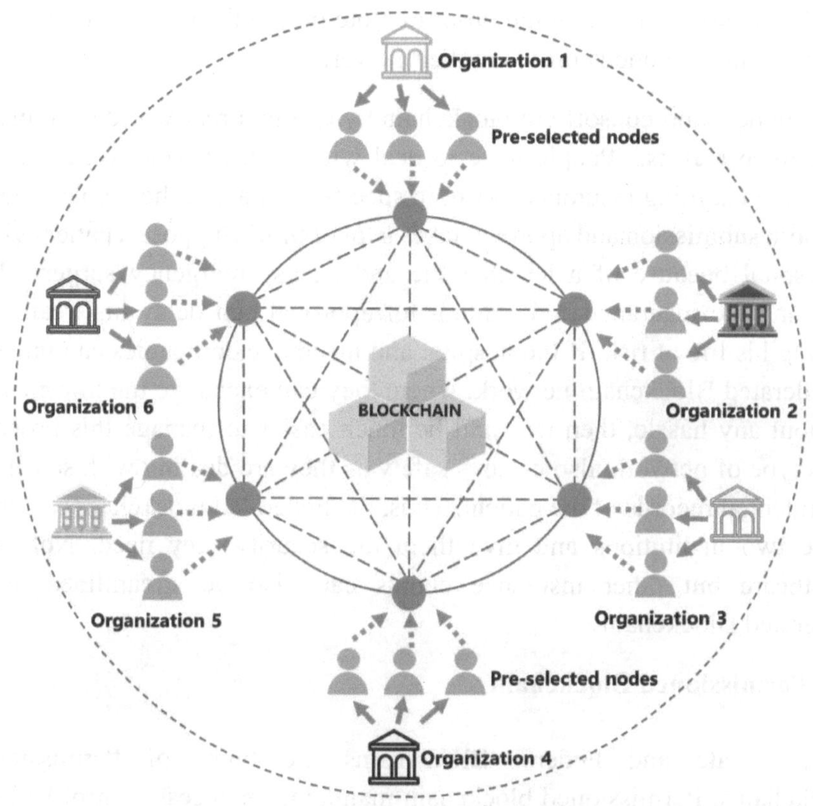

Fig 4-1: Consortium/Federated Blockchain

For example, let's assume there is a consortium of 20 financial institutes on the blockchain network. From these 20 institutes, the nodes will be pre-selected to make changes on the network. These nodes have the authority to read or write transactions, and they can also allow or restrict participants on the network. But none of the nodes alone can add a block to the Blockchain. To add a block, every single node has to approve the block. The mechanism of reaching a decision to add a block is based on the voting system, also referred to as the **Proof of Vote** mechanism. The purpose of this mechanism is to follow up on the selected nodes. Here every node will need to vote in order to validate a block. The number of votes required will be pre-determined in order to reach a decision of adding the block to the Blockchain. This means that it has been decided in the code that for fifteen selected nodes, it might take ten nodes' votes or even fifteen nodes' votes to validate a block. By using the Proof of Vote mechanism, the network helps to ensure that no one is misusing their power.

Let's understand consortium blockchain by taking a real-world example of **insurance claims**. People have to deal with a lot of paperwork when it comes to claiming insurance. Also, in specific scenarios, the whole process of claim submission and approval takes a lot of time. Suppose a patient visits a hospital because of a health issue and needs emergency surgery. But claiming the insurance and waiting for approval can delay his treatment, putting his life at risk. If the hospital and insurance companies can unite in a Federated Blockchain network, where they can exchange the information without any hassle, then it would be much easier to manage this process. This type of network also ensures safety as they are dealing with sensitive, confidential records of the patient. Thus, the Federated blockchain can unite these two institutions and give them the security they need. Not only healthcare but other insurance claims can also be streamlined using Federated Blockchain.

4.4. Permissioned Blockchain

Both Private and Federal Blockchains are types of Permissioned blockchains. Permissioned blockchain maintains an access control layer to allow certain actions to be performed only by certain identifiable participants. On such Blockchain platforms, there is a need of special permissions to read, access, and write information on them. The platform will allow anyone to join the Blockchain network after suitable verification of their identity. Then permissions are allocated and designated to perform only certain activities on the network. The roles of each participant who can access and contribute to the blockchain are defined.

Let's understand permissioned blockchain through an example. Say a farmer in the USA cultivates a medicinal plant that he ships to multiple markets across the globe. The supply chain involves multiple stakeholders like the customs department, which gives clearance for the product to enter their respective nation, shipping companies, and warehouse operators who need to maintain the product within a specified temperature range. The farmer finalizes a particular price and quantity for selling his produce to a buyer in India and another price and quantity to another buyer in Australia. The information about the agreed prices between the farmer and buyers should not be revealed to the other entities involved, like the customs department, the shipping company, and the warehouse operator. They simply need access to limited information, like quality specifications and quantity, to perform their necessary function in supporting such deals. This is a perfect use case for the application of a permissioned blockchain that can allow such restricted implementation and limited permission to the various participants.

Permissioned Blockchain has many other applications like payments, KYC validation, escrow, insurance claims, charity, music publishing, and much more. In a nutshell, the permissioned blockchain offers a secure business environment with customization that allows its wider industry adoption across multiple enterprises.

4.5. Hybrid Blockchain

The fourth type of Blockchain is Hybrid Blockchain, the blockchain which combines the best of both private and public blockchains *(Fig 4-2)*. Simply put, a hybrid blockchain provides controlled access and freedom simultaneously. In other words, the hybrid blockchain lets organizations set up a private, permission-based system alongside a public permissionless system. With such a system, organizations can control

- who can access what data on the blockchain,
- what data can be opened up publicly,
- and what data needs to be kept confidential on the private network?

Fusing different features from private and public blockchains ensures that an organization can work with its stakeholders in the best possible way.

- Like a consortium blockchain, a hybrid blockchain has the privacy benefits of a permissioned blockchain.
- But, unlike a consortium blockchain with multiple participants collectively helping to maintain the network, a hybrid blockchain can have a single entity network administrator.

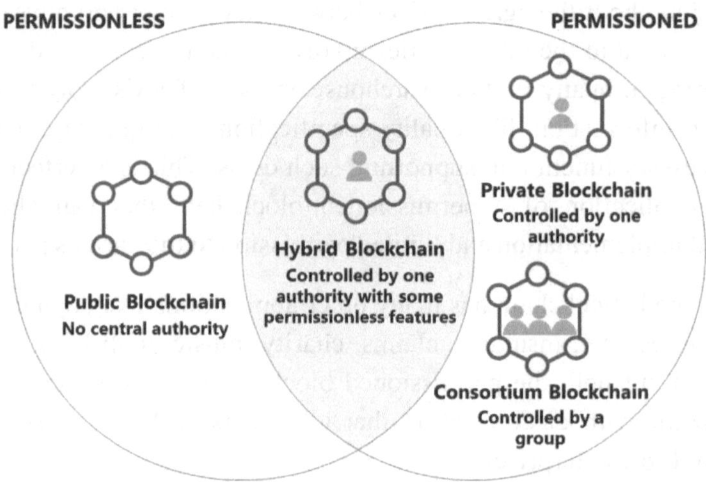

Fig 4-2: Hybrid Blockchain with features of both public and private blockchains

A transaction in a private network of a hybrid blockchain is usually verified within that network. But users can also release it in the public blockchain to get it verified *(Fig 4-3)*. Even though transactions and records in a hybrid blockchain are kept private and not made public, they are always open for verifiability on the public blockchain whenever required.

In the hybrid blockchain, there are two different types of users/nodes based on the level of information that they can access:

- The first type of users/nodes are those who are part of the private blockchain and have all the controls over the blockchain, and can decide the level of security permissions for a particular user.
- And the other type of users/nodes are those who are part of the public blockchain and can just access the data released on the blockchain.

Even though a set of individuals control the hybrid blockchain network, they cannot change the transactions' immutability and security. They can only control which transactions are made public and which are not.

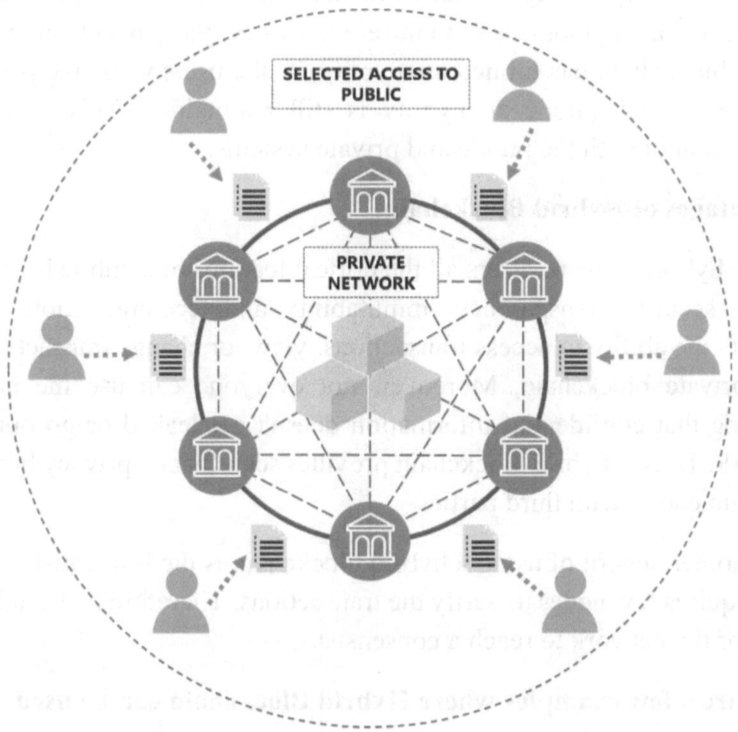

Fig 4-3: Components of Hybrid Blockchain

How can a user join the private network of a hybrid blockchain?

(i) A user is required to get permission to join the hybrid blockchain network and become a node on the private network. Once he joins the network, he can fully participate in the blockchain's activities, like the rights to do transactions, view them, or even append or modify them.

(ii) The identity of the user is kept secret from other participating users to protect that user's privacy. His identity is only revealed to the party/user he is dealing with.

(iii) To ensure that the identification process of a user is done correctly, companies and organizations carry out KYC (Know Your Customer) to make it work. Financial institutes, especially, need to handle the KYC process correctly as they cannot allow the transaction to be carried out by a user who is anonymous or not entirely known to the blockchain. Thus the hybrid blockchain has limited anonymity for the users who take part in the network, though public anonymity is still maintained. This leads to an intersection of both the public and private systems.

Advantages of Hybrid Blockchain:

(i) The hybrid network offers all the critical features of a public blockchain, such as security, transparency, immutability, and decentralization, but also restricts the ability to access transactions, view, or change transactions like in a private blockchain. Moreover, not everyone can use the network, ensuring that confidential information doesn't get leaked or go out of the network. Thus, a hybrid blockchain provides security and privacy but allows communication with third parties.

(ii) Another benefit of using a hybrid blockchain is the low transaction cost as it requires few nodes to verify the transactions. Therefore it also takes less time for the network to reach a consensus.

Here are a few examples where Hybrid Blockchain can be used:

(i) An area where hybrid blockchain technology can be implemented is the Hybrid IoT (Internet of Things). It is not secure to manage the IoT on public blockchains as it will give hackers free access to data to map nodes and hack them. But with a hybrid blockchain, the IoT devices can be placed in a private network with selective access to people who need them. Conversely, the managing authority decides which aspects of the network should be made public depending on what data needs to be shared.

(ii) The second application of hybrid blockchain is in government activities like voting, creating public identification databases, automating acquisitions, providing social/ humanitarian assistance, etc. The hybrid blockchain offers the government the necessary control and enables the public to access it. Totally private or public blockchains will not work as they either hinder users' access or reveal too much data. The hybrid blockchain can ensure that the government stays in control of the data and, at the same time, gives access of data to the public. Thus, maintaining transparency in government operations.

(iii) The third application of hybrid blockchain is in real estate. Companies can use a hybrid blockchain to run systems privately but show certain information, such as listings, to the public.

(iv) Hybrid blockchains have applications in various other sectors like supply chains, banking, finance, trade, enterprise services, etc.

To decide on which type of blockchain technology to be implemented for your organization or project, you have to consider the following two critical factors:

- Does the access to the network need to be restricted or permissionless or a combination of both?
- Does the network operate on a global level or an organizational level?

Different blockchains offer trade-offs in terms of scalability, transaction speed, transparency, and security within these parameters. After considering all the parameters, you can decide which type of Blockchain technology is best suitable for your business or project.

Chapter 5: Merkle tree in Blockchain

The data/transactions in a block are not stored as plain text; instead, they are stored in a data structure called the Merkle tree. In other words, the Merkel tree serves as a summary of all the transactions in a block. Every transaction in a block is uniquely hashed by hash functions like MD5, BLAKE2, SHA-1 or SHA-256 to produce a digital fingerprint of the entire set of transactions. Each pair of hashed transactions is hashed together by the hash function, and this process continues until there is one hash for the entire block *(Fig 5-1)*. Structurally, the Merkle tree is a type of binary tree, where the hashes of the transactional data on the bottom row are referred to as "leaf nodes," the intermediate hashes as "branches," and the hash at the top as the "root." Merkle tree is also called the Hash tree. Each block in the Blockchain has one Merkle root.

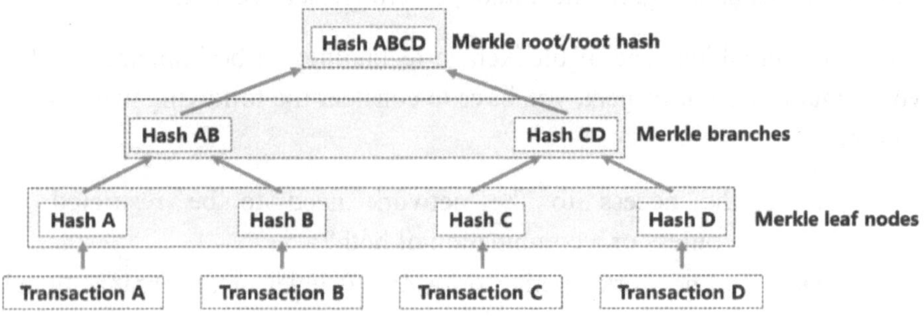

Fig 5-1: The Merkle tree of transactions A, B, C, and D; Hash ABCD is the Merkle root/root hash

5.1. A Basic Merkle tree

To make it easier, let's understand the Merkle tree with the help of an example. Suppose there are four transactions in a block as shown in *Fig 5-1*. Each of the four transactions (A, B, C, and D) will have a unique hash (Hash A, Hash B, Hash C, and Hash D). Then each two hashed transactions are combined to create another hash. In this case, hashed transaction A pairs with hashed transaction B and hashed together to generate the Hash AB. On the other hand, hashed transaction C pairs with hashed transaction D and hashed together to create the Hash CD. The Hash AB and Hash CD are the branches of the Merkle tree. The Hash AB and Hash CD are then grouped and hashed again by the hash function to produce the Hash ABCD, which is the Merkle root/root hash.

Merkle root is stored in the block header *(Fig 5-2)*.

A block is composed of a header and a body. The block header contains Merkel root, Timestamp, Block Version number (indicates which set of block validation rules to follow), Difficulty Target, Nonce, and Previous Hash. On the other hand, the block body contains all confirmed transactions within the block.

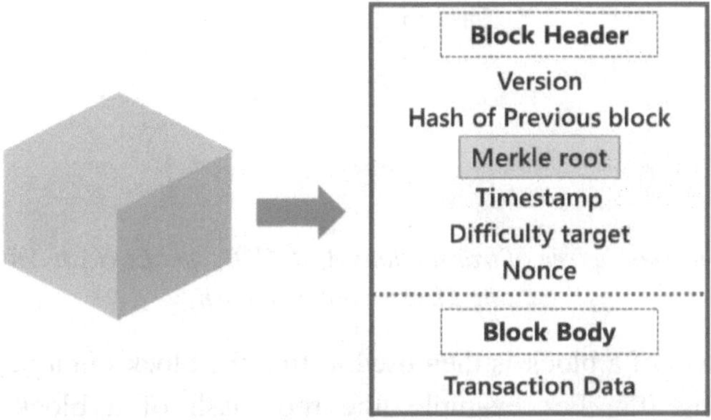

Fig 5-2: The Merkle root is stored in the block header of the block

5.2. An Unbalanced Merkle tree with an odd number of transactions

The above example illustrates the fundamental case of a Merkle tree. There are just the correct number of Merkle leaves at every level to form exact pairs. What happens if you have an odd number of transactions, leading to the formation of an odd number of Merkle leaves? For example, suppose there are five transactions in the block *(Fig 5-3)*. Each of the five transactions (A, B, C, D, and E) will have a unique hash (Hash A, Hash B, Hash C, Hash D, and Hash E). The pair of hashed transactions A and B is hashed again to produce the Hash AB. Similarly, the pair of hashed transactions C and D is hashed to produce the Hash CD. But hashed transaction E is left without a pair to hash into a new branch. Since the Merkle trees are binary in nature, they require leaf nodes to be even for them to work. Therefore, if there happens to be an unpaired hash, then that hash is copied and paired with itself. In this example, Hash E is duplicated to pair with itself to be hashed again to form Hash EE. The Hash AB and Hash CD are grouped and hashed to create Hash ABCD. On the other hand, Hash EE gets duplicated and pairs with it itself to be hashed to form Hash EEEE. The hashes ABCD and EEEE are again grouped and hashed to produce one hash, i.e., the Merkle root.

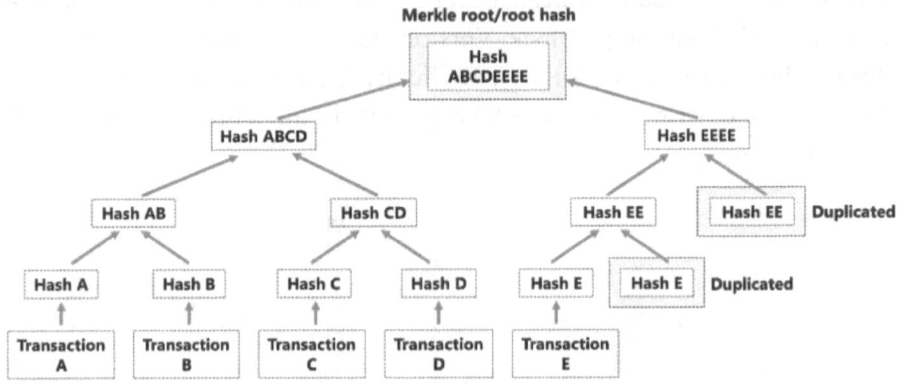

Fig 5-3: The Merkle tree of transactions A, B, C, D, and E; Hash ABCDEEEE is the Merkle root/root hash

The root hash of a block is then used to find the block's unique, valid hash with leading 0's. For example, the root hash of a block #72608 is a1c6d67c992a70fca66188e178d9ca7c20d5c775393948f19955be7f0952c0fa. The root hash is then combined with other information of the block (block number, the previous block's hash, the timestamp, the difficulty target, and the nonce) and run through a hash function to produce the block's unique and valid hash with leading 0's: 00001a03b7328189f5f7154681c5827a1b2fce2fcb5301a8e412e22ea9a7859. Once the block gets the valid hash, it becomes a part of the Blockchain, and new blocks can be added to this block.

5.3. Advantages of Merkle tree

1. Each block has a unique hash value, calculated from the Merkle root. The block also contains the previous block's hash, thus linking one block to another in the Blockchain. If there is a change in any transaction, then the hash of that transaction changes. This change cascades up to the Merkle Root, changing the value of the Merkle root and thus making the block

invalid. This then is reflected in the succeeding block, leading to a change in its hash, thus making the rest of the Blockchain invalid. Therefore, the Merkle tree makes an immutable record of transactions in the block.

2. Blockchains are usually made up of hundreds of thousands of blocks; and each block can contain up to several thousand transactions, thereby making memory space and computing power the two big problems while validating the data. If the Blockchain did not have the concept of Merkle trees, then every single node on the network would have been required to keep a complete copy of every single transaction that has ever occurred on the Blockchain. While confirming a transaction, a node would have been required to compare each entry line by line to make sure its own records match exactly with the network records. If there was any discrepancy between the records, it could compromise the security of the network. Therefore, the computer used for validating the data would have required much higher processing power to compare the records to ensure that there had been no changes.

On the other hand, Merkle trees solve this problem by considerably reducing the amount of data that has to be maintained for verification purposes. They hash all the records in the ledger, which effectively separates the proof of data from the data itself. Users can verify individual blocks and can also check transactions by using hashes. Thus, reducing the amount of computing power required to validate the transactions.

3. Merkle trees help eliminate modifying transaction records and double-spending within a Blockchain. For example, if someone tries to hack an entry on the Blockchain to make it appear as if he has more cryptocurrency than what is available in reality, any such false entry would not be in line with the rest of the hashes in a Merkle tree and thus would be rejected by the network. This is because when a transaction happens on the Blockchain, it is not stored as such; instead, it gets verified. The transaction is hashed by the hash function, and then its hash is verified with every other hash on the Blockchain to prove that nothing has been altered or tampered with.

Since the hash function is **deterministic**, it generates the same hash whenever the same input is passed through it. Therefore, if an individual tries to double-spend his digital currency, a hash will be generated for that transaction. If that hash matches with the existing records present on the Blockchain, that transaction is rejected. Hence, double-spending is prevented.

5.4. Merkle proofs

Merkle proofs allow for the verification of a specific transaction/content in a large body of data. In Blockchain systems, there are two types of nodes:

(i) The nodes holding a complete history of blockchain are called "full nodes."

(ii) And other nodes are called "lightweight nodes." A Lightweight Node contains only a partial list of Blockchain, which usually includes just the block headers (containing Merkle root) instead of its entire transaction history. The lightweight node can validate transactions included in a block without the need to download the whole Blockchain.

When a lightweight node wants to verify a specific transaction, it uses the hash function to obtain the hash value of that transaction. The full node sends all the hash values to the lightweight node required for verification, based on the structure of the Merkle tree. Next, the lightweight node repeats the hash operation to compute the root hash value. Then the root hash value obtained by the process is compared with the root hash value sent by the full node.

Suppose a lightweight node wants to verify whether transaction D has been lost or tampered with. For this, the full node sends the hash values Hash C, Hash AB, Hash EFGH, and Merkle root to the lightweight node *(Fig 5-4)*. First, the lightweight node finds the hash of transaction D, i.e., Hash D using the hash function. Then Hash D, along with the values Hash C, Hash AB, and Hash EFGH, are recomputed to generate Merkle root/root hash. If the computed Merkle root and original Merkle root match, then it can be verified that the Hash D is a genuine leaf of the Merkle tree, and thus, transaction D is a part of the Merkle tree.

On the contrary, if the computed Merkle root and original Merkle root do not match, then it can be confirmed that transaction D has been tampered with.

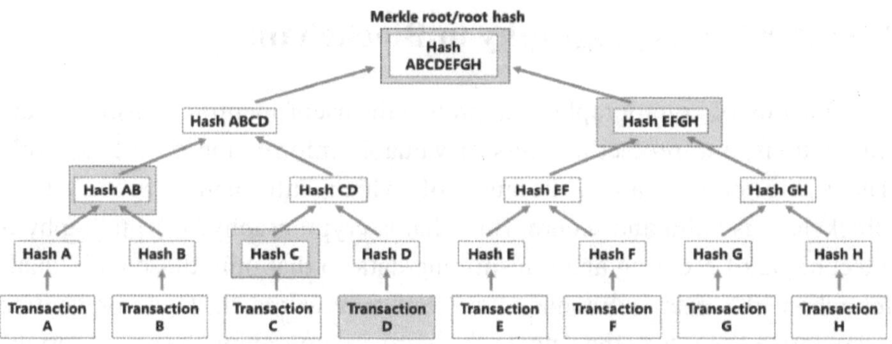

Fig 5-4: Merkle proof for transaction D

Chapter 6: Cryptography in Blockchain

The function of cryptography is to protect the users' identities, ensure secure transactions, and protect all sorts of valuable information on the network. Thanks to cryptography, because of which information recorded on Blockchain is valid and secure. But what is cryptography? Cryptography is a technique of securing and transmitting data so that only those individuals for whom the data is intended can read and access it. Thus, preventing unauthorized access to the data. In the word cryptography, the prefix "crypt" means "hidden," and the suffix "graphy means "writing."

6.1. Encryption and Decryption

Encryption and decryption are the two critical functionalities of cryptography *(Fig 6-1)*.

Encryption: Encryption is the process of transforming the original information (plaintext) into random numbers that appear to be meaningless (ciphertext).

Decryption: Decryption is the process of converting ciphertext into its original form of plaintext.

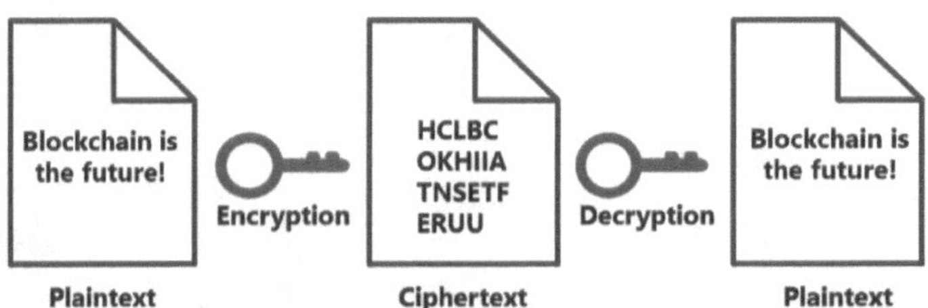

Fig 6-1: Encryption and decryption of data

Plaintext refers to any information that humans or a machine can directly read and understand. This may be English sentences, a script, or Java code. If one can make sense of what is written, it is said to be in plaintext. On the other hand, ciphertext or encrypted text is a series of random letters and numbers which humans cannot make any sense of.

An encryption algorithm takes in a plaintext message, and the key (a string of characters) within the encryption algorithm locks and encrypts data to convert it into ciphertext. Only someone with the right decryption key can unlock or decrypt the ciphertext and convert it into plaintext.

There are various ways by which plain text can be modified to obtain ciphertext. For instance,

(a) Substitution: It involves replacing characters of plaintext with other letters, numbers, or symbols. For example, with a shift of +1, A would be replaced by B, B by C, and so on. Therefore,

Plaintext: BLOCKCHAIN IS THE FUTURE

Ciphertext: CMPDLDIBJO JT UIF GVUVSF

In this case, the encryption key will be +1.

(b) Transposition: In the transposition technique, the positions of the characters of plaintext are changed to create the ciphertext. For example, in *Fig 6-2*, "HCLBCOKHIIATNSETFERUU" is the ciphertext for the plaintext "BLOCKCHAIN IS THE FUTURE" using the encryption key 7421635.

1	2	3	4	5	6	7
B	L	O	C	K	C	H
A	I	N	I	S	T	H
E	F	U	T	U	R	E

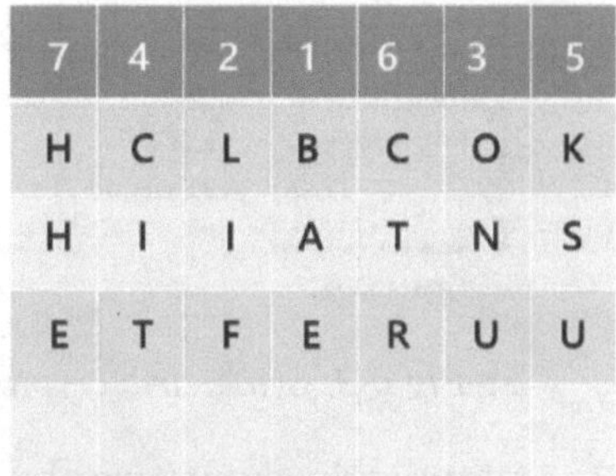

7	4	2	1	6	3	5
H	C	L	B	C	O	K
H	I	I	A	T	N	S
E	T	F	E	R	U	U

Plaintext: **BLOCKCHAIN IS THE FUTURE**
Ciphertext: **HCLBCOKHIIATNSETFERUU**
Key: **7421635**

Fig 6-2: Transposition technique to convert plaintext into ciphertext

Although the above examples illustrate how cryptographic keys can turn plaintext into ciphertext, cryptographic keys actually used are far more complex and can scramble a text beyond human recognition to generate the ciphertext.

6.2. Types of cryptography

Based on the types of key and encryption algorithms used, cryptography can be divided into three types:

6.2.1. Symmetric cryptography

Symmetric cryptography, also known as secret-key cryptography, is an encryption system where the same secret key is used to both encrypt and decrypt the data *(Fig 6-3)*. The entities/parties communicating via symmetric encryption must exchange the key with recipients so that it can be used in the decryption process. Symmetric cryptography is faster and simpler, but the problem is that the sender and receiver have to somehow exchange the secret key securely.

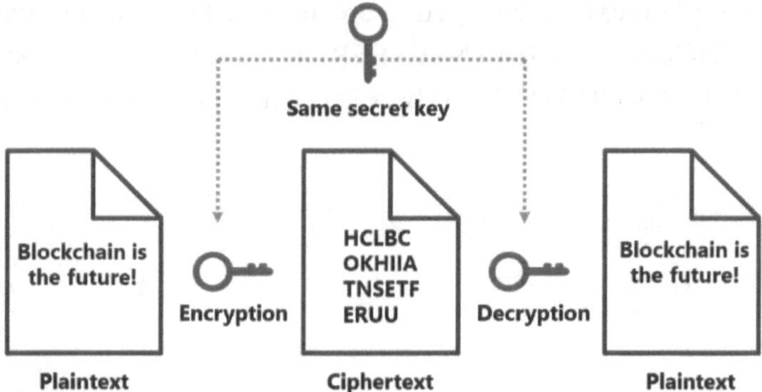

Fig 6-3: Symmetric cryptography uses the same secret-key

6.2.2. Asymmetric cryptography

Asymmetric cryptography, also known as public-key cryptography, is an encryption system that uses two keys- one is used for encrypting data, while the other key is used for decrypting the data *(Fig 6-4)*. Unlike symmetric cryptography, if one key is used to encrypt, that same key cannot decrypt the data; instead, the other key shall be used.

Out of the two keys used, one key is kept private and is called the "private key," while the other key is shared publicly and is open to be used by anyone; hence it is known as the "public key." Therefore, the private key must be kept secret and should not be shared with anyone to keep it from becoming compromised. So, only the authorized person, server, or machine has access to the private key. On the contrary, the public key can be shared with any other entity. For ease of understanding, consider your public key as your bank account number and private key as your bank account password. For someone to send you money, they just need to know your public (bank account) address. However, only you can access the funds in your bank account because you are the only one who knows your password or has access to your private key.

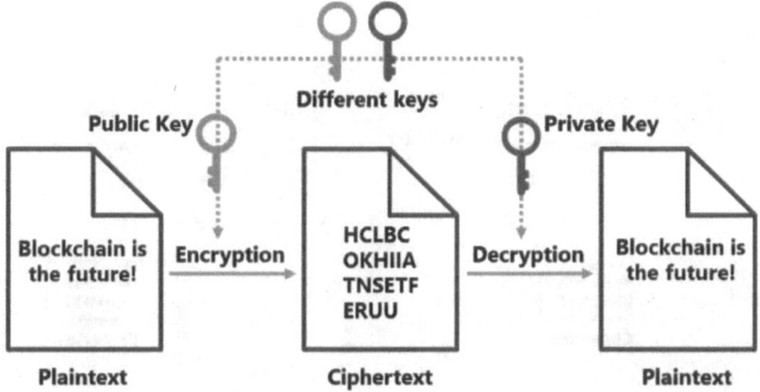

Fig 6-4: Asymmetric cryptography uses different keys

The mathematical relation of the keys is that the private key cannot be derived from the public key, but the public key can be derived from the private key because a public key is a mathematical result of its associated private key. This leads to a more robust level of security for the data.

How asymmetric cryptography works?

Let's assume A wants to send an encrypted message to B; then, he can encrypt the message with the intended recipient B's public key before sending it. After receiving the message, B can decrypt the message using his related private key *(Fig 6-5a)*.

And on the other hand, sender A can also encrypt the message with his own private key before sending it to B. In this case, B uses sender A's public key to decrypt the message *(Fig 6-5b)*. This proves that the message originates from A, and nobody else. Since anyone can access A's public key, the message encrypted by A's private key won't be a secret per se, but it can be used to prove the authorship of that message or information. This is also called digitally signing the message.

Therefore, encrypting the information with the receiver's public key makes the information readable only by the receiver. On the other hand, encrypting the information with the sender's private key proves the identity of the sender.

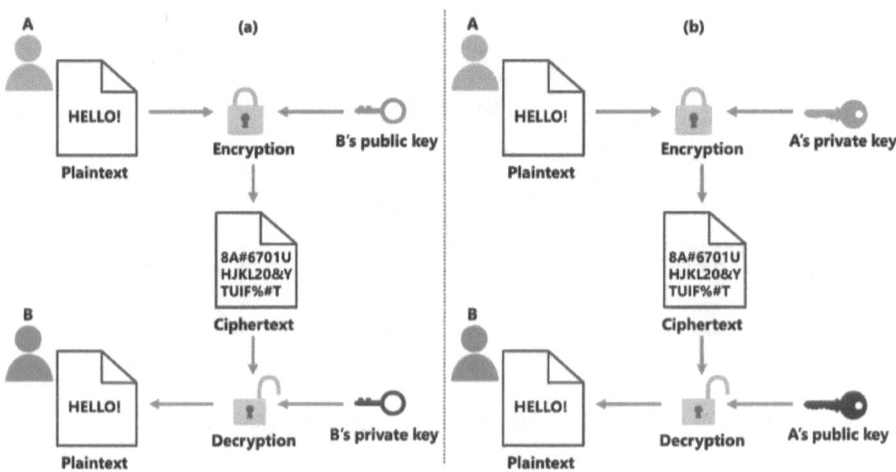

Fig 6-5: Encrypting information with (a) receiver B's public key and (b) sender A's private key

6.2.3. Cryptographic Hashing/Hashing

Both symmetric and asymmetric cryptographic functions are two-way functions meaning that you can encrypt some data, and then the person who receives the encrypted data can decrypt it to obtain the original data. But now, we need to understand that cryptographic Hashing is a one-way function. Hashing is a technique or process of generating a fixed-length output "hash" for any input data, irrespective of its size and length. This is done by the hash functions/ algorithms like MD5, BLAKE2, SHA-1, SHA-

256, etc. The input can be a single character, an MP3 file, an entire book, or an excel sheet of your banking history. But the hash function generates a fixed length of the output. This type of encryption doesn't use keys, unlike symmetric and asymmetric cryptography.

Blockchain uses two types of cryptographies: asymmetric cryptography and cryptographic hashing.

6.3. Importance of Cryptographic Hashing/Hashing in Blockchain

Provides security and immutability: A slight change in the data can result in a significantly different output, i.e., Hash. For instance, "Blockchain is the Future" and "Blockchain is the Future!" (with just one extra exclamation mark) will have completely different hashes *(Fig 6-6)*. This property of hashing makes the data reliable and secure on the Blockchain because any changes in the data will lead to the changes in hash value of the block to which it belongs and subsequently changes the hashes of the following blocks, making the Blockchain invalid. Thus, hashing is essential in keeping an immutable record of transactions/data on the Blockchain.

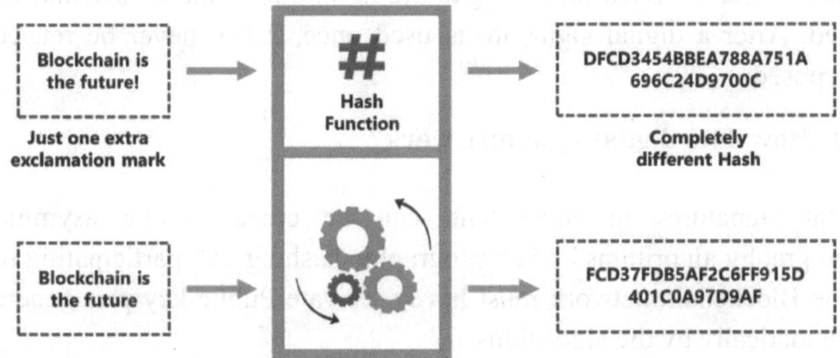

Fig 6-6: Different hashes for different inputs

Additionally, cryptographic hash functions work as one-way functions that encrypt the data. It is mathematically impossible to decrypt the data in any other method other than randomly guessing input until you're able to recreate that hash output. In simple words, if you have a hash, you can not decrypt it to find the corresponding input. So in a real-life scenario, even if a hacker gets access to a hash output, it is completely useless as he can't decrypt it to get the input. The hash is used to agree between all parties that no transaction/data in the history has been tampered with because any alteration in the block data can lead to inconsistency and break the Blockchain, making it INVALID.

Therefore, cryptographic hashing is one of the key components which enables security and immutability on the Blockchain.

6.4. Digital signature in Blockchain

In addition, Blockchain relies on digital signatures, as they are primarily used to verify the authenticity of transactions. It is common in the real world to use handwritten signatures on paper to bind a person to an agreement. For example, say Steve buys a car for $15,000 and writes a cheque as payment. The signature guarantees that only Steve could have signed the cheque. Therefore, Steve's bank must pay the cheque.

Similarly, a digital signature binds a person to the digital data, i.e., provides verification that the transaction was created by a known person and was not altered in transit. Each digital signature is unique to the transaction being signed. After a digital signature is used once, it can never be reused or repurposed.

6.4.1. How does digital signature work?

Digital signatures in Blockchain can be created using asymmetric cryptography algorithms and cryptographic hashing. All participating users on the Blockchain network must have a Private-Public key pair generated mathematically by the algorithms.

Let's understand digital signature through certain examples. Every transaction that is executed on the Blockchain is digitally signed by the sender using his private key.

Example 1: Suppose Phil wants to send a document/message to Jane on Blockchain.

(i) To create a digital signature, the signer Phil has to feed the document data to the hash function, which generates the one-way hash of the electronic data to be signed. The value of this hash is unique to the document.

(ii) The private key of the Phil is used to encrypt the hash. For this, the hash value and private key are fed to the signature algorithm (e.g., ECDSA), which produces the digital signature on a given hash *(Fig 6-7a)*.

(iii) Phil then sends the data with the digital signature to the intended receiver Jane. Additionally, the digital signature + the public key of Phil are enough for nodes to verify that the private key associated with Phil has been used to make such a signature. Hence, it can be proved that the transaction is authenticated, and the document has been sent by Phil.

(iv) After receiving the data and signature on it, the receiver, Jane, can verify it. This would involve two steps, generating the hash of the sent data and decrypting the encrypted hash. By using the signer's public key, the hash can be decrypted *(Fig 6-7b)*.

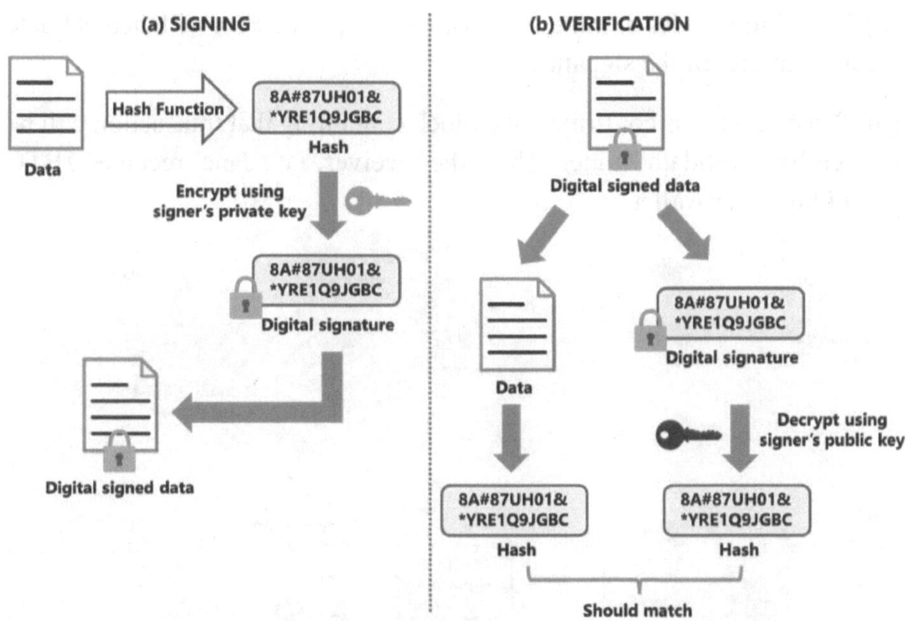

Fig 6-7: (a) Signing the data with the signer's private key and (b) verifying the data with the signer's public key

If the decrypted hash matches a second recomputed hash of the same data, it proves that the data hasn't changed since it was signed. On the other hand, if the two hashes don't match, it indicates that the data has been tampered with.

Example 2: Suppose Phil wants to send 1 Bitcoin (BTC) to Jane. To achieve this, each account owner in the network needs to have a digital wallet that assigns them a public/private key pair. The public key is the address of the digital wallet. You are safe sharing it with others when you want them to send you bitcoin/cryptocurrency. On the other hand, the private key is used to assign and authorize the cryptocurrency to be spent or sent elsewhere.

To send 1 BTC to Jane,

(i) The transaction details, including the amount to be sent (1BTC), recipient (Jane) address, etc., are hashed, and the hashed transaction is then signed using Phil's private key. The signed transaction is then sent to nodes on the network *(Fig 6-8)*.

(ii) The mining nodes or miners, who know his public key, will then validate the authenticity of the signature.

(iii) Once validity is confirmed, the block containing that transaction will be created by a validator/miner. Thus, the receiver, i.e., Jane, receives 1BTC from Phil in her wallet.

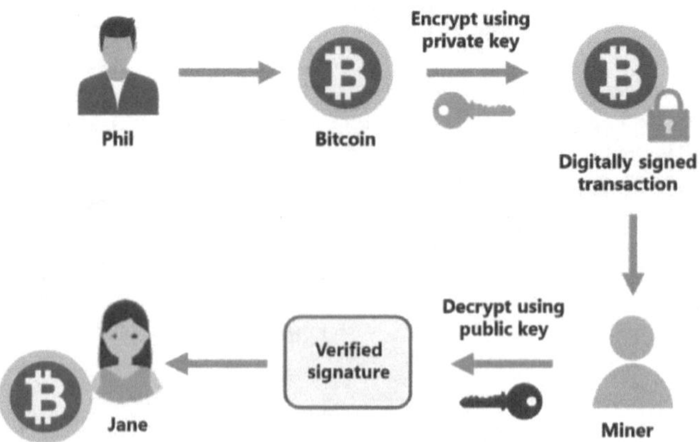

Fig 6-8: Digitally signed bitcoin transaction on Blockchain

Therefore, the digital signature ensures that only the account owner can move money out of the account.

6.4.2. Advantages of digital signature

(i) Authenticity: Digital signature enables the receiver to confirm data authentication by validating the digital signature with the sender's public key. Also, the receiver can be sure that he/she is communicating with the person they intend to.

(ii) Data integrity: Digital signatures ensure that the data has not been illegally accessed and modified by any hacker. For instance, if a hacker has access to the document and alters it, the hash of the modified document and the output hash provided by the decrypting digital signature will not match. Hence, the receiver can safely deny the document assuming that data integrity has been breached.

(iii) Non-repudiation: Digital signatures also provide non-repudiation of the data. Non-repudiation means that participants cannot deny the transaction in the Blockchain. For example, A sent a signed document to B, so A cannot deny that he didn't send the document to B. This is because the person who sent the document had to be in possession of a private key to sign the document. Therefore, the receiver can present the document and digital signature to a third party as evidence if any dispute arises in the future.

Chapter 7: Consensus mechanism for Public Blockchain- Proof of Work (POW)

Unlike centralized systems like banks, there is no central authority involved that makes the decisions on what, when, or how information gets stored on the Blockchain network. Since Blockchains operate as a decentralized system, they need to have a reliable, robust, efficient, and secure consensus mechanism. Consensus means reaching an agreement about something within a group of people *(Fig 7-1)*.

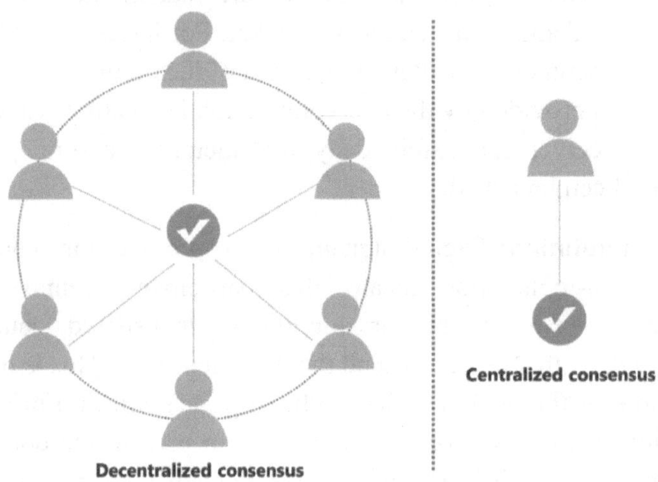

Fig 7-1: Types of consensus: Decentralized and Centralized

The purpose of a consensus mechanism is to validate and verify that the data being appended to the Blockchain is valid. There are various mechanisms for consensus that are used currently. Each of them serves the same purpose of validating the data being added to the Blockchain, though they do it differently. And quite naturally, each one of them has its own pros and cons. The major difference between these mechanisms is in the way they reward and delegate the verification of transactions.

Consensus mechanisms for public blockchains: The two most notable Consensus mechanisms for public blockchains are - Proof of Work or POW and Proof of Stake or POS.

Proof of Work (POW)

Proof of Work is one of the older consensus mechanisms that came into existence in the 1990s. It is a consensus algorithm to confirm the transactions and create a new block to the Blockchain. It has been used by various crypto projects like **Bitcoin**, **Litecoin**, and **Ethereum 1.0**. Proof of Work uses the computational power of the computers on the network to create new virtual coins. In this algorithm, miners (a group of nodes validating the transactions on a Blockchain network) compete against each other to solve complex mathematical problems, i.e., finding the nonce value in order to complete the transaction on the network. The nonce is responsible for generating a valid hash value for the block to make it valid and adding it to the existing Blockchain. The process of validating transactions and adding them to the Blockchain is called mining. As soon as a miner successfully creates a valid block, he gets rewarded with new virtual coins, for example, Bitcoins in the Bitcoin network.

7.1. How POW and mining work?

Let's understand how POW and mining work in the context of the Bitcoin Blockchain.

7.1.1. Validating transactions by nodes

(i) When a user submits a new Bitcoin transaction to the network, it goes through transaction verification. It means that transaction is validated by every computer holding a copy of the Bitcoin blockchain. These computers are called nodes.

(ii) Two types of verification are done: one is, verifying the authenticity of each transaction, and the second is, ensuring whether the user actually has the Bitcoins in his account balance that he wants to spend.

(iii) Each transaction is signed with a private key (digital signature). Since the public key is the sender's address, it can be used to identify if it is the correct key for the given address from which the transaction has been done *(Fig 7-2)*. Hence the authenticity of each transaction can be verified. If the transaction fails this verification test, it gets discarded. In this way, each transaction is validated for knowing its authenticity.

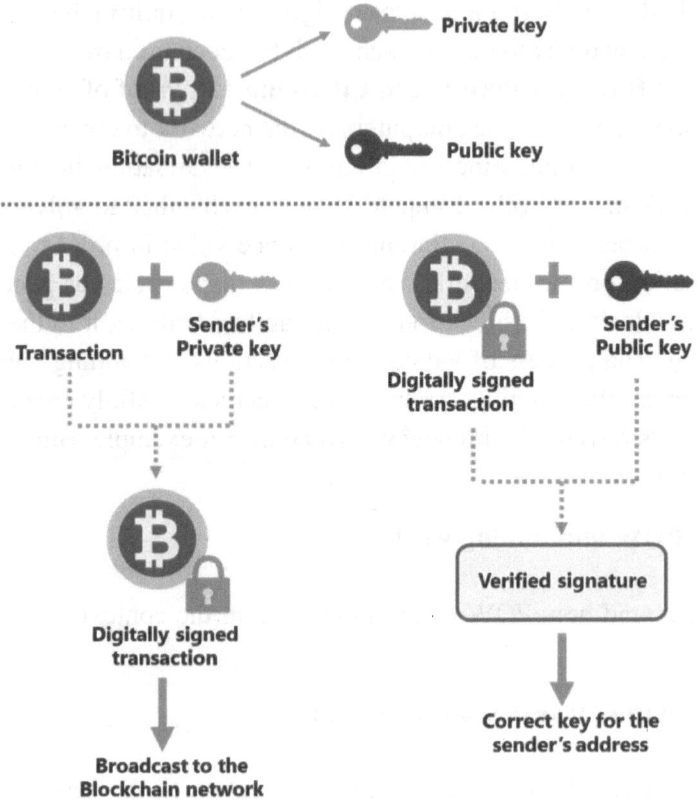

Fig 7-2: Verification of transaction using sender's public key

(iv) Nodes hold a full copy of the Bitcoin blockchain, which is a universal ledger system. The ledger contains the complete transaction history of all previous bitcoin transactions. To perform transactions on the blockchain, you need a wallet that allows you to store and exchange your bitcoins (BTC).

But how does a node keep track of your account balance and ensure that you are spending the Bitcoins that you have in your wallet?

The Blockchain ledger does not keep track of the account balances of users; instead, it only records every transaction that is broadcasted, verified and approved within the network. For example, a user Phil generates a transaction request to send 5 BTC to Jane. To complete the transaction, the nodes verify all the links to previous incoming transactions of Phil that add up to at least 5 BTC *(Fig 7-3)*. These links are called "inputs." Then the nodes verify and ensure that these 5 BTC inputs have not been spent yet. The spent transactions are called "outputs." Therefore, the nodes need to analyze and verify all the previous transactions (inputs and outputs) that ever took place on the whole network connected to your wallet. By referencing to the previous transactions on the Blockchain, nodes ensure that the sender of a transaction is not spending the same BTC twice and has the Bitcoins in his account that he wants to spend. This also solves the problem of "double-spending."

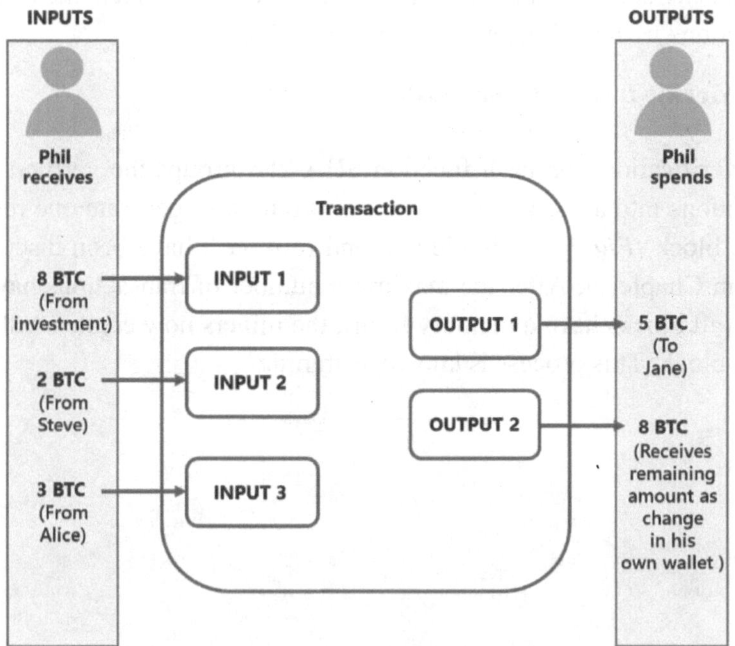

Fig 7-3: Transaction Inputs and Outputs

(v) After the successful verification by the nodes, the transaction goes into the memory pool known as the mempool of each node. A mempool is a waiting room for the transactions where these transactions sit and wait to be picked and packed into a block of transactions by the mining nodes/miners. Until added to a block, they are referred to as "unconfirmed" transactions.

7.1.2. Picking of transactions by miners from mempool

A block can hold a finite number of transactions. In the Bitcoin Blockchain, the limit of a block is 1 megabyte, which limits the number of transactions that can be included in one block to 1500-3000. But the transactions are happening all the time, sitting in the mempool, waiting to be confirmed. So how do miners prioritize which transactions to pick up from the mempool and create a block? The answer lies in the transaction fee that the miner gets after adding the transaction into a block. This fee is non-compulsory and is decided entirely by the user - a user can pay zero fee or a higher transaction fee. When a miner successfully creates a block, it gets the fee attached to all the transactions included in that block. So, the miner picks up the transactions with the highest fee to create a block.

7.1.3. Merkle tree and Root hash

After verification, the hash function SHA-256 groups the verified hashed transactions into a Merkle tree, which is required to generate one root hash for the block *(Fig 7-4)*. Merkle tree and root hash have been discussed in detail in Chapter 5. After the maximum number of transactions have been added (all blocks have a memory limit), the miners now create a valid hash for the block. This process is known as mining.

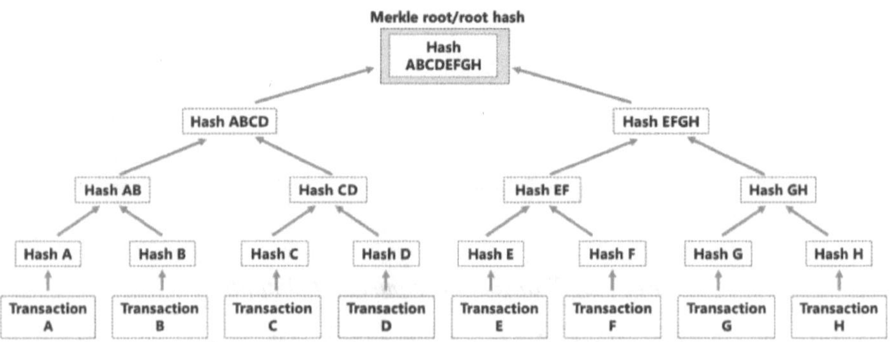

Fig 7-4: Merkle tree and Root hash

7.1.4. Difficulty level and Nonce value

A valid hash for the block is a hash that meets a certain difficulty level and is less than or equal to the "hash target." For example, suppose the hash target is 000032c2d3e965, then any hash less than or equal to the hash target is a valid hash for the block *(Fig 7-5)*. Additionally, the difficulty determines the number of predefined zeros at the beginning of the valid hash. Like in this case, the valid hash should be less than or equal to the hash target and must begin with 0000. More zeros at the beginning of the hash mean a higher difficulty.

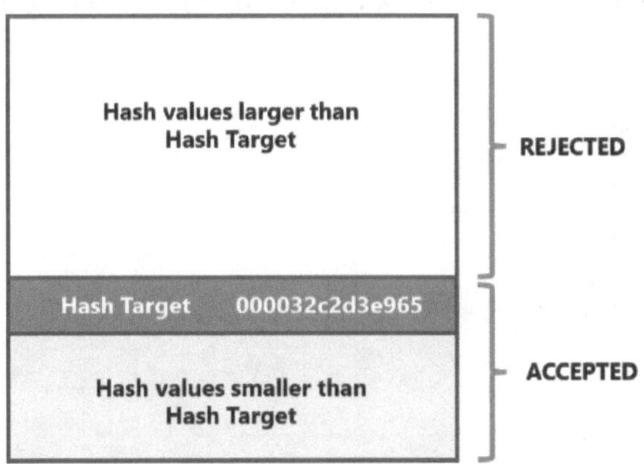

Fig 7-5: Valid hash for the block contains a value less than or equal to the hash target

To create a valid hash for the block that meets the difficulty level, the miners compete to find the nonce value that is required to generate a valid hash for the block. The nonce here stands for "number used only once"; it means each time the nonce is changed for the same block, a new hash is created. A nonce is an integer number, and along with the block number, data, and previous hash, the nonce serves as an input for the SHA256 hash function to calculate the current block's valid hash, that begins with predefined 0's and whose value is less than or equal to the hash target.

Since miners can't alter the previous block's hash or the Merkle root, they randomly choose a nonce value to generate a hash for the block. If the hash produced does not have sufficient number of 0's, then the miner discards the hash and tries a new nonce. This process is repeated continuously until a miner discovers a nonce value that produces a hash of the desired difficulty.

The nonce is the only parameter of the block that a miner can change, with all other parameters remaining static.

For instance, in the given *Fig 7-6*, for Block 1, the miner inputs nonce value as 1. The block is invalid as the hash doesn't start with 4 O's. The miner will then try to change the nonce numbers one by one from 1,2,3,…, and so on, run the SHA 256 hashing algorithm until he inputs the nonce value 30555, which gives a valid hash that matches the mining difficulty level, i.e., starts with 4 0's and its value is less than the hash target 000032c2d3e965.

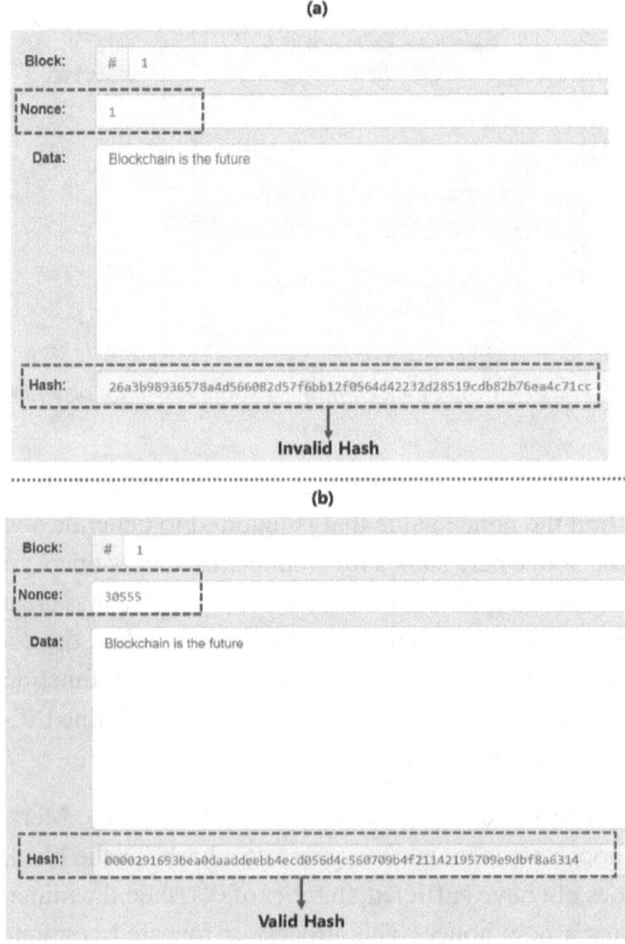

Fig 7-6: (a) Invalid hash for the block (b) Valid hash for the block as it contains four leading 0's and the value is less than or equal to the hash target

Finding a valid hash is computationally very intensive and is the "**work**" in itself. Hence the consensus mechanism got the name **Proof of work**.

If a miner finds such a nonce, called a golden nonce, and successfully completes the proof-of-work, the block is broadcasted to the rest of the network. Other miners on the network then stop the proof-of-work mining. They validate the solution and update the copy of the Bitcoin transaction ledger with the transactions that the winning miner chose to include in the current block. The mining process is challenging, i.e., it is difficult to find the nonce value, but it is very easy to verify the correct solution by the network, i.e., to check whether the hash has a value less than the hash target and has the predefined leading zeroes. After verification, if the block is found to be valid, it is added to the Blockchain. Thus, the consensus mechanism allows the network to achieve consensus on the current state of the Blockchain. It allows only a single block to be added, and this addition is broadcasted to every node in the network. Miners are then rewarded in the form of Bitcoins upon the successful verification and addition of a block to the global Blockchain. Every single node on the network stores a copy of the Blockchain, so when the Blockchain is updated, this update is broadcasted to all the nodes.

The mathematical puzzle of solving nonce value doesn't require any particular skill set of the user. It is achieved through brute force, i.e., they have to go through an intense race of trial and error to find the nonce for a block. In this puzzle-solving, the odds of solving the puzzle can be improved by acquiring more computational power. Therefore, the mining computers/miners with powerful processors will succeed more often, but due to laws of statistical probability, it is highly unlikely that the same miner will be the winner every time.

7.1.5. Increasing difficulty level

The average time for solving a puzzle is 10 minutes. And once a puzzle gets solved, the block gets added to the Blockchain. So over time, if the miners start finding it easier to solve the puzzle, the block generation time gets reduced from the proposed 10 minutes. Therefore, if mining happens too quickly, the hash computations become complex. On the contrary, if the mining is happening too slowly, the hash computations get easier to ensure that the average time for adding a block to the Blockchain is 10 minutes.

The difficulty level of the puzzle is revised after every few days. For instance, while mining Bitcoin, it is revised after the creation of every 2,016 blocks, which approximately takes around 14 days (one block in every 10 mins = 6 blocks per hour, 6 x 24 in a day, and 6 x 24 x 14 = 2016 blocks in 2 weeks). As the difficulty increases, the target value for the hash decreases. This means there have to be more leading zeros at the start of the hash number. The probability of finding a lower hash value decreases, so miners have to test more nonces. This, in turn, means that more computational power is required to successfully solve the puzzle to find the valid hash with the desired difficulty.

7.2. Mining Reward

When the verified transactions form a block, and this block is appended to the existing Blockchain, new Bitcoins are created/mined. The miner who first solves the puzzle and adds the block to the Blockchain is rewarded with newly mined Bitcoins *(Fig 7-7)*.

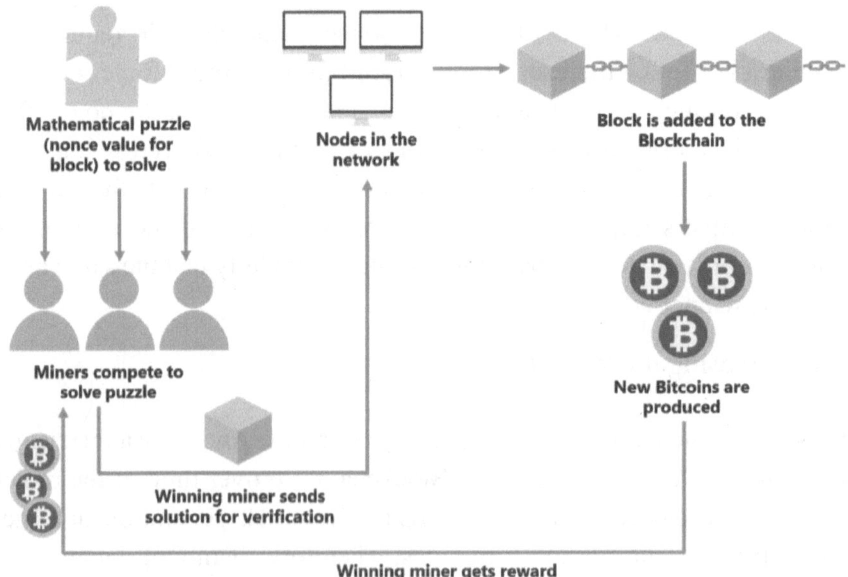

Fig 7-7: Mining reward to the winning miner

Additionally, the miner also gets the transaction fees attached to the transactions that were inserted in the block. Currently, in 2022, on average, 144 blocks are mined daily, and with each block, new 6.25 Bitcoins are created. Thus around 900 (144*6.25) new bitcoins are mined daily; in other words, they are added to the Bitcoin supply.

7.3. Bitcoin halving

Furthermore, the Bitcoin reward gets halved for every 210,000 blocks added. This process is known as bitcoin halving. It currently takes around four years to add that many blocks, so Bitcoin halving occurs approximately every four-year interval. In 2009, when Bitcoin was launched, the reward for successfully mining a Bitcoin block was 50 BTC. The first halving occurred in November 2012, which reduced the mining reward to 25 BTC. In July 2016, the reward was reduced to 12.5 BTC, and the current bitcoin halving occurred in May 2020, which reduced the reward to 6.25 BTC. The next bitcoin halving is expected to occur in 2024, and the last halving is predicted to occur in 2140. Once 21 million bitcoins have been created, no new bitcoins will be produced. From that point onward, Bitcoin miners will profit solely from the transaction fees given by network users, the people who buy and sell bitcoins.

Bitcoin halving is essential as it:

- Ensures that the amount of bitcoin mined with each block decreases, making bitcoin more scarce and, ultimately, more valuable. In other words, if the new supply of bitcoins decreases, their demand will increase.
- Halvings are also associated with huge surges in the price of bitcoin. It provides miners with the incentive to mine more, although their rewards are halved. For instance, upon the first halving in 2012, the price of bitcoin rose from a mere $12 to around $1,000; after the second halving in 2016, the bitcoin price increased to $20,000. In January 2022, the price of bitcoin was more than $40,000.

7.4. Importance of increasing the difficulty level of the mathematical puzzle

It is important to revise the difficulty level of the puzzle to find the valid hash for the block. If the difficulty is not adjusted, there would be a linear relationship between the hashing power and block rewards. As more miners join the network and hashing power increases, there would be a corresponding increase in the Bitcoin rewards. This would undermine the inflation controls on the Bitcoin protocol.

7.5. Longest chain rule

Since solving the mathematical puzzle is complex, the probability that two or more miners complete the blocks at similar times is rare. Even if they do it, two or three branches are created in the Blockchain. Imagine that the Blockchain is 1000 blocks long, and three miners simultaneously find the 1001st valid block and broadcast them to the network. Therefore, three branches will be created with the three 1001st blocks: 1001A, 1001B, and 1001C *(Fig 7-8a)*. So which of these blocks will become part of the valid Blockchain? This depends on the "longest chain rule." This problem is solved when the 1002nd block is mined. If this block is added to the 1001A block, then the chain with the 1001A block becomes longer than with the 1001B and 1001C blocks. The longest chain in the Blockchain created by the 1001A block is accepted and trusted, and therefore, everybody switches to the longest chain *(Fig 7-8b)*. As a result, all other subsequent blocks will be added to the longest chain.

The transactions of 1001B and 1001C simply go back to mempool, which the miners again pick to pack them into the blocks *(Fig 7-8c)*.

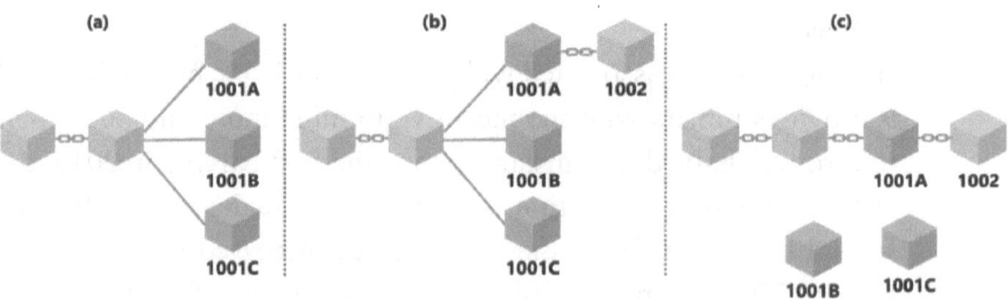

Fig 7-8: (a) Three branches of Blockchain with 1001 block, (b) 1002 block gets added to 1001A block, (c) Longest chain created by 1001A block is accepted

7.6. Mining pool

The mining process can be carried out either individually (individual mining) or in a group (mining pool). In individual mining, the user has to register his/her device as a miner. As soon as the nodes verify the transactions, all the miners in the Blockchain network will pick up the transactions and solve a mathematical puzzle to pack the transactions into a valid block. The first one to solve the complex mathematical puzzle gets rewarded and has the privilege of adding the block to the Blockchain.

On the other hand, in the mining pool, miners group together to form a pool. In other words, they combine their mining power to compete more effectively to solve the mathematical puzzle. If the pool manages to win, the reward is split between the pool members, depending on how much mining power each of them contributed. In this way, even small miners can join the mining process and hence have a chance of earning Bitcoin.

7.7. Advantages of Proof of Work (POW)

(i) Proof of work makes it extremely difficult to alter any block/transaction of the Blockchain since such an alteration would require re-mining of the altered block and all subsequent blocks because each block contains the hash of the previous block. If one block is tampered with, the old hash becomes invalid, and a new hash is generated for the block. This affects all the subsequent blocks in the Blockchain, thus making all of them invalid.

(ii) To consistently create malicious yet valid blocks, you'd need over 51% of the miners on the network controlling a majority of the network's computing power to achieve consensus on adding a block containing fraudulent transactions to the network. However, such an attack is highly improbable in a widely distributed ledger with many nodes.

(iii) Mining also solves the double-spending problem. Because of the verification done by nodes, one can't attempt to send the same digital asset to various parties at once. Therefore, if one attempts to double-spend the currency, that transaction will be rejected during verification.

7.8. Challenges of Proof of Work (POW)

(i) The biggest challenge of proof of work centers on the computational capabilities needed to solve mathematical puzzles in authenticating Blockchain transactions. Therefore, for mining, one needs a powerful computer equipped with advanced hardware.

(ii) Powerful computers inherently consume a lot of electricity and energy. Moreover, these machines require effective heat management or cooling system to remain operational; and prevent overheating and associated damages to hardware components due to internal heat build-up. As of the reports in 2021, Bitcoin miners were responsible for the consumption of around 90 terawatt-hours of electricity annually. That's more than the electricity used annually to power Finland, which is a country of 5.5 million people. And also is almost 0.5% of global electricity consumption worldwide.

The drawbacks of POW represent a significant reason why other Blockchain platforms have utilized alternative consensus mechanisms like proof of stake.

Chapter 8: Consensus mechanism- Proof of Stake (POS)

The other type of consensus mechanism, Proof of stake or POS, was introduced in 2011 to solve the problems of Proof of work or POW (discussed in Chapter 7). While they both share the same goal of reaching a consensus in Blockchain, the process is different. The first cryptocurrency to adopt the POS mechanism is Peercoin. Initially, Peercoin used the Proof-of-Work mechanism for mining, and after all the coins were mined, the transition to Proof of Stake took place. The first "clean" coins that worked on POS from the very beginning were Blackcoin and NXT.

Forging and forger: In the proof of stake consensus mechanism, blocks are considered to be forged or minted instead of mined. And the nodes who validate the blocks are not known as miners; instead, they are known as validators or forgers.

8.1. Validators and how are they selected

In the Proof of stake or POS consensus mechanism, a pseudo-random process selects a node to validate the next block. The chosen node is called a validator. The selection of validator is based on various factors like:

(i) Node's wealth: Individuals must have cryptocurrency coins with them to participate in the POS consensus mechanism. They are required to stake coins by depositing them to a node *(Fig 8-1)*. The nodes then compete for the opportunity to validate transactions. This is where the term "stake" comes from. The size of stake determines the chances of a node being chosen as the validator/forger for the next block. The forger validates transactions and creates new blocks in the network. The process of creating new blocks in POS system is known as forging. The higher the stake, the higher the chances of getting selected as the validator to forge the next block in the network.

Therefore, unlike the proof of work mechanism, in which the miner creates new blocks by performing computational work, a proof of stake system requires the validator to show ownership of a certain number of cryptocurrency units to add a new block to the Blockchain.

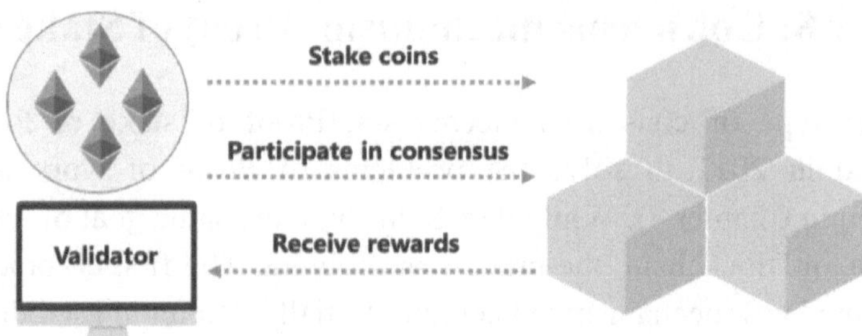

Fig 8-1: POS mechanism requires the validator to stake cryptocurrency to participate in consensus

To ensure that the POS process does not support the dominance of only the richest nodes in the network, other methods like coin age and randomized block selection are added to the selection process.

(ii) Coin age: The coin age selection method selects nodes based on for how long their coins have been at stake. It is determined by multiplying the number of coins at stake with the number of days the coins have been held at stake. For instance, the staking age for 100 tokens held for 30 days is 3000. The nodes who have staked larger sets of coins and have also staked for a long time have a greater chance of being assigned to forge the next block. The age of the coins is reset to zero as soon as a node forges a block. He/she needs to wait for at least 30 days before being able to create another one. This prevents the dominance of large share nodes in the Blockchain.

An important point to note here is that in order to participate in the forging process, the crypto coins must have been at stake for a minimum of 30 days. If it's less than 30 days, the node cannot participate in validation. The stake-holding duration is essential in order to avoid repetitive selection of a forger having more number of coins and to make the process semi-random.

Additionally, the maximum period for which the coins can be at stake is 90 days. It prevents the nodes with a significant stake from dominating the participation by holding the stake for an extended period of time. Thus, giving a fair chance to all the nodes to participate in the validation process.

Peercoin cryptocurrency uses the coin age selection process combined with the randomized selection method to select who will get the chance to forge the next block.

(iii) Randomized Block Selection: In the randomized block selection method, a node with a hit value below the target value is selected for forging the next block. To calculate the hit value, each forger encrypts the hash of the previous block using his private key. The encrypted value is 64 bytes, which is then hashed by SHA 256 hash function. The first 8-bytes of the hash output are referred to as hit value. Since each forger's private key is unique, the use of a private key in calculation generates a unique hit value for each forger in the network. The forger having the hit value below a target value is then selected for the process of forging. The calculation of the target value involves the amount of coins staked by the forger. Consequently, the target value of each forger in the network is different, and the value is higher for a forger having more coins at stake.

The target value T is calculated by the formula:

$$T = T_b * S * S_e$$

Where T_b is the base target value calculated by multiplying the previous block's target value and the amount of time that was required to forge that block, S is the time (in seconds) since the last block was forged and S_e are the coins at stake. As can be seen from the formula, the target value increases with an increase in S because of each passing second since the timestamp of the previous block. With more coins at stake, the value of Se increases, and as a result, the target value becomes high, which provides an opportunity for the hit value to be less and the forger to be selected.

Therefore, forger with the highest stake and hit value below a target value is selected for the process of forging the next block in the Blockchain.

Nxt and BlackCoin are two cryptocurrencies that use the randomized block selection method.

In a nutshell, the staking age and random block selection processes promote a healthy and decentralized forging network.

8.2. How does POS work?

(i) For the node to become a validator, an individual must "stake" a specific amount of coins. For instance, Ethereum 2.0 Blockchain will require atleast 32 ETH (ether) to be staked before a node can become a validator.

(ii) Validators are then selected in a pseudo-random way depending on their wealth by the randomized selection system to validate the block *(Fig 8-2)*. This system randomizes who gets to "forge" rather than using a competition-based mechanism like proof of work. In other words, contrary to the POW where the block creation depends on the computational power, the block creation in POS is directly proportional to the node's holding of the cryptocurrency or the underlining token of the network.

(iii) When a node gets chosen to forge the next block, it will check if the transactions in the block are valid. Each transaction is signed with a private key of the sender (digital signature). The public key, which is also the address of the sender, can be used to identify if the transaction is authentic. The validator also verifies that the sender of a transaction is not spending the same cryptocurrency twice and actually has the coins in his account that he wants to spend. This solves the problem of "double-spending." Then, the hash function SHA-256 groups the number of verified hashed transactions into a Merkle tree, required to form a block containing one root hash.

(iv) After verifying the transactions, the forger signs the block using his private key and broadcasts it on the network. Other validators on the network not chosen for forging are called **attestors**. A number of attestors are required to "attest" that the block is valid and is signed by the appropriate forger. For instance, in the case of Ethereum 2.0 Blockchain, 128 validator nodes are selected from the entire pool of validators to attest the block. At least attestations from 2/3rd of attestors are required for the block to become finalized and add it to the Blockchain. The attested block can never be reverted or changed, thus becoming an immutable and permanent part of the Blockchain.

(v) Time in proof of stake is divided into slots and epochs. One slot is the time set to create a block. For instance, in the case of Ethereum 2.0 Blockchain, one slot is of 12 seconds. 32 slots make up an "epoch," thus one epoch is 6.4 minutes. Each slot represents the opportunity for a block to be added to the Blockchain. Under normal operation, each slot will generate a block, but if a forger misses an assigned duty, a slot may be empty.

At the end of an epoch, a new group of 128 validators is formed for the next validation. Out of them, 1 is forger, and 127 are attestors. This regular and random selection process increases security preventing collusion and other bad acts.

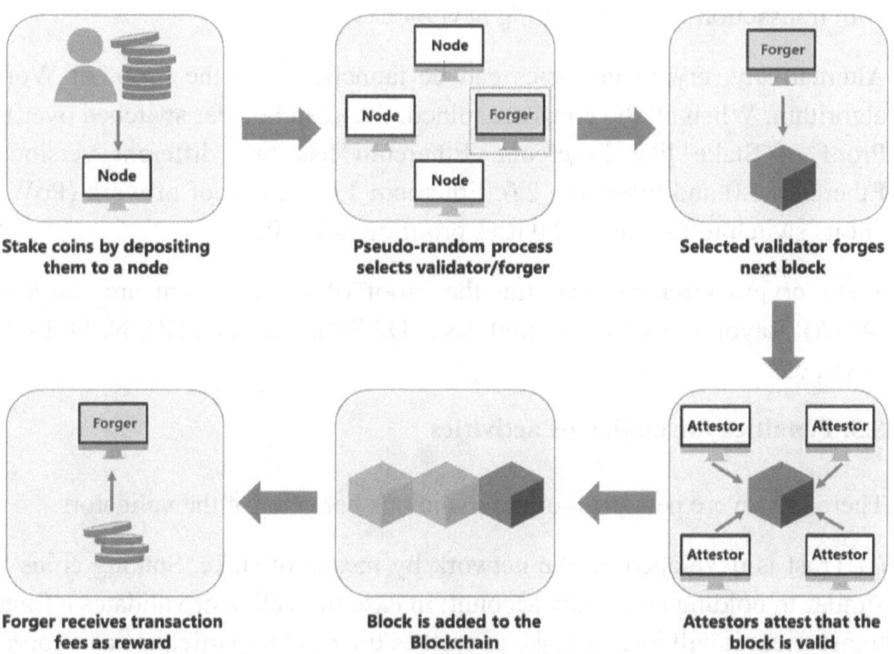

Fig 8-2: Proof of Stake consensus mechanism

(vi) After the block has been validated and added to the Blockchain, the node that got the chance to forge the block gets a reward. As a reward, the forger receives the transaction fees that are associated with the transactions in the block. The attestors also get rewarded for making correct attestations. Different cryptocurrencies that use this mechanism have their own way of calculating and distributing rewards.

Additionally, to provide the network with some time to check the validity of the transactions, the stake as well as the reward received are locked up for some time. They are only released once the network verifies that the transaction isn't incorrect or fraudulent.

Mining coins in proof of stake: In the Proof of Stake mechanism, cryptocurrency units are created initially at the time of launch of the currency, and their numbers are also fixed. Because the energy consumption in Proof of Stake is negligible as compared to Proof of work, the block creators are not rewarded with the network coins. Instead, they are rewarded with transaction fees for creating new blocks.

Alternatively, cryptocurrencies can be launched with the Proof of Work algorithm. When all the coins are mined, they can be later switched over to Proof of Stake like Ethereum. Ethereum has two different versions, Ethereum 1.0 and Ethereum 2.0. Ethereum 1.0 uses proof of work (PoW), but its switch to Ethereum 2.0 uses proof of stake (PoS).

Other cryptocurrencies that run the proof of stake system are Cardano (ADA), Raydium (RAY), Digital cash (DASH), Tezos (XTZ), NEO, EOS, NAV, etc.

8.3. Penalties for malicious activities

There are severe penalties for the malicious behavior of the validators.

(i) Trust is developed on the network by means of stake. Staking coins is similar to holding an escrow account; in case the validator validates a fraud transaction, it will lose its stake as well as the right to participate as a forger in the future. So, as long as the stake is higher than the reward, the validator who tries to participate in fraudulent activities would lose more than what it would earn. Therefore, staking cryptocurrency acts as a financial motivator for the validators to perform their job honestly.

(ii) In order for a validator to receive the full reward amount, the entire process of validation and signing block must take place within a 12-second 'slot.' Time taken over 12 seconds leads to a reduced reward, and in case it misses the slot, then it receives no reward.

(iii) Validators are also penalized for not following through with their responsibilities when it is their turn to do so, i.e., if they are offline.

However, penalties for being offline are relatively mild. So, if a validator participates correctly more than half the time, the rewards will be a net positive.

(iv) Additionally, if a validator wants to quit the forging process, its stake, along with the earned rewards, will be released only after verifying that there are no fraudulent blocks added to the Blockchain by it.

(v) There is also the risk of chosen validator not doing the job it is assigned to do. This is solved by appointing backup validators.

8.4. Benefits of Proof of Stake mechanism

(i) The proof of stake mechanism is much less wasteful as compared to the proof of work mechanism. Unlike POW, POS doesn't require high-powered computing to achieve consensus. Therefore, it's better for the environment. It uses owned cryptocurrency as the stake to participate in the consensus mechanism.

(ii) Proof of stake mechanism can be run on any average computing device. It does not require expensive equipment for mining. This is why proof of stake attracts many validators, ensuring that the system grows while also making it more robust. But only a few validators are selected in a random fashion that can verify the block, thus making the system more decentralized and secure.

(iii) When using a POS consensus mechanism, it would not make financial sense for an individual/node to attempt to perform a 51% attack. A 51% attack is defined as the event where a group or individual gains more than 50% control of a Blockchain network. For this to be achieved, the bad actor would be required to own 51% of the total amount of staked cryptocurrency. For instance, the 51% attack on Ethereum 2.0. Blockchain will cost between 55 to 85 billion USD. If he attempts to do malicious activity, he would lose all of his staked coins. As a result, he would end up spending significantly more than he could gain from the attack.

8.5. Issues with Proof of Stake mechanism

Nothing at stake problem: As already discussed in POW, the miner can only mine one chain at a time according to the "longest chain rule." Additionally, choosing the wrong chain is costly. For example, suppose a fork in Blockchain creates two chains, A and B *(Fig 8-3)*. A miner can choose to mine one chain or the other one. But it's not possible to mine both the chains. It is because mining requires the miner to use high-powered computation devices. Therefore, if the miner chooses to mine the wrong chain, the money that went into mining the block goes wasted.

Fig 8-3: Fork in Blockchain creates two chains, A and B

On the other hand, in the case of POS, the validator can forge both chains. Thus, when there is a fork in Blockchain, validators have three choices:

(a) work only on the chain A

(b) work only on the chain B

(c) work on both chains A and B

Also, choosing the wrong chain is not costly because it costs a validator nothing to validate transactions on multiple chains. Also, if validators forge both (or more) chains, they will collect transaction fees regardless of which chain is confirmed *(Fig 8-4)*. Thus, the problem is called "nothing at stake."

Fig 8-4: Both chains A and B can be forged in the POS mechanism

The solution to the "nothing at stake" problem

There are three possible ways by which the nothing-at-stake problem might be addressed:

(i) Punishment to validators for choosing to validate two different versions of the same block.

(ii) Punishment to validators for validating the wrong block, regardless of whether or not they double-attested.

(iii) The network contains validation software that will not allow for forging all chains, so validators would need to choose a "true" chain for forging.

Casper: To eliminate the issue of nothing at stake, Ethereum developers have designed the Casper protocol in which the validators will be penalized for the fraudulent activities. To reduce the likelihood that validators forge all chains, they would need to deposit security on the Blockchain. If validators are found to validate blocks on both chains or found to validate wrong blocks, they will be penalized by losing a portion or all of their security deposit. The security deposit attaches a cost to being dishonest; thus, it is in the best economic interest of all of the validators to behave honestly.

Chapter 9: Other consensus mechanisms for Public Blockchain

9.1. Delegated Proof of Stake (dPoS)

As discussed in Proof of stake (Chapter 8), data verification is assigned to network nodes that have staked or locked their cryptocurrency coins as collateral. The larger the number of coins a user stakes, the higher the chances of getting their device selected as the validator to validate the next block in the network. Delegated Proof-of-Stake (DPoS) consensus mechanism is a variant of POS, in which users still stake their cryptocurrency coins. However, rather than becoming responsible for validating the block themselves, users (or stakeholders) stake their coins to delegate the work by voting on the node that would validate the block on their behalf. Thus the consensus mechanism got its name "Delegated Proof-of-Stake."

Once the nodes have been elected, they're responsible for reaching a consensus among themselves to validate transactions and add blocks to the Blockchain. Using DPoS, you can vote on nodes by pooling your crypto coins into a staking pool and linking those to a particular node. You are not required to physically transfer your tokens to another wallet but instead utilize a staking service provider to stake your tokens in a staking pool.

9.1.1. Technology-based democracy

The Proof of Work consensus mechanism is operated as direct democracy. As discussed in Chapter 7, all nodes have the equivalent role for transaction verification and block creation in the Bitcoin Blockchain. On the other hand, in Delegated Proof of Stake, stakeholders vote for a number of nodes to process and validate transactions on the network, thus allowing a more diverse group of people to participate in the process. This is a representative democracy.

The election of the nodes is based on their reputation and trustworthiness. If an elected node misbehaves or does not work efficiently, it will be quickly expelled and replaced by another one. Therefore, the delegates are motivated to be honest and efficient, or they get voted out.

9.1.2. How does DPoS work?

Voting

Voting is the most important component of DPoS. The users/stakeholders 'vote' to select the nodes they trust to validate transactions, and the nodes who have collected the most votes earn the right to validate transactions *(Fig 9-1)*. Users can also delegate their voting power to other users called delegates, whom they trust to vote for nodes on their behalf. A user must stake coins in order to vote. Staked coins are locked in smart contracts during the voting rounds. Votes are weighted according to the size of each user's stake. More coins translate into more votes. A user is allowed one vote per node. But he can vote for multiple nodes. Refer to Chapter 11 for a detailed explanation of smart contracts.

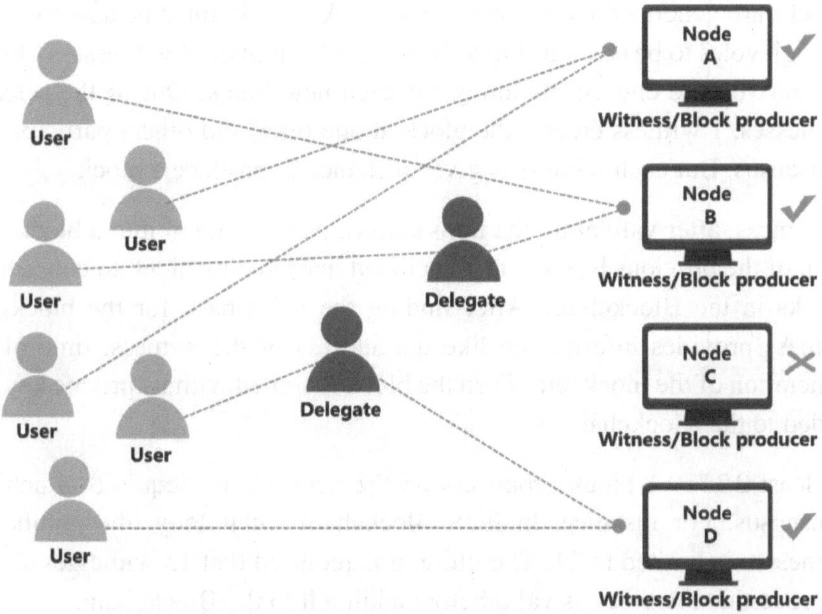

Fig 9-1: Users and delegates vote to select the nodes to become witnesses/block producers that will validate transactions

To become a validating node, the owner of the node must convince the stakeholders in the network that they have all the requirements to be a validating node. Ceratin factors that favor a node being elected are:

(i) Team behind the node

(ii) Hardware capacity, location

(iii) No. of coins staked in the network. The larger the stake, the larger the reward after validating transactions.

The nodes selected by voting are referred to as witnesses or block producers.

They are able to create blocks by validating transactions. After all transactions in a block are verified, the witnesses receive a reward that is then shared with every user who voted for that witness.

Block producers/Witnesses

Blocks are generated by witnesses in turn. A witness must be able to obtain enough votes to be elected *(Fig 9-2)*. A limited number of witnesses between 20 and 100 are chosen randomly for each new block. Out of the selected witnesses, 1 witness creates the block at one time, and others participate in consensus. But each witness is given a chance to produce a block.

A witness, after validating the transactions, package them into a block. The hash of the previous block is also included in each new block to connect the blocks in the Blockchain. After finding the valid hash for the block, the witness provides information like the address of the witness, time of the generation of the block, etc. Then the block is signed with its private key and added to the Blockchain.

At least 2⁄3rd + 1 block producers on the network are required to achieve consensus. For instance, in EOS Blockchain technology, the number of witnesses is limited to 21. Therefore, it is required that 15 witnesses should approve that the block is valid before adding it to the Blockchain.

The witnesses of one block might not be the witnesses of the next. The elected witnesses receive the transaction fees from the validated block, and that reward is then shared with users who pooled their tokens in the successful delegate's pool. The more the stake, the higher the share of the block reward user receives. The rewards are shared based on each user's stake, so if the user's stake represents 5% of the total staking balance, he will receive 5% of the block reward.

Additionally, because there are a limited number of validators, DPoS allows the network to reach consensus more quickly.

Even though a witness can keep certain transactions out of a block, they cannot change the transaction's information.

Why are witnesses trusted?

It is important to note that voting is a real-time and continuous process, which means that witnesses can be voted out if the selected witness is non-performing and fails to validate the transactions within the allotted time. If the block is missed, which means that none of the transactions is verified, then it is passed to the next active witness. Also, the reward of the missed block would be given to the next active witness who ends up verifying all transactions in that block. When this occurs, the block is considered stolen. If the block is missed frequently by a witness, it is considered non-performing and can be kicked out of the network. Then the stakeholders vote for a new witness.

On the other hand, if the witnesses are found to be dishonest to the network, they will lose what they staked. The election of the nodes is based on their reputation. If the node performs well, its reputation value will gradually increase; otherwise, the reputation value will gradually decrease. The reputation determines the credibility of a node. So obviously, the nodes with a good reputation are preferred to be voted by the users. Additionally, reputation is also the primary incentive against malicious behavior. Therefore, it is in the witnesses' best interest to be a valued member of the community to avoid getting replaced.

Delegates

Delegates are also elected by stakeholders via voting in a manner similar to witnesses. Apart from voting on behalf of stakeholders, delegates are active members of the network. They examine the performance of the entire Blockchain protocol, improve the Blockchain by developing new features, and may even propose to change the rules of the Blockchain. The changes proposed can be changing the size of a block, changes in transaction fees, or the amount a witness should be paid in return for validating a block. After the majority of delegates are in favor of a proposed change, the changes are done via voting by the stakeholders. It ensures that the direct power is in the hands of users rather than either the delegates or witnesses. Even the delegates may be voted out if they are found to be involved in fraudulent activities.

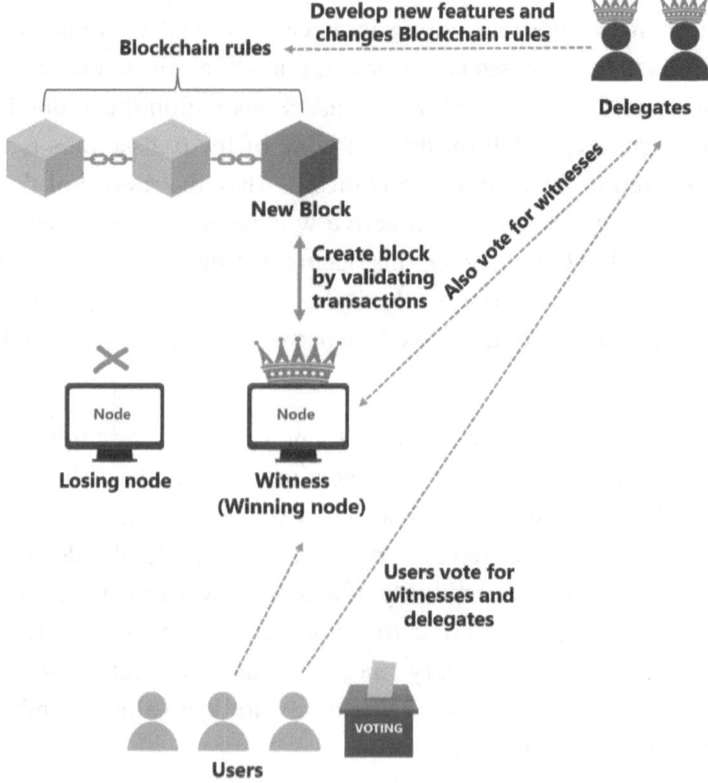

Fig 9-2: How does DPoS work?

Block Validators

Block validators in DPoS refer to full nodes who verify that blocks created by witnesses follow the consensus rules. Any user can run a block validator and verify the network. There is no financial incentive to be a block validator.

9.1.3. Blockchains using DPoS consensus

EOS (21 witnesses), Cosmos, Lisk (101 witnesses), Ark (51 witnesses), Bitshares (101 witnesses), etc.

9.1.4. Advantages of DPoS systems

(i) Since there are a limited number of validators, DPoS allows the network to reach consensus more quickly and therefore provides much faster processing of transactions than Proof of Work and Proof of Stake systems. The transactions are confirmed in an average of just 1 second. Because of this reason, DPoS systems are more scalable and can be used for many applications.

(ii) Witnesses can be voted out as soon as they are found to be performing malicious activities; therefore, they have an incentive to perform their role honestly.

(iii) Also, stakeholders lose their stake if the network does not operate smoothly. Therefore, it is in the best interest of stakeholders to replace the witness if it is found to be non-performing or involved in fraudulent activities.

(iv) No specialized equipment is required to become a user, witness, or block validator. A normal computer with good computation power is enough.

(v) They are energy-efficient, cost-efficient, and environment-friendly compared to Proof of Work hashing algorithms.

9.1.5. Limitations of DPoS systems

(i) Having a small group of elected witnesses can make DPoS vulnerable to centralization. For instance, EOS Blockchain has only 21 witnesses/block producers to validate transactions. This is a fairly high amount of centralization.

(ii) Because fewer nodes/witnesses (20-100) are in charge of keeping the network alive, it's easier to organize a "51 percent" attack.

(iii) Vote strength is determined by how many tokens the individuals have, which means that people who own more coins will influence the network more than people who own very few. Thus, DPoS users with small stakes will have less incentive to vote as they might think their vote doesn't matter in comparison with the votes of bigger stakeholders. Thus, low participation in the voting process can further generate centralization in the network by placing the power in the hands of a limited number of coin holders.

9.2. Proof of Activity: A Hybrid consensus algorithm

Proof of Activity is a hybrid consensus mechanism that is a combination of two other Blockchain consensus mechanisms: Proof of Work (POW) and Proof of Stake (POS). It attempts to leverage the best of both PoW and PoS consensus mechanisms to validate and generate new blocks in the Blockchain.

9.2.1. How does Proof of Activity work?

(i) The mechanism in Proof of Activity goes through two phases before a new block is ready to be added to the Blockchain.

First phase: The first phase uses the approach from Proof of Work. The miners on the network, with higher computing power, compete to be the first to solve a complex mathematical puzzle to find a valid hash for the block. After finding the valid hash, a new block is generated. The new block will have a header and the reward address of the winning miner. The block header contains information like: Merkel root, Timestamp, Block Version number, Difficulty Target, Nonce, and Previous Hash.

Second phase: Once the block is generated, the system is directed into the second phase, i.e., Proof of Stake. In this phase, a group of validators is randomly selected from the network. The chances of getting selected increase with the number of coins a participant owns in that network — just like in traditional Proof of Stake. The validators will be in charge of validating the generated block and signing it to confirm its validity.

Once the selected validators have signed or confirmed the block, the block is completed. The complete block is then added to the Blockchain.

(ii) The winning miner and the validators who played a role in contributing to the new block will be rewarded.

9.2.2. Advantages of Proof of Activity

(i) PoA mechanism makes the Blockchain more secure than either POW or POS separately. The probability of a 51% attack drops nearly to 0%. A successful attack means gaining control of over 50% of a Blockchain network. This can happen if an individual or a group has control of at least 51% of the entire network's mining computing power like in PoW, plus at least 51% of the coins that are staked in the network are required to be owned like in PoS. As a result, the loss is significantly more than anyone could gain from the attack.

9.2.3. Disadvantages of Proof of Activity

(i) Proof of Activity carries with it problems that POW has been criticized for. Similar to POW, Proof of Activity uses high computational power for solving the mathematical puzzle. This means that this consensus mechanism also requires relatively high-power consumption and powerful hardware.

(ii) Proof of Activity doesn't have any solution to stop the double signing by the validators.

9.2.4. Blockchain platforms using Proof of Activity

Decred (DCR) and Espers (ESP)

9.3. Leased Proof of Stake or LPoS

In the Proof of Stake (discussed in Chapter 8), users are required to stake their cryptocurrency coins by depositing them to nodes. The stakeholders with low amounts of staked coins are unlikely ever to get the chance to add a block —just as in Delegated Proof of Stake, where the users with small stakes will have less incentive to vote for the nodes to add blocks. Because of this reason, many stakeholders with low amounts of coins never actively participate in the network, so maintaining the consensus is left to a limited number of larger stakeholders. This creates unwanted centralization in the Blockchain network.

Leased Proof of Stake or LPoS consensus mechanism is a variant of POS and was introduced to solve the problems associated with POS and DPoS.

Leased Proof of Stake works exactly like PoS but uses leasing to provide nodes with small stakes, an incentive to take part in the consensus. In other words, the users can lease their coins to the nodes that participate in validating transactions and adding blocks to the Blockchain.

9.3.1. How does LPoS work?

(i) To start leasing, the coin holder needs to create a lease transaction and specify the recipient node address along with the number of coins to be leased. There is always an option to stop leasing by placing a cancel lease transaction.

(ii) The leased funds remain in full control of the coin holder/leaser. The coins don't leave the wallet of the leaser, but they can link the coins to the nodes to whom they want to lease. The coins are not transferred to the node; they just remain unspendable: they cannot be transferred or traded until the leaser cancels the lease.

(iii) LPoS enables the leasers to participate in the consensus mechanism because the larger the amount that is leased to a node, the higher the chances for that node to be selected to generate the next block. For instance, two leasers lease their coins to node B *(Fig 9-3)*. The tokens that are leased to the node are used to increase the stake weight of the node, which in turn increases their chances of getting selected to validate transactions and add the next block to the Blockchain.

(iv) Upon winning, the node packs the waiting transactions into a block. The winning node then receives the transaction fees as a reward.

(v) Upon receiving the reward, the node operators share a percentage of their node rewards with their leasers. The higher the leased amount, the more is the reward for the leaser.

9.3.2. Blockchain platforms using LPoS

Waves and NIX. In the Waves platform, the node must have at least 1000 WAVES in order to participate in generating blocks. The node's balance can be zero but there should be enough coin holders wishing to lease their coins to the node, thus, generating a balance of 1000 WAVES to make the node eligible to produce the block. If the node is selected to produce the next block, the leaser(s) will receive a percentage of the transaction fee collected by the node.

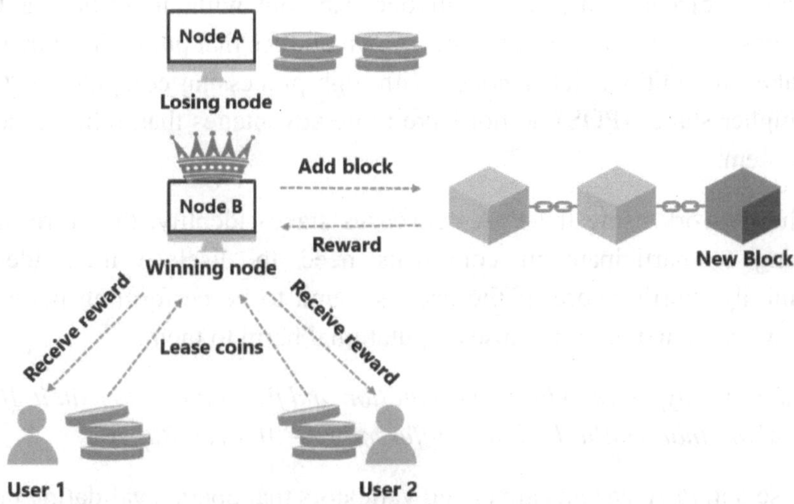

Fig 9-3: How does LPoS work?

Chapter 10: Consensus mechanisms for Private/ Permissioned Blockchain

10.1. Proof of Authority (PoA)

As discussed earlier, Blockchains can either be permissionless or permissioned. Unlike permissionless Blockchain, where anyone can become a node, in the permissioned Blockchain, all nodes are pre-selected. One of the types of consensus mechanisms used in permissioned Blockchains is Proof of Authority, abbreviated as PoA. It is also a variant of the Proof of Stake consensus mechanism where instead of coins, the network users stake their identity and reputation. This means that, unlike POW and POS consensus mechanisms, where anyone can join without disclosing their identities, users in PoA systems are known entities that put their reputations at stake. In addition, richer nodes with high processing computers (POW) and higher stakes (POS) do not have more advantages than other nodes in the system.

As the network using the PoA consensus stakes identity, therefore, users wishing to participate in consensus need to disclose their identity voluntarily. Furthermore, if the user is found to be performing malicious activity on the network, it causes reputational harm to them.

"It takes twenty years to build a reputation and five minutes to ruin it. If you think about that, you'll do things differently." – Warren Buffet

The users in PoA systems are called validators that operate validating nodes to validate the blocks and add them to the Blockchain. Therefore, the validators that are considered to be trustworthy are allowed to participate in achieving the consensus.

10.1.1. How to establish authority?

To be elected as a validator, a candidate should comply with the following conditions:

(i) It should not be easy to obtain the right to be elected as a validator. A potential validator is required to obtain a valid notarial license because the notary data is publicly available. In addition, the notary license attests to the absence of a criminal record and a candidate's good moral standard.

(ii) The identity must be formally verified on the network with the possibility of cross-checking the information in the public domain.

(iii) There should be complete uniformity in the checks and procedures for establishing authority.

(iv) In order to ensure honest validators and the integrity of the Blockchain, the identity of the selected validators must be periodically verified.

Thus, PoA using Blockchains is secured by the validating nodes that are randomly chosen to serve as trustworthy entities. It uses a limited number of block validators, around 25, making the system highly scalable.

10.1.2. How does PoA work?

(i) PoA based network is an automated process; it is not mandatory for the validator to constantly monitor their computers/validating nodes. However, the software is required to run to put transactions in the blocks.

(ii) The validator nodes are selected randomly. Out of the selected nodes, one validator node is the leader node that validates the transactions and creates a new block. A leader node can only sign one block in the round in its validation time *(Fig 10-1)*.

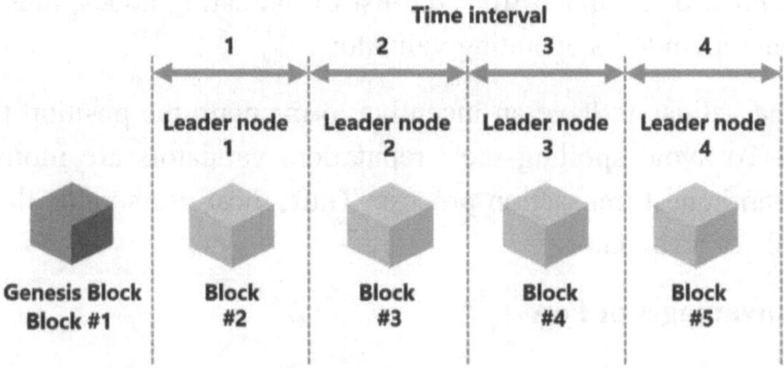

Fig 10-1: Generation of a block by one leader node in its validation time

Other selected validator nodes confirm the validity of the signed block, and then the block is added to the Blockchain *(Fig 10-2)*. At each time interval, the leader role is passed to the next validating node from the list of validating nodes. PoA allows every selected validator node to have an equal opportunity to be assigned to produce blocks.

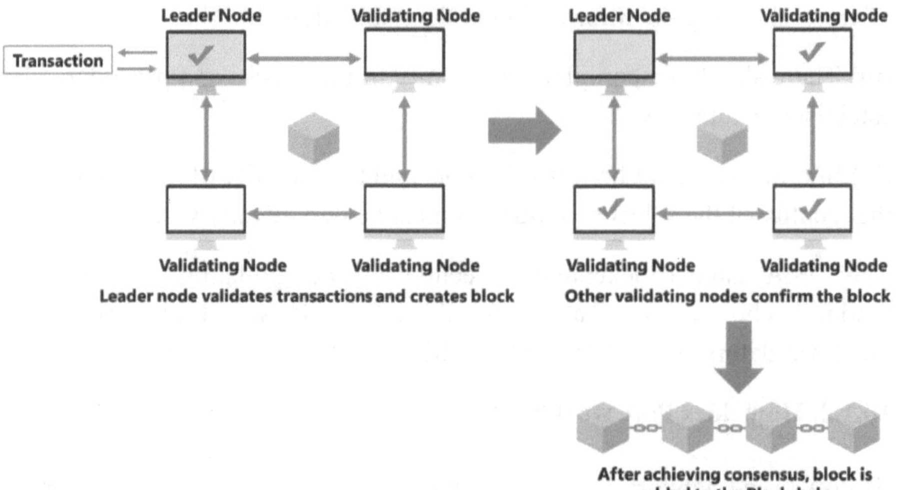

Fig 10-2: How does PoA work?

(iii) If the leader node misses generating a new block in the round, it will be marked 'inactive' by other honest nodes. An inactive node will be considered "active" once it creates a new block again.

(iv) If the validating node processes a malicious or fraudulent transaction, it can be banned or excluded from the list of validating nodes, thus causing reputational harm to its operating validator.

(v) So, the validators have an incentive to maintain the position that they received. To avoid spoiling their reputation, validators are motivated to maintain an honest transaction process. Thus, most users value their hard-earned role of a validator.

10.1.3. Advantages of PoA

(i) Like PoS, proof of authority requires minimal computational effort and does not need specialized equipment. Thus PoA platforms are incredibly cheap to run and maintain.

(ii) PoA system is based on a limited number of block validators; thus, it allows the network to reach consensus more quickly and therefore provides much faster processing of transactions than Proof of Work and Proof of Stake systems. The transactions are confirmed in less than 1 second. Because of this reason, PoA systems are more scalable.

10.1.4. Limitations of PoA

(i) PoA networks typically have a relatively small number of validating nodes. This makes a PoA network more centralized.

(ii) PoA networks typically accept entities with an established reputation as their validators, meaning attaining that role is typically out of reach for an ordinary person.

(iii) PoA is suitable only for enterprise applications as it requires users to trust validators, but it can not be used for public blockchains, as public Blockchains aim to be trustless.

10.1.5. Blockchains using PoA

Vechain, Ethereum Express, PoA network, and Microsoft Azure

10.1.6. Applications of PoA

The PoA mechanism works best in a centralized way because of the small number of validators. It aims to make centralized systems better and more efficient. Thus, it is a practical, efficient solution for Blockchain networks, especially the private Blockchain where some level of trust and familiarity already exists among the members.

For instance, the PoA consensus mechanism may be applied in a variety of scenarios and is deemed a great option for logistical applications such as supply chains but can not be used in the crypto community. The faster speed of the PoA mechanism allows logistics operators to track any products in real-time for maximum efficiency of deliveries.

10.2. Proof of Elapsed Time (PoET)

Proof of elapsed time, developed by Intel Corporation in 2016, is another consensus algorithm used by permissioned Blockchain networks.

10.2.1. How does PoET work?

(i) PoET follows a time-lottery system that spreads the chances of every participating node winning equally in the network. For the node to participate in consensus, it downloads the trusted code and requires code attestation by Intel Software Guard Extension (SGX). SGX functions as a Trusted Execution Environment to run the code, thus ensuring that the nodes are running the trusted code necessary for the consensus mechanism and it can not be altered by anyone. The node then sends SGX's attestation to the network in order to get approved by other participants. SGX also uses an asymmetric key approach to generate the private/public key pair for the node.

(ii) In each round of consensus, the nodes receive a signed timer object from the trusted code, which is completely randomized. The random timer object generates a random wait time for each node; each node must sleep for that duration or do another task for that random wait time. The random timer operates independently at every node, generating different wait times for each node. This randomization ensures that every node is equally likely to be the winner. Also, the signed timer object mitigates any potential malicious actor from taking control of the system and attempting to consistently receive a shorter timer so that they can produce more blocks.

(iii) The node with the shortest wait time will wake up first and win the chance to verify and sign the new block using his private key, then add it to the Blockchain. This information is then broadcasted to the whole network. The same process then repeats for adding the next block.

10.2.2. Advantages of PoET

(i) PoET is time and energy-efficient. It doesn't require much electricity consumption, and the nodes can "go to sleep" while they wait for their turn.

(ii) It allows the network to reach consensus more quickly, allowing faster processing of transactions. Thus, it is easily scalable.

10.2.3. Blockchains using PoET

Hyperledger Sawtooth—designed for enterprise uses like supply chain and logistics, uses the PoET consensus mechanism.

10.3. Practical Byzantine Fault Tolerance (pBFT)

Any technology, including Blockchain, is based on the basic assumption that the system has faults and should survive even when the nodes deviate from their normal behavior. The deviation can be also be non-malicious, like the crashing of a node or no response from a node, which can happen if the node has not received the message due to faults in communication protocol or the node is offline.

So, Blockchain technology can have two types of fault tolerance systems:

Simple fault tolerant system: This mechanism prevents the system from failing when the node(s) crashes or goes offline. It does not take care of the nodes behaving maliciously.

Byzantine fault tolerant (BFT) system: In a decentralized distributed system, like Blockchain, the participants often communicate with each other in an uncontrolled, open, and permissionless system. Their action may vary based on their individual interests and can be malicious. A BFT system ensures that it will continue to operate where the node(s) fail or are malicious.

10.3.1. The Byzantine Generals Problem

The Byzantine problem was first referenced in the paper titled 'The Byzantine Generals' Problem,' published in 1982.

The problem is how to ensure that multiple entities, separated by distance, are in absolute full agreement before an action is taken. In other words, how can individual parties find a way to achieve full consensus? Let's understand the problem and how it relates to Blockchain technology. Imagine several battalions of a Byzantine army surrounding an enemy city. Each of the battalions is camped several miles from the other, and each is commanded by its own general. The generals can communicate with each other only by messenger. After observing the enemy, they must agree on a battle plan. However, some generals may be traitors, trying to prevent the loyal generals from reaching an agreement to attack the enemy city. In order to achieve consensus, the generals must agree on the same decision as to whether attack or retreat.

10.3.2. pBFT consensus

Imagine generals are actually the computers/nodes on a network. And byzantine node refers to the traitor node, which could intentionally lie or mislead other nodes in the network.

Practical Byzantine Fault Tolerance (pBFT) is a consensus approach that resists a system getting into the Byzantine Generals' problem. It also means the system should stay intact even if one of the nodes (or general) fails. The objective is that the

- distributed computer network should function correctly by mitigating the influence of these malicious nodes on the correct function of the network by propagating incorrect information to other nodes in the network,
- and the right consensus is reached by the honest nodes in the system.

10.3.3. Nodes in the pBFT model

(i) All of the nodes within the system communicate with each other, and the goal is for all of the honest nodes to come to an agreement through a majority.

(ii) Nodes not only have to prove that messages came from a specific peer node but also need to verify that the message was not modified during transmission.

(iii) For the pBFT model to work, the assumption is that the amount of malicious nodes in the network cannot simultaneously equal or exceed 1/3rd of the overall nodes in the system. In other words, the pBFT consensus algorithm requires at least 3f+1 nodes in a system of f faulty nodes (byzantine nodes). Because as long as there are 3f+1 nodes, the majority of the non-faulty/honest nodes will always be able to reach a consensus no matter how the f faulty nodes interfere with the process.

10.3.4. How does pBFT work?

(i) There are three types of nodes in the pBFT model:

Client nodes: The client nodes are responsible for sending transaction requests.

Leader node: Each consensus-reaching process has only one leader node that receives the request from the client.

Replica nodes: Replica nodes that are responsible for finalizing blocks. Each consensus-reaching process involves multiple replica nodes, and they all proceed in a similar way.

Both leader and replica nodes are **consensus nodes**.

(ii) A client sends a request to the leader node to broadcast the message and start the execution of consensus.

(iii) The leader node then broadcasts the request to the replica nodes.

(iv) The replica nodes verify the request's legitimacy and then broadcast a corresponding prepare message to other nodes.

(iv) After certain nodes gather, 2f+1 prepare messages and verify if these messages are all consistent with the ones they sent out. Then these nodes send a commit message to the client.

(v) When the client receives f+1 commit messages from different nodes with the same result, it confirms that the consensus is reached on its request. Here f represents the maximum number of potentially faulty nodes.

Suppose a consensus cannot be reached among all consensus nodes in the distributed system. In that case, the view-change protocol will be executed, and a newly elected leader node will initiate a new consensus procedure.

10.3.5. Blockchains using pBFT

The Hyperledger Fabric project uses the pBFT protocol to achieve high transaction throughput in a permissioned Blockchain. Zilliqa is another project that uses pBFT in combination with a PoW consensus mechanism.

10.3.6. Limitations of pBFT

(i) pBFT model is susceptible to a Sybil attack, where a malicious node creates many duplicate accounts in the network and operates unauthorized actions. This may out-vote honest nodes, thus compromising the network.

(ii) pBFT is a promising consensus solution when the group of nodes is small but becomes inefficient for large networks. Because of this, scalability and the high-throughput ability of the pBFT model are reduced. Thus it needs to be optimized or used in combination with another consensus mechanism.

Chapter 11: Smart Contracts

Smart contracts are the self-executing programs stored on a Blockchain that run when predefined conditions are met. They are the digital versions of the standard paper contract, whose terms of the agreement are written in the lines of code. They automatically execute transactions if certain conditions are met without requiring the help of a third party to manage or approve the transaction. This third party could be a government organization, a lawyer, or any other entity. For instance, in traditional paper contracts, a document outlines the terms of conditions between two parties, which is enforceable by law. If one party A violates the terms, party B can take Party A to court for not complying with the agreement. Whereas, in the smart contract, such agreements are written in code, so the conditions of the agreement are automatically enforced without any third party getting involved *(Fig 11-1)*.

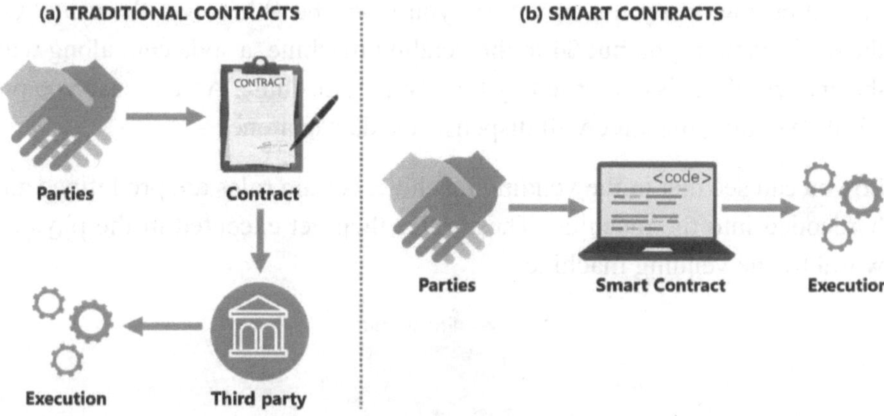

Fig 11-1: Third-party is not involved in the execution of smart contracts

The concept of smart contracts was first proposed in 1994 by Nick Szabo, an American computer scientist and cryptographer who invented a virtual currency called "Bit Gold" in 1998.

11.1. A metaphor for Smart Contracts

One of the real-life metaphors for a smart contract that many of you may have interacted with is the Vending Machine! The smart contracts on the Blockchain and vending machines share a lot of commonalities.

Certain rules are hardcoded into the vending machine that decides what happens when certain conditions are met, and based on these conditions, the vending machine triggers automatic actions *(Fig 11-2)*. For instance, if you want a can of soda, then:

(i) You select a product i.e., can of soda

(ii) The vending machine tells the amount required to purchase the selected product

(iii) You insert the correct amount

(iv) The vending machine verifies you have inserted the correct amount

(v) The vending machine dispenses the product of choice

Suppose the cost of a can of soda is $3. If you have only $1 in your pocket, no matter how many times you try, you won't be able to get the drink. On the other hand, if you put $4 in the vending machine, a soda can, along with the change of $1, is dispensed by the vending machine. And in case you put $3, the vending machine will dispense a soda can alone.

So you can see that in the vending machine, certain rules are predefined and hardcoded into the machine. These rules then get executed in the physical world by the vending machine.

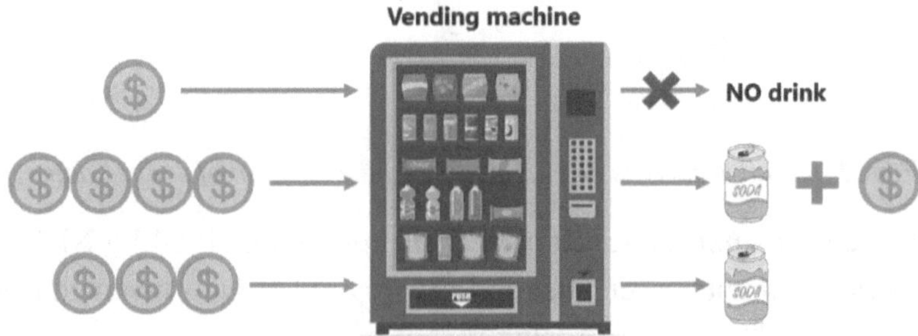

Fig 11-2: Vending machine: a metaphor for smart contracts

Similarly, smart contracts are rules defined and executed by the lines of code on the Blockchain.

11.2 How do smart contracts work?

The life cycle of smart contracts consists of four consecutive phases: creation, deployment, execution, and completion.

11.2.1. Creation of smart contracts

Before any transaction, the contractual parties determine the terms of the contract. It is important to note that lawyers or counsellors may be required to help parties draft an initial contractual agreement, but for the execution of the agreement, a third party is not required. After the contractual terms and conditions are finalized, they are translated into programming code called a smart contract. Basically, the code represents a number of different conditional statements that describe the possible scenarios of a future transaction. They work by following simple "if…then…else" statements that are written into code on a Blockchain. The "if" statement is the most basic conditional statement that is used to make a decision on whether the statement or code will be executed or not.

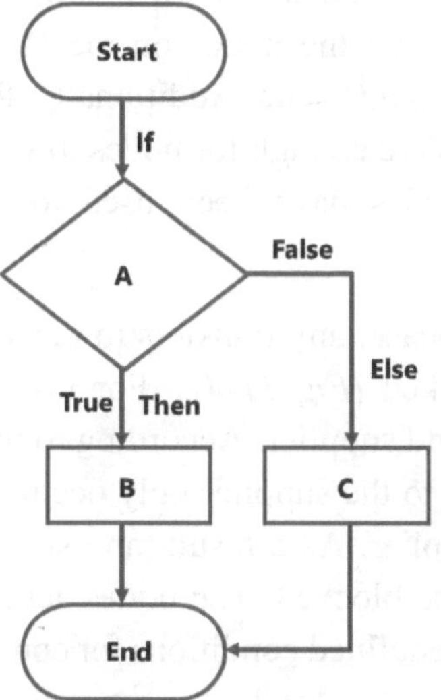

Fig 11-3: If-Then-Else flow diagram

"If" the condition is true, "then" the statement will be executed, while if the condition is false, then else (other) statement will be executed. For instance, in *Fig 11-3*, if A is true, then B will be executed, else C will be executed.

11.2.2. Deployment of smart contracts

When the smart contract is created, the parties can agree to the terms and conditions by applying their digital signature on the contract. A digital signature is a cryptographic technique that binds a person to digital data. Private keys of the parties are used to create digital signatures. Digital signatures have already been explained in detail in Chapter 6. Then the smart contract is stored on the Blockchain network, which can not be altered/modified, making them immutable. Any correction or revision in the contract requires the creation of a new contract. For that reason, you must pay special attention to writing and testing code to avoid introducing bugs in the contract that will never be fixed.

Because of storing the smart contracts on Blockchain, they become decentralized. It means that smart contracts are not controlled by a single machine/human. In fact, all the nodes on the Blockchain store the same contract with exactly the same state. Additionally, the digital signature + the public key of the parties are enough for nodes to verify that the private keys associated with the parties have been used to make signatures on the contract.

Moreover, during this phase, any transfers to the smart contract's receiving wallet address are blocked *(Fig 11-4).* For instance, a smart contract is signed between buyer and supplier. According to the contract, fund transfer from the buyer's wallet to the supplier only occurs once the buyer receives the goods from the supplier. As a result, any sort of funds transfer on the supplier's wallets will be blocked. The nodes act as a governing body that validates whether the predefined conditions for contract execution have been satisfied.

11.2.3. Execution of smart contracts

After the deployment of smart contracts, the contractual terms are monitored and evaluated by all the Blockchain nodes in the network. Once the predefined conditions are met, the smart contract is self-executed. The funds in the form of coins are released from the buyer's wallet to transfer them to the supplier (as a commitment of exchanging goods). The released funds create a transaction triggered by the criteria met. Consequently, the executed transaction is validated by the nodes on the Blockchain to ensure fulfilment of the contract conditions. This verification process is done by consensus mechanisms. The verified transactions and the updated state of smart contracts are then stored on the Blockchain.

11.2.4. Completion of smart contracts

According to the predefined conditions on the smart contract, after the buyer receives the goods from the seller, the seller's wallet is unlocked. Therefore, the funds get transferred from the buyer to the supplier's wallet. This marks the completion of the smart contract, which is then closed and recorded on the Blockchain.

It is important to note that a sequence of transactions has been executed during the deployment, execution, and completion phases of a smart contract. Therefore, all three phases need to be recorded on the Blockchain.

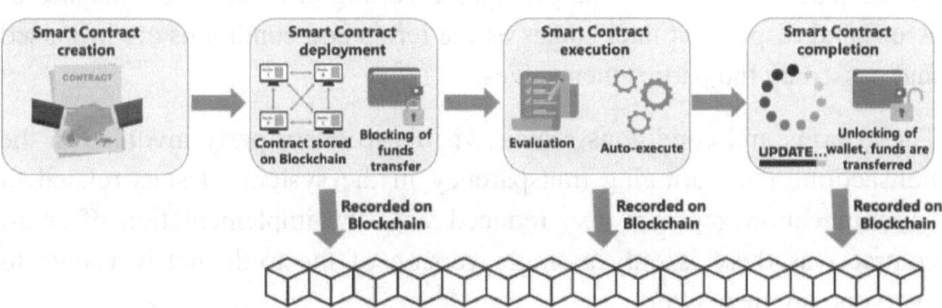

Fig 11-4: Life cycle of smart contracts

11.3. Advantages of smart contracts

(i) Trust: One of the most significant benefits that smart contracts have over traditional contracts is that they are automatically executed when the agreement conditions are met. There is no need to wait for a third party to execute the result. In other words, smart contracts remove the need for trust.

For example, if an employer wants to write a contract that holds funds in escrow for a hired person, allowing them to withdraw funds after the completion of an assigned task. In this case, a third party like Upwork initiates the contract and holds the payment in escrow. Once the hired person completes the work, the employer reviews the work. If the employer is satisfied, he notifies Upwork, and the payment is released. For this, both parties have to rely on the reputation of the intermediaries like Upwork.

On the other hand, the smart contract would work in a fully automated way, ensuring that the hired person receives the money after completing the task. And the employer gets the task completely done. For this, the parties don't have to rely on intermediaries. Once conditions have been met, nodes on the Blockchain validate the transaction, and the money is released to the hired person. Smart contracts can also hold funds. For example, you could write a smart contract that holds funds in escrow for a child, allowing them to withdraw funds after a specific date. If they try to withdraw the funds before the specified date, the smart contract won't execute.

(ii) Transparency: Another property of smart contracts that makes them so critical is the transparency they bring along with them. As discussed earlier, smart contracts contain a detailed list of terms and conditions agreed upon by the parties involved. This pre-agreed setting eliminates the chances of issues and disputes at later stages as the terms and conditions are proposed and passed by the parties themselves.

These terms and conditions remain visible to every party involved in the transaction. Thus bringing transparency in the system. Issues related to communication gaps are also reduced with the implementation of smart contracts as there is only a single version of the truth that is visible to everyone on the network.

(iii) Immutability: Smart contracts are immutable, which means their code and conditions can not be changed or updated once they are deployed on the Blockchain. Moreover, they are stored and duplicated throughout the whole distributed blockchain system and are thus, traceable and auditable. As a result, malicious behaviors like financial fraud can be greatly mitigated. If you want to change an existing smart contract, you will have to deploy a new version in a new address. For that reason, you must pay special attention to code writing and testing to avoid introducing bugs that will never be fixed.

(iv) Better Time Efficiency: The fourth significant benefit of implementing smart contracts is better efficiency. In the traditional system, with the paperwork involved, it generally takes days to get a request processed. There is a lot of unnecessary duplication of documents at various stages of the process. Further, the involvement of a large number of intermediaries makes the process more complex, cumbersome, and time-consuming.

But with the implementation of smart contracts, all these redundant and unnecessary steps are eliminated from the process, which significantly reduces the time taken to complete the transactions.

(v) Safety and security: Smart contracts along with Blockchain are tamper-proof, reliable, and secure. This characteristic of security and safety brings in more value and trust in the associated transactions.

11.4. Ethereum smart contracts

Smart contracts lie at the heart of Ethereum Blockchain. The smart contracts on Ethereum Blockchain run on the Ethereum Virtual Machine or EVM, which is present on every node in the network. The purpose of EVM is to execute smart contracts.

11.4.1. Gas and gas fees

Executing a smart contract in EVM comes with a price. Any operation in the EVM requires CPU cycles, disk access, and the memory of the hosting machine. Each computation happening in the EVM for executing lines of code on smart contracts needs some amount of gas. Simply put, gas is a unit used for measuring the amount of computational effort required by the EVM to perform transactions on the Ethereum Blockchain. Therefore gas is used for assigning fees to each transaction with a smart contract. The more complex the computation is, the more the gas is required to run the smart contracts. For every transaction that you submit on the Ethereum Blockchain platform, you must pay Gas in the form of Ethereum's cryptocurrency Ether

(ETH). Gas prices are paid in gwei; each gwei is equal to 0.000000001 ETH (10^{-9} ETH).

Transaction fee = Gas units used (limit) * (base fees + priority fees)

Where base fees is the gas price per unit, meaning the fee for every unit of gas that is burned or disappears upon successful completion of the transaction. In addition to the base fee, a priority fee is added, again per unit of gas, the value of which depends on how quickly you want the transaction to go through.

The gas limit refers to the minimum amount of gas a user is willing to consume on a transaction. More complicated transactions like smart contracts, minting NFTs, etc., require more computational work, requiring a higher gas limit than a simple payment. For instance, a standard ETH transfer requires a gas limit of 21,000 units of gas. Let's say Alice has to transfer 1 ETH to Phil. The base fee for ETH transfer is 200 gwei, and Alice adds a priority fee of 10 gwei. Therefore, transaction fee for 1 ETH transfer would be: 21,000 * (100+10) = 2,310,000 gwei or 0.00231 ETH. On the other hand, the gas fee is much higher for the execution of the smart contract that is more complex in terms of the actions to be performed. The transaction fees increase with the complexity of the contract. While the gas fee for minting NFTs is most expensive relative to other sorts of operations performed on the Ethereum Blockchain.

11.4.2. Solidity

On Ethereum, smart contracts are written in a programming language called Solidity.

Other Blockchain-based smart contract platforms: Although Ethereum is currently the most important smart contract platform, this is not the only one. Other blockchain platforms suited for designing smart contracts are Hyperledger fabric, Waves, NEO, Polkadot, Tezos, Solana, Cardano, etc.

11.5. Smart contract real-world examples

Smart contracts have a broad spectrum of applications from financial transactions to the insurance industry, supply chain, and many more. Now let's have a better understanding of these contracts through practical, real-life examples:

11.5.1. Insurance industry

The current issue with the insurance industry is the claim processing time, i.e., it takes weeks and sometimes even months to get the claims settled. The processes are outdated and manual. This increases the overhead cost for the insurer, and in turn, customers have to pay higher premiums. Insurance companies can use smart contracts to automate these insurance policies.

In these smart contracts, conditions and rules are defined under which the claim will be approved or rejected. For example, in the event of any catastrophic natural disaster, quantifiable parameters such as the speed of the wind or the magnitude of an earthquake can be recorded onto the Blockchain. When the parameters meet the defined conditions in the smart contract, the claims processes are triggered immediately, and the complete payout amount is released without any human intervention. Implementation of smart contracts not only reduces the overhead costs for the insurer but also brings trust and transparency in the system.

11.5.2. Supply chain

Another good use case for smart contracts is the supply chain which has become quite complex owing to more porous international boundaries and the involvement of a large number of intermediaries. The supply chain involves the flow of products and goods from its initial stage till its final stage, for example, from a producer who produces raw material to a consumer who ultimately consumes them.

Let's take the example of the Pharma supply chain and understand how Smart contracts can disrupt this space. Certain drugs like vaccines are sensitive to temperature changes. If kept at an unsuitable temperature, these vaccines become inactive and ineffective. But in the current scenario, there is no foolproof way to establish that a vaccine has been kept at the right temperature throughout its journey and is fit for medical use. But with the implementation of smart contracts along with the Internet of things or IoT, it is possible.

But what is IoT? IoT is the concept of connecting physical devices like sensors, cars, kitchen appliances, fitness devices, etc., to the internet. It gives the IoT devices the ability to gather and share data over the internet about how they are used and the environment in which they are operated. Thus, allowing them to communicate with people and other IoT-enabled devices. It's done using sensors that are embedded in the devices. The sensors continuously emit data about the working state of the devices. The combination of Blockchain and IoT enables sensors embedded in IoT devices to send data to Blockchain networks to create tamper-resistant and immutable records of transactions.

For instance, smart IoT temperature sensors will be installed on the vaccine packets, which will record its temperature throughout its journey, and this information will be recorded on the Blockchain. Smart contracts will be predefined for this supply chain. One of the conditions defined in the smart contract will be: if the temperature rises above the expected range (6°C), the manufacturer will be notified, and the drugs will be sent back to him for inspection *(Fig 11-5)*. Therefore, removing ineffective drugs from the system.

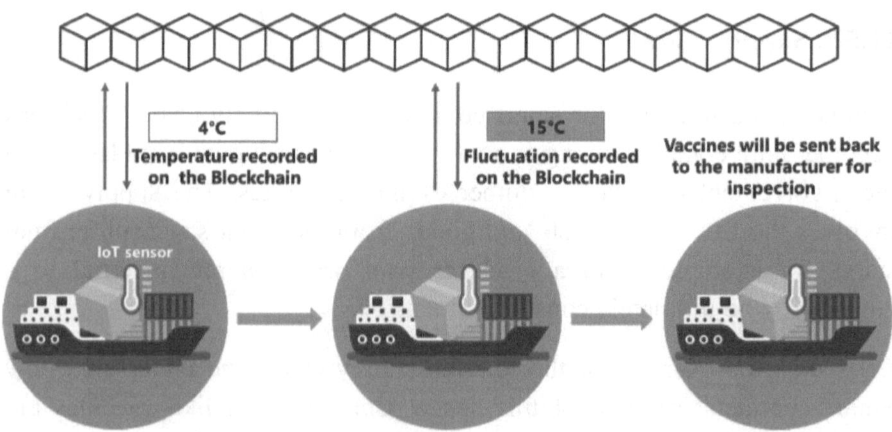

Fig 11-5: IoT sensors record the temperature of vaccines during transportation, and any fluctuation in temperature is recorded on the Blockchain

These are just some of the few examples of the limitless possibilities of Smart Contracts. Though smart contracts are still in their infancy, the future holds a great promise for them with their applications ranging from regular day-to-day agreements to huge government and enterprise agreements on a global level.

Chapter 12: Layer 1 Blockchain and scaling solutions

12.1. Blockchain trilemma

Decentralization, security, and scalability represent the core features of Blockchain technology. Blockchain developers and engineers can only choose two features to have in the network while compromising the third one. For instance, if the Blockchain system excels in providing decentralization and security, it lags when it comes to scalability. So this is called Blockchain Trilemma, a term that Ethereum founder Vitalik Buterin coined. In other words, Blockchain Trilemma means a trade-off between these three features: decentralization, scalability, and security *(Fig 12-1)*.

(i) Decentralization: Rather than being managed by a single central entity, Blockchains distribute control over the network equally to all participants. However, obtaining optimum decentralization tends to decrease the network throughput. Furthermore, as more nodes secure the network through consensus mechanisms, transaction speeds slow, which is considered a hurdle to wider adoption of Blockchain technology.

(ii) Security: Blockchain networks should have the ability to withstand frauds and attacks like 51% attacks. Therefore, Blockchain security is an essential component of the Blockchain network that must never be compromised.

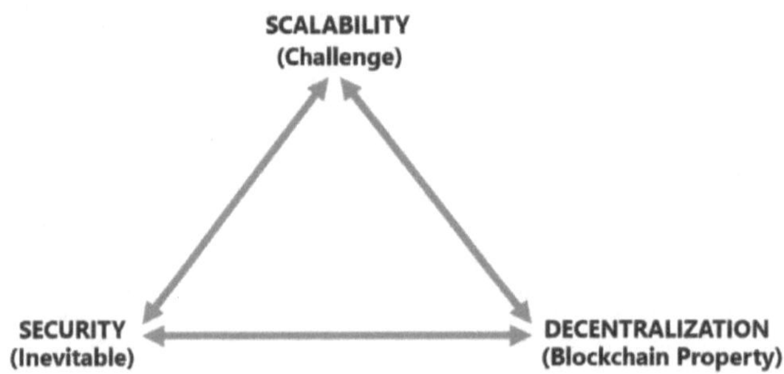

Fig 12-1: Blockchain trilemma

(iii) Scalability: Blockchains, such as Bitcoin (BTC) and Ethereum (ETH), process a huge amount of information and securely verify transactions. Blockchain has outgrown its cryptocurrency roots and is now ready to reshape the supply chain, Fintech, real estate, and many other industries. To achieve its full potential, Blockchain has to grow exponentially without getting slower, congested, or crashing the computers on which it runs. That means making Blockchain scalable is the need of the hour! It's because as the Blockchain grows, so does the amount of data stored on each node/computer in the peer-to-peer network, and more information needs to be managed. According to the Blockchain Trilemma, more scalability is feasible, but security, decentralization, or both would suffer as a result.

While many Blockchain systems have achieved decentralization and security, scalability remains a crucial problem for today's leading decentralized networks. So to solve the Blockchain trilemma and simultaneously achieve decentralization, security, and scalability, Blockchain scalability solutions are designed.

The scalability solutions can be divided into two types: Layer 1 and Layer 2 solutions.

12.2. Layer 1 Blockchain

Layer 1 Blockchain term is used to describe the parent or base layer Blockchain network. Bitcoin, Ethereum, Solana, and Litecoin are a few examples of layer 1 Blockchain networks.

On the other hand, Layer 2 is an overlaying network that lies on top of the underlying Blockchain *(Fig 12-2)*. So, with layer 1, the scaling solution is directly on the main Blockchain.

The scaling solutions can be divided into two categories: consensus mechanisms and sharding.

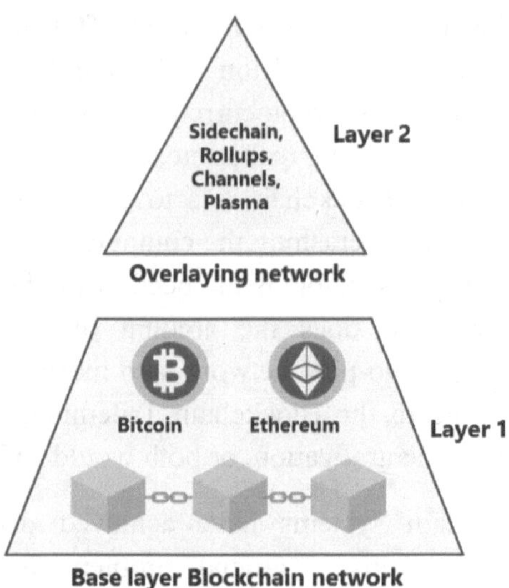

Fig 12-2: Layer 1 and layer 2 Blockchain

12.3. Consensus mechanism improvements

Some consensus mechanisms are more efficient than others. For instance, the Proof of Work (PoW) consensus mechanism used by Bitcoin and Ethereum 1.0 Blockchains is secure but highly computing-intensive, making it slow. For instance, Bitcoin can process up to 4-7 transactions per second, and Ethereum 1.0 Blockchain can process 15-30 transactions per second. But the processing of transactions is too slow compared to the electronic payment network Visa, which can process around 1700 transactions per second. In order to compete with the existing centralized systems, Blockchain technology must match or exceed these high levels of scalability. On the other hand, in the case of the Proof of Stake (POS) consensus mechanism, instead of requiring miners to solve mathematical puzzles using substantial computing power, POS systems allow the nodes to process and validate new blocks of transaction data on the basis of their stake in the network.

The transaction speed is better with POS than POW. That's why many newer Blockchain networks favor the POS consensus mechanism. Ethereum 1.0 has also transited to Ethereum 2.0, which utilizes a POS consensus mechanism *(Fig 12-3)*. This can increase the scalability of the Ethereum network while maintaining decentralization and network security.

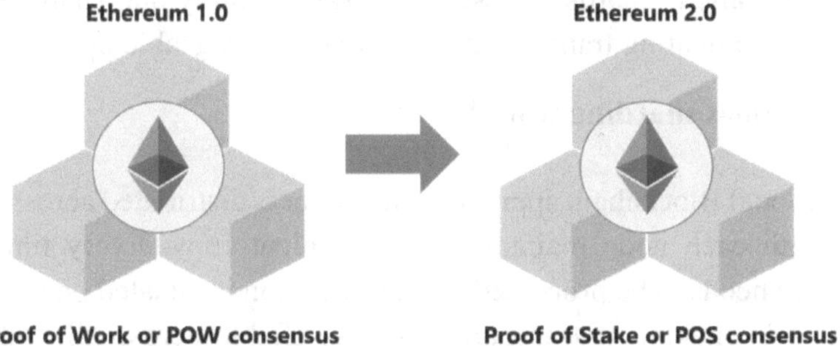

Fig 12-3: Consensus protocol improvements

12.4. Sharding

The workload on Layer 1 Blockchain has increased with the increase in the number of users. Because of this, processing speeds and capacities have dipped. The scaling solution for this problem is Sharding, adopted from distributed databases sector. It is the process of splitting a database horizontally to spread the load, which allows data from a single database to be stored across multiple servers *(Fig 12-4)*.

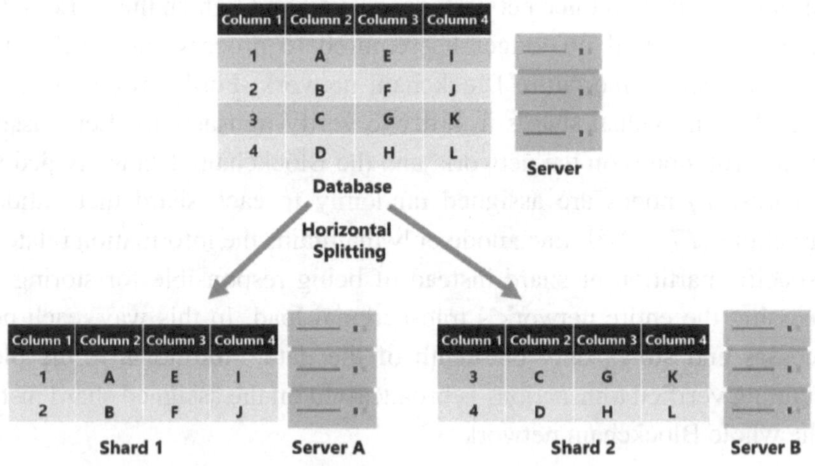

Fig 12-4: Sharding of database

Similarly, in the Blockchain context, sharding is meant to split the computing and storage workload from the Blockchain network by creating new chains called "shards" or "subnetworks." Simply put, sharding breaks the work of validating transactions into small, manageable pieces.

12.5. How does sharding work?

In a traditional Blockchain approach, the ledger is distributed across multiple nodes, with each node maintaining a complete copy. Every time a new transaction needs to be processed, the information is updated on all nodes of the network, making it transparent and verifiable across all nodes. Any transaction is added to the ledger only when the nodes come to an agreement on it. Therefore, as the number of transactions grows, so, does the ledger's size, resulting in more data to be processed and stored on each node. Deploying additional nodes worsens the problem because more time is needed for verification. Because of this, the following issues arise:

- decrease in transaction throughput,
- increased network congestion,
- increased transaction fees,
- and high storage costs.

Sharding is done to reduce network congestion and lighten the workload for each node who will no longer be required to process and verify every transaction across the entire Blockchain network. Furthermore, nodes are assigned to individual shards in order to verify transactions. Let's assume there are 100 nodes on the network, and the Blockchain data is divided into 10 shards. 10 nodes are assigned randomly to each shard that validates transactions *(Fig 12-5)*. Each node only maintains the information related to its specific partition or shard instead of being responsible for storing and processing the entire network's transactional load. In this way, each node processes and stores only one-tenth of the data. Additionally, the block containing verified transactions is broadcasted on the assigned shard instead of the whole Blockchain network.

Also, by breaking the Blockchain network into shards, each shard will have a unique set of smart contracts and transactions. The basic idea behind sharding is to process multiple non-conflicting transactions in parallel simultaneously, then after running consensus, the global state of the Blockchain is updated.

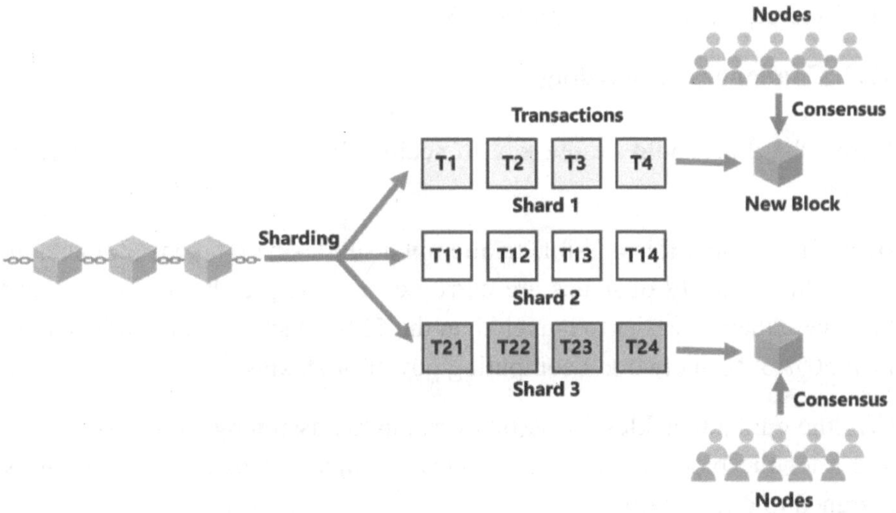

Fig 12-5: Sharding in Blockchain

12.6. Benefits of sharding

(i) Speed up transactions: Fewer nodes have to process transactions; therefore, more transactions can be processed in parallel. It also reduces the number of times computation is run for a single transaction.

(ii) Reduced storage requirements: The size of each shard is only a percentage of the total Blockchain, meaning that storage requirements for node operators drastically decrease to only the size of the shard because each node has to handle a fraction of the data. Therefore, this also lowers the barrier of entry to becoming a node. Thus, the more shards the network has, the more information it can process in parallel.

(iii) Decentralized and secure: Sharding allows the Blockchain to remain decentralized and secure. The information contained in a shard can be shared among other nodes. It keeps the ledger decentralized and secure because everyone can see all the ledger data; they simply don't process and store all the information. In addition, since the location of data is mapped on the Blockchain, it is easier to find and verify by the interested node.

Examples: A Blockchain that uses sharding relies on the Proof of Stake consensus mechanism. Sharding has been implemented in different projects like Ethereum 2.0, Zilliqa, and MultiVAC.

12.7. Challenges of sharding

While sharding could be the key to scaling Blockchain securely, hurdles remain.

(i) With sharding, it is possible to attempt a single-shard takeover attack, in which the majority of nodes are corrupted in a single shard. Single-shard takeover attack is easier to launch than the 51% attack, which requires more than 50% of the network's computing power or staking.

(ii) Ethereum 2.0 tackles this issue by randomly assigning a node to a shard, and after the block is produced, nodes are then reshuffled and randomly assigned to other shards.

Chapter 13: Layer 2 Blockchain and scaling solutions

Layer 1 solutions aren't the only option available to scale Blockchains. Layer 2 scaling solutions establish an additional protocol that is built on top of Blockchains like those of Ethereum and Bitcoin.

13.1. Layer 2 Blockchain

While Layer-1 is the term used to describe the underlying main Blockchain architecture, Layer-2, is an overlaying network that lies on top of underlying main Blockchain layer 1. It is called layer 2 because it is not written into a code that affects layer 1. Consider Bitcoin and Lightning Network. Bitcoin is the layer 1 network, while the lightning network is layer 2 *(Fig 13-1)*.

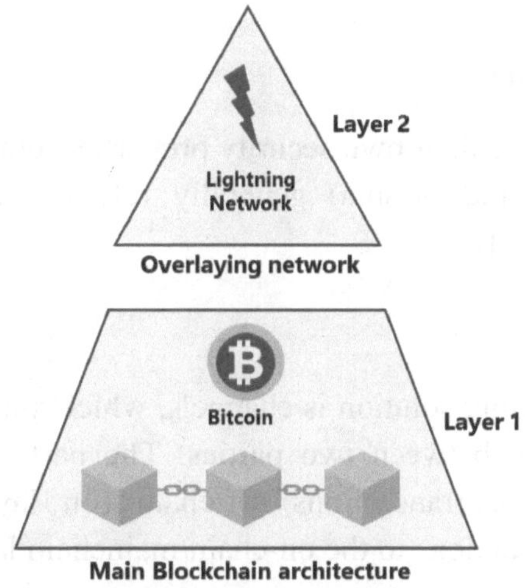

Fig 13-1: Layer 1 and layer 2 Blockchain

Other Blockchain layer 2 examples are Ethereum's Plasma, Polygon, and so on. The layer 2 scaling solutions don't require changes in the layer 1. It can be just built on top of the layer 1 using the existing elements, such as smart contracts. Layer 2 also leverages the layer 1's security by anchoring its state into layer 1.

Layer 2 scaling solutions help with increasing the capabilities of layer 1 by handling transactions off-chain. The two main capabilities that can be improved are transaction speed and transaction throughput. For instance,

Ethereum can currently process around 15 transactions per second on its base/on-chain/mainchain layer 1. Ethereum 2.0 has already scaled Ethereum 1.0 Blockchain to some extent. It uses Proof of Stake and sharding that increased the transaction throughput on layer 1. But layer 2 scaling solutions can enable Ethereum 2.0 to handle hundreds of thousands of transactions per second.

On top of that layer 2 solutions can greatly reduce the transaction fees (gas fees in the Ethereum blockchain).

Layer 2 scaling solutions can be divided into 4 categories:

- channels
- roll-ups
- plasma
- and sidechains

While sidechains have their own security properties, other layer-2 solutions (channels, rollups, and plasma) generally rely on the security of the mainchain, i.e., layer 1.

13.1. Channels

The first type of scaling solution is channels, which allow the creation of a peer-to-peer channel between two parties. The parties can exchange an unlimited amount of transactions off-chain (on layer 2) while only submitting two transactions to the on-chain/mainchain layer 1, which are:

(i) One is the first transaction that opens the connection between mainchain layer 1 and channel layer 2.

(ii) Another transaction stored on layer 1 is the transaction that closes the connection between layer 1 and layer 2.

By taking most of the transactions away from layer 1 (off-chain transactions), layer 2 channels improve transaction speed and reduce network congestion, transaction fees, and transaction delays.

The most popular types of channels are state channels and payment channels. Payment channels deal with payments, and state channels deal with general state updates.

13.1.1. State channels

State channels deal with the state update on a Blockchain network. Let's understand state channels through an example. Suppose two players want to play game tic-tac-toe on Ethereum Blockchain. For this,

(i) First, the players create a multi-signature smart contract on the Ethereum mainchain that contains the rules of tic-tac-toe, information about the players, and prize money 1ETH for the winner.

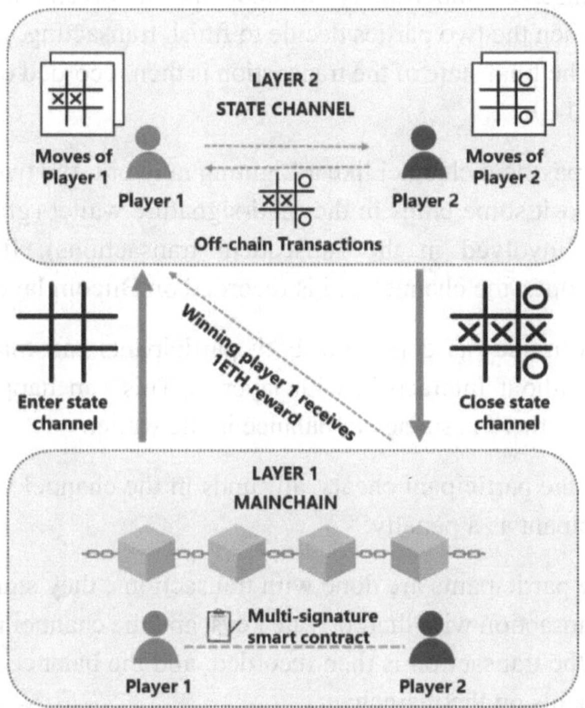

Fig 13-2: State channels to play tic-tac-toe game on Ethereum Blockchain

(ii) Then, players enter the state channel and begin playing the game. Each move of the player creates an off-chain transaction. *(Fig 13-2).*

(iii) When there's a winner, the players close the channel by signing the final state and submitting it to the multi-signature contract. The final state of the contract is then stored on the Ethereum mainchain, and the prize money 1ETH is transferred to the winner.

13.1.2. Payment channels

Payment channels are similar to state channels, but they deal with payments only. For instance, the payment channel used by Bitcoin Blockchain is the Lighting network, and the payment channel used by the Ethereum Blockchain is Raiden. The channels enable the creation of peer-to-peer payment channels between two parties. The two parties can transfer funds between themselves indefinitely without the involvement of layer 1. Eventually, when the two parties decide to finish transacting, they can close the channel. The final state of the transaction is then recorded on Blockchain layer 1 *(Fig 13-3)*.

(i) To open a payment channel like a Lighting network, the two participants must first deposit some coins in the muti-signature wallet (greater than the total amount involved in the subsequent transactions). It is the first transaction to open the channel and is recorded on Bitcoin layer 1.

(ii) After the money is deposited, both participants can make unlimited transactions without interaction with layer 1. This can happen unlimited times as long as there is sufficient balance in the wallet.

(iii) If one of the participant cheats, all funds in the channel will be sent to another participant as a penalty.

(iv) When the participants are done with transactions, they sign on the final state of the transaction with their private keys, and the channel is closed. The final state of the transaction is then recorded, and the balance is transferred to the participants on the mainchain.

Only two transactions (opening and closing of payment channel) are recorded on the main Blockchain. This significantly reduces the transaction load on the Bitcoin network.

Examples: Examples of other channels are the Celer network, Connext, Kchannels, etc.

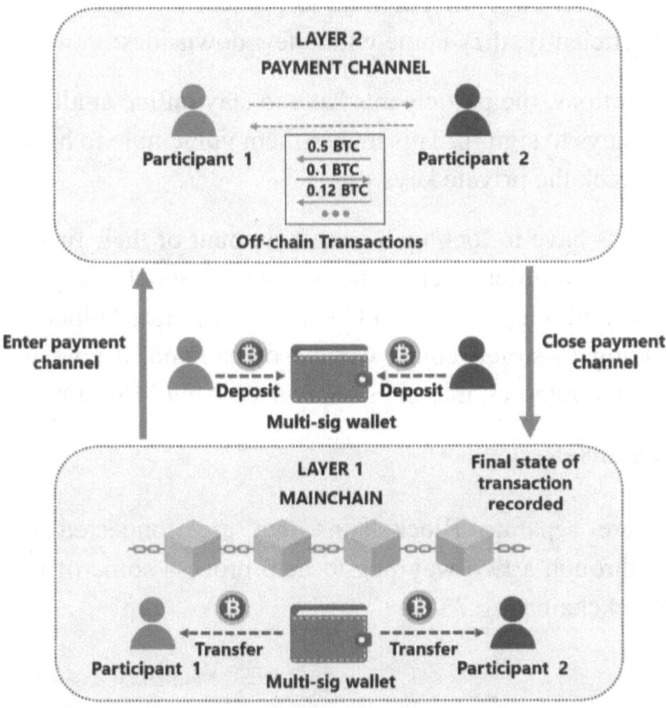

Fig 13-3: Payment channels to handle payment transfers

13.1.3. Benefits

(i) By taking transactions away from layer 1 (off-chain transactions), layer 2 decongests the layer 1 network and subsequently increases the transaction speed. For instance, the main Bitcoin Blockchain (layer 1) can handle around 10 transactions per second, but the Lightning Network (layer 2) can handle thousands to millions of transactions per second.

(ii) Because of the decrease in transaction fees, **micropayments** are feasible. For instance, the payment channels may even allow users to pay for even smaller goods and services, such as coffee, without affecting the main Blockchain network.

13.1.4. Limitations

Although channels have the potential to process thousands of transactions per second efficiently, they come with a few downsides:

(i) For transactions, the participants have to stay online at all times and use their private keys to sign in. This makes them vulnerable to hacks and thefts if attackers crack the private keys.

(ii) Participants have to lock up a certain amount of their funds in a multi-signature wallet in order to open the payment channel. Keeping coins in a hot wallet on a mobile, server, or PC makes them more vulnerable to online attacks, leading to stolen coins. On the other hand, a cold wallet is not connected to the internet, making it more secure but less convenient.

13.2. Sidechains

Sidechains are separate Blockchains that are connected to the main Blockchain through a two-way peg to help process some of the data from the main Blockchain *(Fig 13-4)*.

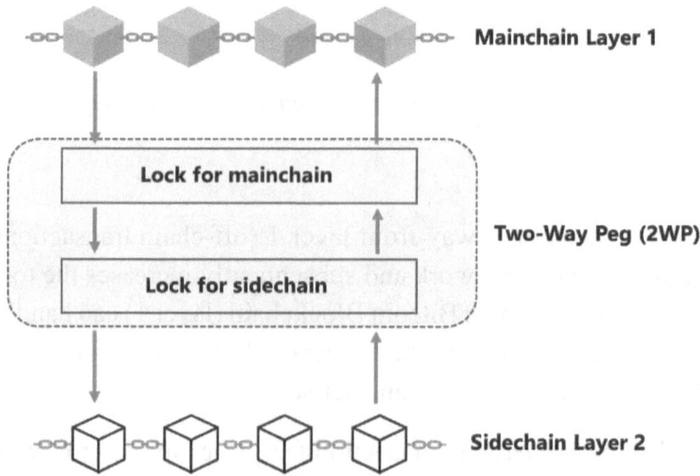

Fig 13-4: Sidechains are connected to the mainchain through a two-way peg

Each of these chains has its own set of rules, functionalities, and purposes. Unlike other layer 2 solutions- channels, plasma, and roll-ups, which leverage the security of layer 1, sidechains are responsible for their own security. Another important point about sidechains is that they need their own nodes to validate transactions and create a block. They also have their own consensus mechanisms (such as POW, POS, Proof of Authority, DPoS, etc.) and block parameters. The block validating nodes earn the rewards for their work in a sidechain in the same manner that all other Blockchains work. Although sidechains remain independent from one another, together they form an entire ecosystem.

13.2.1. How do sidechains work?

The main job of sidechains is

- processing and validating data for the mainchain
- or adding functionality, such as running smart contracts for Blockchains that are unable to do that, like Bitcoin.

Sidechains communicate with the mainchain via a two-way peg (2WP); thus, the sidechains are also called pegged sidechains.

(i) Two-way peg (2WP): The 2WP acts as an intermediary to facilitate the transfer of assets or coins from the mainchain (layer 1) to the sidechain (layer 2) and vice versa. Under the hood, coins are not transferred; instead, they are temporarily locked on the mainchain by creating a transaction. A second transaction is generated to unlock the same amount of equivalent coins in a sidechain. The coins on the mainchain can be unlocked only when the equivalent amount of coins on the sidechain are locked again *(Fig 13-5)*. This is done to avoid the presence of free coins on both chains and prevent a double- spending problem. 2WP system enables the interested parties to get into a transaction on the sidechain without revealing the information to the entire network.

(ii) Presence of the third-party: The third-party/authority is in charge of the locking and releasing functions between the sidechains and mainchains. A transaction to lock coins is initiated. After the consensus is reached among the nodes, the signed block is submitted to the mainchain. This automatically locks the coins on the mainchain.

The trusted authority who controls the 2-way peg then issues an equivalent sum of coins in the sidechain to the transaction parties. The parties can then have a bunch of transactions within the confines of the sidechain. Once the transactions are done, the authority then verifies the transactions and releases the corresponding coins in the mainchain by unlocking the coins.

The whole sidechain construct is based on the 2-way peg and the trusted authority for maintaining the integrity of transactions between the two chains. The presence of authority can bring centralization in the network by giving it too much power.

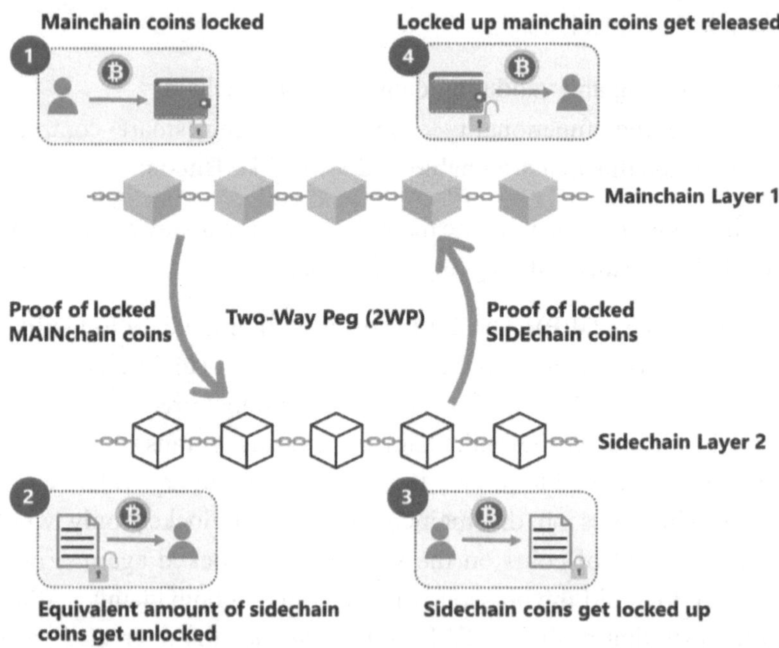

Fig 13-5: Locking and unlocking of mainchain and sidechain coins

(iii) SPV proofs: SPV (Simple Payment Verification) proof is a way to cryptographically prove that the coins are locked on the mainchain for their use on the sidechain. Rather than checking all the previous transactions, which would be slow, an SPV also proves whether the transaction initiated on the mainchain is valid and is a part of the valid block. Through SPVs, the nodes on the sidechain are not required to download the whole main Blockchain every time the verification process is needed. The Bitcoin and

Ethereum Blockchains support SPVs in the form of Merkle proofs. The Merkle Proofs include the Merkle Root and the Merkle Path.

Each pair of hashed transactions is hashed together by the hash function and so on until there is one hash for the entire block, which is called Merkle Root or Root hash. On the other hand, the Merkle path is the set of hash values required for generating root hash. For instance, the Merkle path for transaction D will be the hash values Hash C, Hash AB, Hash EFGH, and Merkle root *(Fig 13-6)*.

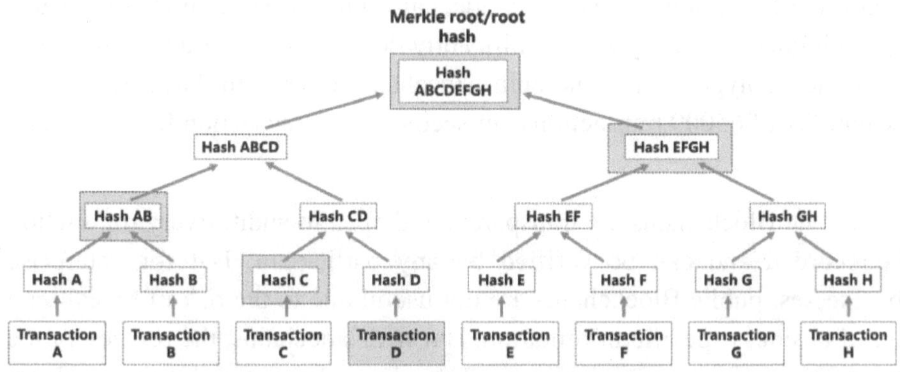

Fig 13-6: Merkle path for transaction D

The nodes of the sidechain repeat the hash operation to compute the root hash value. If the root hash value obtained by the process matches with the root hash value present in SPV, it means the transaction has been initiated that locked coins on the mainchain.

13.2.2. Sidechains of Bitcoin and Ethereum Blockchains

Examples of sidechains of Bitcoin Blockchain are the Liquid Network and Rootstock (RSK). With the Liquid network, blocks are added every minute, compared to Bitcoin's 10 minute block time. By adding the RSK sidechain to Bitcoin Blockchain, **Bitcoin can use smart contracts**, thus, broadening its functionality. Therefore, RSK can add an Ethereum-like layer to the Bitcoin protocol and thus enable the Bitcoin protocol to develop DApps using smart contracts.

xDai Chain, POA network, and Polygon (formerly known as Matic network) are a few examples of sidechains of Ethereum Blockchain. Interoperability of sidechains with Ethereum mainchain is made possible by using the same Ethereum Virtual Machine (EVM). So contracts deployed to the Ethereum base layer can be directly deployed to the sidechain.

13.2.3. Benefits

(i) Sidechains increase the transaction throughput by taking away the majority of transactions into their sidechain and processing transactions at a much higher rate. They also significantly decrease the transaction fees. For example, Polygon, an Ethereum sidechain, claims to have reached a scalability of 65000 transactions per second, with transaction fees of around $1.

(ii) Public Blockchains are transparent and open to audit. Every transaction is recorded and can be verified by any participant. But for enterprise businesses, public Blockchains are not useful due to the risk of revealing a lot of business-specific information. But with sidechains, the privacy of the transactions can be maintained. The data about the business-related transactions reside in the sidechain, and the mainchain acts as a record store for verification of hashed data. While the mainchain is public and permissionless, the sidechain is designed private & permissioned to cater to business needs. The business-specific data can be stored securely in the sidechain and hence much more secure and immune to hacking.

13.2.4. Challenges

Most sidechains are a little more centralized than the mainchain because of which they provide a security trade-off for speed. Therefore, the information that is outsourced to the sidechain can be selected, with the most sensitive details remaining on the mainchain to maintain Blockchain security.

13.3. Plasma

Plasma is another layer 2 scaling solution. Plasma leverages smart contracts and Merkle trees to create an unlimited number of child chain copies of the parent Blockchain mainly (Ethereum Blockchain). Offloading transactions from the mainchain (layer 1) into child chains (layer 2) allows fast and cheap transactions. Like sidechains, each child chain is treated as a separate Blockchain with its own consensus mechanism, nodes, block size, and block time.

Like channels, plasma leverages the security of the mainchain. The mainchain and child chains are tied together through 'smart contracts' that contain the rules guiding each child chain. The contracts act as the bridge that lets the participants move digital assets/coins between the mainchain and the child chains. Initially, all transactions have to be created on the mainchain.

If any suspicion or fraud is detected in the plasma child chains, plasma users can exit the plasma chain and move to the mainchain.

13.3.1. How does Plasma work?

(i) The child chain operator lays down the rules in which the child chain will operate.

(ii) Processed transactions stay at the plasma chains. But the block headers (containing Merkle roots) of each block of the plasma chains are submitted and recorded in the blocks of the mainchain. This reduces the mainchain network congestion and thus, allows tens of thousands of transactions to be processed simultaneously.

(iii) The data on child chains is validated using "fraud proofs." Fraud proofs are a mechanism by which anyone can determine if the data is invalid using Merkle proofs. For example, when fraud occurs in a plasma chain, whether it is a double-spending case or one cash out more than they have in all accounts, anyone can provide a fraud proof to prove the transaction is invalid. If the transaction is proven fraud, it will be rolled back.

13.3.2. Benefits

(i) Plasma chains are more favorable than channels because one can send assets/coins to anyone, whereas with channels, the transaction can occur between two parties only.

(ii) The advantage of Plasma chains over sidechains is that the plasma chain is secured by the mainchain. If the sidechain gets attacked, nothing happens to the mainchain, but the mainchain can't do anything to protect users on the sidechain. While, since the plasma chains leverage the security of mainchain, in the case of any attacks, plasma chain users can exit and move to the mainchain. Thus, the security of plasma is more than the sidechains.

13.3.3. Limitations

(i) One of the drawbacks of plasma is a long waiting period for users who want to withdraw their coins from layer 2 and transfer them to layer 1.

(ii) The users have to wait for at least 7-14 days for the withdrawal. This time duration is required to verify that the withdrawal transaction isn't fraudulent.

Examples: The project that leverages the power of Plasma on Ethereum is OMG.

13.4. Rollups

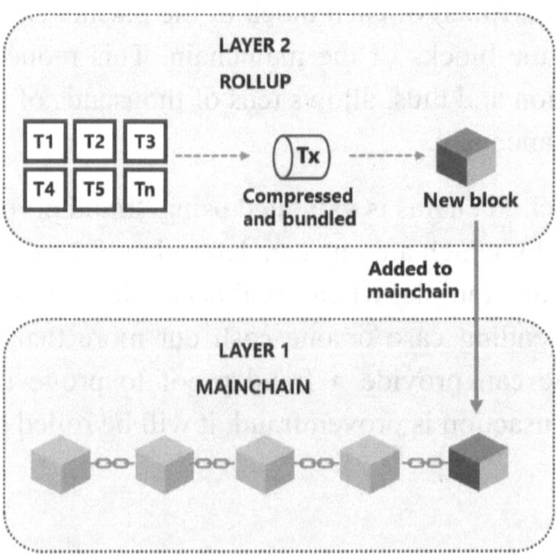

Fig 13-7: Rollups bundle executed transactions into a single block and post it to the mainchain layer 1

Like channels, sidechains, and plasma, rollups are also scaling solutions that use both layer 1 and layer 2 Blockchains. In rollups, the transactions initiated on the mainchain are executed on layer 2. Then the data of the executed transactions are bundled or rolled up into a single block and then posted to the mainchain layer 1 *(Fig 13-7)*. Thus the scaling solution got the name "rollups."

A version of the Ethereum Virtual Machine or EVM is run inside the rollup layer. It means that any transaction possible on the Ethereum mainchain is possible to execute on the rollup. Additionally, it allows the existing Ethereum applications to migrate to rollups without writing any new code.

Advantages over plasma: The advantage of rollups over plasma is that the data of each batch of executed transactions is bundled and is posted on the mainchain. But with Plasma, only the Merkle roots are recorded on the mainchain. The amount of data posted on the mainchain is the minimum amount required to validate the rollups transaction. By putting data on the mainchain, anyone can detect fraud. Therefore, rollups give much higher security than Plasma chains.

13.4.1. How do rollups work?

(i) There's a "rollup contract" on the mainchain that stores the state root of the rollup layer 2 *(Fig 13-8)*. The state root is the Merkle root of the current state of the rollup. Merkle tree is derived from all the transactions on the rollup.

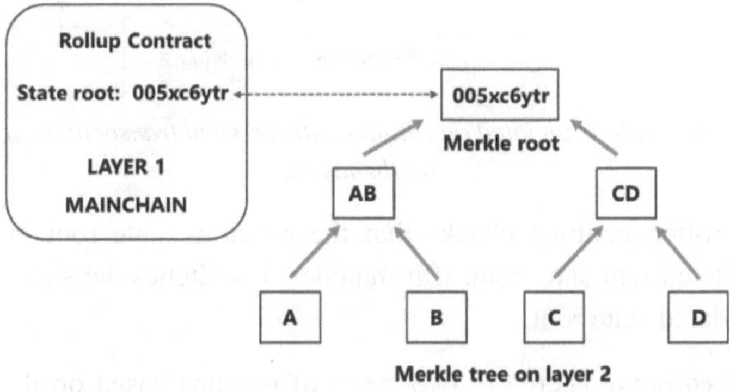

Fig 13-8: Rollup contract on the mainchain contains state root of the layer2

(ii) When transactions happen on the rollup layer, state root (Merkle root) changes. That means the state root needs to be updated on the rollup contract on the mainchain. For this, the executed transactions are compressed, batched, and posted on the rollup contract together with the updated state root *(Fig 13-9)*. Along with the updated state root, the batch of executed transactions includes data like account balances of the users, addresses, contract code, etc. The entire Merkle tree is stored on the layer 2 rollup, not on the mainchain.

(iii) The batch of executed transactions is stored on the mainchain in a highly compressed form along with the previous state root (Merkle root before processing transactions) and the new state root (Merkle root after processing transactions).

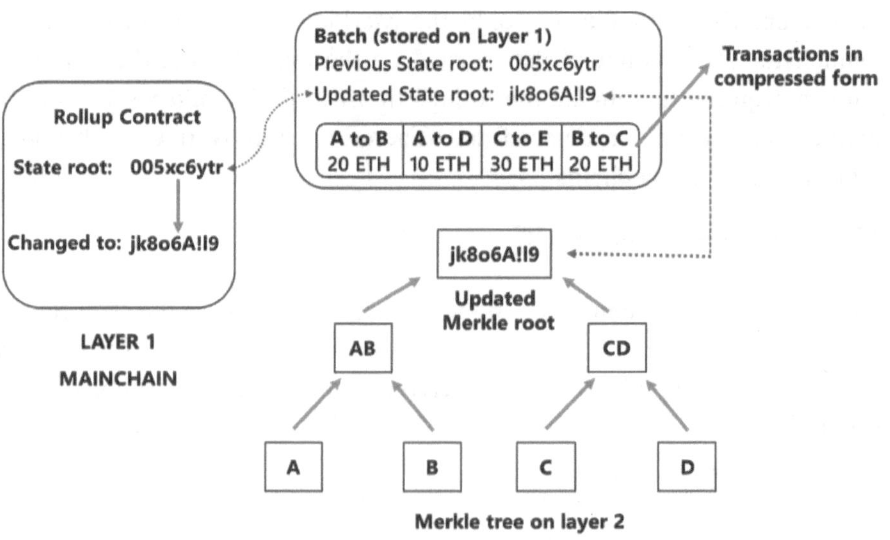

Fig 13-9: State root is updated on rollup contract when transactions are executed on the layer2

(iv) The rollup contract checks that the previous state root in the batch matches its current state root; if it matches, it switches the state root to the newly updated state root.

Types of rollups: There are two types of roll-ups based on the proofs to validate that the state roots in the batches are correct.

- Zk roll-ups
- Optimistic roll-ups

13.4.2. Optimistic rollups

A new batch of transactions is compressed, bundled, and posted to the mainchain along with the state root. The rollup contract keeps track of the entire history of the state roots of each batch. At the time of posting, it is not actually validated that the transactions have been executed correctly. In other words, we are "optimistically" posting the new state root and transaction data to the rollup contract on the mainchain. If someone discovers that one batch with incorrect state root has been published to the rollup contract, they can generate a "fraud-proof." The fraud-proof incudes:

- Proof of pre-state root, or the Merkle root that should be before processing transactions
- Proof of new state root, or the Merkle root that should be after processing transactions
- Proof of the executed transactions

The fraud-proof is posted to the rollup contract on the mainchain. The rollup contract verifies the proof and compares the result to its state root. If there's a mismatch, the contract rolls back the batch and all the batches after it until it reverts to the last known valid batch.

Examples of Optimistic rollups include: Optimism and Arbitrum

A major limitation of Optimistic rollups is the longer withdrawal time. If anyone suspects a transaction to be fraudulent, they can challenge it and submit fraud-proof within the time duration of 7 days. Thus, users have to wait around one week to withdraw their assets from layer 2 rollups.

13.4.3. Zero-knowledge rollup (ZK Rollup)

Since the optimistic rollups work on the "Innocent until proven guilty" belief, ZK rollups rely on the "Don't trust, verify" belief. The batch of bundled transactions is updated on the mainchain only when validity proof called SNARK (succinct non-interactive argument of knowledge) is submitted. SNARK is cryptographic proof that proves the new state root is the correct result of executing the batch of transactions in the ZK-rollup layer. The validity proof is posted to the rollup contract, so anyone can use it to verify transactions in a particular batch on the rollup layer.

SNARKs are also called Zero-Knowledge Proofs or ZK Proofs because they allow anyone to verify that the transactions are valid without revealing any information about the transaction. In other words, anyone can verify that the data existed, even if they don't have access to the data itself.

Examples of rollups include: Loopring, Hermez and Starkware

13.4.4. Limitations

(i) Since the data of executed transactions is bundled and posted on the mainchain, the scalability gets limited. The scalability with rollups can be up to 100x, but they can't scale the Blockchain infinitely.

(ii) Though the mainchain network congestion is eased as all the computation work is done off-chain on the rollup layer 2, the transactions are executed by running a version of the EVM in the rollups. Thus, on the rollups as well, the same execution is being performed as the Ethereum mainchain, and the users are charged gas fees. But gas fees on the rollup layer are much cheaper than on Ethereum.

Chapter 14: Web 3.0 Decentralized Applications or dApps

14.1. What is Web 3.0?

Web 3.0, also referred to as Web3 is the third generation of the internet after Web 1.0 and Web 2.0. These three generations show how the internet has evolved and disparities in how users interact with the internet.

Web 1.0: Web 1.0 is the initial version of internet between the years 1991-2004. This was the age of static webpages retrieved from servers, meaning that whenever you loaded them, they just showed some stuff and that was it. It was just read only, there wasn't any logging in, viewing analytics or any interaction capabilities. The majority of users of web 1.0 were consumers of content. So web 1.0 is also known as "read-only web."

Web 2.0: From around 2004-until now, web evolved a lot. One of the biggest changes was the interactivity of the internet. Web 2.0 allows the users to create content. It also enables social media kind of interactions. Users can interact in the form of likes, comments, tagging, sharing their photos, blogs, podcasts or videos, etc. Web 2.0 also enables the tech giants to collect information from us like Facebook, YouTube, Google, Twitter, Amazon and many other centralized companies, and use the algorithms to decide the information that we consume so that they could serve us better content which in turn would make us stay on their websites much longer. This means the big centralized companies control how our personal data will be used and even sell it to advertisers to bring more traffic. Thus, Web 2.0 is the age of targeted advertising and lack of privacy for the users.

Web 3.0: It is the next evolution of the internet utilizing Blockchain technology and tools of decentralization. In Web 2.0, our data is under the control of centralized organizations. But with Web3.0, the data will reside on Blockchain networks, making users the owners of their own data. The owners get to decide the ways in which they want to share it. It focuses on more data privacy and security for users.

14.2. Web 3.0 dApps

Web 3.0 dApps or decentralized applications are digital applications or programs that are run on a decentralized, peer-to-peer Blockchain network.

Let's consider the examples of Web 2.0 traditional apps like Facebook, Twitter, YouTube, etc., where the backend code runs on centralized servers, owned and operated by an organization, giving it full authority over the app and its workings. There may be multiple app users, but a single organization controls the backend.

On the other hand, the backend code of dApps runs on the decentralized peer-to-peer network. That means the apps are run on a network of computers instead of a single computer; thus, dApps are not under the control of one person or entity. For example, one can create a YouTube-like dApp and put it on a Blockchain where any user can post videos. Once posted, no one, including the app creators, can delete the videos.

14.3. Web 2.0 App architecture

To understand how dApps work, it is essential to understand the architecture of a web 2.0 app. Every mobile or web application has two parts: the frontend and a backend server.

Frontend: The frontend of the web application is the part with which the user interacts directly. Therefore, it is usually referred to as "client-side." The front end consists of everything that the user sees while interacting with the app, such as text colors and styles, graphics, images, tables, buttons, navigation menu, etc. The main languages used for frontend development are- HTML, CSS, JavaScript. The frontend code runs on the client's browser for the web application.

Backend: On the other hand, the backend is the server-side of a web application. It is responsible for receiving user requests and sending appropriate data back to the user once the logical processing is complete. While the backend doesn't interact with users directly, it includes all the code to power apps from behind the scenes. In a nutshell, without a proper backend, the frontend won't work properly. It is the brain of any app. For example, filling your credentials in a registration form is managed by the frontend, but when you click 'enter' and get registered, the backend makes it work. The backend has three components: server, database, and APIs *(Fig 14-1)*.

(i) Server: The server is a computer that can be present on-site or in the cloud. The application running on the server listens for requests, retrieves information from the database, and sends a response. The languages used for writing the backend code are- JavaScript, PHP, Python, Java, etc., which can interact easily with the frontend.

(ii) Database: A database is a part of the backend that makes the web application dynamic. Whenever any user makes a request, like searching for a product in an online store or searching for restaurants for food delivery, the database is responsible for accepting the query, processing it, fetching the data, and returning it to the user. The database is also accountable for accepting new data and editing the old data, as desired by the user.

(iii) APIs: Application Programming Interface or API is a software intermediary that allows two applications to talk to each other. Let's understand APIs through a real-life scenario. Imagine you're sitting at a table in a restaurant and want to order a sandwich. The kitchen is the part of the restaurant that will prepare your order. The waiter is here the critical link to communicate your order to the kitchen and deliver your food back to you. In other words, the waiter is the messenger or API that takes your order and tells the kitchen what to prepare. Then the waiter delivers the response back to you; in this case, it is the sandwich.

Here is a real-life API example, if you want to purchase something from an online store, the backend manages the actual monetary transactions. While the frontend makes sure that the check-out button is appropriately positioned on the page, the backend interacts with the third parties (your bank or PayPal) for the payment. The entire process of transactions happens behind the scenes in the backend.

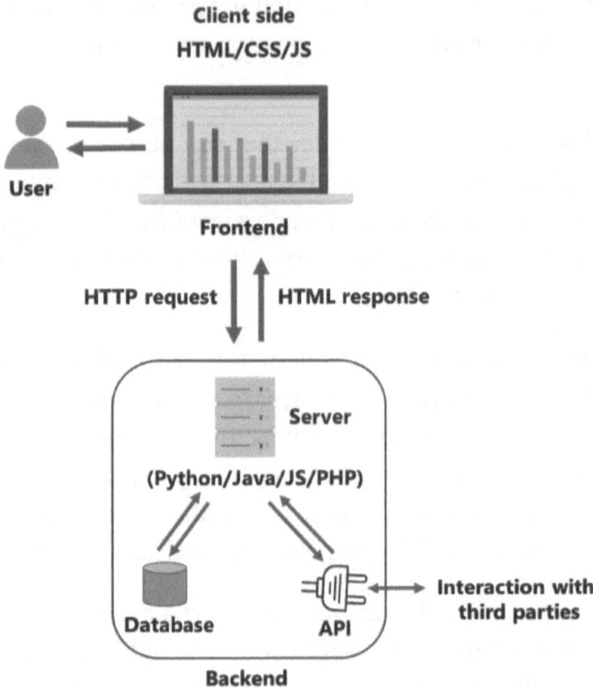

Fig 14-1: Web 2.0 application architecture

How do frontend and backend work together?

Frontend and backend communicate with each other via Hypertext Text Transfer or HTTP requests. In the web application, when a web address or URL is entered in the browser, the browser then makes a request to the server using the HTTP protocol to locate the address of the requested resource corresponding to the entered URL *(Fig 14-1)*.

The server then accesses the database to get the information and returns an HTML page. HTML is the language used to write the contents of the web page. This response is sent to the user browser that requested the resource. The browser then interprets the HTML code and draws the screen showing images, buttons, and all the information on the requested page.

14.4. Web 3.0 dApp architecture

With decentralized applications or dApps, there is also a frontend client and a backend server. But unlike Web 2.0 applications, Web 3.0 eliminates the need for a centralized database and a centralized web server; instead, the Blockchain is used. The most used Blockchain Blockchain platform for implementing dApps is Ethereum. Other Blockchain platforms that are also available for dApp implementation are Hyperledger Sawtooth, Hyperledger Fabric, EOS, NEO, etc.

Frontend: Like web 2.0 applications, the frontend of the dApp is written using HTML, CSS, and JavaScript programming languages.

Web3.js: Web3.js is a Javascript library that enables your frontend to interact with the Ethereum network *(Fig 14-2)*. To connect with the Blockchain, you need to connect to a node. It can be done by running a node on your computer. And if you don't want to run a node, you can connect with a third party who is running the nodes, e.g., Infura. The nodes that you connect with to interact with the Blockchain network are often called "providers."

Smart contract: Smart contract is a self-executing program that runs on the Ethereum blockchain and defines the logic of a dApp. Smart contracts are written Solidity language. Because the smart contract code is stored on the Ethereum Blockchain, anyone on the network can inspect the code.

Additionally, smart contracts can also connect to any API by integrating Oracle. This helps the smart contracts to extract external data like weather information, market data, etc. One can also make payments through a bank on dApp because of Oracle.

Ethereum Virtual Machine or EVM: EVM executes the logic defined in the smart contracts and processes the updates that happen on the globally accessible Blockchain. The EVM doesn't understand Solidity language, which is used to write smart contracts. Instead, the code written in Solidity language is compiled into bytecode, which the EVM can then execute.

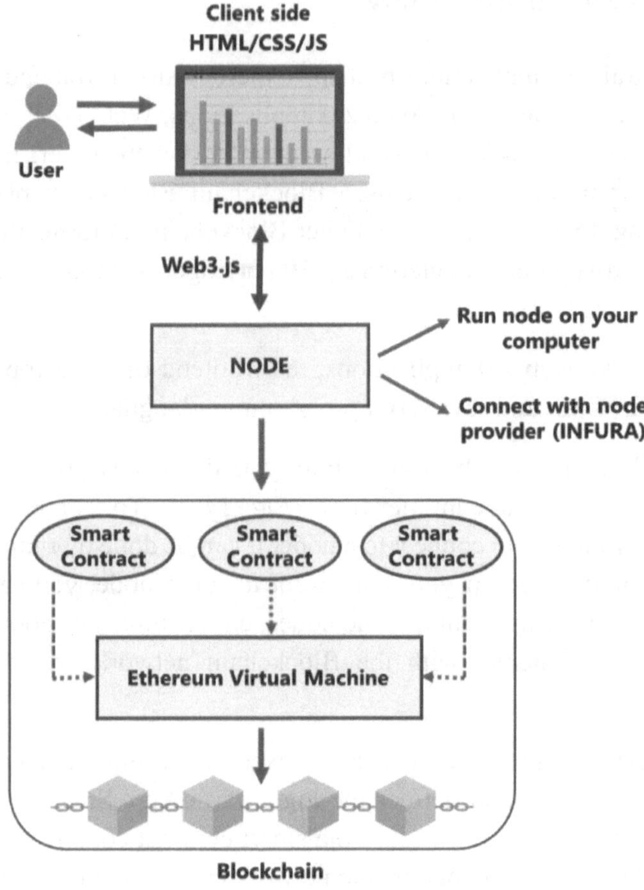

Fig 14-2: Web 3.0 dApp architecture

14.5. How does the frontend of Web 3.0 dApp communicate with the Blockchain network?

Because of the decentralized network, every node in the Blockchain network is required to keep a copy of the full Blockchain, including the code associated with smart contracts. Once you connect to the Blockchain through the node, you can submit the transaction to the Blockchain only after signing it using your private key. For instance, imagine you have a dApp that lets users view or post videos to the Blockchain. You might have a button on frontend that allows anyone to view the videos. Viewing videos on the

Blockchain does not require a user to sign a transaction. However, when a user wants to post a new video onto the Blockchain, the dApp asks the user to sign the transaction using their private key; only then transaction, i.e., the new video will be posted. Otherwise, the nodes wouldn't accept the transaction.

For "signing" the transactions, the third-party Metamask is required, which stores the private keys of a user in the browser. Whenever the frontend needs the user to sign a transaction, it calls on Metamask to sign the transaction and submit it on the Blockchain. *(Fig 14-3).*

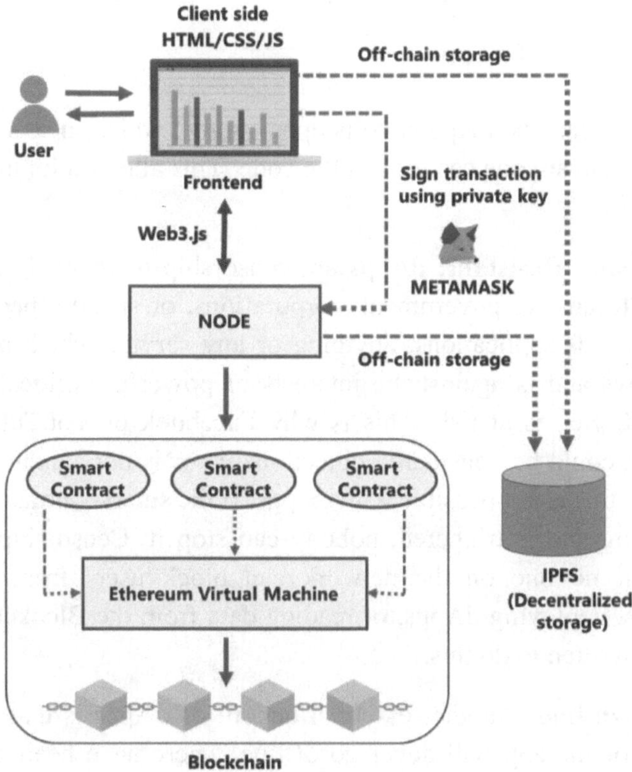

Fig 14-3: How frontend of Web 3.0 dApp communicates with Blockchain

Storage on Blockchain: The smart contracts are stored on the Ethereum Blockchain. But storing every dApp data on the Blockchain gets really expensive. The user needs to pay every time they add new data to the

Blockchain. Asking your users to pay extra fees for every new transaction on your dApp is not a good experience for the user. This issue can be solved by using a decentralized off-chain storage solution, like the Interplanetary File system abbreviated as IPFS. Instead of storing data in a centralized database, the IPFS system distributes and stores the data in a peer-to-peer network.

Additionally, you can host the frontend code of your dApp on the cloud as in Web 2.0, but that creates a centralization for your dApp. If you want to build a completely decentralized app, you might choose to host your frontend code on decentralized IPFS.

14.6. Advantages of dApps

(i) Open source: The dApp code is open source, which means the code is transparent, and anyone can look at the code. This allows a lot more trust in the application.

(ii) Censorship Resistant: dApps are censorship-resistant. It means they don't have to answer government, corporations, or specific people. In the case of web 2.0 applications, anything or any service which may violate codified laws and is against the interests of powerful political groups or government, etc., is at risk. This is why Facebook or YouTube removes content that could be considered objectionable or is not conducive to their growth. But this is not possible with dApps. If the smart contract is coded to do something and is triggered, nobody can stop it. Censorship resistance ensures that no one on the network can block users from submitting transactions, deploying dApps, or reading data from the Blockchain unless the code is written to do this.

(iii) No downtime: Another essential benefit of dApps is that there is no downtime, or the app will never go offline. There have been times when Facebook or YouTube are down, maybe because of a single point of failure like the servers have a bug, or there is an outage. Since dApps run on Blockchain, they will actually never go down because they are run by hundreds and thousands of computers all around the world. It would be infeasible to turn them all off.

14.7. Challenges of dApps

(i) It is challenging to modify smart contracts once deployed.

(ii) Also, it becomes difficult to fix any issues in dApps because fixes require every node in the network to update all the copies in the network.

15.6. Few examples of dApps

(i) Social network dApps: Sapien, Steemit, Sola, e-Chat, etc.

(ii) DeFi (Decentralized Finance) Apps: AAVE, IDEX, EOSFinex, etc.

(iii) Insurance and banking dApps: AiGang, Everledger, etc.

(iv) Streaming dApps: DTube, UjoMusic, Theta EdgeCast, etc.

(v) Gaming dApps: Cryptokitties, Zed Run, Splinterlands, Alien Worlds, etc.

Chapter 15: Interplanetary File system or IPFS

In the traditional web application, the data is stored on centralized servers owned and operated by an organization, giving it full authority over the app and the data *(Fig 15-1)*. Also, centralized data storage may have availability issues. Let's say you want to download an image abc.png from the domain xyz.com. For this, you tell the computer exactly where to find the image. The location of the image is the URL address, i.e., xyz.com/abc.png. This is called "location-based addressing." But suppose if the server is down, or the file has now been removed from the servers for whatever reason, you won't be able to access the image anymore. However, there is a probability that someone else has downloaded the image before and has a copy of it. But yet, there is no way of connecting to them and grabbing a copy of the picture from that person.

To solve this issue Interplanetary File system, abbreviated as IPFS storage solution protocol, is used, which uses "content-based addressing" instead of "location-based addressing."

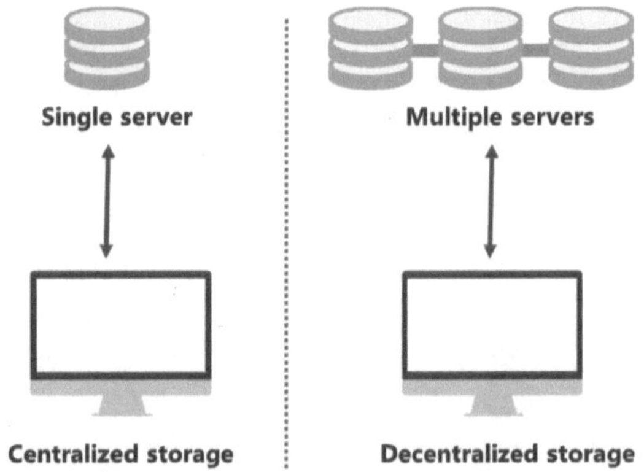

Fig 15-1: Centralized and decentralized data storage

15.1. IPFS and Content-based addressing

IPFS is a peer-to-peer (P2P) decentralized protocol for storing Blockchain-based data. In a P2P network, a group of computers are linked together with equal permissions and responsibilities for processing data. Unlike traditional client-server network systems, no devices in a P2P network are designated solely to serve or receive data.

In a P2P network, instead of saying where to find a resource, you just say what it contains. Also, rather than referring to objects as pics, articles, or videos, IPFS refers to everything by the hash on the file. Every file has a unique hash, which can be compared to a fingerprint. Therefore, when you want to download a certain file, you will ask the network, "who has the file with this hash?" and someone on the IPFS network will provide it to you. The hash function allows you to check the integrity of the obtained file by comparing the requested hash with the hash of the received file. If the hashes match, it means you received the file as it is; it has not been modified.

The hash function also helps de-duplication, such that no file with the same content can be submitted twice since the same content generates the same hash. This optimizes the storage requirements and also improves the performance of the network.

15.2. How can Blockchain data be stored on IPFS?

Blockchain is an expensive medium for data storage. It costs around $100 per GB of storage. For efficient storage of extensive data and content, Inter-Planetary File System, abbreviated as IPFS, can be used which is a distributed, decentralized file system and a platform to store data and files with high integrity and resiliency.

Let's now understand how data is stored in the IPFS system:

(i) Files are stored as IPFS objects. 256 kB of data can be stored inside one IPFS object. Therefore the file up to size 256 kB can be stored in a single IPFS object. But what about the files that are larger than 256 kB, like an image or a video file? Such files are split up into multiple IPFS objects that are all 256 kB in size and are stored across a network of nodes. Nodes of the IPFS are incentivized for providing storage space on their computer or server for hosting/storing files. Anyone can install and run an IPFS node on their computer.

Each IPFS object is identified with its own hash. For example, suppose you want to store a file of size 1MB, whose hash is, say, 85bcd. The file will be split into 4 chunks of 256 kB each, and each chunk will have its unique hash (content identifiers or CID), say 09afg, 6efab, 45af, and 23hbc *(Fig 15-2)*. When the chunks are assembled together, based on their hash value, it recreates the original file.

(ii) IPFS system also creates an empty IPFS object that contains an array of links to IPFS objects of the file. These links of IPFS hashes are stored into the Blockchain smart contracts to provide traceability and authenticity. And the content of the files is stored on IPFS.

If there is any change in the content of the digital document, the hash changes, which indicates that the original content was modified and altered.

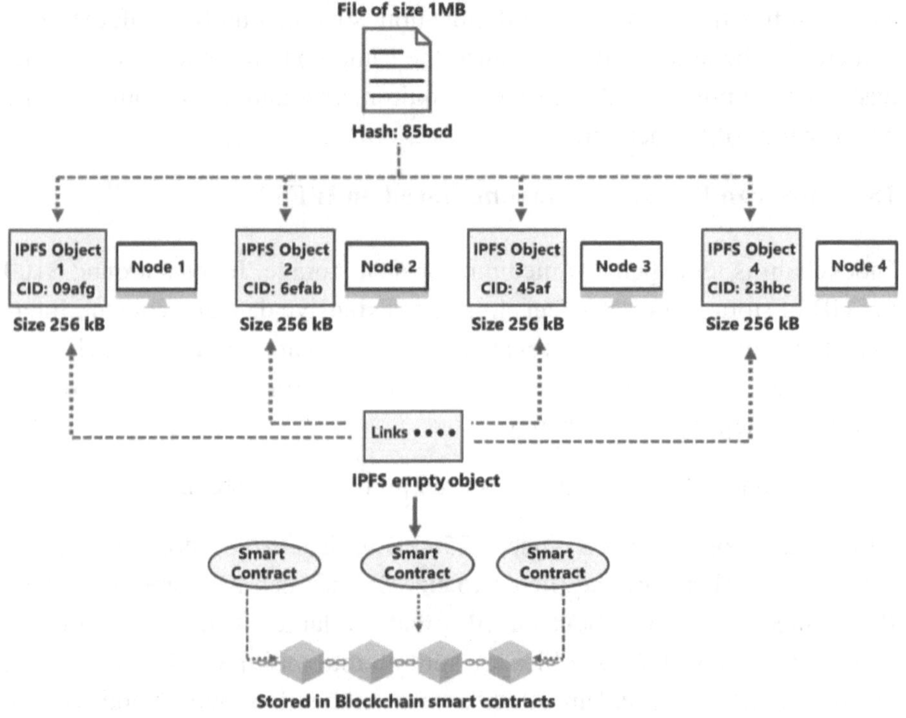

Fig 15-2: How can Blockchain data be stored on IPFS?

15.3. How to share files on the Blockchain with IPFS?

Suppose you have uploaded a PDF file on the IPFS network. The hash of the file is stored on the smart contracts of the Blockchain. Anyone knowing the hash of the file can retrieve the file from IPFS and read its data.

Asymmetric Encryption: Since as long as anyone has the hash of the PDF file, they can retrieve it from IPFS. So sensitive files can not be stored as such on the IPFS network. This problem can be solved by using cryptographic public and private keys. You need to encrypt the file with the intended recipient's public key so that only they can decrypt it. A malicious party who retrieves the file from IPFS can't do anything unless it is decrypted. Coming to our example- suppose you uploaded a PDF file on the IPFS network that only Mat can access *(Fig 15-3)*. After knowing the hash of the file, Mat can retrieve the encrypted file from the IPFS network. He can now decrypt the file using his private key and know its contents.

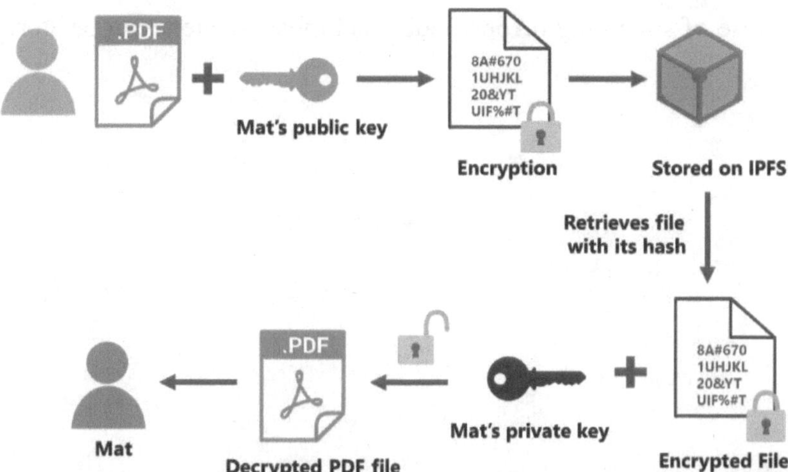

Fig 15-3: Asymmetric encryption to securely share files on the Blockchain with IPFS

16.4. Few use cases of IPFS in storing Blockchain data

(i) Non-Fungible Tokens or NFTs: A NFT is a type of digital certificate that guarantees ownership of a unique digital asset such as a song, an image, art, videos, a game, etc. NFTs, digital assets, and everything can't be stored on Blockchain, as storing that much data on the Blockchain is expensive and consumes a lot of electricity. Here is where IPFS comes in. The specifics of the NFT, including the sale agreement, information regarding the creator of the work, royalties, etc., can be stored directly on the smart contracts. But the digital assets associated with NFTs can be stored in IPFS. A unique hash is generated for every uploaded file on the IPFS server, which is then stored on the smart contract and can be accessed by authorized users.

(ii) Storing Electronic Health Records (EHR): IPFS also allows for safer storage of patients' health data, and smart contracts on Blockchain limit the data access to only authorized users, e.g., healthcare providers, insurance companies, etc.

(iii) IPFS can be an excellent tool for dApps as it can be used to store any dApp data. For example, in the case of educational dApp, course content, assignments, blogs, articles, etc., can be stored on decentralized IPFS. And in the case of streaming dApps, video and music content can be stored on IPFS.

Chapter 16: Blockchain Interoperability

Blockchain interoperability refers to a Blockchain's ability to actively communicate and freely exchange data with other Blockchains. A common analogy is that of emails; someone with a Gmail account can send emails to someone with a Yahoo or Hotmail account.

16.1. Types of Blockchain Interoperability

Blockchain interoperability would allow users on any Blockchain layer to transact or send messages to an outside chain. Interoperability can be split into two parts:

(i) Exchange of digital assets: This means the ability to transfer and exchange assets originating from different Blockchains. For instance, making bitcoin spendable in distributed applications (Dapps) built on Ethereum. Or, while you are working with an application on the Ethereum network, you can make a direct payment to a separate chain like Cardano or Cosmos.

(ii) Exchange of data: This is the ability to exchange data or send messages between two or multiple Blockchain platforms.

16.2. Blockchain interoperability solutions

16.2.1. Notary Scheme Solutions

In this solution, the transactions between the two users on different Blockchains are managed by a trusted third-party called a notary. The notary's job is to verify that a Blockchain event occurred and feed this information to a second Blockchain. For this, the notary should have accounts on both the Blockchains, i.e., source and target. Suppose the transaction has to happen between two users; one user is on Blockchain A, and another is on Blockchain B. For this, user 1 on chain A transfers the assets to the notary account (on source chain A). The notary will lock and confirm the assets and then transfer the corresponding assets from its account (on target chain B) to user 2 on chain B.

Two types of notaries may be used; a single-signature notary or a multi-signature notary.

Single-signature notary: A single-signature notary, also known as a centralized notary, collects transaction data from the source chain Blockchain A, validates it, and initiates the execution of the transaction on the target chain Blockchain B. The notary group consists of many nodes, each of which should have funds in the notary account. Each node, also called a notary, has a reputation value in the notary group, and all members in the notary group jointly maintain the party's credit standing. The node with sufficient funds and with high reputation will be randomly selected, and that single node will undertake the tasks of data collection, verification, and transaction confirmation in the process of the cross-chain asset or data excahange.

Limitations: (i) Single-signature notary schemes are one of the simplest ways to achieve cross-chain interoperability with high transaction speed. However, it requires depending on a centralized body, which is against the Blockchain's decentralized nature. (ii) An additional disadvantage is its vulnerability to the failure or misbehavior of any node.

Multi-signature notary: With a multi-signature notary, a cross-chain request initiated by user 1 on 'Blockchain A' needs to be successfully verified by the majority of nodes/notaries. Once verified, the signatures of multiple nodes are published on the corresponding transaction to be executed on 'Blockchain B.' In order to tolerate Byzantine faults, a Byzantine-fault-tolerant consensus algorithm is used, according to which the cross-chain transactions can be processed and transmitted to the target Blockchain only if more than two-thirds of notaries achieve consensus and sign the transaction.

Examples of platforms using notary solutions for Blockchain interoperability: Herdius (a decentralized exchange platform) and Bifrost use notary schemes to facilitate cross-chain transactions on multiple Blockchain platforms.

16.2.2. Hash locking technology

Hash-locking or hash-time locking is another technique for the cross-exchange of assets on different Blockchain platforms without the need for trusted third parties/notaries. The cross-exchange of assets is also called **atomic swap**. This technique does not permit the transfer of a token from one Blockchain to another but enables users to hold its ownership by the user on a different Blockchain. By that, users are free to choose on which Blockchain they want to keep their assets.

The atomic swap takes place with the help of a special type of smart contract between the users on different Blockchains called a hashed time lock contract, or HTLC. One of the users (user 1) must be the first to time-lock their assets into an HTLC. These assets remain locked and illiquid until either the swap is completed or the HTLC expires. After getting confirmation that user 1 has locked assets on chain A, user 2 would time-lock their assets into the corresponding HTLC on the other chain B, completing their side of the collateral. After the locking of assets from both users, they can each claim their swapped assets; otherwise, the locked assets are transferred back to the users.

Time lock: It is a type of locking or a restricting mechanism that locks out the assets until a preset or a predetermined time is not reached. In terms of cryptocurrency, it means that a certain amount of coins will be locked out and will not be spent until a preset or predetermined time is reached.

How hash-locking scheme works?

Suppose the transaction has to happen between Alice and Bob, who possess accounts in Bitcoin and Ethereum Blockchain networks, respectively. They come to an agreement whereby Alice will give Bob 10 BTC in exchange for, say, 12 ETH.

(i) Alice's contract generates a secret key (random number), e.g., s, and computes its hash value, e.g., h = hash(s), then sends the hash value h to Bob. By doing so, Bob only has access to verify the locked Alice's 10 BTC, but Bob cannot access or withdraw the funds – at least not yet.

(ii) After verification, Bob also locks his assets, i.e., 12 ETH, into a smart contract until a certain lock time. He also needs to send the hash of his secret key to Alice. Smart contracts have certain pre-defined rules:

- If the secret s is provided by Alice to Bob within lock time, i.e., 2t, then Bob can verify 10 BTC locked by Alice and can claim his ownership over them; otherwise, the BTCs are sent back to Alice.
- On the other hand, if Bob provides the correct secret to Alice within the pre-defined time t, then the ownership over 12 ETH is transferred to Alice; otherwise, the ETHs are sent back to Bob.

(iii). After verification of assets by both the users, the ownership of assets is transferred, and its transaction is stored on both the Blockchains to prevent double-spending.

16.2.3. Cross-chain bridges

A Blockchain bridge, also known as a cross-chain bridge like a physical bridge, that connects two Blockchains. It facilitates communication between two Blockchain networks by facilitating the transfer of data or digital assets.

How do cross-chain bridges work?

The cross-chain bridges do not permit the transfer of a token from one Blockchain to another in the sense that a specific amount of assets is locked on the source Blockchain, and the same number of equivalent assets are released on the target Blockchain. This is generally performed using smart contracts.

Users send their tokens to a smart contract on the source Blockchain. Once the smart contract locks and has custody of the user's crypto coins, it automatically communicates this to a smart contract on the target Blockchain, which then releases the equivalent amount of coins. In some cases, the released coins may be freshly minted, whereas in other cases, they are derived from the liquidity pools on the target chain.

Binance Bridge, Celer cBridge, Multichain, and Wormhole are among popular cross-chain bridges.

16.2.4. Sidechains

Sidechains, layer 2 scaling solutions also provide Blockchain interoperability. Sidechains are separate Blockchains that are connected to the main Blockchain through a two-way peg to improve the scalability by helping process some of the data from the main Blockchain. It also adds an interoperability function by validating data from other Blockchains. And has the ability to import and export digital property (i.e., coins, assets, etc.) from other Blockchains at an agreed-upon price or exchange rate. It allows the transfer of digital properties between the two Blockchains using Simplified Payment Verification (SPV) proofs. Through SPVs, the nodes on the sidechain can verify if the transaction has been initiated on the other Blockchain and are not required to download the whole main Blockchain every time the verification process is needed.

The 2 way peg, abbreviated as 2WP, acts as an intermediary which locks an asset in one Blockchain to reserve it until the transfer to the other one is completed. Sidechains have already been discussed in detail in Chapter 13 while discussing Layer 2 scaling solutions.

Chapter 17: Criteria for choosing Blockchain

Before diving into the use cases of Blockchain technology, let's first understand when you should use Blockchain for your business. There are certain criteria that you should keep in mind in order to decide whether it makes sense to start a project with this technology.

17.1. Number of Intermediaries

If your business is subjected to high costs and work delays because of the involvement of middlemen or intermediaries, then Blockchain is a good fit for your business. With the implementation of Blockchain, these issues can be resolved as it will remove these intermediaries. As a result, it will cut down the high costs of the middlemen and will further expedite the work.

For instance, in the case of the entertainment industry, Blockchain can really prove to be a game-changer. In the entertainment industry, there is a long chain of intermediaries involved between the creative artist and the final consumers of his creation. With the implementation of Blockchain, the artist or the creator will have absolute control over his content, and he can be paid directly, instead of going through a chain of intermediaries, for sharing his creative talent with the world.

17.2. Secure Database

If you need to manage a database in your business that is fundamentally secure, tamper-proof, and you need to share it with multiple parties, then Blockchain is a good option. Blockchain itself can not be used to store massive data, but Blockchain with IPFS can store and manage data with high integrity. It is also a good approach to avoid data manipulation and perform data exchange in real-time.

For instance, in a business related to supply chain management, multiple stakeholders are involved at various stages of the process, and it also lacks transparency and real-time updates about the consignment. For such a scenario, Blockchain can be a perfect solution. In a Blockchain-based system, stakeholders involved in the supply chain will record the information about the consignment on the Blockchain platform once they receive it. This in turn, will make it feasible to get real-time updates and information about the consignment, and the location of a consignment will be clearly visible to all the stakeholders involved throughout its journey.

17.3. Trust

Another critical point to consider is the trust factor. Trusting other parties is essential when doing business. There could be many reasons why a third party should handle some business data. But, it always creates trust issues due to a lack of transparency. It is because, in a centralized system, malicious and fraudulent actions can be performed easily. Also, the information stored in a centralized system can lead to a single point of failure, and moreover, a centralized database is prone to hacking activities as well. But with the implementation of Blockchain, the issue of a single point of failure can be avoided due to its distributed nature. Further implementation of this technology can even make your business, data, and transactions transparent, tamper-proof, and immutable. In our example of a supply chain business, the implementation of Blockchain technology will make it nearly impossible for any party involved in the process to forge the documents of the consignment or introduce fake products into the supply chain.

17.4. Collaborations

One of the other crucial criteria to look upon while considering blockchain is the level of collaborations required in your business. If your business requires coordination between a large number of stakeholders, Blockchain can be a great solution.

The concept of creating smart contracts can help in automating collaborations. A traditional contract defines only the terms of a business relationship, but a digitized smart contract also defines conditions under which the contract will be executed. For instance, defining the criteria under which the payment shall be made, and once those conditions are fulfilled, smart contracts automatically release the payment. Thus smart contracts can eliminate human intervention for payments and play an important role in automating cross-company collaborations.

17.5. Type of Blockchain

If you agree that your business requires Blockchain technology, it is essential to figure out whether you want to use public or private Blockchain. If you don't want your confidential data to be public, you have to choose a permissioned or private Blockchain that allows you to keep data private and give access only to specific parties. In such a case, do not opt for open public Blockchains like Bitcoin and Ethereum, where anyone can join the network and access the transactions.

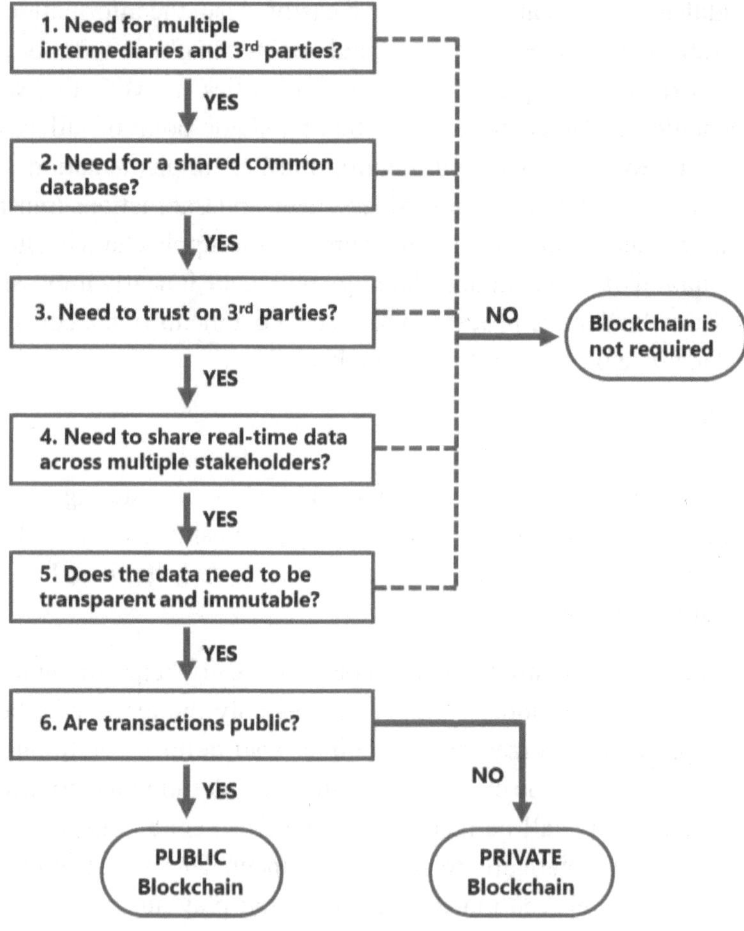

Fig 17-1: Blockchain decision criteria

Section 2

Blockchain and the Internet of Things or IoT

Chapter 18: Blockchain and IoT

There is a huge impact of IoT, or the Internet of things, on everything, from how we travel and do our shopping to the way manufacturers keep track of their inventory. But what is IoT, and how does it work?

18.1. What is IoT, and how does it work?

IoT refers to the concept of connecting any physical device to the internet and other devices. Similar to the way in which Internet has changed how we work & communicate by connecting us globally, IoT aims to take this connectivity to the next level by connecting various devices to the internet, generating a giant network of connected things– all of which collect and share data about the way they are used and about the environment around them. Thus, allowing the devices to communicate with people and other IoT-enabled devices.

There are five main components of IoT:

(i) IoT Sensors or smart sensors: Any device is called an IoT device or smart device when it is equipped with a smart sensor that helps in collecting very minute data from the surrounding environment. An IoT device may also have multiple sensors. For instance, simple watches can be used to see the time and date only, but smart IoT watches with different sensors like optical heart rate sensor, oximetry sensor, calorie counter, pedometer sensor, etc. allow a user to monitor heartbeat rate, oxygen level, calorie count and steps walked. There are also many other types of sensors used by different smart devices like temperature sensors or thermostats, pressure sensors, humidity sensors, CO_2 sensors, light sensors, motion sensors, RFID tags, etc.

(ii) IoT gateway: IoT gateways, as the name suggests, are the gateways to the internet for IoT devices. The data collected from various IoT sensors embedded into a variety of devices is sent to the cloud via IoT gateways *(Fig 18-1)*. In other words, the IoT gateway acts as a bridge that connects multiple IoT devices to the cloud. The devices are connected to the IoT gateway through low-power wireless networks like ZigBee, Bluetooth, Z-wave,

LoRaWAN, etc. IoT gateway collects data from different smart sensors, pre-processes it locally, and sends it to the IoT cloud via the internet. Pre-processing of data means aggregating, summarizing, filtering, and synchronizing traffic from different IoT devices so that the volume of data that needs to be forwarded to the cloud is significantly minimized. This reduces power usage, response time, and network transmission costs.

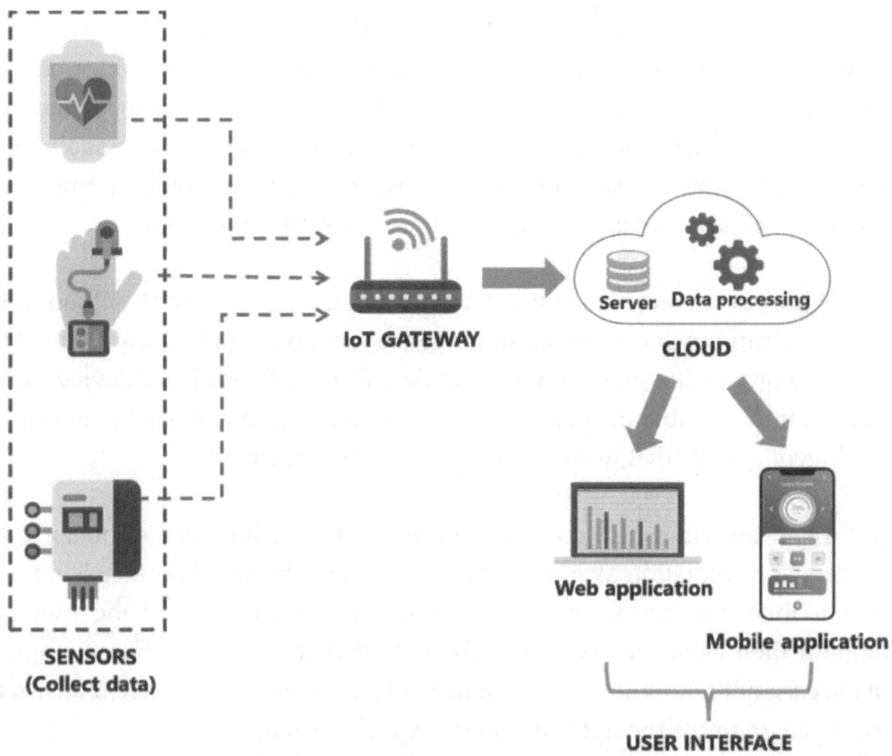

Fig 18-1: How does the Internet of things or IoT work?

The wearable devices connected with Bluetooth often use a mobile phone as their gateway. This works well as long as the phone and the devices are nearby. On the other hand, other smart devices like home automation smart devices can't use mobile phones as the gateway as the phones don't stay in a fixed location. These require a gateway box plugged into the wall, which receives information from IoT devices using Zigbee, LoRaWAN, etc. and then forward the information to the cloud via the Internet. Also, the devices don't receive the information from the cloud directly; it is received through the IoT gateway. Thus, gateways have a role in **both sending data to the cloud and then receiving information from it**.

(iii) IoT Cloud: The IoT devices collect massive amounts of data that must be managed efficiently. The IoT cloud offers tools to collect, process, manage and store a huge amount of data in real-time. Some examples of IoT cloud platforms are Google cloud IoT, Azure IoT, Amazon Web Services (AWS) IoT, etc. Basically, the cloud is a sophisticated, high-performance network of servers optimized to perform high-speed data processing of billions of IoT devices, traffic management, and deliver accurate analytics. Industries and businesses can easily access these data remotely to improve products and services and make critical decisions when necessary.

(iv) Data processing: Once the data is collected and gets to the cloud, the machine learning and artificial intelligence tools process the acquired data. The data processing means converting data from billions of IoT devices and sensors into valuable insights which can be interpreted and used to perform intelligent actions that make all our devices 'Smart Devices.'

(iv) User interface: Lastly, there needs to be an interface to make the processed information available to the end-user. The user interface is either in a mobile application or a web-based application. It helps the user to monitor their smart devices remotely and interact with them. For example, in the case of home automation, the user interface provided will help the user to switch on or off the lights or fan in a specific room.

The alert notifications can be sent either by triggering alarms on their phones, and the app also offers you options to make changes to the conditions. For example, if the temperature of the AC is too high, the app can suggest you adjust it to something more suitable *(Fig 18-2)*.

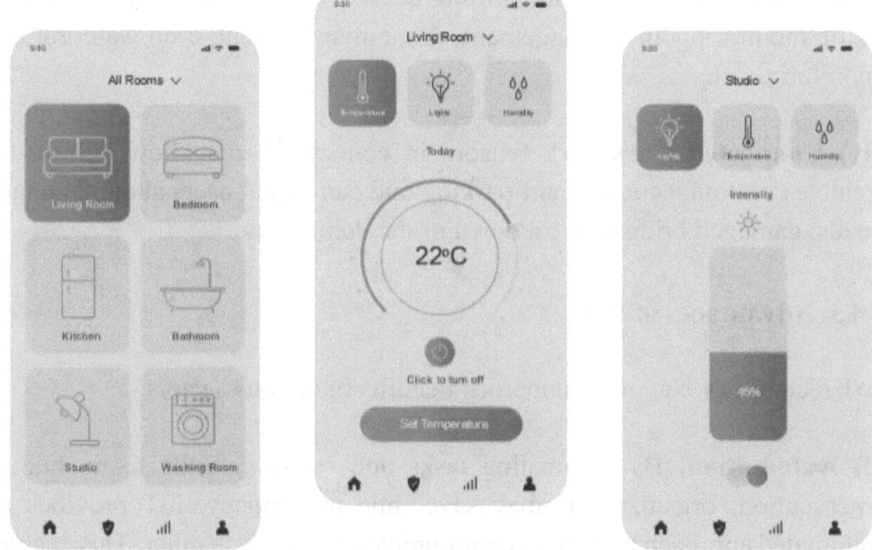

Fig 18-2: A user interface for a smart home app

18.2. Few examples of the Internet of Things

IoT can transform traditional objects and devices into smart devices by exploiting technologies such as sensors and the internet. Internet of Things (IoT) has many applications in various areas such as healthcare, agriculture, home automation, wearables, augmented reality, transportation, and many more. A few examples of IoT or smart devices are as follows:

(i) Smart wearable health devices: These devices are IoT-enabled and analyze all of our data, like real-time patient monitoring, pulse, heart rate, blood pressure, etc., to improve our lifestyle and health. The data can also be passed to the clinicians directly on their remote devices.

(ii) Smart home devices: IoT enables home users to create a network of smart home appliances such as smart thermostats, smart locks, smart doorbells, smart light switches, smart speakers, etc.

(iii) Smart Farming: Smart farming devices monitor weather conditions, cattle monitoring and management, drone management, crop watering and monitoring, etc.

(iv) Connected Cars: IoT sensors in connected cars allow vehicle-to-vehicle communication, smart parking and can signal users about damaged roads, damaged bridges, breakdown of the vehicle, etc.

18.3. Advantages of IoT

IoT technology can offer numerous benefits in various sectors:

(i) Automation: By automating tasks and requiring little to no human intervention, organizations may save time and money. IoT provides an automated approach to devices communicating with each other. This enables devices to automatically identify or even predict a fault and inform the maintenance team. Thus, allowing you to reduce downtime and unexpected or unnecessary maintenance costs.

(ii) Save time and resources: By reducing human effort, IoT devices allow you to accomplish cumbersome tasks faster and with optimum energy utilization. For example, if your home has smart lights that turn on only at times when people are moving through areas, this saves the unnecessary use of electricity.

(iii) Better customer experience: With so much data and information collected by IoT devices, organizations now have greater access to data related to their customers and products than ever before. With real-time operational insights, they can monitor customer behavior, understand their requirements, and deliver better-personalized experiences that engage the customers at a deeper level and increase customer loyalty.

(iv) Better business insights: IoT devices can help organizations gather data to identify insights about their business, both internally and externally. They can be beneficial in asset tracking, monitoring, inventory management, energy optimization, etc. For instance, logistics firms can use IoT devices to align the delivery locations and schedules that make the most efficient use of their vehicles and employees. Businesses can also use IoT to reduce their time to market for new products or services and amplify their ROI.

18.4. Challenges with IoT

Although IoT provides enormous benefits, it comes with its own share of problems too:

(i) Single point of failure: Most IoT devices depend on centralized architecture by connecting them to cloud servers to store and collect information. This centralized architecture can introduce a single point of failure, which means that a component of a system can interrupt the running of the entire network if it crashes. This is undesirable in any system as it can compromise the availability of the entire data.

(ii) Security: Secondly, the largely unregulated and centralized IoT market makes the IoT devices vulnerable to being hacked. In case a hacker is able to access control of an IoT device, there would be two main risks associated with it:

- The hacker would be able to access and steal sensitive data of the IoT device users.
- The hacker could be able to take remote control of the device itself. For instance, a hacker could take control over a self-driving car with someone in it or make purchases based on access levels given to an IoT system.

Therefore, robust cybersecurity is a must.

(iii) Additionally, IoT devices lack the ability to identify compromised IoT devices, data leaks, and hackers. According to a report, less than half of IoT businesses can detect if any of their devices have been breached.

18.5. Blockchain- The Solution

Blockchain technology aims to solve the challenges associated with IoT:

(i) Security: Because of the decentralized nature, Blockchain technology offers various potential benefits and allows a smart device to function autonomously without the need for a centralized authority. The transactions are timestamped and then inserted into blocks; each block is cryptographically protected by a hash. The transactions refer to the IoT data exchanges that occur in the network. The blocks are linked together to form a chain, referred to as a Blockchain. No centralized entity is commissioned to monitor or process the transaction; instead, a block containing transactions is added to the Blockchain only after achieving the consensus among the nodes. It empowers all the network nodes with validation rights to check the correctness of IoT data. This prevents the hackers from attacking or manipulating data once the data is added to the Blockchain. Hacking Blockchain is difficult because if one block is hacked, the attacker must hack every subsequent block because every block contains the previous block's hash. This piece of information is what links one block to another. Tampering with a block changes its hash and hashes of the subsequent blocks, making the whole Blockchain invalid. Therefore, it is nearly impossible to tamper with the data, thus making the whole network safe and secure.

(ii) No single point of failure: Adopting a decentralized peer-to-peer network to process the transactions reduces the costs associated with maintaining large centralized data centers by distributing computation and storage needs across the nodes of the Blockchain network. This will prevent failure in any single node in a network (either because of a power outage or the node goes offline) from bringing the entire network to crash and compromise data. Thus, the adoption of Blockchain in IoT can overcome the single point of failure problem and serve as an adequate means to efficiently and securely store and process IoT data.

18.6. Challenges in implementing Blockchain in IoT

There is no doubt that integrating Blockchain with IoT would have many advantages that may improve many of the IoT issues, but at the same time,

Blockchain technology has its own flaws and challenges that need to be addressed:

(i) Processing Power and Time: Due to the block size constraints, many Blockchains have lengthy processing periods for transactions to be written into the chain of confirmed blocks. For instance, in the case of Bitcoin Blockchain, the block size limitation is 1MB, and the average transaction size is 500 bytes; therefore, around 2000 transactions can be stored per block. And the block time is set to be 10 minutes, which leads to a maximum throughput of 7 transactions per second.

In IoT systems, the IoT devices continuously stream data. Therefore, the number of transactions in the IoT ecosystem would far exceed the Blockchain limits. Thus, the challenge is to boost Blockchain's throughput to meet the need for frequent transactions in IoT systems.

(ii) Scalability issues: Current Blockchain platforms have scalability issues because of restricted transactional throughput (transactions/second), efficiency, and high computational cost. If all transactions are to be processed and saved on the main Blockchain, the ledger over time will become extremely large. Every time a new transaction needs to be processed, the information is updated on all nodes of the network to make it transparent and verified across all nodes. Therefore, as the number of transactions grows, so does the ledger's size, resulting in more data to be processed and stored on each node. With the block size and block time constraints, one has to wait for a long time for the validation of a transaction.

Since the magnitude of IoT data would grow rapidly, it makes the processing of high volumes of data extremely complicated and lengthy on the Blockchain, reducing the overall performance of the Blockchain.

Due to these limitations, certain Blockchain scalability layer 1 and layer 2 solutions have to be implemented before integrating Blockchain with IoT *(Fig 18-3)*. These will increase the transactional throughput, increase the number of confirmed blocks per second, and decrease the block time.

Layer 1 scaling solutions: Layer 1 scaling solutions are applied to the main Blockchains to increase their performance and transactional throughput.

They are divided into two categories: consensus mechanism improvement and sharding, each of them has been discussed in Chapter 12.

Layer 2 scaling solutions: Layer 2 scaling solutions don't require changes in the main Blockchain layer 1. They establish an additional protocol that is built on top of main Blockchains like those of Ethereum and Bitcoin. Layer 2 scaling solutions are of 4 types: channels, rollups, plasma, and side chains. Each of them has been discussed in detail in Chapter 13.

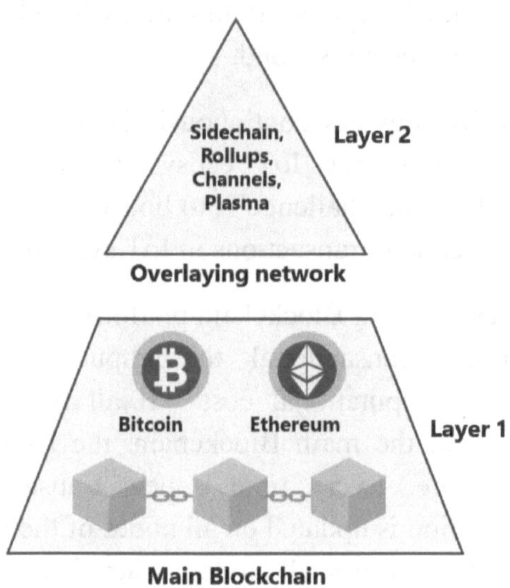

Fig 18-3: Layer 1 and layer 2 Blockchain

(iii) Handling massive data on Blockchain: In the Blockchain network, every participant/node maintains a copy of the complete distributed ledger. Upon the confirmation of a new block, the block is broadcast throughout the entire network, and every node appends the confirmed block to their local ledger. Therefore, the management of huge data on Blockchain puts a burden on nodes' storage space, making Blockchain very expensive for storing all the data collected by IoT devices. To overcome this issue, InterPlanetary File System (IPFS) can be used.

IPFS: IPFS is a content-addressing, peer-to-peer network for storing and sharing data in a distributed file system. Instead of storing every data in the blockchain network, IPFS can be used to store the entire digitized content with high integrity, and only the hash address of the data needs to be stored on the Blockchain. In other words, the Blockchain can be used to store the address of the data, while IPFS can be used to store the entire data securely. Furthermore, since IPFS is distributed, it has no single point of failure.

18.7. Proposed architecture for Blockchain and IoT integration

(i) Type of Blockchain: A permissioned private Blockchain, more specifically, a consortium Blockchain, can be used instead of a permissionless public Blockchain. The IoT devices that interact with consumers and gather their sensitive information have profound privacy implications, like in the scenarios such as a smart door lock that records what times of the day the door is open and closed or the data collected by a pacemaker and sent to a hospital. This type of information should not be available to the public. Therefore, a consortium Blockchain being a private Blockchain, would be suitable for the IoT. Additionally, unlike permissionless public Blockchain, where anyone can become a node, in the permissioned Blockchain, all nodes are pre-selected.

(ii) Consensus mechanism: The consensus mechanism used can be Proof of Authority, abbreviated as PoA, where the network users stake their identity and reputation. This means that, unlike POW (POW) and Proof of Stake (POS) consensus mechanisms, where anyone can join without disclosing their identities, users in PoA systems are known entities that put their reputations at stake. The faster speed of the PoA consensus mechanism allows the network to reach consensus more quickly. It, therefore, provides much faster processing of transactions than other consensus mechanisms like POW and POS.

(iii) Smart contracts: Smart contracts, written in Solidity language, are the self-executing programs stored on a Blockchain that run when predefined conditions are met. Smart contracts can settle service disputes between consumers and IoT service providers, restrict data access to only the desired parties, and securely share data with the stakeholders.

(iv) Integration of Artificial Intelligence (AI): Integration of AI tools is essential for converting raw data captured by IoT devices into meaningful, useful insights that can be interpreted and used to perform intelligent actions by the devices.

(v) Layer 2 scaling solution: Layer 2 scaling solution Sidechains can be used. Sidechains are separate Blockchains that are connected to the main Blockchain through a two-way peg to help process some of the IoT data from the main Blockchain. The IoT devices can be grouped together; each sidechain network is responsible for maintaining a secure log of the IoT data operations that occur within it. For instance, the IoT devices in the entire smart city can be grouped as sub-networks like smart transportation, smart medical, smart home, etc. Each of these sub-networks has independent businesses and runs in parallel on their assigned sidechains *(Fig 18-4)*. Then these sidechains can share data through the mainchain to provide a more valuable service. The mainchain is also responsible for managing successful or failed requests to access IoT data. A sidechain with its own protocols and implementation runs independently and is completely isolated from the main chain. Therefore, sidechains provide scalability and increase the transaction throughput by taking away some of the IoT transactions into their sidechain and processing transactions at a much higher rate.

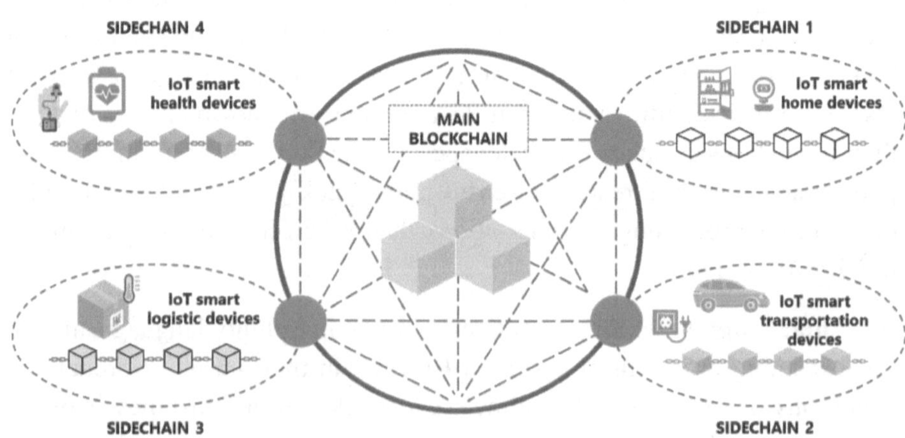

Fig 18-4: Each of the IoT sub-networks runs in parallel on their assigned sidechains

In case the main Blockchain is hacked or compromised, the sidechain can still operate; likewise, the cyberattacks on the sidechain cannot affect the operation of the mainchain.

Another advantage of using sidechains is that public Blockchain can also be used for IoT data management. While the mainchain is public and permissionless, the sidechain is designed private & permissioned to cater to IoT data. Thus, the public mainchain will be used as a reference chain to keep the IoT device information record, and maintaining and processing IoT data will be done on the private sidechains.

(vi) IPFS: Both the main Blockchain and sidechains are connected to IPFS for storing the entire IoT data. The hash address of the IoT data will be stored on sidechains and Blockchain *(Fig 18-5)*.

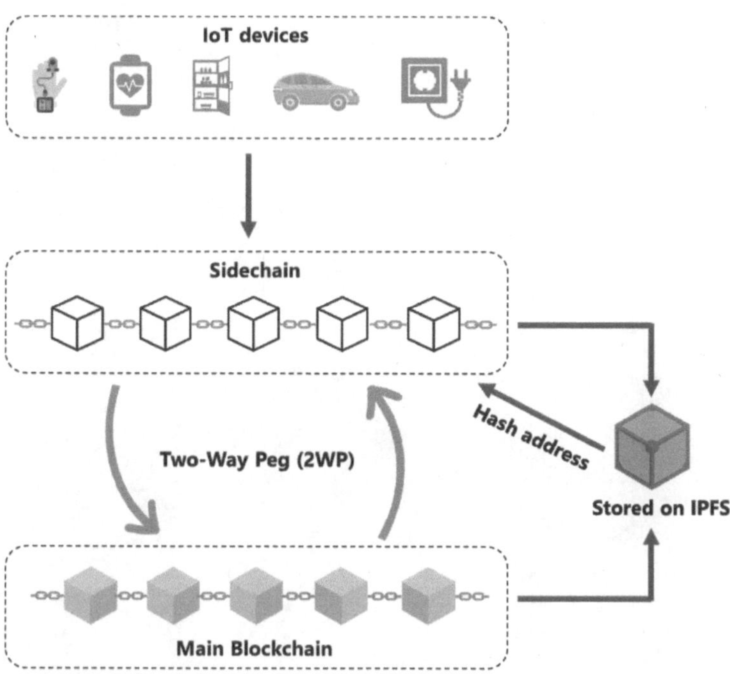

Fig 18-5: IoT data is processed by sidechain and stored on IPFS

(vii) dApps: dApp refers to a distributed web application, a user interface that can interact with Blockchain using the smart contract. Unlike a conventional app, dApp is no longer controlled by a single entity or an organization once deployed on the Blockchain network.

When a new IoT device is added to a smart system, the device should be registered to the Blockchain network through the dApp. It enables the user to monitor their smart devices remotely and interact with them. Any notifications or alerts are also sent on the dApp.

Chapter 19: Blockchain and IoT in smart homes

A smart home may be defined as a "residence equipped with the Internet of Things or IoT devices that send and receive data in real-time to anticipate and respond to the needs of the residents, promoting their comfort, convenience, security, and entertainment within the home and connecting them to the world. The IoT technology provides automation to various home devices, making them smart such as smart TVs, smart lights, smart refrigerators, smart locks, smart coffee makers, and so on *(Fig 19-1).* For instance, a smart coffee maker can prepare the perfect coffee for you as soon as you wake up, a smart microwave can differentiate between a perfectly cooked pizza from a burnt pizza, and a smart air conditioner can send a maintenance service request on its own in case it breaks down.

Fig 19-1: Smart home with various IoT devices connected to the internet

19.1. IoT smart home challenges

Home is a private space where individuals perform different activities while carrying out their daily routines. They need to feel secure and enjoy emotional and physical comfort when they are inside their house. But by connecting home devices to the internet, security issues arise.

(i) Security and privacy challenges: The data collected from the sensors embedded into IoT devices is sent to the cloud via IoT gateways. The devices are connected to the IoT gateway through low-power wireless networks like ZigBee, Bluetooth, Z-wave, LoRaWAN, etc. IoT gateway collects data from the sensors, pre-processes it locally, and sends it to the cloud via the internet. Additionally, various IoT devices communicate with each other through the gateway. The gateway thus becomes the main target for the hackers to steal sensitive data of the residents or to take remote control of an IoT device. For instance, a hacker could take control of a smart door lock to break into the house. Even the hackers could also hack smart home devices to send malicious emails and spam messages, making them the main target to cause cyberattacks.

(ii) Restricted access challenges: In super-connected smart homes, there will be many situations where you will want to give limited access instead of complete access of your home to the other party. For example, when you hire a pet sitter for paying a half an hour visit to feed and look after your dog. In such a situation, you would want him to access your lobby only and not the entire house.

In today's IoT-enabled smart homes, this pinpoint access is not feasible. We can give complete access of our home to the sitter through our mobile app, but we can't choose what devices or services he can access and what devices and services should be kept off-limits for him.

19.2. Proposed Blockchain architecture for smart homes

Because of the decentralized and peer-to-peer network, Blockchain technology overcomes the challenges IoT devices face and enables them to operate in a decentralized manner without relying on a trusted or centralized intermediary.

The architecture will contain four layers: the smart home layer, Blockchain network, IPFS, and application layer *(Fig 19-2)*.

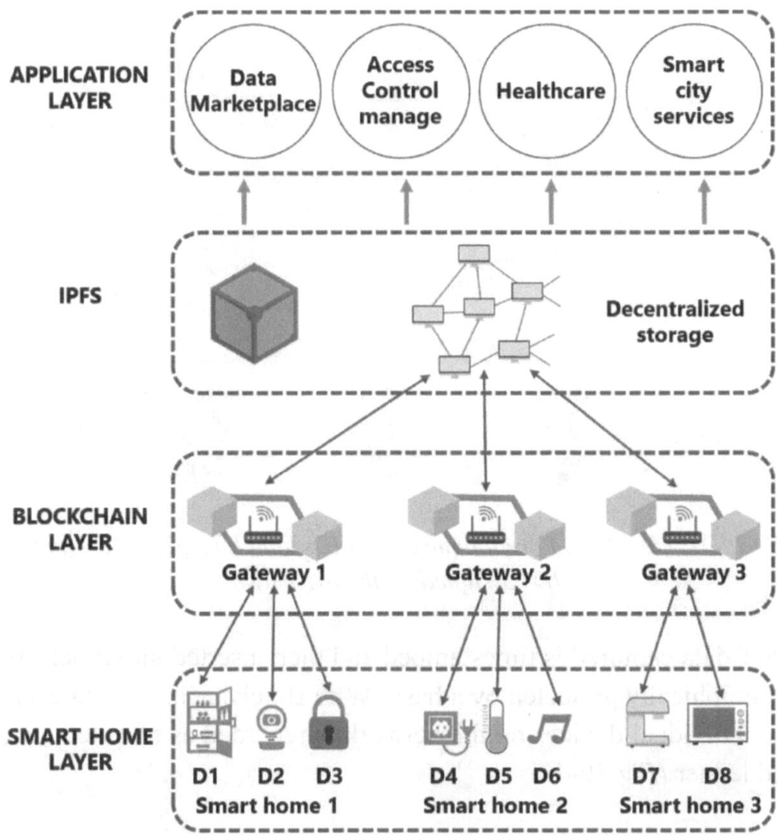

Fig 19-2: Proposed Blockchain architecture for smart homes

(i) Smart home layer: Smart home layer consists of many IoT devices like a security system, smart lights, smart refrigerators, smart thermostats, and so on. These devices have sensors that collect real-time data and transmit it to the gateway.

(ii) Blockchain layer: Blockchain can be applied to the smart home gateways for transmitting data with integrity and confidentiality between devices and other media. All of the smart devices of a home are connected to one gateway. Each IoT device and gateway needs to be registered on the Blockchain network and is given a fixed unique ID. Similarly, each user on the network is assigned a unique User ID *(Fig 19-3)*.

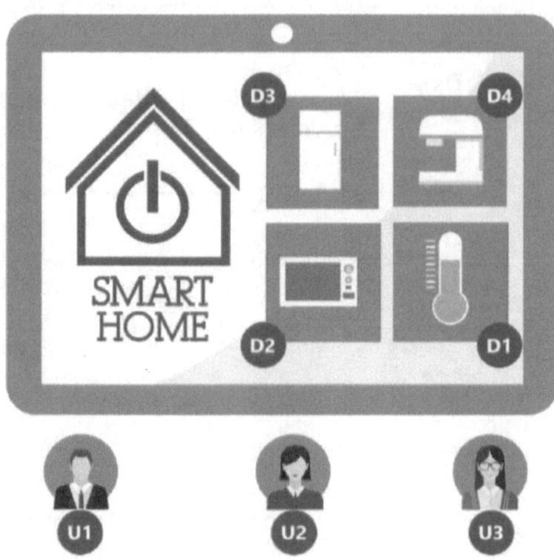

Fig 19-3: D1, D2, D3, D4 are unique device IDs, and U1, U2, U3 are unique user IDs assigned on the IoT network

The IoT data captured is timestamped and then inserted into blocks that are cryptographically protected by a hash. With Blockchain, all data exchanged by the individual devices on the network is recorded as transactions on the shared ledger *(Fig 19-4)*.

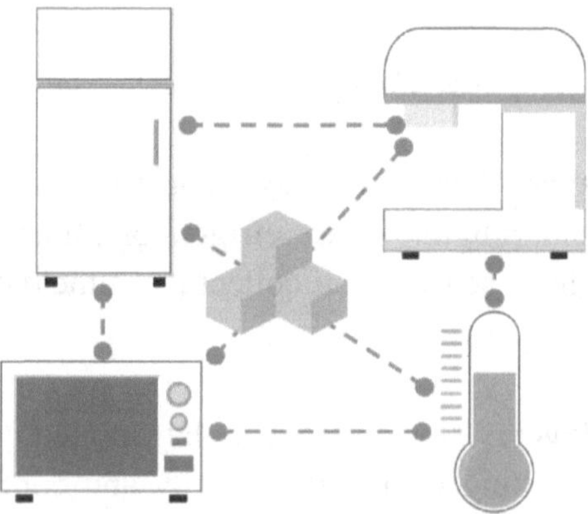

Fig 19-4: Data exchanged by smart devices are recorded on Blockchain

For better clarity, let us understand it through a real-life scenario, Jaime got a new thermostat for his smart home. When the device is added on to the network - the device is given a unique ID, say TH1. His cousin Robert visits his home for the weekend, but Jaime has to leave for a colleague's party. He gives access of the thermostat to his cousin so that he can feel comfortable in his absence. As soon as Robert is granted access to the thermostat, a unique user ID, say C1, will be generated for him. All his interactions with the thermostat will be recorded on the ledger as immutable transactions *(Fig 19-5)*.

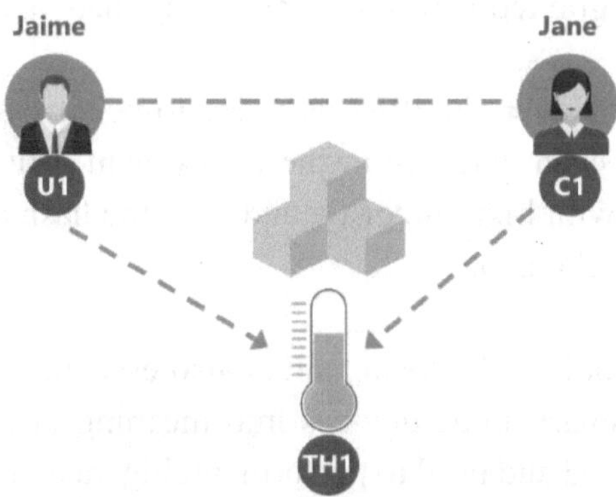

Fig 19-5: Access of thermostat given to Jane on Blockchain

A home server computer may be considered a validating node responsible for verifying and adding transactions to new blocks, while smart contracts on the Blockchain follow predefined rules and facilitate decentralized transactions.

Generally, a **permissioned private Blockchain** is used in a smart home network to maintain privacy and reduce overhead costs.

The communication between devices and gateway is done through pre-shared keys.

- When a device intends to communicate with the gateway, the gateway requests its ID.
- The gateway encrypts the gateway information and sends it to the device. Devices with pre-shared keys decrypt the encrypted messages.

- The registered devices also send encrypted data to the gateway, which then decodes the transmitted data to verify that they received data from the authorized registered devices.
- The gateway stores the decoded data, pre-processes it, and sends it to the IPFS.
- Only those smart devices can communicate with each other that the owner has granted permission by giving them a shared key.

(iii) IPFS: The third layer, the IPFS, is a peer-to-peer network that stores the data processed by each gateway in the Blockchain. IPFS stores the entire digitized IoT data with high integrity, and only the hash address of the data is stored on the Blockchain.

Integration of AI tools and Blockchain is also essential for converting raw data captured by smart home devices into meaningful and useful insights that can be interpreted and used to perform intelligent actions by the devices.

(iv) Application layer: The fourth layer, the application layer, is created to facilitate communication of various smart home devices with other existing Blockchain platforms such as data marketplace, access management, homecare or healthcare, automated utility payment, smart city services, etc.

19.3. Smart home data marketplace

Data marketplace is an online platform where entities can trade data. In a conventional data marketplace, data providers and potential consumers contact each other directly or via a third party. In such cases, trust is the main issue that hinders the transparency of the trade. There are certain real-life cases in which malicious actors have fraudulently tampered with the customer data to illegally increase their benefits. But through the Blockchain, a decentralized and secure data marketplace can be created, which has two advantages: The first is continuous data availability for IoT device manufacturers. And the second is the availability of a diverse set of data for the AI and ML startups. This data is then processed by these companies using their specialized algorithms to produce useful insights. For instance, data from smart coffee makers can be used to get insights into people's choice of the coffee brand and preferences for the strength of the coffee in a specific region.

19.4. Smart home access management

To maintain privacy and enhance the smooth operation of a smart home, it is required to integrate a customized access control system that permits third parties on demand. The access to third parties can either be "Approved" or "Rejected" by the user using a smart contract *(Fig 19-6)*. The user can even define a time limit for the access, after which the access status will be changed.

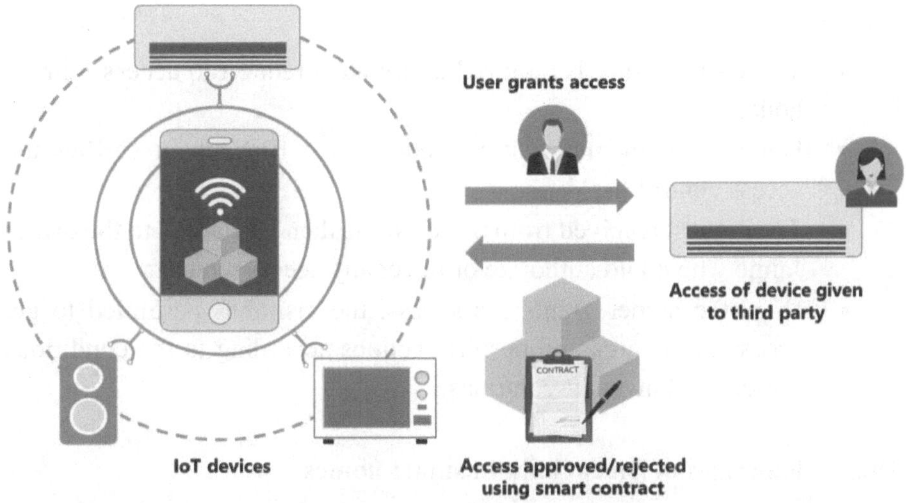

Fig 19-6: Access granted to third-party through a smart contract

Let us take a scenario to understand it in a better way: Jaime has a lovely dog named Miller. He knows that he will be late from work today. Therefore he hires Smith, a pet sitter, for Miller's evening walk. Jaime gives a digital key of his house to Smith, and that too only for today, so as to avoid any unwanted accident *(Fig 19-7)*. This time-bound access can only be given with the implementation of Blockchain, which is not possible otherwise.

Fig 19-7: Time-bound access of home on Blockchain

For this,

- The visitor Smith is required to initiate a request to access Jaime's house.
- Upon receiving the visitor's request, the Blockchain verifies the access control list.
- The request received from the visitor is then forwarded to the owner Jaime who could authorize or reject any access request.
- Once the owner grants the access, the visitor is permitted to get access of the area and perform actions according to the conditions pre-defined in smart contracts.

19.5. Advantages of Blockchain in smart homes

Blockchain can overcome certain challenges faced by smart homes. These challenges can be classified under these major four heads:

1. Network Security
2. Identity Management
3. Privacy
4. Resilience

These security issues are a big pain point for the IoT devices, but with the implementation of Blockchain, these issues can be mitigated, and the IoT networks can be made more secure, reliable, and robust.

Network Security - The first critical issue that Blockchain mitigates is network security. The software of any IoT device is the most crucial component that supports its functioning. Once a specific device is installed in the IoT network, its software needs to be updated with time to address the identified issues or to further add new functionalities.

For a better understanding, you can compare this with the updates that your mobile apps get to fix the latest identified issues or add new functionalities. These upgrades in the IoT devices are not secure and prone to hacking, resulting in a compromised network. Any hacker can use this lacuna in security to introduce a harmful update instead of the proposed update by the manufacturer, thus leading to a serious security breach.

But with the implementation of the Blockchain, the whole network can be made secure and robust. It is much easier to validate the authenticity of the software update once the Blockchain is introduced into the network.

Blockchain can further ensure that all the devices on the network are updated and are using the latest software version released by the manufacturer.

Identity Management - The second critical issue that Blockchain mitigates is Identity Management. Every device on the IoT network is authenticated to satisfy its identity management requirement.

During the authentication process, only trusted devices are added to the network, and unsecured or unauthorized devices are rejected. However, current IoT systems don't have a foolproof mechanism to enforce these measures. But with the implementation of smart contracts, this can be made foolproof and much more robust.

Privacy - The third critical issue that Blockchain mitigates is Privacy. IoT devices in the smart home network generally capture sensitive and very personal data of the users. Therefore permission handling process is a must-have requirement in the network. In such a scenario, whenever a third-party entity tries to exchange data with any of the devices in the smart home network, the user is required to authorize this exchange. This exchange can either be Approved or Rejected by the user using a smart contract. The user can even define a time limit for the data exchange, after which the data exchange status will be changed.

Resilience - The fourth critical issue that Blockchain mitigates is Resilience. Resilience in the system is built by detecting and mitigating unauthorized access and intrusion. For this purpose, a private Blockchain network can be used where network access to any unauthorized user will be prohibited. Thus, keeping the network robust and resilient.

19.6. Challenges in implementing Blockchain

Undoubtedly, Blockchain technology has the potential to open new opportunities for state-of-the-art smart home applications. However, several issues need to be investigated before mainstream adoption of the Blockchain in the smart home IoT ecosystem.

(i) Delayed response: The IoT devices continuously stream data, but the employment of Blockchain may cause delayed response because of lengthy processing periods for transaction validation. For instance, the block time of Bitcoin Blockchain is 10 minutes, which leads to a maximum throughput of 7 transactions per second. As a result, the traditional Blockchain technology is unsuitable for time-sensitive smart home IoT applications, where a minimum delay results in severe consequences.

(ii) Scalability: As the number of IoT devices increases, the processing of high volumes of data will become extremely complicated and lengthy on the Blockchain because of restricted transactional throughput (transactions/second), efficiency, and high computational cost. Thus, reducing the overall performance of the Blockchain.

These issues can be overcome by implementing certain Blockchain scalability layer 1 and layer 2 solutions before integrating Blockchain with IoT. These solutions will increase the transactional throughput and decrease the block time. Thus, reducing the delayed response to make it near real-time system while maintaining its security and tamper-proof properties for a sustainable smart home Blockchain ecosystem.

Chapter 20: Blockchain and IoT in smart healthcare

Healthcare is an essential part of life, and technology is disrupting this space day in and day out. The current technology in healthcare and the general practice of medicine can be enhanced by using the Internet of Things or IoT systems. Let's understand how these IoT systems and smart devices can enhance the healthcare services and create a positive impact on our health:

20.1. Benefits of IoT devices for healthcare

The benefits of IoT devices for healthcare are numerous.

Improve lifestyle: Smart wearables like Fitbits, Apple watches, health bands, etc. have many monitoring features to help you create goals and improve your fitness. Various sensors embedded in smart wearables track your activity levels, sleep cycle, and nutrient intake while checking your progress and making goals. There are certain other smart wearable pain relief patches like Thimble Bioelectronics which can send electric currents to chronic pain spots. This means treating pain the same way we treat a cut by putting a bandage on it and letting it heal. Other IoT devices like glucose monitoring devices provide continuous, automatic monitoring of glucose levels in patients. These devices eliminate the need to keep records manually, and they can alert patients when glucose levels are problematic.

Simultaneous monitoring and reporting: IoT health devices have the potential to collect real-time information about the patient and report this to the physician remotely. The IoT devices can collect information like blood pressure, heart rate, blood glucose level, etc., of a patient and store it on the cloud, and then this information can be shared with the authorized physician *(Fig 20-1).* This technology can save unnecessary clinical visits, allow healthcare providers to provide better care to their patients, and even facilitate remote consultation irrespective of place or time.

Essentially, these devices can improve access to healthcare resources while reducing strain on healthcare systems and giving people better control over their own health at all times.

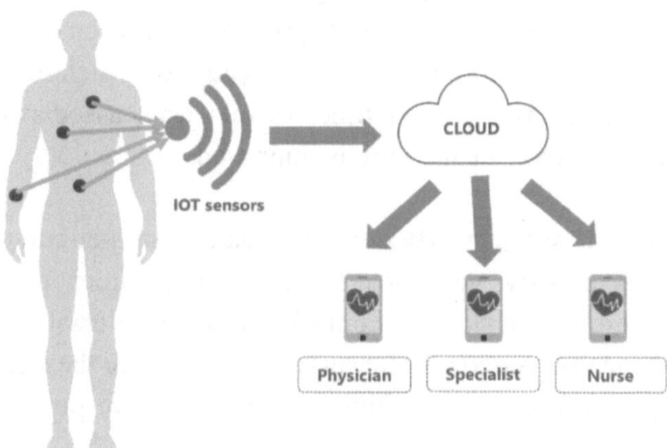

Fig 20-1: IoT devices collect and store information about patient's vitals on the cloud, then share it with healthcare providers

Improved disease management: Another important advantage of IoT devices is that emergency situations like heart attacks and asthma can be analyzed by healthcare professionals remotely. For instance, a heart monitoring device continuously monitors heart rate, and in situations like fluctuations in heart rates and heart attacks, the healthcare professionals are notified by the device itself *(Fig 20-2)*.

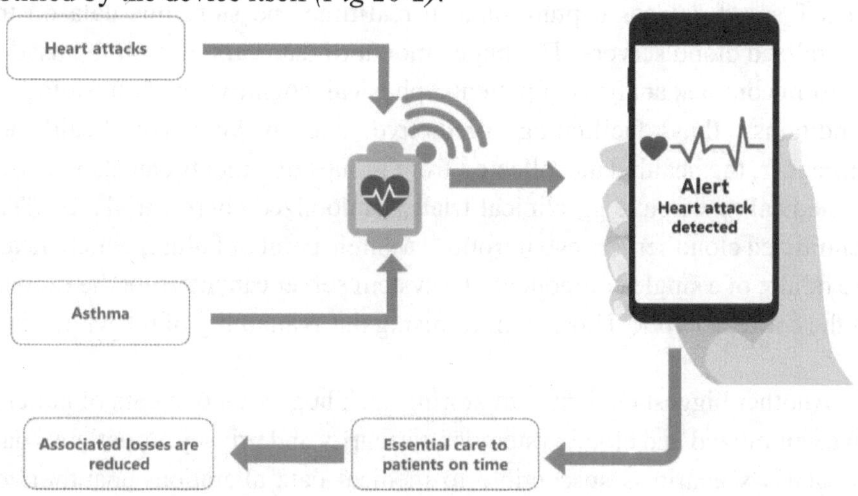

Fig 20-2: Through IoT devices, healthcare providers can remotely analyze emergency situations

Because of IoT devices, the healthcare providers can even get access to the patients' profiles way before their arrival because of which they can deliver essential care to the patients on time. In this way, associated losses are reduced, and emergency health care is improved.

IoT-aided robotic surgery: By deploying small Internet-connected robots inside the human body, surgeons can perform complex procedures and surgeries with more precision and control than is possible with human hands. At the same time, IoT-aided robotic surgeries can reduce the size of incisions required to perform surgery, leading to a less invasive process and faster healing for patients.

The IoT-aided robotic devices can also interact with doctors and interpret complex conditions inside bodies to make the right decisions about proceeding during a surgery.

20.2. Challenges faced by IoT devices

But there are certain challenges that IoT devices face:

(i) IoT smart devices capture data in real-time and store this data on the centralized cloud servers. The huge amount of data captured can be used to perform complex analysis of patients' physical, cognitive, and physiological conditions, thus facilitating predictive and preventative healthcare. Moreover, the health data collected from groups of patients can also be used in medical research, e.g., clinical trials, randomized control trials, etc. The centralized cloud servers can introduce a single point of failure, which means the failure of a single component of a system/server can interrupt the running of the entire network. Thus, compromising the availability of the whole data.

(ii) Another biggest challenge of storing such huge sensitive data of patients on a centralized and cloud system is its security and privacy. A patient's data in such a scenario is susceptible to medical data alteration, unauthorized sharing, data theft, data loss, etc. The patient's data can be used to create fake IDs to buy drugs and can even be used to file fraudulent insurance claims. Moreover, cybercriminals can achieve complete remote control of wearable devices and pose a threat to a patient's life. For instance, a hacker can take control of the smart insulin pump (commercialized by Johnson & Johnson) to overdose diabetic patients with insulin, causing them harm.

20.3. Blockchain- The Solution

The decentralized and peer-to-peer Blockchain technology can provide the required solution to solve security issues IoT health devices face as the data stored on the Blockchain will be resistant to hacking and tampering. Additionally, Blockchain technology will also prevent failure in any single node in a network (either because of a power outage or the node goes offline) from bringing the entire network to crash and compromise data.

Type of Blockchain used: Private permissioned Blockchain can be used instead of a permissionless public Blockchain to avoid costs associated with transactions on the public Blockchain and ensure patient's privacy. The IoT health devices gather sensitive health information of the patient, which is then shared with the healthcare provider. This type of information should not be available to the public. Therefore, a consortium Blockchain or a private Blockchain, would be suitable for the IoT. Additionally, unlike permissionless public Blockchain, where anyone can become a node, in the permissioned Blockchain, all nodes are pre-selected. In the Blockchain, healthcare providers, medical experts, and researchers who should be able to access patient records act as nodes.

IPFS: Storing data on Blockchain is very expensive and energy-consuming. Therefore, it is recommended to store massive health data generated from the smart wearables in secured off-Blockchain peer-to-peer distributed file system IPFS and the hash from IPFS will be stored on the main Blockchain.

Smart contracts: Smart contracts on Blockchain eliminate the need for a mediator by automatically defining and enforcing rules and duties set out by the participants in the network.

20.4. Proposed Blockchain architecture

The Blockchain platform should be patient-centric in which the patient has complete control over their data. He should have the ability to grant and revoke access to the records as and when they wish to do so. Granting and revoking access to records is possible with the smart contracts on Blockchain.

(i) The patients and healthcare providers will be required to register themselves to become part of the Blockchain network.

(ii) Once the patient Login to the platform, Blockchain can enable the patients to share the LIVE data captured by IoT devices with the doctor.

(iii) The doctor will be required to get permission to access the patient's data. Then the doctor will get complete access to the medical report along with the real-time data captured by the IoT devices like LIVE ECG of the patient to find the malfunction of the heart.

(iv) Blockchain technology also promotes collaboration among healthcare providers and research organizations to do qualitative research. The medical experts and researchers must take permission from the patients to access their medical records. The doctors and researchers are only allowed to go through those records to which the patient has permitted them.

Hence, through Blockchain technology, a patient can control and share their information without violating the privacy policy.

Better integration of data of IoT devices with Electronic Healthcare Records: IoT smart health wearables like Fitbit, health bands, watches, blood glucose monitors record the daily data and activities of a user like calories, step counts, miles, heart rate, quality of sleep, blood pressure, blood glucose level, etc. With Blockchain technology, all this daily data from a user's smart health devices can be clubbed with the patient's Electronic Health Records *(Fig 20-3)*. These devices collect the real-time data of a patient, and because of this, doctors can see a patient's condition in real-time. As data is acquired continuously, there is no need to conduct all the tests when the patient visits the hospital. This will reduce the costs of conducting basic tests and save valuable time for both the doctor and the patient. This could really be a boon for emergency cases where providing timely treatment is the biggest challenge.

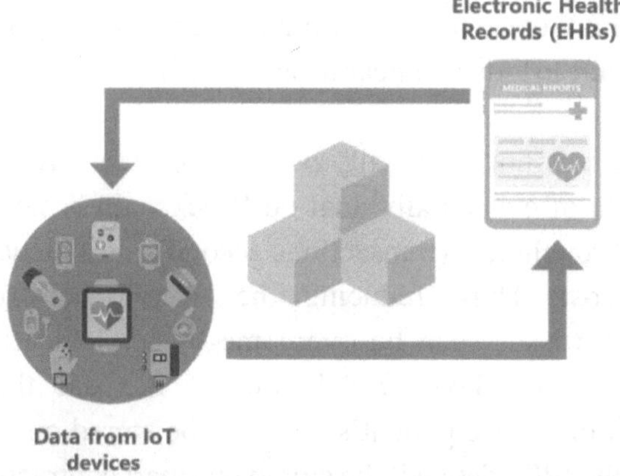

Fig 20-3: Better integration of data of IoT devices with EHRs on Blockchain

20.5. Challenges of implementing Blockchain in smart healthcare

(i) Interoperability: Healthcare interoperability means exchanging medical information with each other in the Blockchain network. In the Healthcare sector, ensuring proper interoperability can be a challenge due to the presence of different players like hospitals, insurance companies, physicians, private doctors, etc.

(ii) Hesitation among hospitals in sharing information: Some hospitals can be reluctant to share their patient-related and other medical records, such as in for-profit situations, as they will want to charge fees from different customers. Thus, it can be competitively advantageous for them to keep the fees-related data with themselves. Therefore, it is essential to build trust between the parties and convince them to share their data for a better healthcare ecosystem.

(iii) Hesitation among patients to share their medical records: Trust building among the most crucial stakeholders, the patients, is very important for the success of a Blockchain-driven medical and healthcare system. Many patients can be hesitant to share and disclose their medical records in the public domain with third-party entities. So, it is essential to build trust and confidence among the patients regarding the security and privacy aspects of the Blockchain and IoT-driven healthcare system.

(iv) Scalability: It is not practically possible to maintain electronic health data and IoT data of every individual on Blockchain because of restricted transactional throughput (transactions/second), efficiency, and high computational cost. Thus, reducing the overall performance of the Blockchain. These issues can be overcome by implementing Blockchain scalability layer 1 and layer 2 solutions to increase the transactional throughput. And the entire patient's data can be stored on IPFS, while the hash address of the IPFS data will be stored on smart contracts. Thus, scaling solutions and IPFS can handle the Blockchain's scalability and storage issues.

Chapter 21: Blockchain for connected and self-driving cars

The future belongs to cars that are connected to the internet. They can communicate via IoT devices and enable the vehicle to vehicle communication. Through IoT devices, connected cars can connect to traffic, weather, location, and travel conditions. But there is still a time when these connected cars will be available for mass adoption, as many critical issues still need to be addressed before making them available for the masses. One of the biggest challenges that bother these connected cars is security. The more they are connected to IoT devices, the more they become susceptible to cyber attacks.

Enter Blockchain. Blockchain has the ability to safeguard the information exchange through IoT devices, thus making them resistant against any attack by fraudsters. Let's see how Blockchain will work for connected cars:

21.1. Edge, and Cloud computing in connected cars

In a connected and self-driving car, there are smart IoT sensors that can collect information on everything from location, weather, damaged roads, and damaged bridges, to parking availability, congestion, and even about the breakdown of the vehicle.

Edge computing: Let's understand edge computing by taking an example of an autonomous or self-driving car running on a highway. After seeing an obstacle, the car has to apply a brake instantaneously to avoid an accident. Here, sending the data back and forth from the car to the servers on the cloud either directly or via a gateway, in order to be processed and then waiting for cloud triggering to apply brakes can create latency in the response time, and the consequences can be dire where even a millisecond lag can be the difference between life and death. Here comes the need for edge computing with integrated artificial intelligence (AI) tools. With the help of Edge Computing, the live video can be processed closer to the IoT sensor that captured it; in other words, computation takes place at the edge of a device's network. Because of this, processing will be fast, and real-time action can be taken without any adverse effects. For this, the edge server may be present in the autonomous car itself, or the data may be sent from the car to the geographically distributed nearest edge server, which processes the data, and the processed results are notified directly to the vehicles, thus, improving the real-time performance *(Fig 21-1)*.

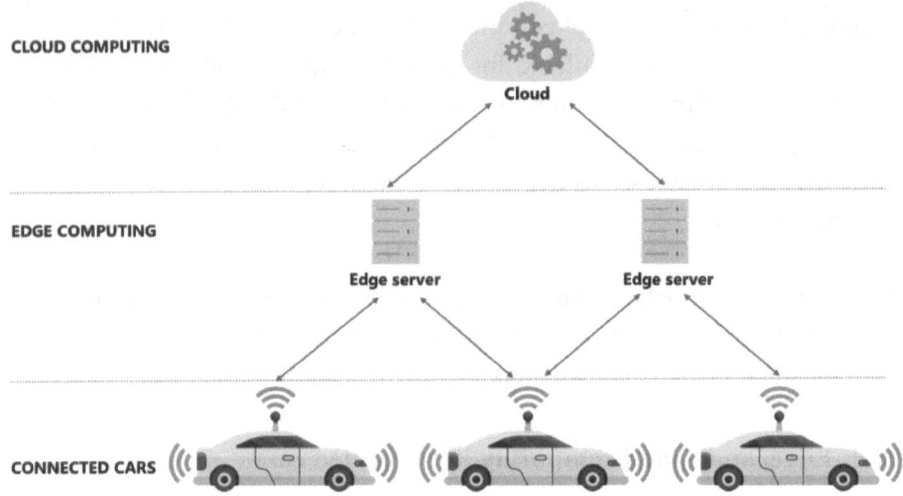

Fig 21-1: Edge computing

Edge computing has many other use cases too. For instance, in the case of rash driving, data collected from the car's sensors, accelerometer and gyrometer can be computed at the same place where it is gathered and generates the corresponding required alerts to maintain the safe driving standards. Similarly, on-board diagnostics tools and interfaces in the car help in detecting real-time problems within the car and generate the required alerts for the drivers. Data received from the onboard diagnostic tools can be continuously monitored with the help of Edge Computing, and any failure or risk can be predicted before actual damage.

Through edge computing, every connected vehicle can become a repository of data. This data can be used by third parties to offer services such as route guidance for travelers, ride-sharing, and providing information that can guide traffic flow control by road authorities.

Cloud computing: Edge computing is not the replacement for the cloud; it helps to offload some of the resource-intensive work from the cloud. With edge computing, data sent to the cloud could be minimized. It can process and analyze that data at the edge, which requires a quick response, and other data is transferred to the cloud via the internet. The cloud stores the IoT data and processes it to get real insights into the vehicle, geographical locations, consumer usage patterns, and environmental changes. For instance, smart cameras at the edge can detect movement in real-time, and a nearby edge server can process the data and determine whether the movement poses a threat. And the cloud can collect and analyze IoT data over the long term to help businesses understand environmental patterns.

Challenges with edge computing: Undoubtedly, edge computing is an innovative computing method, but it faces a series of security risks, as edge servers, and IoT devices are vulnerable to cyberattacks. There have been a number of incidents in which attackers hijacked IoT devices within an edge computing infrastructure. Security breaches can compromise sensitive data and put trade secrets or other corporate information at risk. They can also interrupt or even halt business operations entirely. The hackers may even turn an autonomous vehicle into a dangerous weapon by taking its control.

21.2. Blockchain-enabled Edge computing

A permissioned Blockchain network must be created to prevent hackers from hijacking edge servers and accessing or manipulating sensitive information. Each edge server together with the IoT devices connected to it will be the nodes that form the local network. The IoT sensors will generate data and send it to their assigned edge server. The edge server will then verify the data and broadcast it to the other edge servers of the network. After achieving the consensus from the network, the verified data is uploaded as a transaction on the Blockchain. Communication between IoT devices, between devices and the edge server, or between edge servers are recorded as transactions and stored on the Blockchain. Edge servers process real-time requests, and the processed data is also stored as a transaction on the Blockchain *(Fig 21-2)*.

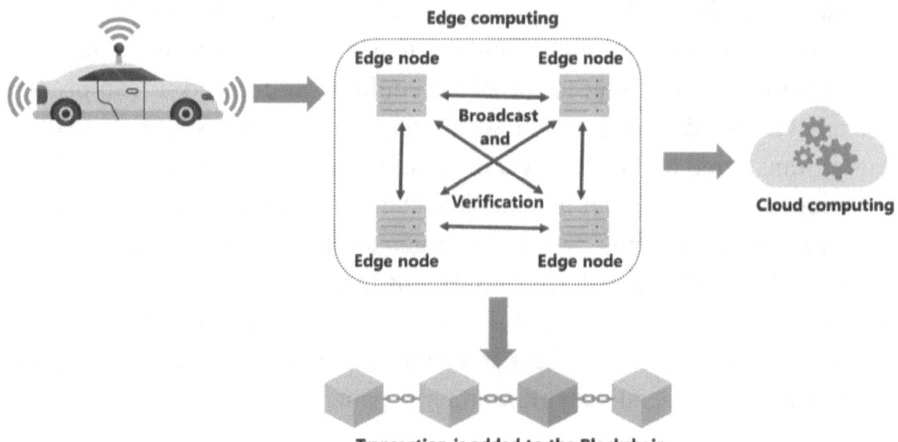

Fig 21-2: Blockchain-enabled Edge computing

Each node has a unique ID and a pair of private and public keys. Whenever a node sends data to the edge node, it signs the data with its private key. Other nodes in the network can verify the identity of a sender node by its public key. Thus, it makes hacking of edge servers and IoT devices difficult and secures the data received from devices. It is essential to secure the IoT and edge server's data at all times because any hacking activity on this data can even cost lives. Therefore, uploading data derived from IoT devices on Blockchain is very critical for making it secure and resistant to hacking.

21.3. Vehicle-to-vehicle (V2V) and vehicle-to-infrastructure (V2I) connectivity

As the name suggests, vehicle-to-vehicle connectivity allows connected vehicles to communicate with each other on the road by sharing data about speed, road conditions, etc. This technology provides great promise in reducing vehicle accidents and traffic congestion on the roads. There's also vehicle-to-infrastructure (V2I) communication, which allows cars to connect with various road infrastructures like traffic lights, road signs, lane markings, construction zones, and school zones. This would help your car find the safest and most efficient route to your destination in real-time. But if the malicious actors hack the devices responsible for V2V or V2I connectivity, they may mislead the information and create chaos on the road. Further, data falsification attack is another security issue in connected cars where vehicles rely on information received from other vehicles. To avoid any such incidents, Blockchain can provide the required safety and security to the data so that hackers can not view or alter the data collected by these devices. In case any IoT device is compromised by the hackers, the respective authorities and other nodes that are part of the Blockchain may be able to identify and take immediate actions against that compromised IoT device. Similarly, for self-driving cars, data hacking can be disastrous. In these cars as well, Blockchain can provide the much-needed safety net to make its data secure.

21.4. Responsible driving behavior

Blockchain technology may also ensure customer safety during cab riding. In the Blockchain network, the vehicles need to be registered and will be considered as nodes which are further divided into validating/miner nodes depending upon their service criteria. The authenticity of a new vehicle or IoT device joining the network is verified in order to avoid network failures. The vehicle number, current and previous vehicle ratings, along with the data captured by IoT devices are stored on the Blockchain network. Therefore, even if the hacker or cab driver hacks one or more IoT objects to gain their benefits, the nodes or vehicles present in the network will be aware of the information registered under that compromised IoT device. Thus, any compromise in any IoT device would be recorded on the Blockchain. Therefore, Blockchain technology ensures the security and traceability of IoT devices or a vehicle's legal or illegal activity information.

21.5. Infotainment

The vehicle infotainment system provides an audio-video experience for car riders. Car owner needs to subscribe to these infotainment services provided by various providers. Blockchain can provide a great application in this scenario as well. Blockchain can enable vehicle owners to make in-car payments for infotainment services like movies, apps, and other services based on predefined contracts.

21.6. Insurance

Imagine a scenario where you have to pay for your car insurance based on how much you actually use your car rather than on a set of predefined insurance policy conditions. Blockchain technology can help insurance companies to create personalized vehicle insurance contracts based on actual driver behavior. A connected car can capture information on driver location, drive duration, mileage of the vehicle, vehicle speed, and other information like the accident history of the car. And Blockchain provides a foolproof means for collecting this data and delivering it in a secure and unalterable manner to the insurance companies. This will make the cost of insurance premiums fairer, and you will pay as you drive or how you drive. Additionally, through smart contracts, automatic payment of insurance premiums can be directly executed.

21.7. Blockchain and IoT for automatic repairing and payment

Another interesting thing that Blockchain and IoT can do is automatic order placing to repair any part of the car and then release automatic payment for the services rendered. In such a system, sensors in the car would first detect the need to repair a particular part. After this, they would contact nearby suppliers for replacement parts, followed by fixing an appointment with a technician for service and repairs. And once repairing is done, smart contracts will get executed, which will automatically process the respective payment for the services rendered.

21.8. Smart car parking and payment

Smart parking is another area that can be targeted through the integration of blockchain and IoT. In this system, IoT sensors will first locate a vacant space in the parking lot. And once the car is parked, they will even calculate the duration for which the car remains parked there. Additionally, during the payment phase, the smart contract will get executed, and automated payouts will be done based on the parking time calculated by the sensors.

Section 3

Blockchain in Supply Chain

Chapter 22: Blockchain and IoT in Pharma Supply Chain

Trust is the foundation of the medical profession. When we fall ill, we trust our doctor's advice and consume the prescribed medicine with the trust that the medicine will help us recover from our illness. And by and large, they do. However, that may not always be true. The medicine you bought might actually be a counterfeit with just its visual appearance similar to the actual one. Some fraudsters, out of their personal interests and monetary gains, exploit the lacunas of the pharma supply chain to introduce these fake drugs into the system.

22.1. Challenges of the Pharma Supply Chain

(i) Complex Supply Chain: Companies today no longer work in silos and are not limited by the physical boundaries. They trade internationally and are a part of the global network. Further, the pharma supply chain is highly fragmented, has various stages, and involves multiple hands changing from product manufacturers to product packagers to logistics partners and finally to a pharmacy from where we buy these drugs.

Furthermore, the current system in the pharma supply chain is not interoperable and unified. For example, when a drug changes hands, there is no system for the receiving stakeholder to verify that the drug he received is an original product from the manufacturer. Therefore, an increased number of stakeholders in the supply chain results in a complex system with very little control and nearly no transparency.

(ii) Temperature Sensitivity: Additionally, several drugs remain active below a particular temperature, and therefore during its journey, it is mandatory to maintain the desired temperature range for the drug to remain active and effective. Any fluctuation in the temperature above the desired range can hamper the effectiveness of the drug and make it unfit for medical use. And there is no way for the consumer or the company to know if the drug has been maintained at the proper temperature throughout its journey and is still active.

(iii) Drug Shortage: Drug shortage leads to delayed treatments of patients and thus poses a significant threat to public health. The issue of drug shortage demands attention and collaboration from everyone involved in providing life-saving medicines to patients. This includes pharmaceutical companies producing medications, wholesalers, distributors, pharmacies, and health care providers.

But because of the complex supply chain, there is a lack of coordination among the players to better communicate their demands. As a result, the manufacturers don't get accurate information about the demand on time, which results in the delayed manufacturing and supplying of the drugs. Shortage of drugs can even force healthcare providers and patients to shift to alternate drugs that, in turn, can lead to a less effective treatment.

(iv) Drug Recall: Sometimes, certain drugs lead to severe side effects, and therefore, removal of such drugs from the market becomes very crucial to protect the customers. In such a scenario, manufacturers are required to withdraw the drug from the market at the earliest possible.

But the biggest challenge in such a scenario is that there is no direct contact between the company and consumers who have bought this drug. Drug recall announcements are generally made online or through advertisements. Therefore customers are subject to their awareness, and there are very high chances that they can miss out on the announcement of this drug recall.

(v) Regulatory Challenge: It is very challenging for a regulatory body like the FDA to monitor and regulate various players involved in the supply chain. Therefore it becomes challenging to weed out the illegal companies who claim to be legal entities through false paperwork.

(vi) Counterfeit Drugs: Counterfeit drugs are one of the biggest challenges that this industry faces today. The worldwide counterfeit drug market is valued at over 200 billion USD. Counterfeit drugs are responsible for killing

more than 500,000 people every year. According to WHO estimates, 1 out of every 10th medical product sold-including pills, vaccines, and diagnostic kits-is fake or substandard.
According to the European Pharmaceutical Review, around 30% of drugs sold in developing countries are fake. Due to this growing challenge of counterfeiting, many countries have introduced strict regulations for tracking the drug in the pharma supply chain. For instance, the Drug Supply Chain Security Act passed by the US government mandates all the drug manufacturers to provide a unique ID on the drug for weeding out the counterfeit drugs.

22.1.1. How do counterfeit drugs affect our health?

(i) If a counterfeit drug contains no active ingredient, then

- the drug fails to treat the patients and therefore harms them indirectly
- In the case of counterfeit antibiotics, patients don't respond to the first-line drug, which makes their physician prescribe them the more potent antibiotic. This unwanted use of a stronger antibiotic leads to antibiotic resistance in these patients.

(ii) The second scenario is if the counterfeit drugs have harmful ingredients like toxic paints, contaminated water, colored dyes, floor wax, boric acid, antifreeze, etc. This leads to an adverse effect on the health of the consumer and proves to be fatal in many cases.

For instance, more than 500 children around the world died after consuming counterfeit cough syrup containing an antifreeze agent, ethylene glycol. In another case, counterfeit inhalers for the treatment of pediatric lung disease were found to contain contaminated bacteria that hospitalized them.

(iii) Wrong concentration of the active ingredient in the drug can also have adverse effects on patients' health.

22.1.2. Economic consequences of counterfeit drugs

(i) Counterfeit drugs hijack the brand and infringe the patent rights of legitimate pharmaceutical manufacturers.

(ii) Counterfeiters just copy the appearance of the products and take advantage of the money that has gone into the research and development of these original and authentic medicines.

(iii) For consumers, too, this is a big menace as counterfeit drugs lead to both health and financial loss for them when they pay their hard-earned money for these fake products, and that too with a substantial threat to their health.

22.1.3. How do counterfeit drugs enter the supply chain?

(i) As discussed earlier, the pharma supply chain is quite complex, and a drug changes multiple hands before reaching a pharmacy near you. It may happen that one or more parties in the supply chain are unethical and are involved in illegal practices. They may introduce counterfeit, contaminated products in the supply chain to increase their profit share.

(ii) For any drug to be manufactured, the basic requirement is the raw material. It may happen that the raw material itself is coming from an unauthentic or uncertified source.

(iii) Certain companies and trading partners claim to be certified legal entities by using false and forged papers, and using these certifications, they can easily introduce fake drugs into the supply chain.

(iv) In many cases, fake drugs enter into the pharma supply chain through online distribution and internet sales. According to WHO, more than 50% of the drugs sold online are counterfeit.

(v) Drug shortages can also open doors for counterfeit drugs to enter the market.

(vi) In addition to the above reasons, social stigma is another reason that makes it easier for counterfeit drugs to enter the market. For instance, Viagra is one of the most widely produced counterfeit drugs. Patients may be too ashamed to consult a physician for this drug; therefore, they may unknowingly buy the fake versions of this drug online.

22.2. Blockchain-The solution

Today, pharma companies are exploring new routes to synthesize new drugs, and therefore their raw material requirements have become quite complex. Because of these requirements, these raw materials are sourced from various suppliers, who are geographically scattered across the globe. As the raw materials required run into tens of thousands, it becomes very crucial for the manufacturing companies to have a check on the ingredients and ensure that the suppliers are complying with the guidelines provided by them.

In the current system, there is no clear way to know if the raw material supplied is authentic or if it is some cheap counterfeit. Once the raw materials are sourced from the suppliers, the manufacturing process starts. Big pharma companies generally have multiple plants scattered in various locations. This further adds to the complexity of the supply chain. The manufactured drugs are shipped via third-party cold chain logistic companies to local distributors and various other countries *(Fig 22-1)*. In many cases, these logistic partners don't have the adequate capabilities to maintain these drugs under the required conditions. Thus leading to drugs losing their effectiveness.

But for a manufacturer, it is very difficult to ensure that the drugs were moved under the appropriate conditions as specified by them. If the drug is to be distributed within the same country, it is shipped to thousands of local distributors spread across the country. The distributors then supply these drugs to secondary wholesalers or pharmacies and hospitals, who sell these drugs to the patients.

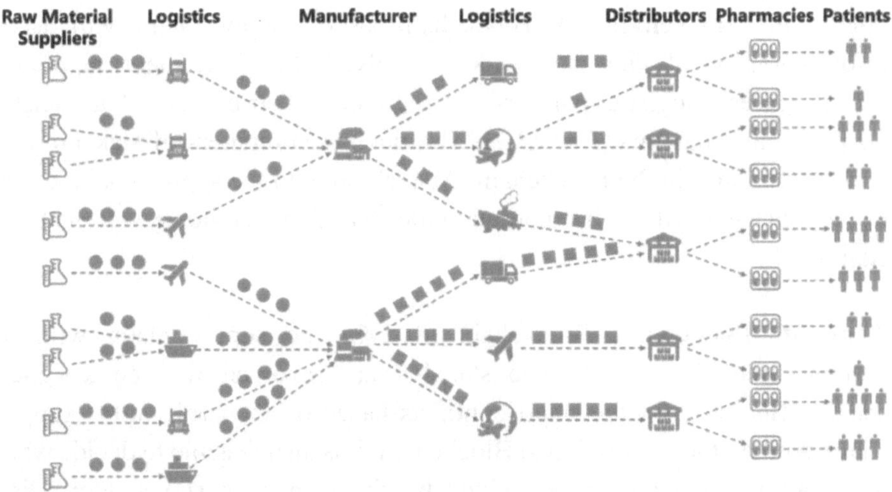

Fig 22-1: Complex pharma supply chain

And in case the drugs are to be exported, they change multiple hands in various countries before reaching their final destination. In such a scenario with a lack of transparency and control, the supply chain becomes vulnerable to counterfeiting.

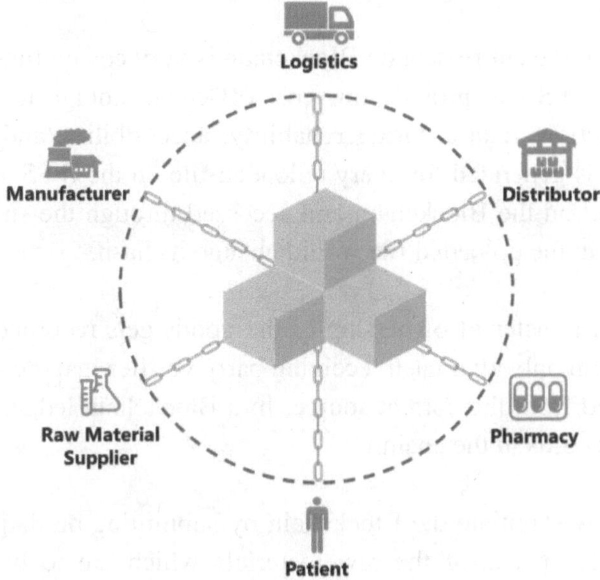

Fig 22-2: Nodes in the Blockchain

Nodes in Blockchain: A Blockchain-based supply chain will have information on all the stakeholders involved, like ingredient suppliers, manufacturers, logistic partners, wholesalers, distributors, pharmacists, hospitals, and patients *(Fig 22-2)*. The devices/computers of stakeholders will act as nodes in the Blockchain. At each node in the supply chain, drop-off and pick-up activity is recorded in the shared ledger along with the time stamp.

Type of Blockchain: Blockchain used in the supply chain will be permissioned Blockchain. The stakeholders involved will be assigned specific functions on the smart contracts based on their role in the supply chain. And on the permissioned Blockchain, it is also feasible to decide what information can be seen and added by the respective stakeholders. For instance, the information about the agreed prices of raw materials between the manufacturer and suppliers should not be revealed to the other involved entities, like pharmacies, wholesalers, customers, etc. They simply need access to limited information, like the authenticity of drugs and performing the necessary functions like placing orders. This is possible with permissioned Blockchains that will allow limited permission to the various participants in the network.

IPFS: Storing the entire data on Blockchain is very costly; thus, distributed file storage IPFS can provide low-cost off-chain storage to store supply chain transactions data ensuring reliability, accessibility, and integrity. A unique hash is generated for every uploaded file on the IPFS server, which is then stored on the Blockchain and accessed through the smart contract. Any change in the uploaded file would change its hash.

The physical transfer of ownership of the goods gets recorded virtually in the Blockchain only after each receiving party verifies that the shipment has been received from the correct source. In a Blockchain ledger, no one can tamper the records in the chain.

1. Suppliers will initiate the Blockchain by submitting on dApp, the serial number on the packs of the raw materials which are to be sent to the manufacturer. The data will be stored on IPFS, and the hash will be stored

on the smart contract so that the data can be accessed later by authorized stakeholders. Additionally, the location of the supplier will also be recorded.

2. The suppliers also need to upload the certificates of the authenticity of these supplied materials. This can be done by getting their facility inspected by a regulatory body and getting a legal certificate proving the same. This information is stored in the genesis block of the Blockchain.

3. When the ingredients reach the manufacturer, the event will be recorded on the Blockchain along with the date of receiving and the respective location.

4. Once drugs are manufactured, they will be placed in bottles, vials, or strips labeled with unique identifiers and will then be grouped and packaged. These packages will have labels that will be scanned and recorded at every point throughout their journey from the factory until it reaches the pharmacy. Information about the drugs, and their unique identifiers present in the labeled package, will be uploaded on the IPFS, and the hash will be stored on the smart contract *(Fig 22-3)*.

5. Whenever these packets exchange hands, the concerned party will scan the label on the packets, and the transaction will be recorded permanently on the Blockchain. If anyone tries to temper the product or the information, its hash will change; thus, it can be detected easily.

6. Similarly, the whole journey of drugs from the ingredient supplier to the pharmacy will be recorded digitally on the Blockchain. In case the drug shipment goes missing due to counterfeiting operations, it is much easier to locate it as the complete transaction is recorded on the ledger, and it can easily be known who was possessing the consignment when the issue happened.

7. The last step in the journey is selling the drugs to the patients. The event of the sale of the drug, including drug information and patient information, will be recorded on the Blockchain. This process will ensure that all the transactions are stored on the Blockchain and can be accessed later by all the

supply chain participants to check the authenticity of the products or, in the case of drug recalls.

8. The consumer can also scan the unique number on the drug and know the origin of the drug, the route that drug has taken, and even the ingredients used to manufacture the drug, provided the customer has been granted access to this information by the manufacturer.

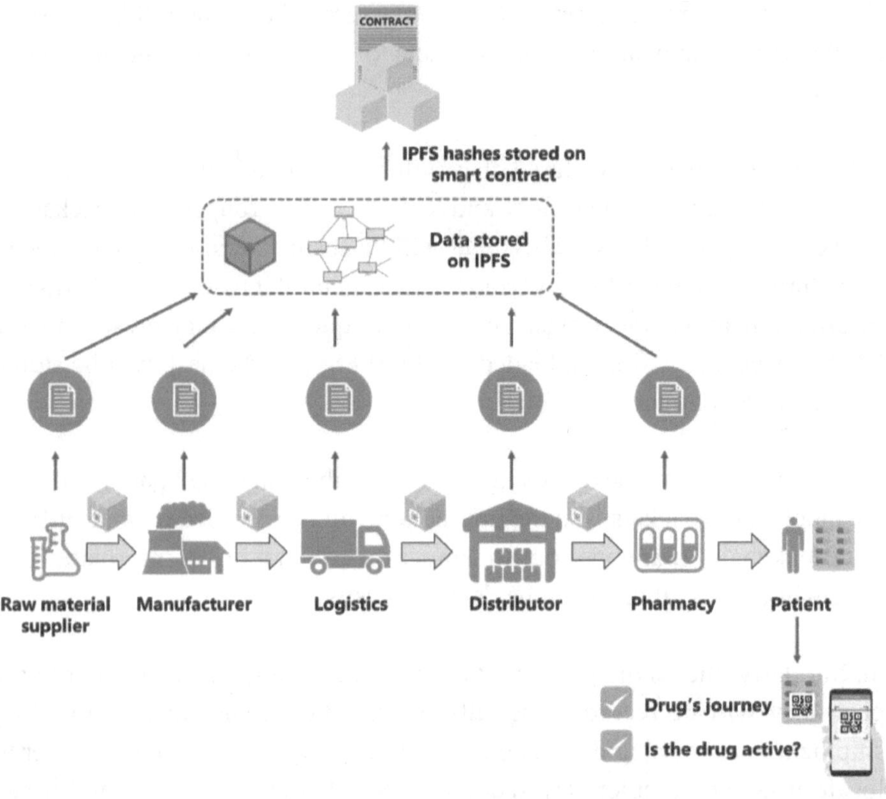

Fig 22-3: Blockchain-enabled supply chain

Because of the decentralized and immutable nature of Blockchain technology, it prevents any single entity from manipulating or modifying the data. It ensures data security as once the information is added to the ledger, it cannot be removed or modified. Transparency of transactions is another important aspect of any supply chain that Blockchain provides.

22.3. Applications of Blockchain in the Pharma sector

22.3.1 Monitoring Temperature Sensitivity of drugs

Many medical aids like vaccines are sensitive to environmental conditions, and any fluctuations in these conditions can make them ineffective. Therefore, IoT sensors are installed on the packages. IoT sensors include a Global Positioning System (GPS) receiver to locate where the package is, temperature sensors to record the temperature of the package throughout its journey, and pressure sensor to measure the pressure differences that detect any opening or closing of the package. Each IoT sensor and gateway needs to be registered on the Blockchain network and is given a fixed unique ID. Any change in the temperature data will be timestamped and then recorded on the IPFS, and its hash will be recorded on the smart contract. If the values for temperature or humidity exceed pre-defined levels, the state of the transport of the package changes to "out of compliance" and is recorded as a transaction inside the Blockchain digital ledger *(Fig 22-4)*. The smart contract will be executed, and an alert will be sent to the relevant parties in the supply chain. Thus through this technology, it can be ensured that the drugs remain in the suggested storage conditions throughout their journey.

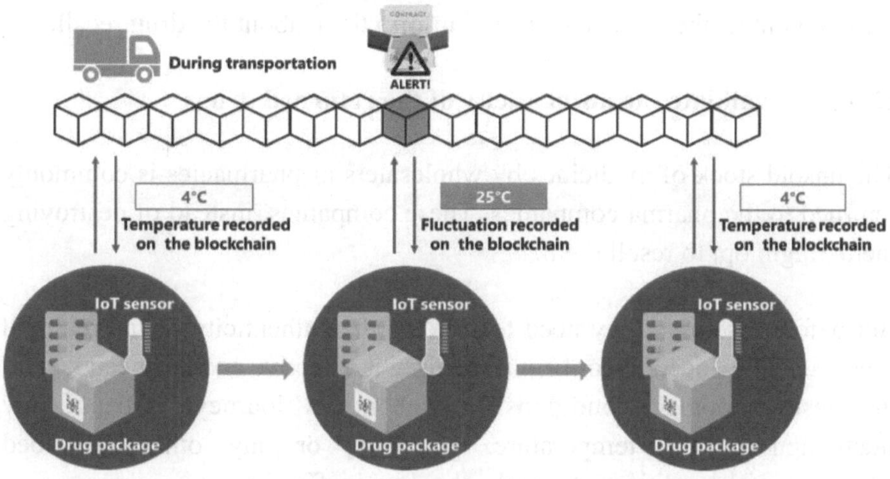

Fig 22-4: IoT sensors record the temperature of drug packages during transportation, and any fluctuation in temperature is recorded on the Blockchain

Additionally, Blockchain technology makes the hacking of IoT sensors difficult; thus, tampering with IoT sensors or manipulating IoT data will not be possible.

Even the consumer, with the help of this shared digital ledger, can easily know if the drug is active by scanning the label on the drug.

22.3.2. Easy Drug recalls

Sometimes severe side-effects of a certain drug are known only when it reaches the market. In such a situation, manufacturers are required to withdraw the drug from the market at the earliest possible.

It is still feasible for a company to recall the drug from the distributors and pharmacies. But the biggest challenge is to contact the consumers who have bought this drug and intimate them to avoid using the drug. Drug recall announcements are generally made online or through advertisements. And there are very high chances that the customer may miss out on the announcement and consume the drug. In such a scenario, Blockchain technology will help manufacturers and pharmacies to keep a record of the people who have bought that particular drug. This will make it easier for them to contact these consumers and inform them about the drug recall.

22.3.3. To validate the authenticity of the returned drugs

The unsold stock of medicines by wholesalers or pharmacies is commonly returned to the pharma companies. These companies, instead of destroying them, might opt to resell them.

But before reselling, they need to validate the authenticity of the returned drugs, i.e., they need to confirm if the drug is effective and has been kept at the desired storage conditions throughout its journey. Because any fluctuation in the temperature, humidity, or any other described environmental conditions can make the drug ineffective.

The companies can scan the returned drugs by their unique ID and track all their journey information. If they find the drug to be effective, then only this drug can be sent for reselling.

22.3.4. To stop the entry of counterfeit drugs

It has become an urgent need to curb counterfeit drugs for the well-being of people. As we have discussed, these fake drugs have serious side effects on human health. Blockchain technology has the ability to minimize these frauds.

A central authority, say a company, will decide who will participate in the Blockchain or, in other words, who will act as nodes like suppliers, logistic partners, distributors, retailers, consumers, etc., and the smart contracts may be issued that will help in establishing the proof of drug ownership.

When the drugs exchange hands, the unique ID will be traced and verified every time. Fake drugs entered into the system will not be verified as they don't have the original unique ID and, therefore, will fail to become part of the network. This will even help to locate the node that allowed counterfeit drugs to enter the supply chain.

When a consumer gets the drug, he can trace all the required information by simply scanning the unique ID on the medicine with his smartphone or by entering the ID on the company's website. In addition, the drugs can be time-stamped, and the technology also ensures that the drug is in its expected geographical region.

Online pharmacies are the main culprits for selling fake drugs to consumers. According to WHO, 50% of drugs bought online are fake. With Blockchain technology, one can identify whether the drug he has received from an online pharmacy is authentic or fake. This technology can save many lives by making them aware of these fake drugs.

22.3.5. Avoiding drug shortages

Drug shortage can lead to delayed treatment of the patients and thus pose a significant threat to public health. To avoid drug shortages, it is essential that the drug manufacturers should get information about the demand on time so as to minimize drug manufacturing and supply delays. But because of the complex supply chain, there is a lack of coordination among the players to better communicate their demands.

The shortage of drugs forces healthcare providers and patients to shift to alternate drugs that can lead to less effective treatment and can even lead to the introduction of counterfeit medicines in the market.

As we know, Blockchain technology will record all the information about the drug from its raw materials until it reaches the consumers. Therefore the digital ledger will also record the sales of medicines from a particular wholesaler or a pharmacy. This, in turn, will update the inventory of drugs available with them on the shared digital ledger. This insight will help the manufacturer to keep his inventory updated and supply these drugs on time to avoid drug shortages in the market.

This will be a win-win situation for all the stakeholders involved. Patients will have timely access to the required drugs. At the same time, the company also won't suffer financial losses due to lost sales because of a drug shortage.

So this is how Blockchain is going to disrupt the pharma industry and bring about a shift in how it works.

Chapter 23: Blockchain and IoT in the Food Supply Chain

Our food supply chain is under constant threat from adulteration, and there is no way to know the origin of the problem. According to WHO, 1 out of every 10th person becomes ill every year after consuming contaminated food, which ends up taking approximately 420,000 lives every year.

23.1. Challenges that the food industry faces

(i) Food Contamination: The biggest challenge that the food industry faces today is the complexity of the global food supply chain. And due to this complexity, it becomes nearly impossible for a retailer to tell the exact provenance of the product. Though retailers have put in place a lot of strict quality checks and measures, but despite that, there has been a lot of food contamination cases recently. Once a contaminated food item reaches the shelves of retailers, the consequences can be quite dire. Such events not only result in big financial and reputation losses for them but also endangers the health and lives of their customers. In the current scenario, if a contaminated food item gets introduced into the food supply chain, it is not an easy task to track and eliminate it. It takes a lot of paperwork and toiling to find the exact item and reach back to its original source to eliminate it from the supply chain.

(ii) Opaque Cold Chain Logistics: Most of the perishable food items like milk and poultry during their transportation must be kept at lower temperatures to keep them fit for consumption. But today, it is nearly impossible to know if these food items stayed at the right temperature during their whole journey and are fit for consumption.

(iii) Food Fraud: The complexity of the food supply chain is exploited by fraudsters as they purposely adulterate, tamper, and substitute one product with another for their economic profits.

Food fraud and tampering can happen at any stage of the supply chain. For example, during the initial stages of procuring and shipping raw materials or during the final stages of product manufacturing and packaging. It may even happen that the tampering is done by some intermediary involved in the supply chain. But in the current system, it is nearly impossible to identify the stage where this tampering is done.

The ramifications of food fraud are many and can range from damage to the brand to financial losses to the retailers and, the worst of them — the poor health of the consumers. Some of the notable instances of food fraud that will make you realize the gravity and seriousness of this menace are as follows:

- In a 2013 food fraud case in the UK, horse meat was mixed with beef and was labeled and sold as beef in the market.
- In 2008, a Chinese infant formulated food was contaminated with chemical plastic named Melamine which hospitalized thousands of infants.
- It has been claimed that around 70% of Kopi Luwak coffee is not genuine. Kopi Luwak coffee is an extremely expensive variety of coffee compared to regular coffee and therefore it is at a very high risk of fraudulent adulteration.
- Honey is consistently in the top 10 food frauds. As honey is one of the most expensive forms of sugar, it is commonly adulterated with other sugar syrups like corn syrup, cane sugar, etc. to increase its volume.
- Virgin olive oil that you use over your salads or vegetables might be adulterated with some other less expensive oils like sunflower oil or peanut oil. In case it is adulterated with peanut oil, it can cause serious health effects to people who are allergic to peanuts.

(iv) Food Mislabeling: Certain food products are highly-priced because they claim to be grown organically or without any fertilizers. But there is no way for a customer to validate if the product is really organic, for which he is paying those extra bucks.

Additionally, certain products are famous or are known because of their specific origin. For instance, French wine is known for its quality across the globe. So obviously when a customer sees the French Wine label on a wine bottle he will assume its origin to be France. But what if the origin of that wine is a different country say Spain. There is no way to validate the provenance of a product in the current supply chain. And this is a real scenario that came to light recently, where millions of Spanish wine bottles were being sold as French Wine.

23.2. Blockchain- The solution

Enter Blockchain. These loopholes in the food industry can be solved by permissioned Blockchain Technology. This distributed ledger technology facilitates a shared digital view of the transaction data to all the permissioned members in the food supply network. Each transaction on the ledger is immutable and is recorded only after the consensus among the members. This innate characteristic of immutability and transparency of Blockchain can really work as an enabler to build trust among the consumers.

There are many stakeholders involved in the food supply chain management and each of them will record the relevant information on the digital ledger that is immutable and decentralized, which means that there is no single server/computer where information is kept. Instead, multiple copies of data are saved on different nodes that can be seen and accessed by all other permissioned members of the network, ensuring traceability.

(i) Food Producers/Farmers: The supply chain starts with the farmers who grow our food. The information that they are required to store on the Blockchain is altitude & location where the plants are grown, irrigation treatment, growth conditions of plants like temperature, humidity, soil, fertilizers used, and other information like date of harvesting and dispatching to the next link in the chain, etc. They also need to provide the certificates if any, to prove that the food they have grown has specific characteristics like being organic or cruelty-free. This information is stored in the genesis block, i.e., the block from where Blockchain originates *(Fig 23-1)*.

(ii) Food Processors: Next link in the chain are food processors. They transform raw food products supplied by the producers into products that meet consumers' requirements. This process is also known as food processing. The food processed in this phase can either be in ready to eat stage or can act as a raw material for further processing by subsequent food processors in the supply chain. For this example, we will assume that the food processed is in ready to eat stage and doesn't require any further processing.

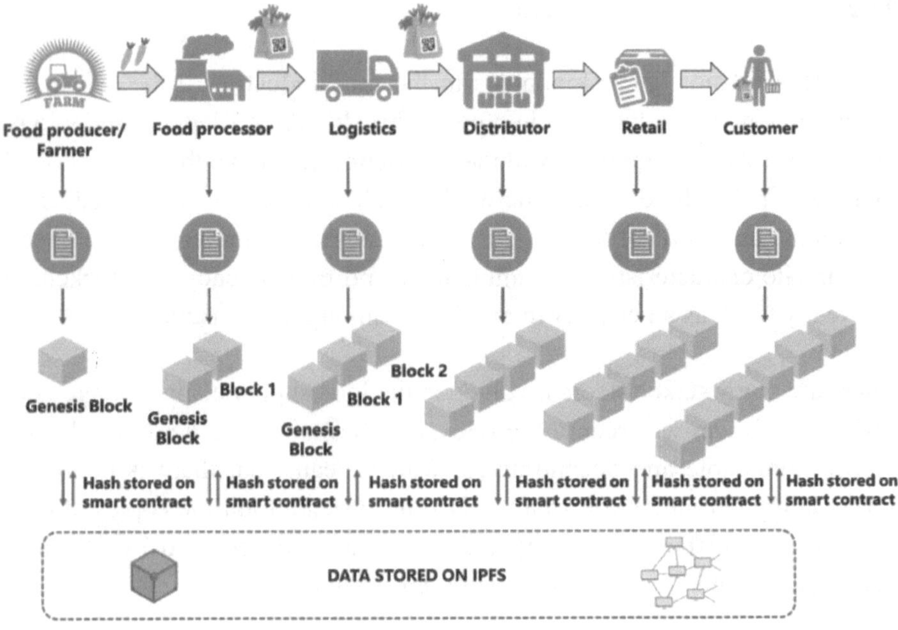

Fig 23-1: Blockchain-enabled food supply chain

At this stage, the food product is assigned a unique ID with a Quick Response (QR) code. With assigning a unique ID, a new transaction is created on Blockchain to claim the food processor's ownership of the food products. The records that they are required to put on the digital ledger include their location, received date of raw materials, sampling details, analysis of the food received, processes and the materials used for manufacturing, storage conditions of the processed food, date of manufacturing, and shelf life of the food, packaging conditions of the food, dispatch date of the processed food to the next link in the chain, etc. Even the ideal temperature range and other conditions required while transportation of the processed food need to be recorded on the digital ledger. The entire information will be stored on IPFS, and its hash will be stored on the smart contract.

(iii) Distributors: Distributors act as a link between food processing companies and wholesalers/retailers. The distributors receive pallets and cartons of processed food from the processors. They then verify the genuineness of the product using the assigned QR code and creates a new transaction on the Blockchain. By doing this, ownership of the product will be transferred from the food processor to the distributor. The information to be stored on the Blockchain at this stage includes: receiving date of the processed food, storage conditions, inventory details, and dispatch date to the subsequent links in the chain. The distributors then distribute the received food through various channels to the end customers. These channels can be wholesalers or retailers, who in turn provide these food products to the final consumers.

(iv) Retailers: Retailers receive these products from distributors and sell these to the end consumers. Retailers need to scan the QR code and record the information like received items, inventory details, storage details, and sales information on the ledger.

(v) Customers: The customer is the final link in the food supply chain who consumes this food; therefore, he should have full rights to see the complete journey of the food he is consuming. With Blockchain technology, he will be able to see all the information that was recorded on the digital ledger throughout its journey. It will only take him a few seconds to trace the origin of the food, its authenticity, and the journey it has taken before entering his shopping cart.

When the QR code on the food product is scanned through a smartphone, the whole history of the food with its unique ID will be shown to the customer right from its origin until it reaches the shelves of the store *(Fig 23-2)*. The information provided will be protected against any unauthorized change as the Blockchain itself is immutable.

Fig 23-2: QR code can be scanned to know the details of the food

Every new transaction creates a separate block. The block contains the previous hash, the data, and the current hash *(Fig 23-3)*. Thus, all the blocks are linked together with hash values. Therefore, if anyone tries to alter the contents of a block, the whole Blockchain will become invalid.

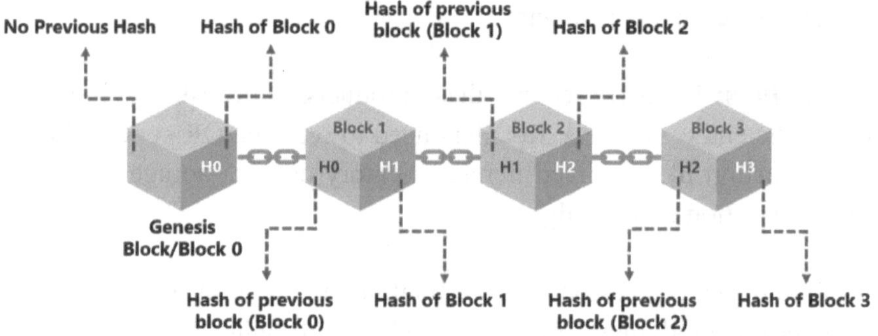

Fig 23-3: Each block contains the hash of the previous block

After verifying the product's information, the customer can buy and make a new transaction on the Blockchain network if the product is valid or deny buying if fake product information is found in the product history.

23.3. Monitoring cold temperature during the supply chain

As discussed earlier, most of the perishable food items like milk and poultry need to be kept at a lower temperature during their transportation. And if the temperature rises above the desired range, it could spoil the food, thus, making it unfit for consumption. But today there is no way to ascertain this fact. Blockchain, together with the Internet of things or IoT, can provide the solution to assure that a food item stays at the right temperature during its whole journey and is fit for consumption.

The packages containing milk will be instrumented with an IoT-enabled temperature sensor. This sensor will record and store the temperature data on the Blockchain. This means that any fluctuation in the temperature will also be recorded on the Blockchain *(Fig 23-4)*.

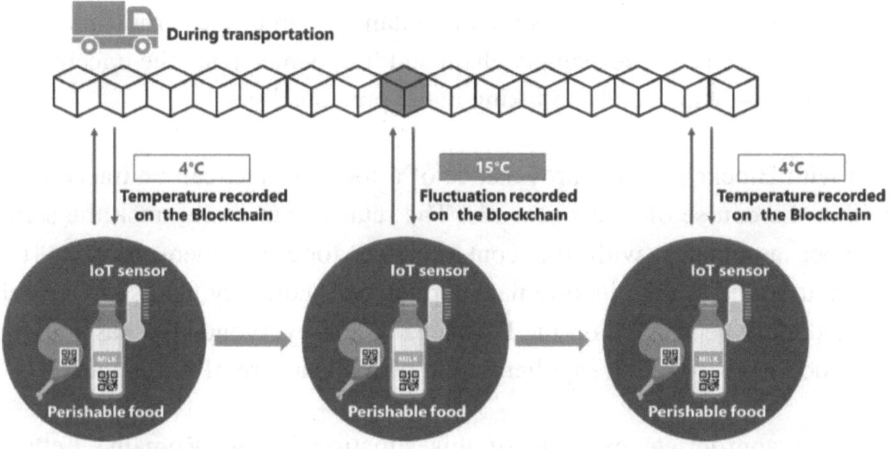

Fig 23-4: IoT sensors record the temperature of perishable food during transportation, and any fluctuation in temperature is recorded on the Blockchain

And when a consumer scans the milk packet, he will be able to view its complete information like its provenance, its expiry date, and other key information, including the temperature conditions at which it was kept during its whole journey. Thus, making him aware of the quality of the milk that he is buying.

Quality of meat products

Further, Blockchain also provides a great solution to know about the quality of animal meat products. By reading a simple QR code with a smartphone, the consumer will be able to see the complete animal details like the animal's date of birth, antibiotics, and vaccinations that it received during its life, whether it was raised free-range, cage-free, or in a cage and even the location where the livestock was harvested.

23.4. Quick traceback of the contaminated Food

The Center for Disease Control and Prevention estimates that each year 48 million Americans become sick because of the consumption of contaminated food. Out of these 48 million, 128,000 are hospitalized, and 3,000 lose their lives to this illness. When a foodborne disease outbreak occurs, it becomes very crucial to identify the source of contamination at the earliest possible. But with such a complex supply chain and fragmented data, the traceback is quite slow — which ends up taking many precious lives.

But with Blockchain, the provenance of a food product can be traced back within the course of a few seconds. The retailer can easily track the serial number associated with the contaminated food shipment back to the distributor and then to its original supplier. Subsequently, that supplier will immediately be flagged on the Blockchain, and everyone who has sourced that food item from that supplier would be made aware of the danger.

A more appropriate example of this situation is The Romaine Lettuce incident, which took place in 2018, where the lettuce contaminated with *E.coli* affected at least 200 people in 36 states of the U.S. and even lead to the death of 5 people. Contaminated canal water used for irrigation was the main cause of Lettuce getting infected with the *E.coli* pathogen strain. It took them months and a great deal of effort to trace the origin point of the problem. If every information would have been on a digital ledger, it would have been much easier to determine the origin of the contaminated batch of Lettuce. And once the origin is tracked, it is much easier to alert everyone and take all the lettuce off the shelves sourced from that particular location, supplier, or farm. This will save the precious lives of the consumers and will also save retailers from the financial losses which they have to bear when they take off all the food items of that category until the source is identified.

Walmart Case Study

To give you a real-life practical example of Blockchain let us discuss the Walmart case study. Walmart conducted a trackback test on a pack of mangoes in one of its stores. It took them more than 6 days to trace back the origin of those mangoes. And when the same test was conducted using Blockchain it took them a mere 2.2 seconds to find the original farm.

So you can imagine how powerful and useful this technology is for the food industry! It will help in quick food recalls and thus reducing the time consumers are at risk.

Chapter 24: Are Blockchain-based QR codes safe?

A quick response code, abbreviated as a QR code, stores information as a series of pixels in a square-shaped grid. The Japanese Automotive Company Denso Wave developed it in 1994. Every QR code is unique and works similarly to that of a barcode, but unlike a barcode reader that is required to read information embedded in barcodes, QR Codes do not require special devices. When a QR code reader application is installed, a consumer can simply point a smartphone's camera at the code to scan and decode the message contained in it *(Fig 24-1)*.

Fig 24-1: QR code can be scanned by a smartphone's camera

24.1. Benefits of QR codes

The data stored in a QR code can be up to 3Kb, which may include website URLs, phone numbers, videos, geolocation, etc. Thus, QR codes can be used to:

- Link directly to websites and product pages. Typing a URL is time-consuming and increases the chances of typo errors. On the other

hand, scanning a QR code is a much faster and error-free process to send users directly to the company's website, signup form, documents, or even download an app
- Send and receive payment
- Track information about the products in a supply chain
- Allow people to scan the code to read more like about animals in the zoo
- and many more.

24.2. Risk of using QR codes

While QR codes offer a great way to store and access information, they come with a fair amount of risk. Inherently QR codes can't be hacked. The security risks associated with QR codes like malware attacks, phishing, or hacking do not originate from QR code technology but instead from the final destination of each code.

(i) Malware attacks: Cybercriminals might embed malicious URLs in the present QR codes so that anyone who scans them gets infected by malware. Sometimes, merely visiting the website might trigger the downloading of malware in the background, which can harm users in several different ways. For example, it might open backdoors for more malware infections or silently steal the victim's information and send it to the cybercriminals. Moreover, these malware infections can give hackers access to the target device's location to monitor the target's every move or open their webcams to carry out live feeds unbeknown to them. At times, these malware infections might even be the ransomware attacks that would hold your information hostage for ransom.

(ii) Phishing attacks: QR codes also serve in phishing attacks. "Phishing" refers to an attempt by cybercriminals to steal sensitive information of the victims, typically in the form of login credentials (usernames and passwords), financial details (bank account information, credit card numbers), or other essential data. For this, a cybercriminal might replace a legitimate QR code with the code embedded with a phishing website URL. The phishing website then prompts users to reveal their personal information that criminals sell over the dark web. Apart from that, they might also coerce them into paying for materials causing them financial gain.

In the case of phishing attacks, the malicious actor pretends to be a trusted person or entity. For instance, phishing websites have slight differences from legitimate websites, making them seem authentic to the victim. They are generally exact replicas of the original website with minor differences, such as the "com" in the domain name can be replaced by something else such as "org" or "in."

To avoid such attacks,

- Don't scan QR codes from sources you can't verify, such as those included in print materials in public places and spam emails.
- Check for code tampering. Is the QR code you are scanning on a poster or flyer, part of the original design, or is it a sticker placed on top?
- When a QR code takes you to a landing page, make sure the URL of the site looks authentic and is the intended site. A malicious domain name may be similar to the intended URL but with typos or a misplaced letter.

24.3. Blockchain-based QR codes

24.3.1. Assigning hash value to QR code

When a QR code is generated, the Blockchain system puts a unique hash value into the QR code. When the user or consumer scans the QR code to access the information or data, the system first cross-checks the hash value in the QR code. It then compares the hash value of the QR code to the hash value in the Blockchain. If it matches, only then can the user access the URL link. The fact is because of the immutability feature of Blockchain; once there is a hash value in the QR codes, nobody can modify or alter it. Also, two QR codes or any two transactions can never have the same hash value; each transaction on the Blockchain has a unique hash value.

24.3.2. Scanning by dApp

But what if the malicious QR code has been put on the products to carry the malware or phishing attacks? It can be prevented by using the dApp to scan the QR code. The dApp will not scan any other QR code unless it is Blockchain-based and has a hash value. The dApp cross-checks the hash value in the QR code and compares it with the hash value on the Blockchain network. If the hash value matches, then only the customer is landed on the web page. On the contrary, if the hash value doesn't match or the QR code points to the malicious link, the dApp will not open the malicious link. This is how Blockchain-based secure QR codes are safe and prevent hacking and attacks.

Chapter 25: Blockchain in Dairy Industry

Cases of contamination and dilution of milk are on the rise. Nowadays, consumers are even ready to pay a premium for genuine quality milk. There are certain questions that bother every customer while buying a packet or a can of milk. What is the source of the milk? Is the milk genuine cow milk, as mentioned on the packet? Whether the milk is from a healthy cow and is the milk fit for consumption, as in many cases, milk gets spoilt during its transportation due to a lack of favorable environmental conditions.

Blockchain-The solution

Blockchain has the potential to provide consumers with a solution through which they will be able to trace the whole journey of the milk from the farm to their mouth. Multiple stakeholders are involved in supplying the milk from the farm to the retail shop from where we buy our milk *(Fig 25-1)*. All of these stakeholders need to register each and every piece of information about the milk throughout its journey on the Blockchain to bring transparency in the supply chain. Since storing the entire data on Blockchain is very costly; thus, distributed off-chain file storage IPFS is used to store supply chain transactions data. A unique hash is generated for every uploaded file on the IPFS server, which is then stored on the smart contract along with its address, which the permissioned stakeholders can access. In other words, anyone knowing the hash of the file can retrieve the file from IPFS and read its data. Any change in the uploaded file would change its hash.

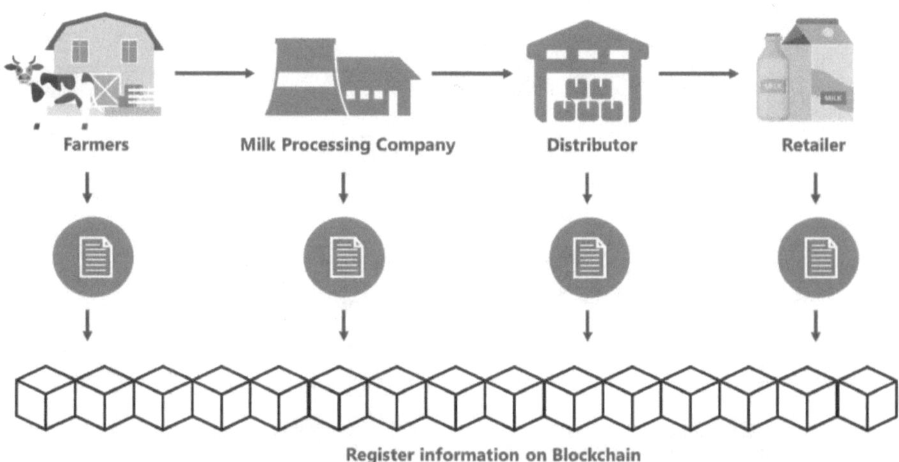

Fig 25-1: Multiple stakeholders in the milk supply chain are required to register every information about milk on Blockchain

1. Starting from farmers, they will be registered on the Blockchain, and a unique ID will be assigned to each of them. They will be required to tag their cows using an electronic tag or RFID tag. A tamper-proof RFID tag is attached to the ear of cows so that each cow becomes uniquely identifiable, and RFID readers can identify each animal via its RFID tag. The unique RFID tag number of each cow needs to be registered on the Blockchain along with its owner.

The information about a cow's health, vaccinations she received, her feed, etc., needs to be recorded on the IPFS along with their relevant proofs, whose hash will be stored on the smart contracts. Farmers will also be required to register other related information on the IPFS and Blockchain, like how the cows are raised, are they allowed to graze in the fields, etc. *(Fig 25-2)*. The recorded data on IPFS along with their hashes on Blockchain, will provide a secure and tamper-proof trail of each animal's history.

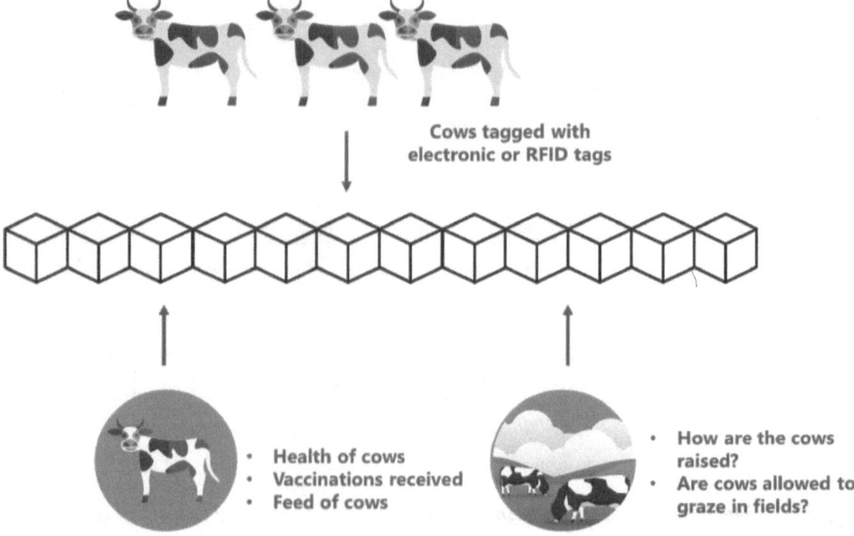

Fig 25-2: Information about the cows, including their health and how they are raised, are recorded on Blockchain

2. The next piece of information to be captured on the Blockchain will be during the milking phase. The milking process can be automatic or manual, which will be recorded on Blockchain along with the yield of milk from each cow.

Then this milk is sold by the farmer to a milk processing company. Before buying milk from the farmer, these processing companies run a quality test on the milk, and once approved, the payments are released to these farmers after a few days *(Fig 25-3)*.

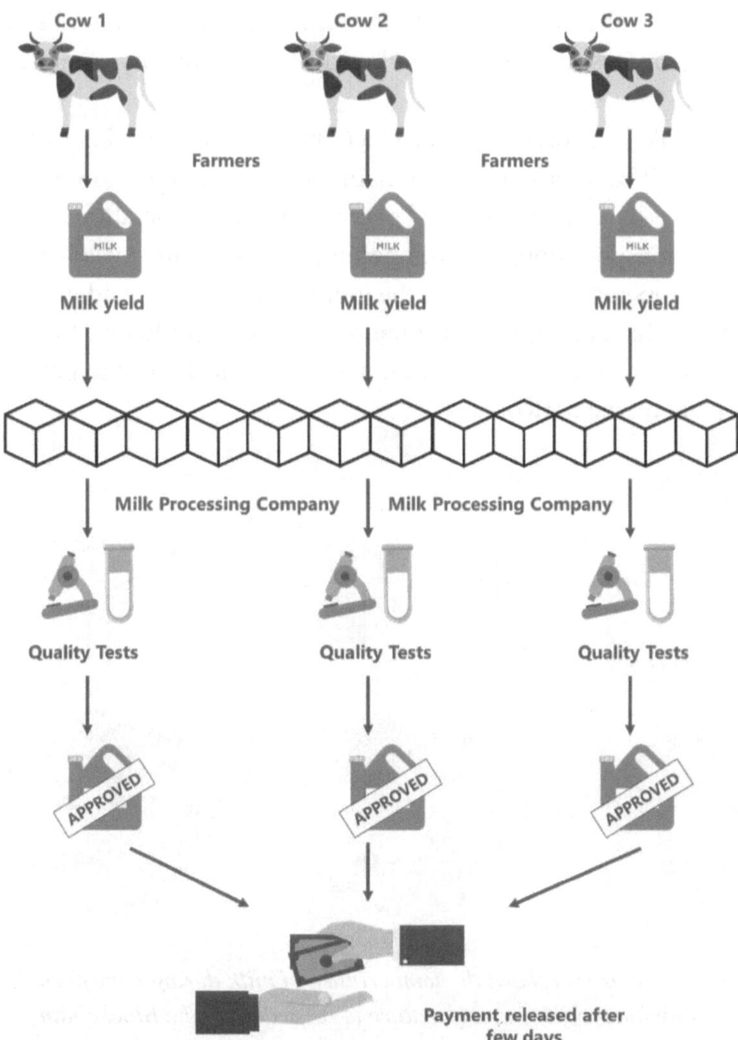

Fig 25-3: Information about the yield and quality of the milk is recorded on the Blockchain

With the implementation of Blockchain and smart contracts, the payment cycle can be shortened for these farmers. Once the quality of the milk is approved, the farmer will be notified about the acceptance of the milk, and a smart contract will be executed that will release an automatic payment, thus shortening the payment cycle for him. And in case the milk does not pass the quality tests, the farmer will be audited for quality compliance.

3. Since milk is a perishable product that needs to be kept at a lower temperature, it becomes crucial to maintain and monitor a low-temperature range during its transportation. To monitor the temperature of the milk during its transportation, IoT temperature sensors are installed that will record its temperature throughout the journey *(Fig 25-4)*. And in case of any temperature fluctuation, the information will be recorded on the IPFS and smart contracts. Additionally, an alert will be sent to all the permissioned stakeholders on the network.

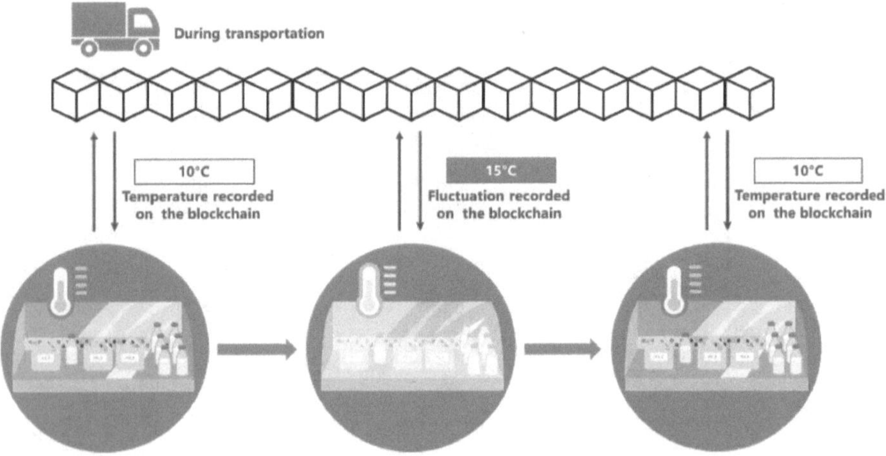

Fig 25-4: IoT sensors record the temperature of milk during transportation, and any fluctuation in temperature is recorded on the Blockchain

4. On receiving the milk supply, the processing company will process and pack the milk in bottles or packets. This whole processing information will then be recorded on the Blockchain. Each milk bottle or packet will be given a unique identification number, i.e., a QR code *(Fig 25-5)*. Then the milk is shipped to supermarkets. During this phase as well, the storage and transportation temperature needs to be recorded on the Blockchain. And once the milk reaches the shelves of a retailer, the retailer is required to keep the milk at the required conditions.

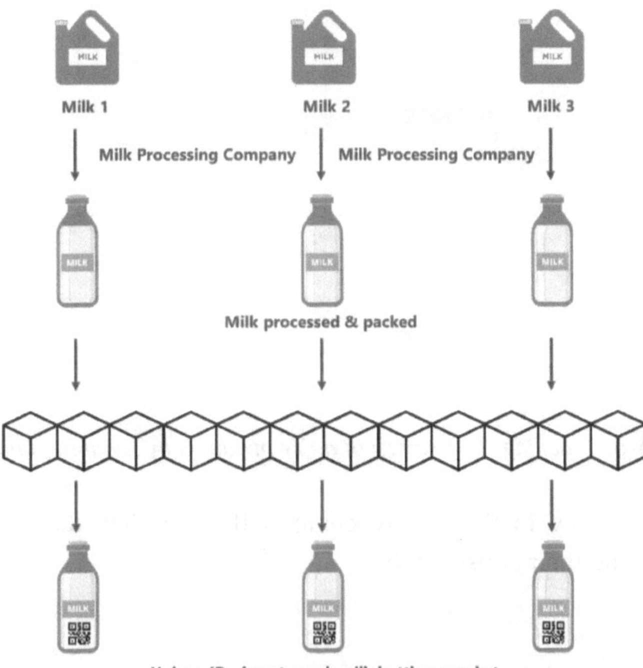

Fig 25-5: Milk is packed in bottles or packets, which are given unique IDs

5. Before buying, the consumer can scan the unique ID on the milk bottle or packet by his smartphone and can trace the complete journey of the milk *(Fig 25-6)*. This information will help him to authenticate and decide if the milk is fit for consumption.

Similarly, other dairy products like butter and cheese can be verified by scanning the unique IDs present on their label covers.

Fig 25-6: Tracking the journey of dairy products by scanning unique ID

This transparency in the supply chain will strengthen the trust between companies and their consumers.

Chapter 26: Blockchain in Poultry Industry

Egg consumption is increasing day by day because it is inexpensive, easy to process, and a rich source of protein. Consequently, growth in poultry farming can also be observed because of the increased demand for eggs and chicken. But still, the quality of eggs and chicken remains a concern for the consumers. For better quality of eggs and chicken, better poultry production needs to be done. Additionally, outbreaks of contamination linked to the eggs and poultry are a major challenge for the food industry. In April 2018, 207 million eggs from a North Carolina farm possibly contaminated with bacteria were recalled.

The consumers, before buying eggs and chicken, have a few questions in their mind like:

- Where and how were the chickens raised?
- What were they fed?
- Antibiotics and vaccinations that the chicken received during its life
- Whether it was raised free-range, cage-free, or in a cage and even the location where the livestock was harvested?
- Where was the chicken processed?
- And most important, is it fit for consumption?

Blockchain-The solution

All the stakeholders involved in the poultry industry will be registered on the Blockchain, and they will be required to record the relevant information on the shared, immutable ledger *(Fig 26-1)*. Precisely, entire supply chain transactions data will be stored on the off-chain file storage IPFS and the hash of the uploaded data, along with its address, will be stored on the smart contract of Blockchain. Anyone knowing the hash of the file can retrieve the information from IPFS.

(i) Producers: The supply chain starts with the producers. The producer will have to provide information like the location of the livestock farm, date of hatching of eggs, antibiotics given to chicken, other details like whether they were raised free-range or cage-free, and departure date of chicken to the slaughterhouse. The poultry should be appropriately managed for better production of poultry items, and therefore producers have to take care towards:

- Maintaining proper body weight of poultry and taking care of its feed and water consumption.
- The stress levels in the poultry should be assessed through body temperatures that are captured through IoT devices.
- From a disease management outlook, it is necessary to spot diseased poultry and separate it before the entire flock is affected because the disease can spread to humans too after consuming the affected poultry products.

The producers will also be required to provide certificates for the proof of managing poultry properly.

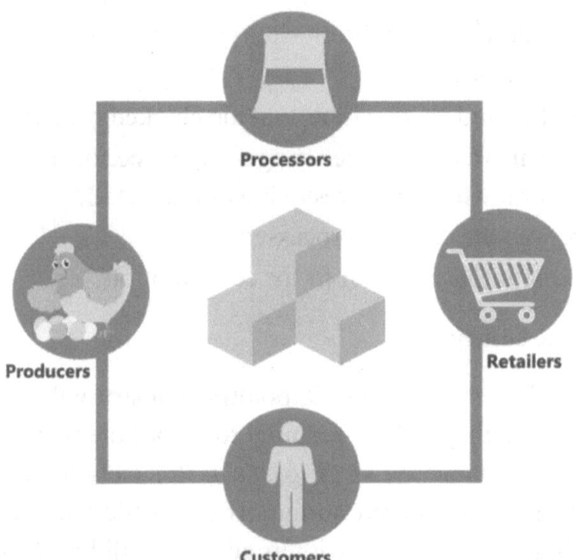

Fig 26-1: Stakeholders involved in the poultry industry are registered on the Blockchain

(ii) Processors: Next comes the processors who process the chicken and eggs. The information they will be required to provide is slaughter location, packaging, labeling location, storage conditions of the processed poultry, product expiry date, and dispatch date of the processed item on the

Blockchain. At this stage, the product will be given a unique identification number QR code *(Fig 26-2)*. Since chicken is a perishable product that needs to be kept at a low temperature during its transportation in order to prevent it from getting spoiled. IoT sensors will be installed on the packets that will sense the temperature of the products and will record it on the Blockchain.

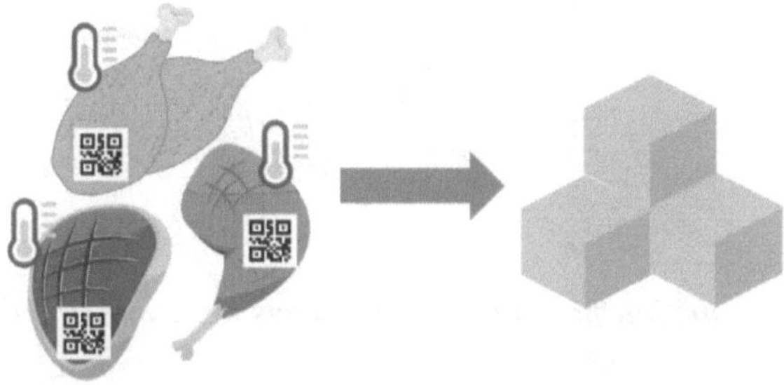

Fig 26-2: Poultry products are given a unique ID, and IoT sensors are installed

(iii) Retailers: Retailers receive these products from distributors and sell these to the end consumers. The retailer will be required to record the received items, inventory details, storage details, and sales information on the ledger.

(iv) Customers: The consumer is the final link in the food supply chain who consumes this food. Therefore should have full rights to know detailed information about it. Through Blockchain, a consumer can know all the information about the poultry, like its health, living conditions, and processing details before buying and bringing it home. The consumer can simply scan the unique ID through his smartphone and get all the information he always wanted to know *(Fig 26-3)*. The information about the provenance of the products will also be available on the Blockchain. Even the transportation conditions of the poultry will also be available on the Blockchain. With all this information at his disposal, he can easily validate if the product he is buying is fit for consumption or not.

Fig 26-3: Tracking the journey of poultry products by scanning unique ID

Chapter 27: Blockchain and IoT in Logistics

In any supply chain, managing the transportation of products is a challenging task. Sometimes materials are improperly shipped, resulting in sensitive products getting damaged. The success of any logistics company lies in efficient inventory management, warehousing, fast delivery, and taking care of safe storage of the goods.

27.1. Challenges in cold chain logistics

The transportation of food, chemicals, and pharmaceutical drugs requires temperature control. A strict predefined temperature is necessary to preserve the desired qualities of these products. Any fluctuation in the temperature can decrease the effectiveness of these products and, in some cases, can even make them unfit for consumption. Human error is the leading cause of mishaps by temperature fluctuations. Some of these errors are as follows:

- If the temperature-sensitive container was to be shipped in the morning but the shipment got delayed to late evening. This delay can cause unwanted fluctuations in the temperature.
- If the lid of the product bottle is not closed correctly in the packaging, it can cause the inside contents to get exposed to high environmental temperature.
- Suppose the frozen packs are not compactly packed, leaving enough space between the product packings. In that case, the products can melt in transit because of uneven cooling and getting exposed to a higher temperature.
- Fluctuation in the temperature of the cold room can damage the pharmaceutical products in case the temperature falls below the acceptable temperature. Thus, reducing the effectiveness of the products.

27.2. Blockchain and IoT in cold chain logistics

In a Blockchain and IoT-based logistics system, the product package will have two components:

(a) The first component will be a unique number assigned to the product package, which will be registered on the Blockchain. Whenever the package changes hands, the information will be recorded on the Blockchain *(Fig 27-1)*. Thus the complete journey of the product from manufacturer till it reaches the customer will be recorded on the Blockchain.

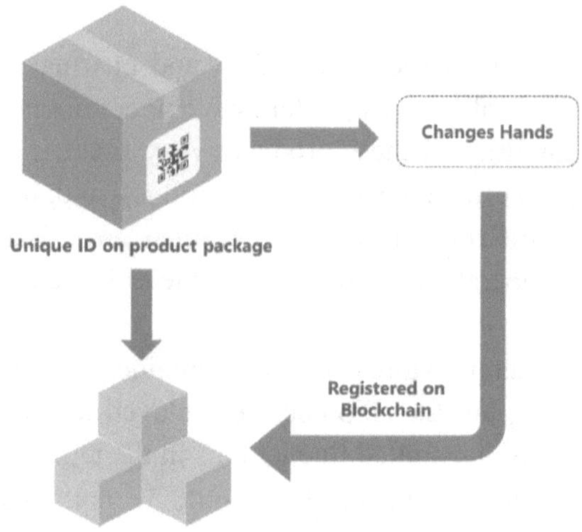

Fig 27-1: The complete journey of the product is recorded on Blockchain

(b) The second component will be IoT temperature sensors attached to the package. The sensors will record the temperature of the product during its transportation, and this information will be recorded on the Blockchain. Besides, any fluctuation in the temperature will also be recorded on the Blockchain, and an alert will be sent to all the relevant stakeholders involved in the supply chain *(Fig 27-2)*.

These IoT sensors can also monitor humidity conditions and physical shock in the storage area of the shipment. Subsequently, all the concerned stakeholders will be able to track this complete information on the Blockchain and then can use this information to notify the truck drivers and shippers of damaged shipments long before they arrive at their premise, and ask for a new and undamaged shipment.

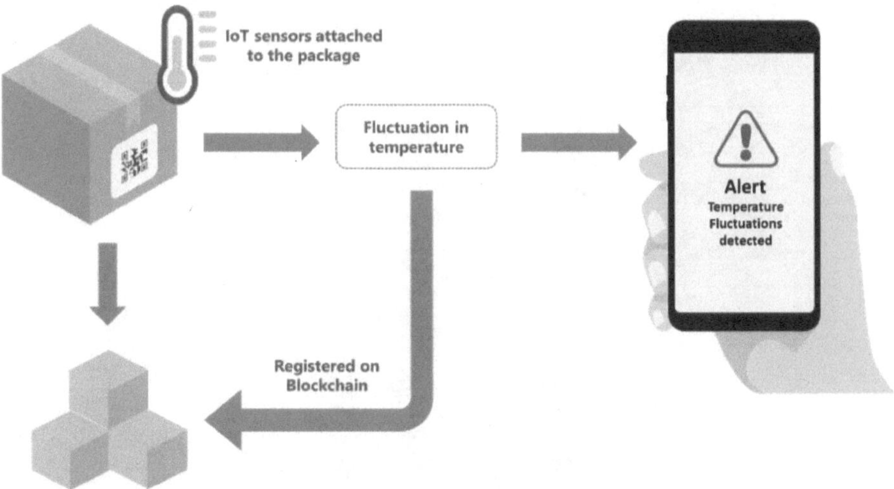

Fig 27-2: Fluctuation in temperature is recorded on Blockchain, and an alert is sent to relevant stakeholders

Other IoT sensors that can be used during transportation can sense the shipment's location and register that on the Blockchain. Thereby informing all the concerned stakeholders about the real-time location of the shipment.

These IoT sensors attached to shipment can even improve the supply chain security and protect the shipment against theft by detecting anomalies like route deviation, hijacking, or tampering. Moreover, the whole information will get registered on the Blockchain and send live alerts to the stakeholders involved.

27.3. Blockchain and IoT in inventory management

Most companies rely on Enterprise Resource Planning (ERP) software to support their business and supply chain inventory needs. The combination of IoT with ERP software can add business value by providing real-time data, giving existing ERPs real-time visibility into the inventory of products and services *(Fig 27-3)*.

Fig 27-3: Real-time visibility into the inventory of products and services by the ERP software

When this whole information gets registered on the Blockchain, the manufacturers can have real-time updates about the inventory of the enterprises. Therefore real-time orders can be placed based on predetermined conditions. In such a scenario, enterprises will receive the shipment without any delay, thereby preventing any loss of sales. Thus, in turn, enhancing the customer experience for these enterprises.

Chapter 28: Blockchain applications in the construction industry

The construction industry is a key driver of economic growth for all nations. This industry has regularly been cited as one of the world's most fragmented yet high-impact industries. For example, the Burj Khalifa project, which had over 12,000 workers from more than 100 countries on-site at the peak of its construction. To manage such an extended supply chain and to keep track of work in progress, schedule, cost, and payments, enormous efforts, and resources are required.

And on top of these challenges, construction projects experience different forms of mistakes, delays, and accidents at various stages and to varying degrees. The lack of accountability in the construction industry has been an ongoing issue for decades.

Enter Blockchain. Blockchain technology can be implemented in the construction industry to overcome these pain points that the industry is currently facing.

28.1. Blockchain in the management of construction projects and settlement of payments

The first application of Blockchain can be in the effective management of construction projects and settlement of payments more transparently.

Every capital construction project involves complex contracts and terms and conditions. Throughout the whole lifecycle of a project, it is always a challenge to ensure collaboration on every level among all the parties involved according to the contract. In addition, late payments and related cash flow issues have been enduring problems of this industry.

Now, let's understand how Blockchain will solve these issues of the construction industry. Let's start with the example of payment to laborers through smart contracts. In the proposed system, every laborer who enters the construction site will pass their ID card for security, health, and safety reasons. The workers' information about the time spent on the construction site will be captured and registered on the Blockchain. This Blockchain-based distributed ledger will be shared between the client, the consultant, and the contractor. Based on the agreed terms on smart contracts with regards to the number of hours worked, the smart contract will be executed, and the respective payment will be initiated to the laborers.

Due to the emergence of very large construction projects, **joint ventures** are becoming an everyday norm in the construction industry. Basically, a joint venture is a commercial alliance between two or more separate entities that enable them to share risk and reward. These joint ventures enable smaller companies to deliver large projects by combining their expertise and resources. Additionally, these joint ventures help companies gain local knowledge in overseas markets. But along with the benefits, there are some challenges as well for these joint ventures. Collaboration between the different entities participating in a joint venture is the prime among them.

With the implementation of Blockchain, the collaboration within a design joint venture (DJV) can be improved and enhanced. In the proposed Blockchain-based system, milestones of the project will be defined on the shared ledger along with predefined instructions on the smart contracts. As the design process starts, the platform will help to collect and record every necessary interaction within the Design Joint Venture or between project participants.

(i) In the project planning phase, different design packages and deliverables will be defined. In the proposed system, once the design is finished, all of the design packages will be added on the Blockchain platform along with the time taken for the design planning. The necessary parties or clients registered on the Blockchain will then be notified to check the document for their acknowledgment and verification. After getting the required approval from the client, the smart contract will be executed, and payment will be initiated following the predefined conditions and hours worked.

Similarly, all other interactions during the project will need to be registered on the Blockchain platform. And based on these recorded interactions, payments and project performance measure updates will be initiated by smart contracts.

Establishing such a collaborative and transparent system can readily improve the way how a construction project is managed and monitored. It can help to minimize misalignments of contracts and can enable collective corrective actions to make a joint venture a success.

(ii) The same concept will be applied during the construction phase. The team that carries out the construction work will need to be registered on the Blockchain, and the tasks assigned to them will also need to be mentioned on the Blockchain platform. During the actual construction, pre-defined specifications and quality assurance procedures need to be followed, which will then be supervised by the site engineer, quality controller, and the project manager. And once the supervision is done, the results of the quality assurance will also be registered on the Blockchain. And if the results are found to be satisfactory in accordance with the predefined conditions, smart contract will release the payment to the workers and will also update the progress of the project.

(iii) But just the registration of work completion is not always enough, the construction projects are far more complex. There are usually unexpected issues, like major health and safety incidents on the site, which can result in additional claims and disputes. In a Blockchain-enabled construction management system, every health and safety incident and record of unsafe working conditions on the construction site can be registered on the shared ledger, and subsequently, the relevant risk mitigation measures can be initiated. For this stage, the use of IoT sensors along with Blockchain can be very useful as these tools can act as a reliable source of data. The critical information obtained by these sensors can be registered on the Blockchain and can then be processed by a smart contract. If certain thresholds and trigger levels are reached, the smart contract can notify the appropriate person on site to prepare for risk mitigation or to change the construction plan.

Let's take the example of a crane; its effective operation is crucial in terms of project progress, but also, at the same time, any mistakes in its operations can cause severe health and safety issues. With IoT sensors installed, the operational status of a crane lift can be easily followed and registered on the Blockchain system. If the sensors record that the crane is lifting a higher weight than its permissible limit or if there are extreme winds that can endanger the safety of workers on site; then through a smart contract, a safety alarm will be triggered that will notify the crane operator and the project manager on site to take appropriate actions to prevent any accidents due to overloading or poor weather conditions.

28.2. Blockchain in the supply chain of the construction industry

Further, Blockchain can also revolutionize the current supply chain of the construction industry and make it more robust. Designers, contractors, and suppliers nowadays are far more concerned about the materials used in construction projects for reasons such as strict quality assurance, health and safety, material standards, and sustainability. Blockchain provides a perfect solution to trace construction materials, such as prefabricated concrete or steel, along the supply chain. Moreover, as every transaction along the supply chain is registered and visible on the Blockchain, it becomes easier to keep track of the delivery of the material.

Let's understand it through the example of a steel beam. The life cycle of a steel beam starts from its production and ends when it is used in construction. In this proposed system, every beam registered on the Blockchain system can be tracked through a unique ID. Additionally, all the fabrication and design specifications of a beam will always be available on the Blockchain. Further, as the steel beam moves through the supply chain - every change of its ownership and its transportation details will also be added to the Blockchain. Thus through this Blockchain-enabled solution, the whole construction supply chain can be made transparent and robust.

28.3. Blockchain in Building information modeling or BIM

Blockchain can also play an essential role in Building information modeling or BIM. But to fully recognize how Blockchain can add value to BIM, it is important to understand the core concept of BIM.

Building Information Modelling or BIM is a process that deals with digital representations of real-life assets. This digital model holds a wide array of information about the asset, such as its 3D geometry, construction management information like time schedules, costs, and operation and maintenance metrics of the asset. BIM is used to design and document building and infrastructure designs. Every detail of a building is modeled in BIM. The model can be used for analysis to explore design options and to create visualizations that can help stakeholders to understand what the building will look like after it's built.

It is important to note that BIM is much more than just the computer model. It also includes the digital working method, which describes how the model fits into the overall project management system, how the incoming and outgoing information will be handled, and how project participants will build, use and manage the model. The implementation of Blockchain can facilitate the development of BIM and can even help to leverage its full potential.

Engineering projects contain vast amounts and types of data and similarly high volumes of corresponding design and managerial decisions. Once Blockchain is implemented in BIM, it can work as a single source of truth for this data. In a Blockchain-based system, the shared ledger will record an audit trail of design approvals, data verification, and project management decisions. And this information will serve as a single source of truth that will cover all aspects of the project and eliminate any kind of disputes between the cooperating parties.

Once Blockchain is implemented, BIM along with other information from the Blockchain, such as supply chain information, the provenance of materials, payment details, etc., will make BIM an even more comprehensive digital representation of a real-life asset.

Thus through Blockchain, the client can ensure the quality of the deliverables by evaluating the designed criteria set by BIM, which the contractor would have to adhere to. This way, quality checks will be highly transparent, and collaborations will simultaneously be made more effective.

Thus, Blockchain would act as an underlying infrastructure to further strengthen any kind of BIM model.

28.4. Blockchain and Digital Twin

Most projects do not stop at the delivery of the asset but continue until the end of the life cycle of the asset, and because of these cases, the Digital twin concept is gaining traction in the industry. The digital twin is a digital representation of a real-life asset. You may wonder how BIM is different from BIM as BIM is also a digital representation. Let's understand the main difference between them - BIM is just a representation of what the real-world object should be. In contrast, a digital twin is a digital copy of an existing asset.

A digital twin embodies a holistic view where the asset management, operation, and maintenance of an asset is performed throughout its whole lifecycle, from initial concept to maintenance and recycling.

Digital twin and IoT: The digital twin of physical objects realize their full potential with the Internet of Things (IoT) sensors. The real-time data captured by the IoT sensors installed on the physical objects/assets can provide real-time information about the performance of the asset to the digital twin. Thus digital twin gets updated and becomes a live information-rich dashboard and reporting tool for asset management. Simply put, a digital twin, along with the input from IoT sensors on a physical real asset, replicates a real-world system and changes with that system over time. Consider a bridge, for example, fitted with IoT sensors for measuring vehicle load and other traffic conditions. The data from these sensors will provide an always up-to-date information to the digital twin—the digital twin updates itself according to the data. Through digital twin, the bridge maintenance team can view areas where the bridge is aging or faulty and needs repairs. Thus, preventive maintenance can prevent equipment failure before it occurs and reduces the risk of accidents.

Blockchain and digital twin: The data captured by IoT sensors will be recorded on the Blockchain, thus, preventing the hackers from attacking or manipulating data once the data is added to the Blockchain. Additionally, the data registered will also serve as an input condition for triggering automatic repairs via smart contracts. For instance, if a certain part of the asset has an unexpected failure, through the Digital Twin and Blockchain, it would be easy to identify exactly which elements caused the issue, who was responsible for its assembly, and which manufacturing companies to be contacted for procuring that part.

Thus integration of Blockchain technology can play a crucial role in improving project performance, especially where the productivity of projects is critical, like Highways, Railways, Bridges, Buildings, etc.

28.5. Scalability concerns

(i) Blockchain used will be permissioned Blockchain. The stakeholders involved will be assigned specific functions on the smart contracts. Storing the entire data about the supply chain, stakeholders, the project's progress, design files, BIM, digital twin, data collected by IoT sensors, etc., on Blockchain is very challenging as it is very costly and will significantly slow down the processing on Blockchain. Thus, distributed file storage IPFS can provide low-cost off-chain storage to store data. IPFS has been explained in detail in Chapter 15.

(ii) To make the Blockchain scalable for its use in the construction industry and increase the speed of transactions, layer 1 (discussed in Chapter 12) and layer 2 (discussed in Chapter 13) scaling solutions will be required to be implemented.

Chapter 29: Blockchain and IoT in the Wine Industry

Wine counterfeiting is one of the major challenges the wine industry faces; the fake wine market amounts to 15 billion USD worldwide.

29.1. How is fake wine introduced into the market?

There are various ways by which fake wine is introduced into the market, some of which are as follows:

(i) Relabeling wine bottles is one of the most common ways through which fake wine is introduced into the market. In some cases, cheaper wines are labeled as expensive wines, while in others, wines are mislabelled with a famous origin because of the premium it commands. For instance, French Wine label on a wine bottle indicates that the wine would be from France, but actually, the origin of that wine is a different country, say Spain, and this is a real scenario that came to light in 2018, where millions of Spanish wine bottles were being sold as French Wine.

(ii) Further, in some cases, original wine is adulterated with some cheap substitutes to increase the profit margins. For instance, wines have been found to contain hazardous components like diethylene glycol to increase their sweetness. Some chemicals may also be used to mask faults and the unpleasant aroma of the wine.

(iii) One of the other prominent ways of wine fraud is through the blending of the original wine. One variety of wine that is touted to be 100% pure is blended with various other cheaper wines. For example, a wine with a dark color is often assumed to be of higher quality, so blending a darker color variety with a cheap lighter wine could enhance the market value of the cheaper wine.

To put a check on the wine fraud, there needs to be a mechanism that can assure a customer that the wine he is buying is authentic and not some cheap counterfeit. Unfortunately, till now, there is no foolproof method to establish this fact, as there are many loopholes in the current wine tracking system.

- The first one being the inefficiency in validating the authenticity of the source information. Since the wine supply chain is quite complex, involves a large number of stakeholders, and the wine changes multiple hands before it reaches the retailers, it is quite feasible to reproduce or forge the information at any point of time.
- Additionally, there is no efficient method to identify counterfeit wine bottles since these bottles are always accompanied by fake provenance histories.

29.2. Enter Blockchain

Blockchain technology has the potential to mitigate these issues of the wine industry and ensure the authenticity and provenance of each wine bottle produced. So let's understand how Blockchain will work for the wine industry.

All the stakeholders involved in the wine supply chain will be required to register themselves on the Blockchain network and, subsequently, will be required to add relevant information on the Blockchain.

(i) As wine is produced from grapes, let's start with grape growers, as they are one of the key stakeholders in the wine supply chain. Grape growers take care of the grapevines and monitor the parameters such as temperature, soil moisture, fertilizers, etc. Once these grapes are ripe, they deliver them to the winery. In a Blockchain-based system, the grape growers will be required to upload information about each plot of the grapevine, location details, the altitude at which the plants are grown, type of the vines, fertilizer requirements, irrigation requirements, and origin of water used for the irrigation. Further, the grape growers will also record information about the dispatch date of these grapes to the next link in the chain, that is, to the manufacturing companies. This information will be stored in the genesis block, i.e., the block from where Blockchain originates.

(ii) Next comes the wine manufacturers, who manufacture wine from these grapes. The information that they will be required to add on the Blockchain includes receiving date of grapes, the variety of grapes, the record of chemical contents, and internal procedures, for example, decantation, fermentation, etc., performed to transform grapes into wine. The winery is responsible for identifying each production run with a batch number. Thus the applicable batch numbers, additives used, transportation, and storage conditions will also be recorded on the shared ledger. After this stage, the wine is sent to bulk distributors, which will also be recorded on the Blockchain along with the dispatch information.

(iii) A Bulk Distributor is responsible for receiving, storing, processing, sampling, analyzing, and dispatching the bulk wine. When the wine arrives, the bulk distributor verifies the supplier information, records all the information, including the amount of wine received, and then takes samples for tasting and analysis.

Irrespective of whether the wine passes or fails the analysis, the results of the wine analysis will be stored on the Blockchain. If the wine is rejected, the wine is returned to the source. For the wine that has passed the analysis, two distinct processes are performed:

- Bulk wine is stored and dispatched without any blending or any other processing. The batch number, in this case, remains the same.
- Or wine blending is performed that involves the blending of different wines and then dispatching the newly blended bulk wine. The complete information about these processes will be recorded on the Blockchain. Finally, a new batch number is allocated, which is different from any other batch number used in the blending process.

(iv) Next comes a filler or a packer who receives the wine from the bulk distributor or transit cellar and fills it into different containers such as bottles, bags, or kegs.

Since the identification and labeling of each wine is done at this stage, therefore it is essential to ensure the consistency of the labeled information with the records stored on the Blockchain for that particular batch of wine. During this step, a unique ID code will be allocated to each wine bottle. The next step is the packaging of these wine bottles into cartons and pallets and then dispatching them to the finished goods distributor.

(v) A finished goods distributor will record the details about receiving, storing, dispatching, and inventory of the finished goods. At this stage, if any re-packing or re-labeling is required, then these details will also be stored on the Blockchain. From the distributor, the finished goods are then dispatched to the retailers.

(vi) After receiving finished goods from distributors, retailers sell these to the end consumers. The retailer will be required to record the received items, inventory details, and sales information on the ledger. When a bottle or a carton is sold, the information will be recorded on the Blockchain so that it is not possible to use the same label again.

(vii) The consumer is the final link in the wine supply chain that consumes this wine. Therefore, he should have full rights to know about the complete journey of the wine he is buying. With the implementation of Blockchain, he will be able to see all the information that was recorded on the digital ledger throughout its journey. Since every bottle is assigned a unique ID, the consumer can easily traceback the complete journey of the wine by scanning the code through his smartphone or by entering the unique ID on the brand's website. After receiving the product ID, the system first identifies the batch of wine and then traces back all information recorded by different stakeholders for that corresponding batch.

Furthermore, since the details of a sold wine are also recorded on the Blockchain, it is impossible to sell another wine bottle with the same ID. Thus, the proposed system makes wine counterfeiting almost impossible. This is how Blockchain ensures transparency and security in the wine supply chain.

29.3. IoT and Blockchain in validating shipping temperature

The wine manufacturer takes special care in maintaining controlled conditions to protect the manufactured wine. Similarly, at the other end of the supply chain, a consumer takes special care of the product by storing it under predefined controlled conditions. Because unwanted change in the environmental conditions can change the perceivable characteristics of the wine. For instance, optimal temperature for storing white wine is between 13-15°C, and for red wine is between 10-20°C. But if the temperature rises above the desired range, it can deteriorate the wine quality and change its color. Unfortunately, in the current scenario, there is no effective method to ensure that the wine remained in its desired conditions during its transportation. Blockchain and IoT can offer a solution to this issue. IoT sensors can be attached to wine bottles and cartons, which can then capture the temperature of the wine during its transportation and upload it on the Blockchain. Consequently, any change in the temperature will also be recorded on the Blockchain. Thus, through Blockchain, each and every stakeholder can ensure that the wine stayed at its correct temperature during its transportation.

29.4. IoT and Blockchain in validating aging conditions of wine

Fine wines have traditionally been bought based on the trust for a particular manufacturer or a brand. Although the buyer shells out a fair sum of money to buy a fine wine but he himself has no means to validate if the wine has aged properly under the desired conditions. During the aging process, a wine undergoes a series of different chemical reactions to improve its taste and quality. These reactions can easily be affected by physical and chemical changes taking place in the environment. For instance,

(i) The storage conditions should be appropriate for wine maturation, including the desired humidity, temperature, and darkness.

(ii) During the wine maturation, a wine should be kept under dark conditions because the UV light can damage wine by degrading stable organic compounds present in it. Just as direct sunlight can negatively affect your skin, it can also damage fine wines.

(iii) Another very critical factor in the aging of wine is temperature. The recommended temperature range for aging wines lies between 13-15°C. Although if the temperature is increased, the maturation process speeds up, it causes undesirable changes in the wine as well. Therefore it is crucial to maintain the recommended temperature range for the perfect maturing of the wine.

(iv) The next important factor is humidity. 60-70% humidity is essential to ensure that a wine ages gracefully. When humidity levels are too low, the wine bottle cork will dry out and will become brittle. Because of this, air will leak into the bottle and oxidize the wine, thus spoiling its taste. And if the humidity levels are too high, it also has undesirable effects on its aging.

But the question here is - how can a customer know and validate all of this information?

IoT, along with Blockchain, has the solution to this issue. IoT sensors can be installed to sense all of these conditions under which wine ages, and these IoT sensors will then record the details on the Blockchain. Subsequently, a consumer can see all this information regarding the wine aging by scanning the unique ID present on a wine bottle.

29.5. Scalability concerns

(i) Blockchain used will be permissioned Blockchain. The stakeholders involved will be assigned specific functions on the smart contracts. Storing the entire data about the supply chain, stakeholders, data collected by stakeholders and IoT sensors, etc., on Blockchain is very challenging as it is very costly and will significantly slow down the processing on Blockchain. Thus, distributed file storage IPFS can provide low-cost off-chain storage to store data. A unique hash is generated for every uploaded file on the IPFS server, which is then stored on the Blockchain and accessed through the smart contract. Any modification in the uploaded file would change its hash. IPFS has been explained in detail in Chapter 15.

(ii) To make the Blockchain scalable for its use in the supply chain of wine or any other industry, layer 1 (discussed in Chapter 12) and layer 2 (discussed in Chapter 13) scaling solutions will be required to be implemented.

Chapter 30: Blockchain in the Coffee Industry

Coffee is the world's favorite drink with diverse flavors and well-known brands. People around the world consume more than 2 billion cups a day.

30.1. Challenges in the supply chain

Yet despite an important significance of coffee in our life, its supply chain has several challenges, such as fragmented production, climate change, and market instability. The supply chain process of coffee beans typically contains seven levels: growing, harvesting, hulling, drying and packing, bulking, blending, and roasting. The entire supply chain is further extended by several intermediaries, including global transporters, exporters and retailers.

(i) Let's start with the origin: the coffee seed grows best in humid climate, with a temperature of approximately 25°C. After around ten weeks, the seed sprouts, but it takes around 4-7 years for the tree to mature and produce the first crop.

(ii) Then, the farmers pick the red cherries by hand. All cherries don't ripe at the same time, therefore, one tree must be inspected several times. This process requires a significant amount of human resources and is not the only manual work that goes into harvesting coffee. After this, the hull and dirt are removed from the cherry, as well as the two beans embedded in the fruit are separated. Then the workers lay out all the beans in the sun to fully dry them into green coffee.

(iii) Once the beans are dried, they are packaged into large sacks and passed on to the exporters. From there, they are distributed to big organizations in the coffee business who take these beans. Then, various measures are applied in the refining process consisting of polishing, sorting, washing, and drying, followed by the roasting process turning coffee brown.

(iv) Then, the roasted coffee beans are packaged and transported to distributors.

(v) Distributors then distribute these roasted coffee beans to retailers like coffee shops, restaurants, and grocery stores from where we buy coffee.

Thus the entire supply chain is linked by several intermediaries. The coffee beans make several stops before arriving at the final destination, be it from crop to drying station, or from individual farmers to processors and roasters. The greater the number of intermediaries, the more complex and opaque is supply chain.

30.2. Blockchain- The Solution

Blockchain has the potential to transform the coffee industry by bringing transparency in its supply chain. The farmers, traders, roasters, and consumers can be fully aware of their coffee's journey. Depending on the product, the supply chain can require many transfers of coffee beans across different countries. Those transfers also require the circulation of invoices and other paperwork among intermediaries, and there can be limited transparency for the end consumer. Blockchain can solve these problems by introducing greater efficiency and transparency to the modern supply chain.

The distributed ledgers record the movements of every batch of coffee beans and determine the exact point of origin.

(i) Through Blockchain technology, roasters will be able to purchase a coffee after accessing all of the previous data on it. They will be able to see information about the farm the coffee comes from, how much was paid for the coffee at that point in time, and more.

(ii) Similarly, on the Blockchain platform, the producer can view what happened to their coffee and how much was paid for it, not just by the person they sold it to but by every other body that purchased their coffee. Thus, they can get a fair price for their produce. Blockchain also provides a platform to directly connect coffee producers with buyers eliminating the role of middlemen.

(iii) Since the quality and transaction values are recorded each time the coffee changes hands, it's possible for us to trace the coffee all the way back to the farm and see how was the coffee traded and how much for simply by scanning unique ID on your coffee. Customers can ensure if their coffee is organic and fairly traded.

Starbucks is embracing Blockchain, powered by Microsoft Azure. The coffee giant has done this to monitor the journey of the coffee right from farms to stores and until it reaches the coffee cup of the customer.

30.3. Scalability concerns

(i) Blockchain used will be permissioned Blockchain. The entire information of the supply chain will be stored on IPFS, and its hash will be stored on the smart contract. All the stakeholders in the network can access the data based on the permissions they have been granted. IPFS has been explained in detail in Chapter 15.

(ii) To make the Blockchain scalable for its use in the supply chain and increase the speed of transactions, layer 1 (discussed in Chapter 12) and layer 2 (discussed in Chapter 13) scaling solutions will be required to be implemented.

Chapter 31: Blockchain technology in Automotive Industry

31.1. Transparency in the supply chain

The Automotive industry is a complex ecosystem with multiple parties involved in the design, production, distribution, marketing, selling, finance, and servicing of vehicles. In the automotive sector, there are several key ERP and manufacturing systems that generate vehicle data and control the manufacturing process. These systems must communicate with hundreds of systems downstream, which rely on data feeds to perform their functions. With the implementation of Blockchain, there would be greater transparency in the flow of information between the different parties and systems involved.

(i) There is a huge problem of authentic-looking but inferior fake parts entering the market because of the complex supply chain and ending up in dealer service centers. These counterfeit spare parts would fail quickly after being installed in cars, causing reputational damage to the automaker and risking the lives of the customers as these fake parts under-perform, causing accidents; for example, imagine a scenario where brakes and airbags are fake. But with the implementation of Blockchain, this issue can be tackled. Each vehicle part, including the spare parts, will have its unique ID, and it will be registered on the Blockchain. Therefore, it will be possible for the car manufacturer, car service center, and customer to verify the authenticity and trace the original supplier and manufacturing date of the spare parts through the Blockchain.

(ii) An automobile manufacturing plant must coordinate effectively with third-party logistics and transportation companies to ensure the timely delivery of orders to different suppliers around the world. Blockchain connected with IoT sensors and smart devices can provide accurate and transparent end-to-end view of the order location, status, and other useful information to all the stakeholders involved in the supply chain. As a result, the original equipment manufacturer (OEM) plant can plan its production schedule more accurately and improve the traceability of the parts that it delivers to its customers.

31.2. Advantages of smart contracts for customers

Smart contracts can be a boon for vehicle owners to process payments. For instance, at the toll booths or after fueling your car with petrol, the smart contracts can get executed, and automatically payments can be released to the respective authority or organization. Similarly, when an electric vehicle owner charges his vehicle at a third-party charging station, the smart contract can be executed, and payment can be made once the charging is done. Further, IoT sensors can sense the parts that need to be repaired, and appoint an authenticated technician for repairing; after that smart contract can get executed, and the payment can be automatically processed to the technician.

31.3. Smart contracts in insurance payment

Blockchain can enable you to pay car insurance based on how much you actually use your car rather than on a set of defined insurance policy conditions. A driver profile, including miles covered by the vehicle, economical usage of the vehicle, and accidental history, is securely stored on the Blockchain. Blockchain provides a foolproof means of collection of this data and delivers it in a secure, and unalterable manner to the insurance companies. This can reduce the cost of insurance premiums, and you will pay as you drive or how you drive.

Further, in case of any accident, IoT sensors will record and take images of the accident, sense the damaged parts and store all this information on the Blockchain. And with this immutable record available on the Blockchain, it would be much easier for the insurers to assess the damage and release the insurance claim. Such a transparent and fair system will benefit the insurer and the customer.

31.4. Targeted Vehicle recalls

There are times when automobile manufacturers need to recall the vehicles if any problem is detected in delivered vehicles which could affect the road and travel safety of the customers. However, because most manufacturers are not able to uniquely identify every part in every vehicle sold, they need to issue the recall for a specific model and model year, which can include several 10s of 1,000s of vehicles even if the defective parts are installed only in a few cars. This process is a loss of money to the manufacturer; moreover, it results in disturbing 1000s of customers.

There is also a concern that sometimes recall notification does not reach the owners, and in case the car has been resold by the original buyer, it becomes a daunting task to contact the 2nd or 3rd owner of the vehicle. But with the implementation of Blockchain, this issue can be sorted out. Blockchain will enable the car manufacturers to uniquely identify every single part, saving a huge amount of time and money in the event of a vehicle recall.

The manufacturer will know exactly which specific vehicles have the defective part fitted into them, and hence they will be able to issue specific recalls for individual VIN numbers.

Also, through Blockchain, it will be feasible for them to track the recall status of the affected vehicles, for instance, how many vehicles are received for repairing and how many vehicles are repaired. This will ease their task of regulatory reporting required to be done to the government.

31.5. Combating odometer fraud

Mileage is one of the most significant parameters while assessing the condition of a pre-owned car. Mileage fraud is widespread while selling pre-owned vehicles. Odometer is generally tampered by vehicle owners while selling their vehicles to conceal mileage.

To combat this odometer fraud, there will be a car connector device that will record the mileage of the car and will store this information on the digital ledger. In such a scenario before buying a second-hand vehicle, you can verify the displayed mileage with the information recorded on the Blockchain. Thus blockchain can serve as a source to verify the veracity of a car's mileage.

Besides, while buying a second-hand car, you will always be able to check every piece of information about the vehicle, like its previous owners, its provenance, repair history, or any other data that can help you to avoid the wrong purchase.

31.6. Car sharing

Most car owners drive their cars alone to work. Thus putting an extra burden on their pocket and our environment. Blockchain can enable vehicle owners to monetize their trips as per the defined smart contracts.

Users and car-sharing providers will be registered on a Blockchain platform, and their identities will be verified on the Blockchain network. The platform can be used to securely exchange data, including the location of the vehicle, agreement details like cost per mile, and the payment details for the user.

The geo-sensors in the car will record the initial coordinates of the boarding point and will also capture the dropping point coordinates. After completion of the trip, the smart contract would be executed, and payment will be automatically deducted from the user's account based on the distance travelled.

Blockchain will also enable the easy renting or leasing of the car. In this case, smart contracts will be executed, and payment will be made once the vehicle has been returned.

31.7. Scalability concerns

(i) Storing the supply chain information, vehicle details, IoT data, odometer readings, etc., on Blockchain is very costly and will significantly slow the processing on Blockchain; thus, distributed file storage IPFS can provide low-cost off-chain decentralized storage to store this data. IPFS has been explained in detail in Chapter 15.

(ii) To make the Blockchain scalable for its use in the automobile sector, layer 1 (discussed in Chapter 12) and layer 2 (discussed in Chapter 13) scaling solutions will be required to be implemented.

Chapter 32: Blockchain in International Trade

When it comes to international shipments or international trade, there are various steps and documentation stages that need to be completed for a trade to be successful.

32.1. How does international trade work?

To give you a clear picture of how international trade works, let's walk you through the whole process in detail:

(i) Export Haulage: The first step is export haulage which involves the movement of goods from the shipper or exporter to the freight forwarders' warehouse. A Freight forwarder is a connecting link or an intermediary who is responsible for transporting goods from one destination to another. Export Haulage usually takes place with the help of a truck or a train or in some cases, both. The export haulage can take a few hours to a few days depending on the distance between the exporter's premises and the freight forwarders' warehouse.

(ii) Exports custom clearance: When goods reach the warehouse of a freight forwarder, he inspects and ensures that everything is transported without any damage. Before the goods can be shipped off from the country, they need to receive customs clearance from the export country. This process is generally performed by customs brokers and requires the submission of cargo details and various other important documents like:

- Bill of Lading
- Commercial Invoice
- Packing List
- Certificate of origin statement
- Packing Declaration Form
- Manufacturing Declaration

(iii) Loading of cargo: Next is the inspection and loading of the cargo on the ship. This is coordinated by the freight forwarder.

(iv) Imports custom clearance: Once the shipment arrives in the importer's country, the authorities in the destination country check the import customs documents. It is the responsibility of the freight forwarder in the import country or the nominated customs broker to perform this clearance by the time cargo arrives.

(v) Destination arrival: Once the shipment cargo arrives in the importer's country, the cargo is handed to the destination warehouse along with the carrier bills and handling bills of the shipment.

(vi) Import Haulage: Next step is the transportation of the goods from the warehouse to the final destination of the intended receiver. This can be facilitated by a freight forwarder, or in some cases, the consignee or the importer can also choose to collect the cargo himself.

This process is followed in both ocean and air freight.

32.2. Blockchain in real-time tracking of ship

Now let's see the challenges faced by this sector and how Blockchain can help in making international trade much smoother.

Real-time tracking of shipment: Tracking the progress of any shipment is a complex process that is prone to human error, fraud and smuggling. But with Blockchain, this issue can be resolved. Blockchain will record all the transactions of shipping in an immutable encrypted format. This information can then be shared with all the stakeholders involved in international trade, including exporters, importers, and customs authorities, and that too in almost real-time. Thus through Blockchain, all the stakeholders will have real-time access about the status and the whereabouts of the shipment.

At each stage of the transaction, the relevant participants will update the Blockchain, and that information will instantly be available to all the parties.

This instant availability of information would eliminate documentation delays. For example, customs clearance delays can be eliminated through Blockchain. If you want to learn more about how Blockchain can facilitate customs clearance, you can refer to the next chapter, "Blockchain Application in Customs."

Recording shipment temperature during transportation: Certain perishable items like pharmaceutical drugs, vaccines, chemicals, and dairy products remain effective only if kept at the desired temperature throughout their journey. IoT sensors installed on the cargo measure its temperature and record the same on the Blockchain. Any fluctuations in the temperature will also be recorded on the Blockchain.

Thus, it will help the buyer to ensure that the goods he received were maintained at the desired temperature according to the manufacturer's guidelines and are effective.

32.3. Blockchain in Trade Finance

With the implementation of smart contracts, payment cycles will be reduced, and manufacturers will get paid for their shipments much faster. International trade involves a lot of complexity owing to various factors such as distance, different sets of rules and regulations in different countries, and difficulty in knowing the other party personally.

Due to this complexity involved, the use of the **letter of credit** has become a common norm in international trade. A letter of credit, abbreviated as LC, is a letter from a buyer's country bank guaranteeing that a buyer's payment to a seller will be received on time and for the correct amount.

In the event when the buyer is unable to make payment for the purchase, the bank will be required to cover the full or remaining amount of the purchase. For instance, a company in the USA seeks to import goods from a supplier in Australia. The importer needs to pay for those goods, but he is hesitant to pay in advance as he wants to assure that the goods he will receive will be as good as he ordered. At the same time, the exporter is also hesitant to ship the goods, as there is no assurance that payment will be received for the goods supplied.

In such cases, the importer's bank issues a letter of credit promising to pay exporter once all the documents of shipment are provided by the exporter.

Thus letters of credit (LC), in essence, provide effective risk mitigation for the trading parties. But still, there are a few challenges that leads to delayed payments to the exporters. For instance,

- LCs are evaluated on the basis of trade documents and not on the actual delivery or quality of goods; therefore, any error in terminology or interpretation of the compliance requirements often leads to disputes between trading parties.
- Further, the letter also mandates the bank to ensure that the documents presented by the seller completely adhere to the LC terms and conditions.

Thus, the issuing bank must carefully evaluate whether the documents submitted by the seller comply with the LC. Therefore, payment delays occur if there is any error in the data entry in the LC contracts.

But this can be simplified with a Blockchain-based system. Using Blockchain, a letter of credit can be issued as a smart contract between the bank and the seller to guarantee payment to the seller. The network consensus mechanism of Blockchain ensures that there is only a single version of the LC draft at any given time and that all parties can view and work on this version based on their access rights. After being reviewed and accepted by the exporter, the LC is finalized as a contract between the issuing bank and the exporter.

Now, all the relevant stakeholders will have visibility into the LC process, and they can easily highlight and resolve discrepancies if any.

Since all the shipment-related documents will be available on the Blockchain, therefore if all the conditions defined in the smart contract are met, the smart contract gets executed, and an automatic payout will be triggered to the exporter without any delays.

32.4. Blockchain in cargo insurance

Cargoes that move internationally, either by sea or air, are insured against losses that can occur during their transportation. Even today the process of cargo insurance has many challenges around it. Blockchain can provide a number of benefits to cargo insurance and can make it a better experience

- **Loss assessment:** The global Blockchain platform will connect all the stakeholders and insurance companies to shared distributed ledgers that will capture data about the loss of cargo and exposure of cargo to unfavorable conditions that can make it ineffective. For this, IoT sensors will be attached to the cargo that will upload information about any loss on the shared ledger. For example, in case a ship sinks or the temperature fluctuates above the desired range, which can spoil the cargo, this information will be recorded on the Blockchain. This recorded information will then help the insurance companies in better assessment and calculation of the insurance claim coverage.

- **Claim Handling:** Through Blockchain, all the stakeholders involved, including the insurers, will have access to all the documents related to the shipment. Therefore in case of any insurance claims, this will reduce the time taken to receive the relevant documents from the concerned parties.

32.5. Scalability concerns

(i) Storing the entire shipment documents, LC, IoT data, etc., on Blockchain is very costly; thus, distributed file storage IPFS can provide low-cost off-chain storage to store this data. IPFS has been explained in detail in Chapter 15.

(ii) To make the Blockchain scalable for its use in international trade, layer 1 (discussed in Chapter 12) and layer 2 (discussed in Chapter 13) scaling solutions will be required to be implemented.

Chapter 33: Blockchain in customs

Any cross-border trade involves a large number of stakeholders, including producers, logistic companies, and distributors through whom vast amounts of goods and wealth travel. Further cross-border trading also involves many legal formalities like contracts, certificates, customs, and approvals from various regulatory bodies. Even though many authorities are involved in any cross-border trade, the most notable authority in any cross-border trade is Customs. The role of the customs is to ensure that all the permits obtained are valid, all the goods have been lawfully declared, and all the defined regulatory requirements have been met.

33.1. Challenges of collecting customs duties

Customs duty is a very crucial component of any international trade; it is an indirect tax levied on both imports and exports by customs authorities for international shipments. This tax is collected by the government to

- generate revenue that is used for the country's development and economic growth of the citizens.
- Prevent smuggling of goods.
- Another essential reason for imposing customs duty is to maintain domestic manufactured products equally competitive with imported goods.

Today's customs handling requires significant manpower to maintain safety, customs evaluation, and regulations. Moreover, customs clearance is a tedious task and takes a lot of time, sometimes even weeks, if proper documentation is not provided or some paperwork is incorrect.

33.2. Blockchain in customs declaration

The shared ledger Blockchain technology can have a huge impact on customs services and help make the whole process swift and transparent. Let's understand how:

(i) Blockchain will record all the trade transactions chronologically, which can then be shared with all the concerned parties involved in the supply chain, thus minimizing the risk of fraud. The complete information about the shipment, including the proof of purchase, clearance form, bill of lading, and insurance, will be recorded on the Blockchain and will be accessible to suppliers, transporters, buyers, regulators, and auditors.

Therefore, through Blockchain, Customs authority could see the necessary data like the seller, buyer, price, quantity, carrier, insurance, etc., that has been tied with the goods that need to be declared for customs clearance.

(ii) With this transparency provided by Blockchain technology, Customs authorities and other border agencies would have real-time updates of any trade happening, which would significantly improve their efficiency for risk analysis and will reduce the burden of manual verification to validate declarations. This, in turn, would lead to faster Customs declaration and reduced end-to-end processing time.

(iii) There are growing concerns about the product quality and authenticity of the products that are traded. Therefore relevant licenses, permits, certificates, and other authorizations are required at the time of Customs clearance, depending on the nature of the declared goods and related national regulatory requirements to keep a check on illegal trading. All of these certificates if uploaded on the Blockchain, can be accessed easily from anywhere. Once implemented, this would also minimize the risk of data manipulation.

(iv) Moreover, as the customs authority will have access to all the shipment related documents present on the Blockchain, it can automatically clear the goods that have been 'pre-screened' by them on the shared ledger at an earlier stage. This would eliminate the need to withhold these goods at the time of declaration, which is the case currently, where the shipment takes a lot of time to get customs clearance, and because of this, the delivery of goods gets delayed.

(v) Further, this would also decrease auditing and accounting costs as well.

33.3. Blockchain in combating Tax Fraud

In many cases of international trade, tax fraud occurs, in which there is a wide gap between the expected value-added tax (VAT) revenues and the revenue that is actually collected. When goods are imported into a country with a VAT regime, import VAT is charged as a percentage of the value of the imported goods.

Because of transparency in the supply chain provided by Blockchain, frauds and errors will be much easier to detect because the system will provide clear and transparent information about all the transactions. Thus making the whole system more robust and reliable.

Additionally, all the transactions between an importer and an exporter can be handled by smart contracts, which are self-executing contracts and get executed when the predefined conditions are met. These smart contracts can be used to automate the VAT collection process and thus bring more transparency to the system.

In this setup, an automatic payment equivalent to the amount of VAT payable will be deducted from the buyer's payment to the seller and will be released to the concerned department at the time of clearance of the goods. The remaining pool of money, after deducting VAT, can then be sent to the seller of the goods.

Thus, minimizing any chance of fraud or false declarations.

33.4. Scalability concerns

(i) Storing all the documents required during customs clearance, including licenses, permits, certificates, and other authorizations, etc., on Blockchain is very costly; thus, distributed file storage IPFS can provide low-cost off-chain storage to store this data. IPFS has been explained in detail in Chapter 15.

(ii) To make the Blockchain scalable for its use in customs, layer 1 (discussed in Chapter 12) and layer 2 (discussed in Chapter 13) scaling solutions will be required to be implemented.

Section 4

Blockchain in Advanced Technologies

Chapter 34: Blockchain in E-commerce

The E-Commerce industry has disrupted the way we shop & live, and Blockchain is on its path to disrupting eCommerce. The E-commerce marketplace like Amazon or e-Bay is a place or a website where one can find different brands of products coming from multiple vendors, shops, or persons showcased on the same platform. The entire marketplace runs on one software infrastructure, allowing all the vendors to sell their goods under the umbrella of one website. In terms of revenue, these companies take a percentage of the sales on any product sold across the platforms. But despite the considerable benefits they provide to both buyers and sellers, marketplace companies constantly are facing common problems and challenges. The implementation of Blockchain technology in the eCommerce marketplace can overcome these problems and ignite a significant shift by establishing a decentralized economy. Let's now study in detail about these problems faced by the eCommerce industry and how Blockchain can transform the eCommerce marketplace.

34.1. Blockchain in payment

Through Blockchain technology, payment methods for eCommerce can be revamped. Payment can be done through cryptocurrencies. Blockchain-based cryptocurrencies are incredibly comfortable to use. Traditional transfers often take long, especially sending money across continents may take up to several days to accomplish. Cryptocurrency transfers, on the contrary, only take up a few minutes.

Also, Blockchain-based currencies are extremely secure to transact with. Because of peer-to-peer and distributed digital ledger technology, it is tough to hack into the process and conduct fraud. Cryptocurrencies don't require the customer to expose sensitive data such as a credit card number. While eCommerce is responsible for billions of transactions each year, there are scores of customers who experience credit card fraud or card-not-present (CNP) fraud, which is also a type of credit card fraud. It can occur when a hacker obtains a cardholder's name, billing address, account number, three-digit security code, and card expiration date to make an online purchase. On many websites, there is a provision to store this information to ease the purchases as every time, the customer is not required to add the credit card details every time to make payments. But if these marketplaces become victims of cyberattacks, the credit card information of the users can be stolen.

Credit card fraud can be mitigated by implementing Blockchain technology. Instead of adding credit or debit card information, the customer authorizes a transfer from his or her own personal wallet to that of a recipient. The transaction details, including the amount to be sent, recipient address, etc., are hashed, and the hashed transaction is then signed using the sender's private key. Anyone on the network with the user's public key can validate the authenticity of the transaction but can never know the details of the transaction and the information about the sender. It is because hashes are one-way functions, which simply means if you know the hash, you cannot decrypt it to find the corresponding input. Thus, making it one of the safest modes of transaction. In addition to being decentralized, secure, and relatively easy to implement, sending and receiving money will become as convenient as scanning a QR code.

34.2. Blockchain in data security

One of the other problems with existing e-commerce platforms is how data is stored. E-commerce platforms are home to a very large amount of data, most of them collected directly from customers and retailers when they are registered on any given eCommerce platform. The customer's data is stored on centralized servers where it is vulnerable to cyberattacks, and thus a substantial amount of data can be stolen. However, with a Blockchain-based e-commerce platform, it is virtually impossible to suffer such attacks since Blockchain platforms are decentralized, which in turn means customer data is also decentralized.

34.3. Blockchain in dispute resolution

Dispute resolution on the Blockchain platform will be easy. On the Blockchain platform, the information about the buyer, the seller, and even the marketplace with a record of the transaction can be stored that is irrefutable, removing the possibility of fraud and dispute that can lead to lengthy resolution at the expense to both the buyer and the seller. Each and every step involved in the purchasing process is recorded and time-stamped on the Blockchain, from the buyer placing the order and making payment to the seller receiving payment, shipping the product purchased, and ultimately the buyer's receipt of the product when the product is delivered.

34.4. Blockchain in supply chain management

Blockchain technology can also improve supply chain management of E-commerce. Supply chain management is perhaps one of the most pressing concerns every eCommerce business faces. Since the supply chain is a critical element of any eCommerce business, Blockchain implementation in this sector will likely solve many problems like:

34.4.1. Provenance Tracking of products

In a Blockchain-based supply chain, record keeping, and provenance tracking becomes easy, as the product information can be accessed with the help of Blockchain-based QR codes and embedded sensors. When a QR code is generated, the Blockchain system puts a unique hash value into the QR code. When the consumer scans the product's QR code to access the information or data, the system first cross-checks the hash value in the QR code. It then compares the hash value of the QR code to the hash value in the Blockchain. By scanning the QR code through dApp, the customer is landed on the authentic web page. On the contrary, the malicious QR code on the products will not be scanned by the dApp. This will also prevent the customers from becoming victims of unethical sellers.

The timeline of a product, right from its inception to where it is at present, can be traced through Blockchain. Every time a product changes hands, the transaction is documented in the Blockchain, creating a complete and permanent history from manufacture to sale. By accurate provenance tracking, it is possible to detect anomalies in any segment of the supply chain. A clearly laid out Blockchain network that can't be tampered with is the key to supporting a fully transparent supply chain where customers can see the order flow of the items they purchase, making a strong foundation for rebuilding consumer confidence.

Thus provenance tracking can also eradicate the risks of frauds and product duplicacy. This also means that retailers can't substitute your purchase with a different, more expensive, or cheaper product. Let's understand it by taking an example.

Suppose the author is selling his digital book for $20 on a Blockchain-powered eCommerce platform. The author can send the digital book to the interested buyer on the Blockchain platform, who could only access it by making a verifiable payment for the correct amount. The amount of the book will be held in escrow. If the transaction satisfies everybody, then the seller gets the payment, and the buyer can access the book. But what if that author tries to cheat? And if he intentionally sends the wrong ebook? This is where the **smart contract** kicks in. The contract stores a book's digital hash code. The buyer has access to that digital hash code before making a purchase. If he receives a book with a different hash code, he can raise a complaint and then the smart contract releases the refund of the full payment that buyer has made for the book.

34.4.2. Blockchain can also be used for Inventory Management

The greater the inventory, the more likely it will be for a customer to find what they are looking for. Because the attention span of your visitors will eventually diminish if they do not find the product that they are searching for, even if they trust the particular eCommerce marketplace for its good customer service. Blockchain technology can help in keeping the real-time tracking of the products which have high demand and, before getting out of stock, will alert the sellers to update their stock on the e-commerce marketplace for customer retention. Thus the management of inventory becomes a whole lot easier by introducing Blockchain in the process.

34.5. Blockchain in curbing fake reviews

Blockchain technology can also help in curbing fake reviews on the online E-commerce platforms. In the case of a face-to-face transaction, the trust issue can be solved easily since buyers and sellers can communicate about the product instantly, and the product is physically presented. But with online purchasing, frequently encountered fake, damaged, or wrong product received makes buyers suspicious about what they saw on the webpage and what they will receive. In this case, recognizing scammers in the sellers before getting them on the e-commerce platform is crucial. Through Blockchain technology, marketplace operators can know the complete information about the sellers, and their customer satisfaction information, thus Blockchain will help marketplace operators to avoid boarding unethical sellers on their platform.

On the other hand, a transparent peer review is also necessary to prevent buyers to buy from untrusted sellers and promote products from trusted ones. Reviews-good or bad also determine the order in which a business appears on an eCommerce marketplace or in a search query result. Sometimes fake reviews deteriorate the reputation of a good company while at the same time promoting a fraudulent one. The reputation of an online enterprise relies on the legitimacy of its reviews. Hence it becomes an utmost concern for online operators to maintain the authenticity of the product service reviews found on their platform. Blockchain technology can be a crucial source to verify the reviews on the products or services and thus can help curb fake reviews by assuring that the reviews are authentic and are provided by those customers who have either used the product or have bought the product from that online marketplace.

Chapter 35: Blockchain-based swarm robotics system

Many upcoming streams are changing the technology landscape, and Robotics is one of them. Robotics has even been referred to as the Next Technological Revolution by many industry experts. Robotics is going to be a multi-billion global industry and is going to have a tremendous impact on many other industries in the coming years.

35.1. Swarm robotics

Whenever we think of robots, we are hardwired to imagine a single, sophisticated robot with jerking movements and a thick voice that we have experienced in various sci-fi movies. Not necessarily; there is a branch of robotics known as "Swarm Robotics" that involves many simple robots. The field of Swarm robotics is inspired by nature. Creatures like insects, fishes, birds, and bees exhibit swarm behavior. These swarms range from a few individuals living in their small natural habitats to millions of individuals living in highly organized colonies. The individuals in these swarms show very poor abilities, but when combined with the intelligence of the whole group, these swarms exhibit great flexibility and robustness in completing complex activities such as path planning, task allocation, and various other complex collective behaviors. Researchers have established the fact that this intelligent collective behavior emerges from local communication and information transmission among these individuals.

Swarm robotics came into being based on this very concept of the collective intelligence of individuals. Swarm robotics is a branch of robotics in which many simple robots are coordinated in a distributed and decentralized way. It operates on the principle of local communication and information transmission between these simple robots. These large numbers of simple robots can perform complex tasks in a much more efficient manner than a single robot. A key advantage of these robotic swarms is their scalability and robustness to failure. And both of these qualities originate from their simple and distributed nature of coordination.

Fig 35-1: Swarm of robots

The number of use cases for robotic swarms is increasing with the decreasing cost of these robotics platforms. Some of the applications include targeted material delivery, where groups of small robots carry big and heavy objects; precision farming, where they support farmers in their agricultural activities; entertainment industry, where groups of these swarm robots come together to form interactive displays; in the nuclear, chemical and biological attack detection, battlefield surveillance, and space exploration, etc.

35.2. Challenges in implementing robotic swarms

However, there are still many grey areas in implementing these robotic swarms, which are proving to be a challenge in their widespread adoption. Some of these challenges include a lack of safety measures, decentralized control, and lack of security protocols for these robotic systems.

Blockchain- The Solution

Enter Blockchain. Blockchain can provide a solution to the challenges faced by these robotic swarms. Implementing Blockchain with these swarm robotic systems can lead to wider adoption of these systems across various industries. Blockchain can make them more secure, reliable, autonomous, and profitable, leading to a mass-scale acceptance of these robotic swarms. In such a system, robots will act as nodes, and the information flow between them will be recorded as transactions on the Blockchain.

Now let's have an in-depth look at the challenges faced by swarm robotic systems and how does the implementation of Blockchain can help to tackle them.

35.3. Blockchain in the transmission of messages

Security is the first and foremost challenge for deploying these systems in large-scale commercial projects. This is very crucial for these systems as the inclusion of any defective or malicious swarm member can compromise the security of the swarm or can put a risk to the completion of the intended goal by the swarm.

Security for robotic swarms fundamentally includes data integrity, data confidentiality, data origin authentication, and entity authentication.
Blockchain technology can be a solution to these security challenges faced by swarm robotic systems as it not only provides a private and reliable peer-to-peer communication network for swarm agents but also has provisions to overcome potential threats, vulnerabilities, and attacks.

Blockchain, with its robust encryption mechanism, including a **public key and digital signature cryptography**, can provide a secure way of transactions happening through shared communication channels. Further, this technology can also prove the identity of a specific agent trying to communicate with other agents. Thus, bringing trust and transparency to the system. The implementation includes generating a pair of private and public keys for each swarm agent. The public key, as the name suggests, will be publicly available in the Blockchain network and provides the address to an agent's main accessible information.

For the sake of simplicity, a public key can be treated as a special account number for the agent. Conversely, a private key can be compared to a password in a traditional system and holds an agent's covert information. Public keys are used for validating the identity of an agent, and private keys are used for executing the transactions. *Refer to Chapter 6 for detailed information on Cryptography and digital signature.*

With public key cryptography, robots can share their public keys with other robots who want to communicate with them. With the availability of these public keys, any robot can send information to any specific robot or robots in the network by encrypting the information with its public key. It ensures that the robot possessing the matching private key can access the information *(Fig 35-2a)*. Since public keys don't have the ability to decrypt messages, the security doesn't get compromised even if it falls into the wrong hands. Besides, this mechanism also prevents information decryption by third-party robots even if they share the same communication channel.

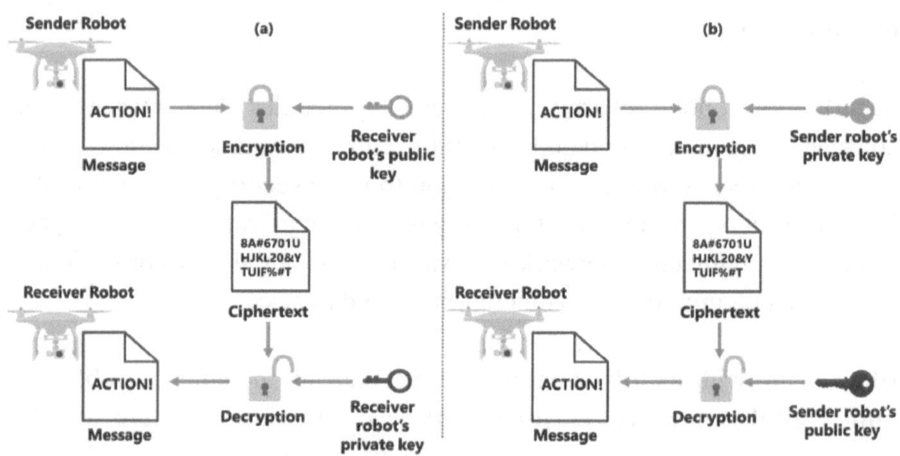

Fig 35-2: Encrypting information with (a) receiver robot's public key and (b) sender robot's private key

Additionally, under digital signature cryptography, these robots can use their own private key to encrypt their messages. In this cryptography, other robots can decrypt the information or the message using the public key of the sender robot *(Fig 35-2b)*. This public key is available to everyone on the Blockchain network. Therefore, the message won't be a secret per se, but it can be used to prove the authorship of that message or information. Because the message is encrypted by a particular robot's private key and therefore it can't be sent by someone else, hence establishing authorship of the message.

Both of these cryptographic techniques can be used to tackle the security loopholes prevalent in Swarm Robotic Systems. On the one hand, public key cryptography ensures that only a specific robot having a specific address can access the content of a message encapsulated in a transaction based on Blockchain technology. On the other hand, digital signature cryptography ensures data origin authentication and entity authentication between robots or third-party agents.

The practical applications of these Blockchain-secured robotic swarms include the **military**, where trustworthy and reliable systems are very much required, and **medical projects** where a team of robots helps in the transportation of medicines and medical records of the patients as in these cases, data confidentiality is the most crucial factor.

35.4. Blockchain in distributed decision making

The individual agents or robots in the swarm are required to reach a global agreement regarding the goal. For example, the path to be taken, obstacles to be avoided, shape to be formed, etc. Therefore, for these swarms to work efficiently, distributed decision-making protocols are required to ensure guaranteed convergence towards a common outcome. Currently, this is still an open problem, and there is no foolproof distributed decision-making protocol that can handle a large number of swarm agents efficiently.

Blockchain is a perfect match for this requirement of robotic swarms. It has the required capability to ensure that the participating agents in a decentralized network always reach a global agreement regarding the end goal. For example, the Blockchain has the provision of distributed voting systems that can be used by these swarm robotic systems whenever they have to reach a global agreement.

Let's understand how this distributed voting system works for these swarms: Whenever a situation arises, when one agent of the swarm needs to get agreement from other agents of the swarm, a special transaction can be issued on the Blockchain network. This transaction will create separate addresses for the possible options that the swarm has to vote on.

For instance, in a scenario, the agents need to decide which path to take out of the 3 paths as visible on the sign board. In this case, the 3 possible options are - Path 1, Path 2, and Path 3, respectively. Now one of the agents will create 3 different addresses for these 3 options. The swarm members can then vote as per their understanding of the situation on these addresses.

As this information is publicly available on the network, every robot can monitor the results of the voting process and act accordingly. In this case, as all of them can see that Route 2, got the maximum votes, the robot swarm will accept it as the group decision, and they all will take Route 2.

Hence Blockchain provides a very good protocol for distributed decision-making where agreements can be obtained swiftly and in a secure and auditable way.

35.5. Blockchain and service robot systems

There are various robotic swarms that have been programmed to find various natural resources, and objects. A very critical part of their activity is to establish the ownership and rights on a found object or resource on behalf of their owner or operator. For instance, a special robotic swarm programmed to do cave explorations finds a hidden treasure in one of the caves. The swarm issues a discovery document on the Blockchain claiming the ownership of that treasure on behalf of their owner. The transaction may include the discovered objects, relevant reports, coordinates of the place of discovery, and images if feasible. A hash is generated along with the time stamp for this document. This, then, gets included as a transaction on the Blockchain as proof of discovery. In this way, Blockchain can provide the required framework for ensuring that robotic swarms operate under a specific legal regulation as they become mainstream and gets integrated into human society.

Thus, it can be said that Blockchain technology could be a game changer for the mass adoption of Swarm Robotic Systems. The amalgamation of these 2 upcoming technologies can open doors for new technological advancements and even new business models that we can't even imagine today.

Chapter 36: Blockchain in 3D printing

3D printing is a process of making physical three-dimensional solid objects from a digital file. The creation of a 3D printed object is achieved using additive processes. In an additive process, an object is created by successively adding material layer by layer. The magic behind 3D printing is that using special equipment, it is possible to join and solidify special materials, like liquid molecules or powder grains, to create a three-dimensional object, all under the control of computer software. Traditional manufacturing relies on subtracting or cutting out a piece of metal or plastic, called a **subtractive process**. On the other hand, 3D printing uses an additive process, carefully layering materials on top of each other to build parts. This is the reason 3D printing is also called **"additive manufacturing."** Also, 3D printing enables you to produce complex shapes using less material than traditional manufacturing methods. 3D printing can even enable people to manufacture objects easily from the comfort of their own homes. So, what can you do with a 3D printer? A lot, it turns out. Does your kid want a new toy? 3D print it! Your door handle has broken? 3D print a new one. Want to custom design a teacup? Go ahead with your 3D printer!

36.1. Steps involved in 3D printing

There are 3 main steps in 3D printing.

(i) The first step is the **preparation** just before printing. Just like a document printer requires a digital document, a PDF or DOC file for printing, 3D printers require digital design files of 3D objects. This 3D file can be created using software or can simply be downloaded from an online marketplace. For example, let's say you want to make a cover for your phone. So, you would first need to custom design or download a digital file with no copyright issue that encodes the design of the phone cover. 3D printing always begins with a digital 3D model, which is the blueprint of the physical object.

(ii) The second step is the **actual printing process**. The 3D digital model is then sliced by the printer's software into thin, 2-dimensional layers and then turned into a set of instructions in machine language for the printer to execute. For printing, you need to choose which material will be best to achieve the specific properties required for your object. The materials that can be used in 3D printing include plastics, ceramics, resins, metals, sand, textiles, biomaterials, glass, and food. Let's come to our example of 3D printing a phone cover. Choose a material for the phone cover, preferably plastic, and load your 3D printer with enough material. A normal Inkjet printer creates a document by depositing ink on paper. A 3D printer creates a physical object by depositing many layers of materials on a print bed. When your 3D printer is loaded with materials, the computer will now send instructions to the 3D printer about how to deposit the material layer by layer to recreate a physical copy of the digital design, like your phone cover in this case.

(iii) The third step is the **finishing process**. When the object is first printed, it can be a final product or an indirect product that requires a mold, assembly, heat, and finishing.

36.2. Applications of 3D printing

3D printing can be used in almost all industries you could think of. Some of the applications of 3D printing include:
(i) 3D printers can be used for rapid prototyping. A prototype is an early sample, model, or initial stage release of a product built to test a concept or process. From an idea to a 3D model to holding a prototype in your hands is a matter of days instead of weeks with the 3D printer.

(ii) Besides rapid prototyping, 3D printing can also be used for rapid manufacturing. Rapid manufacturing is a manufacturing method where businesses use 3D printers for short-run/small-batch custom manufacturing. Automotive companies can print spare parts, tools, and fixtures using 3D printers. Thus, 3D printing can enable on-demand manufacturing to meet individual requirements that would have otherwise been difficult to obtain or have long delivery periods. Also, the ability to print the desired part onsite or closer to operations-as opposed to coming via complex supply chains-saves time and money, reduces transportation costs, reduces labor costs, lowers carbon footprints, and brings agility into the supply chain. Additionally, the production of individual parts and small quantities is also economical.

(iii) 3D printing with concrete can be used in construction. It can be possible to print customized walls, doors, floors, and even complete houses.

(iv) Footwear, eyewear, and jewelry can be created using 3D printers.

(v) 3D printing technology has been used by biotech firms in tissue engineering applications where organs and body parts can be built. Layers of living cells are deposited onto a gel medium and they slowly built up to form three-dimensional structures.

(vi) 3D printed prosthetics are a helpful application of 3D printing. Crowns, dentures, and braces can be created by 3D printing.

36.3. Challenges of 3D printing technology for manufacturing

3D-printing moves through several stages: from initial concept to generating 3D design and then to the actual 3D print. Then comes the post-print process. For additional manufacturing or 3D processes to scale at the industrial level, a series of complex, connected, and data-driven events need to occur. This series of data-driven events is commonly referred to as the **digital thread**. In other words, a digital thread is a single, seamless strand of data that stretches from the initial design concept to the finished part, constituting the information about the design, modeling, production, use, and monitoring of an individual manufactured part.

The ability to dissect, understand, and apply the potentially massive amounts of data throughout the manufacturing process can allow users to enhance and scale their additive manufacturing production and manage the complexities of additive manufacturing. However, the Digital Thread of Additive manufacturing DTAM faces a few challenges like:

- Challenge to create and manage a "digital thread" across the supply chain without being exposed to malicious actors who might tamper with the data and even steal it like crucial 3D designs.
- How to integrate software, multiple printers, and multiple manufacturing locations which are physically disconnected?
- How could the integrity of the "digital thread" across a distributed model with multiple partners can be maintained that may be across diverse geographic locations?
- How could the "digital thread" effectively ensure that raw materials, equipment, processes, and finalized parts meet quality assurance?
- Since the "digital thread" will create significant amounts of data; thus, the challenge is how to record this huge amount of data and events during additive manufacturing or AM process to better understand and utilize this data?

36.4. Blockchain- The Solution

Blockchain technology has the potential to solve the above challenges of the digital thread of additive manufacturing or AM.

Step1 of AM process involves design plus analysis. The 3D image is created using computer-aided software or CAD, which is then analyzed. In this phase, data often switches between CAD systems to analysis tools. This step represents a point of vulnerability in which a 3D print can be corrupted or even stolen, putting the company's intellectual property at risk. On the top of it, the finished state of the printed item can only be as good as the digital instructions the printer receives to manufacture it. As a result, the delivery and security of those digital files are paramount. Here Blockchain technology can play an important role in protecting the 3D files. It can be used to track the origination of each design file and its evolution. The technology can also be used to have a timestamp record of all the changes made to designs and can be distributed across all the concerned departments and multiple organizations. That means every entity involved in any stage of a 3D print is aware of what all the others are doing at any time in a safe and secure manner. Since a Blockchain is decentralized, meaning no single entity owns it, stealing or altering a 3D printed file from a Blockchain is not about tricking a single computer or printer- one has to hack every entity that is a part of Blockchain network, which is extremely difficult, almost impossible. Thus, Blockchain technology will help with cyber risks and Intellectual Property rights (IPR) protection as it is intended to provide an immutable and traceable record of changes.

Step 2 of AM process involves build plus monitor. During this step, the designed 3D image is then sent to the 3D printer. The 3D printer then builds the product by putting down thin layers of material. This is the phase where the digital model created is transformed into a physical product; this is a critical phase as data created in the design phase is used to build a product, and the data used in creation is useful in certification. This phase faces challenges from the distributed nature of AM across the supply chain as product build happens across multiple locations requiring systems and infrastructure to track control, process feedback, and collect data. Additive manufacturing increases not only the importance of digital files but also the number of organizations receiving highly sensitive product data. In the traditional manufacturing model, the company that creates the design files would also handle manufacturing and then shipping the final product. But in the AM supply chain, however, this is no longer the case. In an AM ecosystem, multiple parties attempt to coordinate work together. Thus, 3D printing businesses tend to own a fleet of 3D printers, which can be located in different places. In this scenario, the 3D files can be compromised or hacked, and the design files could fall into unauthorized hands and/or be used to create counterfeit, maliciously modified, or uncertified parts. To make the 3D files resistant to hacking and to ensure that all the 3D printers receive the desired 3D design files, Blockchain can be used to create a distributed network of 3D printers worldwide. Blockchain will record all the transactions of the network of 3D printers and ensure that the printers are printing the desired 3D files. Any modification in the 3D files will be given a new hash and will be recorded in an immutable manner of the distributed ledger. By using Blockchain, manufacturers can monitor and even limit how many copies of a product are printed by the network of 3D printers. This ensures quality standards are met and prevents counterfeits from being made on authorized equipment.

Additionally, the Blockchain ledger will track and store all events associated with the lifecycle of the part design so the provenance of each part can be verified and any errors detected in end products can be traced to their source.

Through Blockchain technology and smart contracts, it can also be possible for an individual or a company to issue licenses to specific users to print a certain number of their 3D images to expand their business. Let's understand it through an example. Suppose company X authorizes company Y to print 100 copies of its IP-protected 3D image. The license will be stored on smart Contract and ensures that only the recipient, company Y, has permission to access the 3D files. Later, company Y's printer verifies the license before starting to print. Additionally, the serial numbers of the separately printed components can be written into the Blockchain to prove the type and quantity having been printed in accordance with the license terms. That lessens or eliminates the possibility of company Y to print only that quantity which is mentioned on the contract rather than printing more copies and then selling them on the gray market.

Step 3 of AM process involves testing, validating, monitoring, delivering, and managing the final product. Test and validate phase of Digital Thread Additive manufacturing involves inspection for both digital design and physical 3D printed product. The major challenge during the test and validation phase is to verify all the records of individual parts with the digital model responsible for its creation. Since Blockchain contains all the transaction records from design concept to physical product thus, it will be possible to understand and track flaws and tolerance measurements, and through Blockchain, it is also easy to validate necessary steps required from creating the design to physical product for the purpose of quality assurance and certifications. All the modifications of data to the original files will also be recorded on the Blockchain, and this whole information may be used for auditing decision trials for better decision-making in the future.

Finally, when a physical part is manufactured, it can be tagged with a unique identification number and then recorded in the Blockchain ledger. By scanning this unique identification number, it is possible to trace back information stored in the digital ledger. The information provides a link between the digital and physical thread that can be used to trace back to its manufacturer. Thus, it would be possible to know if the product is original, copied, or counterfeit.

In the case of manufacturing components in the government and defense sector, the benefits of Blockchain go even beyond protecting against IP theft, as counterfeit parts could threaten safety and national security. In some cases, the original equipment manufacturers can enable suppliers to store designs for replacement parts that they have stopped manufacturing, and thus these suppliers can produce them on the spot with 3D printers. Here, in this case, Blockchain technology can validate that suppliers are using the correct design file and the replacement part is not counterfeit.

36.5. Scalability concerns

(i) Storing all the data about 3D files, analysis, licence, supply chain, etc., on Blockchain is very costly; thus, distributed file storage IPFS can provide low-cost off-chain storage to store this data. IPFS has been explained in detail in Chapter 15.

(ii) To make the Blockchain scalable for its use in 3D printing, layer 1 (discussed in Chapter 12) and layer 2 (discussed in Chapter 13) scaling solutions will be required to be implemented.

Chapter 37: Blockchain-based smartphones

In today's internet world, it is nearly impossible to imagine our phones without internet access. And with the internet in every pocket, the world is increasingly becoming interconnected, and information accessibility is no more a concern. But all of this comes at a cost, which many of us may not even be aware of.

37.1. Challenges faced by cell phones

(i) In this interconnected world, users don't own their digital identities; they don't own their digital data; in fact, they don't even own their personal data. Whether it's behavioral data, commercial data, health data, browsing data, or some other data, all of that is owned by a handful of companies, and users don't have a clue about how this data is used and who all can access it.

(ii) Every app or game you download on your phone wants your personal info, and it will even incentivize you with extra features, easier connectivity, and bonus in-game items in exchange for your personal information. Most of you would have used your social media accounts to sign up for one app or the other on your mobile, but while doing so, you must not have even realized that you're giving them free access to your personal information, which they can use and sell as they see fit. Though some ethical app providers or creators clearly mention that they won't share your data with any third party, there are others that stay silent on this and don't clearly mention if they are sharing your information with third parties or not. That's because they are.

(iii) In today's world, when your mobile acts as your bank, wallet, your personal mailbox, you can't afford to think of losing it. Losing your phone is like losing your keys, wallet, and your personal and critical data. Simply put, it could be devastating if someone stole or found your mobile phone.

(iv) Another security concern arises when users don’t update their phones with the latest software upgrades provided by their Mobile Manufacturer. Most recent and updated version of the operating system of a mobile phone is generally more secure than its predecessors, but the problem is that many Android or Apple users never update the operating system on their phones, which in turn, makes such mobile devices more vulnerable to hacking than the updated ones.

37.2. Blockchain- The Solution

Blockchain-based smartphones can overcome the problems faced by cell phones today.

(i) The biggest advantage of a Blockchain-based smartphone is that it allows you to keep possession of your data, unlike today's smartphones where all of your online data is being held by Google, Apple, or similar tech giants.

A blockchain-based smartphone is effectively an Android phone with all the functionalities similar to what we have in normal smartphones, but one feature that differentiates it from the rest of smartphones is that it has an additional locked area that is nearly impossible to be hacked into. This Blockchain-based smartphone has a parallel micro-operating system that makes it safe, secure, and hackproof.

(ii) Blockchain-based smartphones also support decentralized applications also known as "dApps." The look and feel of these dApps is similar to the normal mobile apps we use today, but these dApps run on public, peer-to-peer networks instead of private servers of big tech companies. From a security point of view, dApps are more resilient and secure than traditional mobile apps. Being decentralized, the major advantage of a dApp is that it would never be subject to centralized control.

For example, consider a centralized application such as Twitter. Twitter users are, ultimately, at the mercy of Twitter. Twitter could conceivably choose to censor or even remove any user from its platform. On the contrary, dApps are leaderless and instead are controlled by their users. Users or members of the decentralized Apps can vote on how the applications should evolve or change. Furthermore, any changes to the dApps can only be performed through consensus.

Refer to Chapter 14 for a detailed explanation of dApps

(iii) Social key recovery is another important feature in Blockchain-based mobile phones. In social key recovery, essentially, a user can choose a small group of contacts and give them parts of his keys. If the user loses his keys, he can recover them piece by piece from his contacts.

(iv) On Blockchain based smartphones, it is much easier for people to use their cryptocurrencies to make micropayments on websites or for using dapps.

37.3. Blockchain smartphones in the market

Blockchain smartphone is not just a concept anymore and multiple companies have already launched their blockchain smartphones in the market. For instance,

(i) **HTC's Exodus 1 smartphone:** This phone aims to provide a secure mobile environment for Blockchain transactions and crypto wallets. For this additional security, the HTC's smartphone provides a safe, encrypted digital space that is separate from the main Android OS.

With the integration of HTC's Zion wallet, the phone serves as a hardware wallet as well. The crypto wallet is configured to store currencies like Bitcoin, Litecoin, and Ethereum. This is much more secure than storing a wallet on your regular phone using an Android app.

In this Blockchain-based system, you hold your private keys and, for any transaction, you need to sign it.

Additionally, there are around 20 apps in this smartphone, including a personal tracker that can sell your data in exchange for cryptocurrencies with your due permission. HTC has also partnered with Opera to allow users to make micropayments to various sites. Micropayments can be a game-changer because with this feature, people will now be able to transfer very small amounts of money without the need to deal with additional transaction fees.

In case you lose your phone, the key recovery mechanism will let you recover your keys. This mechanism splits your key into five different parts so that you can share it among your family and close friends. When you lose your phone, you can call up three out of the five friends to recover it. But you still need your biometrics or password to avoid any possible security breach, which can happen if these contacts get together behind your back to access your key and start signing transactions.

(ii) The second blockchain-based smartphone in the market is **Finney Phone,** launched by a Switzerland-based startup Sirin Labs. The smartphone has a built-in "cold-storage" crypto wallet, distributed ledger consensus, and secure peer-to-peer resource sharing. Let's understand what is meant by cold storage? From a security perspective, there are two kinds of cryptocurrency wallets: "hot" wallets and "cold" storage. Both kinds of wallets store cryptographic private keys, but hot wallets are online and thus more easily hackable while on the other hand, cold wallets are kept offline except for a brief window when funds need to be transferred. A hot wallet might be an app, and a cold wallet may take the form of a USB drive or a dedicated hardware device. For example, the cold storage in the Finney phone is cordoned off from the rest of the device, and to spend cryptocurrency from the phone, the user is required to flip out a second screen that activates that part of the phone. Cold storage has the benefit of making you feel safer and therefore making you store more funds than you would in a hot wallet. But there is an added risk of losing your cold storage if you misplace your phone.

Therefore, if a user loses his phone, then he may permanently lose access to his keys in cold storage.

(iii) The third blockchain-based smartphone in the market is **XPhone,** launched by a Singapore based Blockchain device manufacturer named Pundi X. XPhone will let users switch between a traditional mode that supports Android apps and a "Blockchain mode," which will grant access to decentralized apps (dApps) loaded on the device. This smartphone also allows users to make calls, send messages, and transmit data through a fully decentralized Blockchain network.

(iv) Other Blockchain phones include Samsung KlaytnPhone, LG's Blockchain phone, etc. Solana is also planning to launch its Blockchain phone Solana Saga.

As the cryptocurrency and Blockchain industries continue to grow, it's likely that we'll see more Blockchain phones in the market.

Chapter 38: Blockchain for Big Data

The big data era is upon us. Every single day a huge amount of data is getting generated. Facebook alone has more than 300 petabytes of data which contains personal profiles, pictures, videos, and messages of its users. The generation and availability of such a huge data set has led to the introduction of various new domains like Data analytics, Big data, etc.

Data collection and Data analytics have lead to the understanding of the why, when, who, how, and what of human behavior. And this understanding has fired innovation and development across many fronts, be it economical, social, political, or medical. Big data is undoubtedly a big asset for the global economy.

Big data consists of a massive volume of both structured and unstructured data, which is so humongous that it is nearly impossible for traditional systems to process and analyze it. Though companies are collecting data to give their customers a better experience, there are massive challenges around this data, like data privacy and data security to name a few. There have been many cases of data theft, and misuse of personal data that have lead to a sense of insecurity and distrust in this ecosystem. But at the same time, the potential of big data in making striking contributions to the development of global economy can't be neglected.

And therefore, the need of the hour is to develop an ecosystem where the benefits of big data can be reaped without compromising the security and privacy of the users' data. Enter Blockchain Technology. Blockchain is a perfect companion for big data that can complement it to mitigate these issues. Blockchain further helps in better data management of huge volumes and variety of data that is getting generated incessantly day in and day out. Let's discuss the benefits of Blockchain for Big data in detail:

38.1. Economical Data Storage

As discussed earlier, big data involves massive volume of data and therefore it becomes very crucial to have the right infrastructure to store this big data.

Besides, the volume of this data keeps on increasing day by day. Storing such voluminous data using conventional cloud storage doesn't prove to be an economical option for the businesses. Additionally, in many cases due to certain business requirements, multiple copies of the same data are maintained at different locations, which further leads to an extra burden for the businesses. But with the implementation of Blockchain these costs can be reduced as secured off-Blockchain peer-to-peer distributed file storage system IPFS provides a more economical solution for data storage. The hash of the uploaded data is then stored on the Blockchain and accessed through the smart contract. Any modification in the uploaded file would change its hash. Anyone knowing the hash of the file can retrieve the file from IPFS and read its data. *IPFS has been explained in detail in Chapter 15.*

38.2. Trustworthy External Data

In today's digital age, there are too many touch points that a consumer or a potential consumer interacts with. To get a better understanding of their customer, every business collects data from various sources like social media, external research, purchased lists, etc.. There is always a lack of trust for such external data as businesses can't verify its authenticity. Even though the external data is fed into the internal analytics system but the insights generated are not foolproof and, therefore not reliable. But with the implementation of Blockchain, it is much easier to establish the veracity of this external data as the complete path of the data collected can be verified using the immutable record on the ledger. Therefore implementation of Blockchain in big data analytics brings in a higher degree of confidence for the data collected from external sources.

38.3. Data Traceability and Auditing

With the implementation of Blockchain, datasets become immutable and completely traceable. Blockchain technology provides data visibility and data consistency to all the stakeholders involved the network. The datasets can be audited as the complete data trail is available on the shared ledger right from its source. In particular, supply chain data analytics require this kind of data verification for generation of better business insights.

Additionally, Blockchain technology rejects any dataset that can't be verified and it is even marked suspicious. Because of which the insights are generated only from verified datasets thus making them more valuable and accurate.

38.4. Secure Data

Data security is one of the key concerns for any big data analytics operation. But with Blockchain it can be mitigated. And that is exactly why Blockchain has been getting accepted by many of the financial institutions. Additionally, Retail and Healthcare Industries are ripe for disruption by Blockchain as they are in dire need of a platform that can provide security to the sensitive information residing with them.

38.5. Real-Time Analytics

One of the most exciting use case of Blockchain in Big Data is its potential to detect real-time fraudulent activities. In the current scenario, banking and other related institutions have always relied on reactive or retrospective data analytics to detect any form of fraudulent activities. Simply put fraud can only be identified once it has happened, and there is no way to stop it from happening in real time. But with Blockchain, banking and financial institutions can check every transaction in real time. Thus, predictive analysis can be carried out on this up-to-date data to find patterns of risky or fraudulent transactions on the fly and prevent any possible mishap.

38.6. Scalability concerns

(i)) Storing the entire data on Blockchain is very costly and will significantly slow the processing on Blockchain. Thus, distributed file storage IPFS can provide low-cost off-chain decentralized storage. IPFS has been explained in detail in Chapter 15.

(ii) To make the Blockchain scalable, layer 1 (discussed in Chapter 12) and layer 2 (discussed in Chapter 13) scaling solutions will be required to be implemented.

Chapter 39: Blockchain and Artificial Intelligence (AI)

Whether you know it or not, you are interacting with AI systems day in and day out. For example, when you search on your favorite search engine or shop online from your favorite e-commerce website, the suggestions you see are based on Artificial Intelligence.

Artificial intelligence and Blockchain have been referred to as the major disruptors of the coming decade by many industry experts. In this chapter, let us examine how the interplay of these two technologies can be an irresistible proposition for the stakeholders.

Advantages of Using Blockchain with Artificial intelligence

39.1. Rise of Better Data Models

AI requires data and not just data- it requires a massive amount of data. In the current scenario, business models created by AI depend on the data produced by these businesses and their partners. The first thing that comes to mind when we hear the word data sharing is privacy. So quite naturally, when it comes to data sharing by these businesses for the AI system to work, there is always a risk of data breach, abuse, and misuse of the organizational data.

But for AI, the more data you feed, the more reliable insights and predictions it produces. Therefore the requirement for an AI system to work in a business setting is an unlimited and barrier-free access to information from the complete business ecosystem.

For granting this uninterrupted data access to the AI system, the required data security assurance can be provided by the Blockchain to these businesses. Blockchain and IPFS are safe haven for storing personal and private data of individuals data as the data resides in a decentralized network with no single entity being its owner. Thus, the stakeholders would be more comfortable sharing the relevant data on the Blockchain platform. Data from all the relevant stakeholders and departments can be integrated with a common data mining platform, and then relevant insights can be extracted by the AI analytical tool.

For instance, insights from a smart AI healthcare system can provide an exact diagnosis of your issue based on your medical scans and medical records or the movie recommendations by Netflix or Amazon based on your history.

In these scenarios, the data fed into the AI systems of these service providers is very personal and should remain secure in all possible scenarios. These service providers spend a huge sum of money on securing their customers' private data, as any breach of this data could wreak havoc for them legally as well as financially. But with Blockchain, the data is stored in an encrypted state. Thus, leading to better security management of consumers' data by these service providers along with better consumer insights.

Further smart contracts could be implemented to define the way of usage of the shared data. Hence mitigating any chances of data losing its credibility or its value. Once AI systems get access to this uninterrupted, decentralized pool of data, they can deliver smart insights based on the studied patterns, behaviors, and other relevant aspects of the data. This large pool of data will ensure that the insights are closer to reality. Thus, delivering real business value to all the stakeholders involved.

39.2. Better understanding of the decisions made by AI systems

AI can assess a huge volume of data with a large set of independent variables, based on their relevance to achieving the desired results. And because of the huge complexity involved, many a times, we humans are unable to understand the logic used by these AI systems to reach a specific result or insight.

But with Blockchain, decisions made by AI will be recorded on the shared ledger on a datapoint-by-datapoint basis. This will make it much easier for us humans to audit the decision of AI systems by looking at the decision trail. This transparency in the decision-making process will increase the level of trust in them and their decisions.

39.3. Smarter and Transparent Predictions

AI helps businesses to predict the outcome of various planned and unplanned events before they actualize. Though, many a times these predictions may be incorrect due to faulty data generated by the systems or sometimes due to defective analytical models used by AI systems.

But with the implementation of Blockchain technology, it would be easier to authenticate the data generated, and the working of the analytical methods as the relevant parameters could be regularly monitored on a decentralized system. This increased probability of the availability of error-free data sets will lead to better predictions by the AI systems. For example, in the case of e-commerce and physical retail outlets, AI has enriched the shopping experience for shoppers and monetization for retailers. The smart prediction systems and analytics platform is being implemented by many of these retailers. Retailers can predict the best-suited product for a customer even before the customer walks in the store or visits their online portal.

But there are many grey areas where these AI prediction systems have to work on the unauthenticated or unverified data source to give these predictions. Many times data on the supplier's product quality can't be verified in the current scheme of things. Imagine a scenario where the AI system predicts a product from one of these suppliers as best suited for a particular customer or set of customers, and the product quality is not upto the mark. This could lead to a poor customer experience and a bad brand reputation for the retailer.

But with the implementation of Blockchain, claims about the quality and specs of a product from the suppliers can be easily verified as the complete information about the sourcing, transportation, and its production would be available on the shared ledger. This makes the supplier more accountable, which results in only the best quality products available for sale by the retailing companies

39.4. Birth of Data marketplaces

The rise of Blockchain will give rise to personal data marketplaces. As the data stored on Blockchain is secure, users will start storing their personal data and preferences on Blockchain.

So quite naturally the adoption of Blockchain would first create a cleaner and better organized personal data. The natural progression to this event would be the selling of this organized data on data marketplaces to be consumed by various companies specializing in AI modelling and insight generation. This easy availability of diverse datasets will lead to a rise of many small players and will neutralize the competitive advantage of tech giants who currently have a monopoly over the users' data.

39.5. Increased Trust on Autonomous Virtual Agents

Sometime in the future AI powered autonomous virtual agents will be able to perform tasks without human intervention. You must have seen many sci-fi movies where machines take over the world of humans. Though that is the extreme end of the spectrum but still a plausible one. To avoid any such catastrophic event, a set of rules, directives, and instructions that are secure, tamper proof, and not owned by a single entity will need to be defined.

Blockchain, along with smart contracts, has the perfect solution for this. With the implementation of smart contracts, predetermined conditions will be defined for these AI systems to operate. This will reduce the probability of any faulty operational outcome by these Autonomous Virtual agents as the whole system would be governed by smart contracts residing on a decentralized and immutable ledger. In such a transparent, secure and controlled system, the probability of things going haywire at any point of time are minimal even without any human intervention.

Therefore we can safely assume that the implementation of Blockchain with AI can create a future where instead of imagining those dreadful sci-fi movie scenes, we can imagine a much better and more secure human-machine collaboration.

39.6. Scalability concerns

(i) Storing the users' personal data, business data, data for machine learning, data, predictions, and insights generated by AI tools, etc., on Blockchain is very costly and will significantly slow the processing on Blockchain. Thus, distributed file storage IPFS can provide low-cost off-chain decentralized storage to store data. IPFS has been explained in detail in Chapter 15.

(ii) To make the Blockchain scalable for its use in AI, layer 1 (discussed in Chapter 12) and layer 2 (discussed in Chapter 13) scaling solutions will be required to be implemented.

Section 5

Blockchain in Healthcare

Chapter 40: Blockchain in Electronic Health Records (EHR)

The healthcare industry generates abundant health data from various sources. The meaningful use of health data can improve the decisions of healthcare providers and patient outcomes. The adoption of digitalized healthcare records, referred to as electronic health records (EHRs), provides an opportunity for healthcare data analytics and the coordination of results with the care of patients. For this, timely health information exchange is needed to provide patients with coordinated and efficient care across healthcare facilities. However, there are security and privacy concerns about the sharing of sensitive health data of the patients.

40.1. Cyberattacks

Electronic health records (EHRs) of an individual are very unstructured and controlled by healthcare providers in their respective central databases. These databases lack interoperability, security and are vulnerable to cyberattacks or hacking.

Cyberattacks targeting healthcare institutions have increased exponentially. These attacks can cause serious damage as many healthcare institutes cannot operate after/during a cyberattack, rendering the whole institution useless and thus, devoiding needy patients of their healthcare needs. It is not only the operations of hospitals that are affected; the patients' sensitive medical data are at stake, as hospitals store the patients' data related to the appointment, reports, medical history, and prescriptions, along with other vital information in their central databases.

40.1.1. DoS and DDoS attacks

Most healthcare providers often lose their patients' data due to Denial of Service (DoS) or Distributed Denial of Service (DDoS) attacks. In a Denial of Service (DoS) attack, the attackers overwhelm the target healthcare computer system with a high number of processes, requests, and bandwidth usage. The attackers' goal is to flood the system with more traffic than the server can handle so that it cannot be used for its intended purpose, like preventing patients from scheduling appointments and preventing doctors from sending or receiving important information. These attacks can even crash the system, leading to the loss of patients' data. In the DoS, one attacking machine is used *(Fig 40-1a),* but in the case of a DdoS attack, a swarm of attacking machines is used to exhaust the victim's computer system *(Fig 40-1b)*. Thus, DdoS attacks are more severe than the DoS attacks because the malicious requests to the victim come from different machines, and most of the time, botnets are used for DdoS attacks.

40.1.2. Ransomware attack

In a ransomware attack, the attacker is able to run malware on the healthcare computer system. The malware takes control of the system and encrypts all the data present on the system, rendering it inaccessible. Then, they demand a ransom from the victim in exchange for the decryption key. If the ransom is not paid, the data can be lost forever.

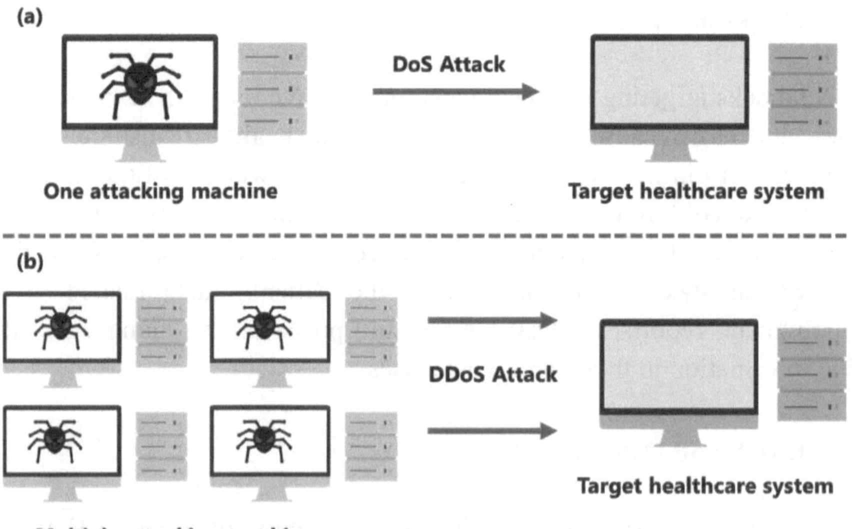

Fig 40-1: (a) DoS attack (from the single machine) and (b) DDoS attack (from multiple machines)

40.1.3. Data breaches

Data breach is a violation in which the confidential and sensitive data of the patients is copied, viewed, stolen, or used by unauthorized individuals. For instance, in 2021, a data breach attack on Florida Healthy Kids Corporation affected 3,500,000 individuals, potentially exposing their personal information such as Social Security numbers, dates of birth, names, addresses, and financial information.

40.2. Challenges in data sharing

Although we have computers in nearly every medical facility and mobile phones in every pocket, we still face difficulty in collecting, exchanging, and sharing our medical history with a new doctor. Sharing medical data between various healthcare providers while maintaining the privacy and integrity of the patient's data is the biggest challenge that health care systems face today.

(i) The health care system is not digitized everywhere in the world. Therefore, many healthcare providers still follow the traditional process and provide prescriptions on paper and graphs. In such a scenario, it becomes difficult for both patients and healthcare providers to refer to these prescriptions whenever required in the future.

(ii) **Lack of interoperability:** The healthcare systems work in silos and lack interoperability. Even the healthcare systems of different departments within the same hospital cannot interact with each other. So you can imagine the level of difficulty when systems of various healthcare providers have to interact with each other.

(iii) **Non-availability of clinic history:** In case of emergency conditions or if a patient wants to change the healthcare provider, it becomes challenging for him to procure his clinical history and share that with the new service provider. All diagnostic tests have to be performed again to know the exact problem, thus resulting in delayed treatment and further aggravation of the issue.

(iv) When the doctor is treating a patient who needs emergency care, it becomes challenging for him to know if the patient is allergic to any specific medicine. Therefore, he has to be extra cautious and has to perform drug allergy tests to validate this because the consequences can be pretty dire if the patient is administered any such medicine that he is allergic to.

(v) It is nearly impossible for hospital pharmacies to have a clear picture of the patient data. This, in turn, becomes a challenge for them to predict the inventory required to meet the needs of hospitals. For example, in the case of a sudden outbreak or some seasonal diseases, the pharmacies can go out of stock due to the non-availability of this data. Further, the drug shortages lead to delayed treatment and force healthcare providers and patients to shift to alternate medicines, decreasing the effectiveness of the treatment.

(vi) Telemedicine, also referred to as telehealth or e-medicine, cannot be used effectively. Telemedicine refers to providing healthcare to patients remotely through phones, computers, etc. It allows the healthcare providers to evaluate, diagnose and treat patients without the need for an in-person visit *(Fig 40-2)*. However, every time a patient consults online, he is required to fill in all his history details. There is no effective way for patients to share their health data with the healthcare provider effectively through remote technology. Moreover, most health reports and consultations are on paper, thus making it cumbersome to be shared online to avail the telemedicine services.

Fig 40-2: Telemedicine

40.3. Blockchain- The Solution

Blockchain technology can provide a secure and sustainable way to share the health data of patients while maintaining control of the patients over their data.

Type of Blockchain used

Private permissioned Blockchain is used when the Blockchain network is required to be created in one healthcare institution only. On the other hand, consortium permissioned Blockchain is used when the consortium of healthcare institutions is intended to become part of the Blockchain network. Permissioned Blockchain means users need to obtain permission to join the Blockchain, which limits the data access of the Blockchain to only authorized users.

(i) Storage of EHR data: The health data for patients who opt to participate in the Blockchain will be encrypted and stored in secured off-Blockchain peer-to-peer distributed file system IPFS. It is because it is very expensive and energy-consuming to store large chunks of data on the Blockchain. The IPFS contains a unified patient medical record database, and the database is distributed across multiple hospitals or different departments of the same network. As it is not a centralized database, loss of any server or workstation does not mean the loss of any patient's data.

Whereas all the transactions referring to EHR requests, exchanges, and the links for EHR data (metadata) will be stored on the main Blockchain.

(ii) Smart contracts: The smart contract on the Blockchain platform is written in Solidity language. It manages the storage of metadata to access EHR data stored on IPFS. Once deployed, the smart contracts can never be modified.

40.4. Proposed Blockchain platform for healthcare facilities

(i) Each healthcare facility will be required to provide at least one Blockchain node, which runs the complete Blockchain on it.

(ii) All the users, such as patients and healthcare providers, can become a part of the Blockchain network through registering on the healthcare dApp. After verifying identities, each Blockchain user will be given a unique ID, represented by a hash value, also called an account address. Two keys are generated: private and public keys *(Fig 40-3)*. The user keeps the private key confidential, and the public key is the account address that can be shared. The private key must sign any transaction related to the account address. A transaction can be defined as a process of uploading, updating, deleting, or exchanging EHR data. All transactions need to ensure the public and private keys are matched before transactions are recorded in the Blockchain.

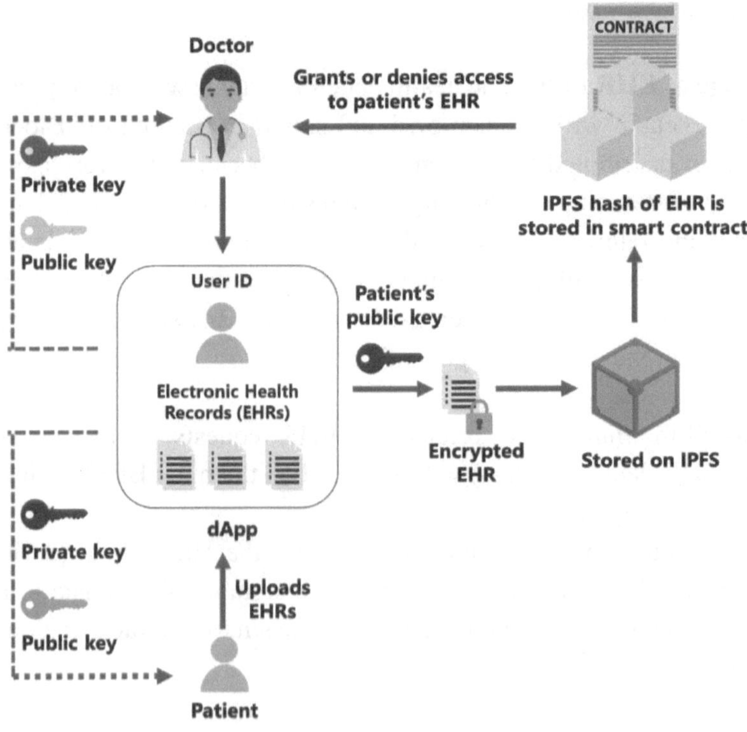

Fig 40-3: Proposed dApp for healthcare facilities

(iii) After registering on the Blockchain network, the healthcare institution or the patients can upload their health records on the dApp. The EHR data of the patients, along with the data of their visits, prescriptions, billing, etc., will be encrypted with their public keys and stored on IPFS *(Fig 40-3)*. Once the documents are uploaded on IPFS, the address of stored documents is stored on the smart contracts. So every time a new document is uploaded, the IPFS hash of the record will be stored on the Blockchain rather than the data. Hence, using IPFS, the space needed to store on blocks is reduced, ultimately reducing every transaction's cost.

The smart contracts on the Blockchain also play an important role in granting, revoking, and denying access to health care providers to retrieve the patients' EHR data from the IPFS.

Therefore, Blockchain and IPFS powered distributed file storage system ensures that everyone on the network has access to the same "data."

40.5. Granting access to EHR data

Blockchain technology, along with smart contracts, will help individuals to maintain their electronic health records and ensure that only authorized healthcare providers can access these Health Records. The individuals/patients will be the owners of their medical data. The hospitals or research institutes will require permission from patients to get access to their data. The patient will have the provision to select who can access his information and for what duration. Individuals can also preauthorize the healthcare providers to see their information during any unforeseen emergencies. Suppose a healthcare provider A wants to access patient X's EHR. For this,

(i) The smart contract on Blockchain verifies the healthcare provider A's permission to access patient X's records.

(ii) When the patient grants permission to the healthcare provider, the smart contract retrieves the patient's metadata, including the location of encrypted EHR data on IPFS.

(iii) Since the patient's HER data stored on IPFS is encrypted with his public key, he has to share his private key, with which the healthcare provider can decrypt his EHR data. For sharing the private key, the patient can encrypt his private key with the public key of the authorized healthcare provider. Thus, the private key of the healthcare provider is used to decrypt the patient's private key, which is then used to access the EHRs. Without the patient's private key, no one can access his data, enabling the patient to control who can access his information.

(iv) The other method of sharing EHRs with healthcare providers without revealing the private key is **proxy re-encryption**. Proxy re-encryption is the process of converting the encrypted data into another encrypted data, which can be decrypted by the recipient's (healthcare provider) private key *(Fig 40-4)*. As discussed, the patient's EHR data stored on IPFS is encrypted with his public key. The patient can use his private key and the healthcare provider's public key to create a re-encryption key.

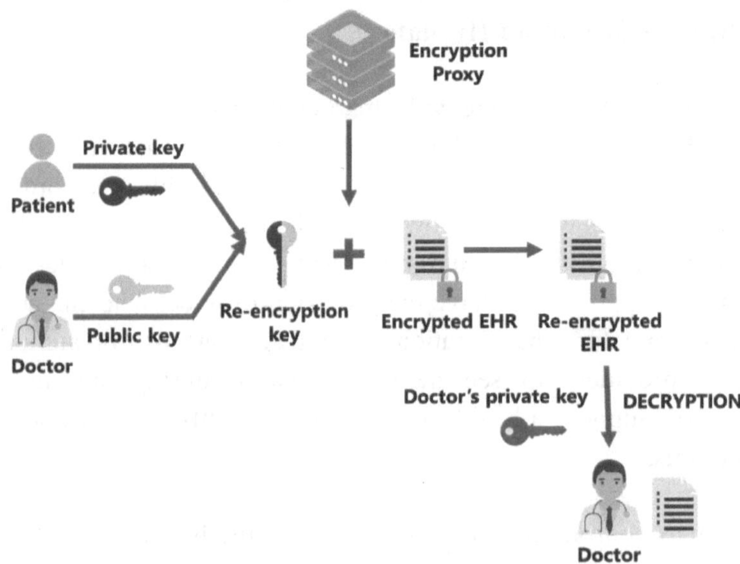

Fig 40-4: Proxy re-encryption to re-encrypt patient's EHR so that it can be decrypted with an authorized healthcare provider's private key

This will allow the encryption server or proxy to re-encrypt the original encrypted data (encrypted with the patient's public key) into a new one so that only the authorized healthcare provider can decrypt it with his private key.

(iv) The Blockchain will also record the timestamp when the healthcare provider received the permission and when they received the EHR data. It allows the patients to revoke access to their records and track how many times their records have been accessed.

40.6. Applications of Blockchain in EHR

40.6.1. Updating EHRs and sharing with multiple healthcare providers

(i) Blockchain technology can provide a truly interoperable network. Whenever a patient undergoes any diagnostic test or consultation, this information can be incorporated into the patient's unique electronic health chain. Even the health-related data collected from smart devices can also be securely incorporated into it. The electronic health record (EHR) data can then be easily exchanged among various health providers as and when needed *(Fig 40-5)*. This would even reduce the cost of healthcare treatment by avoiding redundant diagnostic tests.

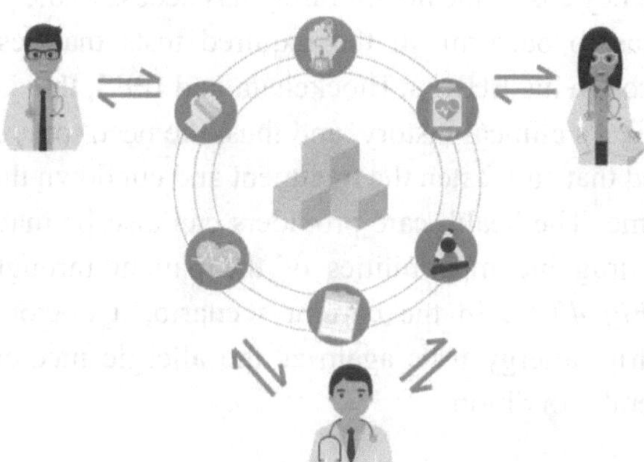

Fig 40-5: EHR data on Blockchain can be exchanged among various healthcare providers

And most importantly, the healthcare provider can provide better patient care based on this accurate data.

(ii) The technology also offers flexibility to individuals either to reveal their identity or share their data anonymously/pseudo anonymously. They can even decide what part of the information should be shared with these healthcare providers.

(iii) Once implemented, the electronic health records on Blockchain will serve as a common and integrated backbone for the health industry. It will also reduce the overhead costs for hospitals and healthcare providers.

(iv) This transparent system can help the government to effectively identify the needed citizens for which the health schemes have been started.

(v) The hospitals can give the controlled and needed access to their pharmacies to maintain the required inventory to prevent the shortage of medicines and thus prevent any delay of medical care to the patients.

40.6.2. Blockchain helps in reducing time delays during emergency cases

During emergency cases, the doctor rarely has access to the patient's clinical history. He has to perform all the required tests that result in delayed treatment. Through his EHR on Blockchain and IPFS, the doctor can easily access the patient's clinical history, and thus, the need to do redundant tests will be avoided that can fasten the treatment and cut down the medical costs at the same time. The health care providers can also be made aware of the allergies and drug incompatibilities of the patient through the EHR on Blockchain *(Fig 40-6)*. In the current scenario, a doctor is required to perform the drug allergy tests again as the allergic medicine can further worsen a patient's condition.

Let's understand it through an example; a patient is allergic to a specific drug, say penicillin. He gets some bacterial infection and visits a doctor for his treatment. Suppose the doctor has access to the patient's medical history. In that case, he will be aware that the patient has an allergy to penicillin, and subsequently, he will prescribe him some other medication avoiding penicillin. Thus, avoiding any unwanted medical error and any further health complications.

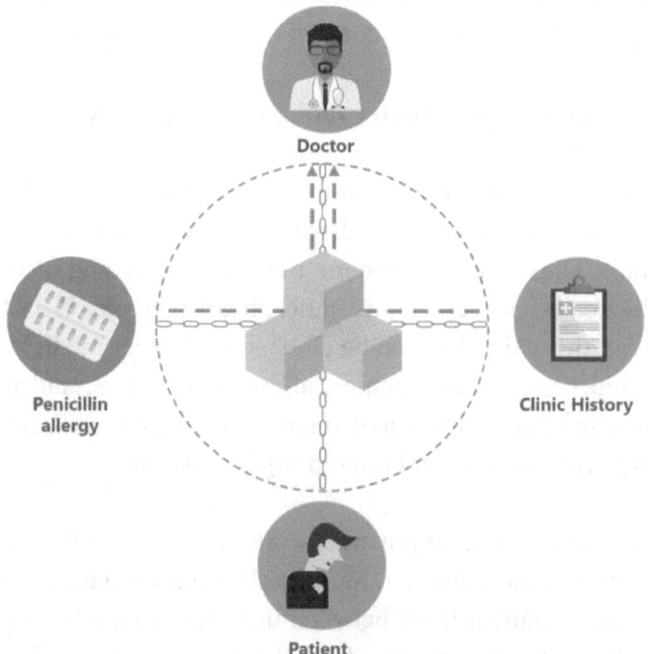

Fig 40-6: The doctor has access to the patient's medical history on Blockchain

40.6.3. Blockchain and Telemedicine can transform healthcare

The distributed Blockchain technology will also play a critical role in better adoption and working of telemedicine and remote monitoring. If the patient cannot physically visit the healthcare provider, he can easily share his EHR data present on Blockchain and get medical advice while sitting at his home. Thus, reducing clinic visits and also saving the commutation time required to visit a clinic. In addition, IoT devices, along with Blockchain and IPFS, can provide real-time data on vital patient measurements such as blood pressure, heartbeat, etc., for better diagnosis. It will also assist in timely follow-ups with doctors, thus making it easier to detect early signs of certain severe health conditions.

Last but not least, this technology would be a great help for the people who live in rural areas and do not have access to good medical facilities. It can be an excellent opportunity for better collaboration between the healthcare providers as well. They can share the patient's information with each other to get an expert advice, with due consent of the patient on the Blockchain.

40.6.4. Blockchain helps in better data integration of Wearables

The growing trend of consumer health wearables like fitbits, health bands, apple health kits, and watches is ushering in a new era of consumerization of healthcare. These devices record the daily data and activities of a consumer like calories, step counts, miles, heart rate, etc. With Blockchain technology, all this daily data can be clubbed with other medical health care data like clinic visits, demographics, allergies, lab tests, and much more. Further, with the implementation of smart contracts, this data can be used to provide better medical care and monitoring by doctors.

Let us understand it through a practical world scenario. Andrew is diagnosed with fatty liver, and therefore, Dr. Steve designed a special exercise regimen for him. A smart contract is set between them to check whether Andrew is sticking to the regimen prescribed by the doctor *(Fig 40-7a)*. Andrew's wearable smart gear logs in his daily movements, exercise regimen, and other essential data points. After every three days, the smart contract verifies if the terms of the contract are fulfilled *(Fig 40-7b)*.

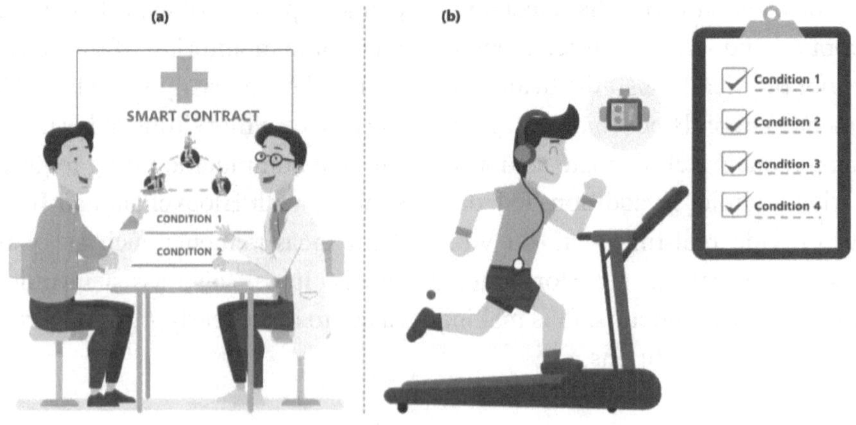

Fig 40-7: (a) Smart contract between the patient and doctor and (b) after every three days contract verifies if the conditions are fulfilled

And Dr. Steve only gets notified if Andrew fails to adhere to his exercise regimen continuously for two times *(Fig 40-8)*. Thus, you can see that smart contracts, when clubbed with Blockchain, can be a game-changer for the healthcare industry.

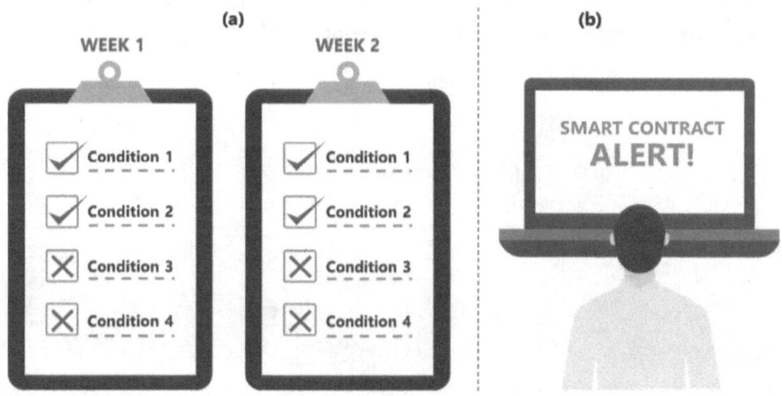

Fig 40-8: (a) Andrew fails to adhere to exercise regimen two times continuously and (b) notification sent to the doctor

40.6.5. Getting compensated for your data

You will be shocked to know that your health data clubbed with millions of other users is sold by health informatics companies to pharmaceutical companies for billions of dollars. Pharma companies use this bundled data for research and marketing purposes. Of course, the name and other crucial identifying details are taken off before bundling and sharing the data of millions of users. The biggest irony here is that this data belongs to you and got recorded against the payment done by you or your insurance company, but it gets sold without your prior knowledge and consent.

With Blockchain, this situation is bound to change where you control your own data. With this technology, you can share your data anonymously or with your actual identity. Once you give your approval on this, your consent will be recorded on the Blockchain. The pharma companies can verify your consent by using a key that connects to the Blockchain and can then use your data for medical research and marketing purposes *(Fig 40-9a)*. Subsequently, you will also be given a pie of the revenue generated from this transaction *(Fig 40-9b)*.

Additionally, it will be a great help for these pharma companies because having a direct relationship with the patient will help them get more valuable insights, which is not feasible in the current world.

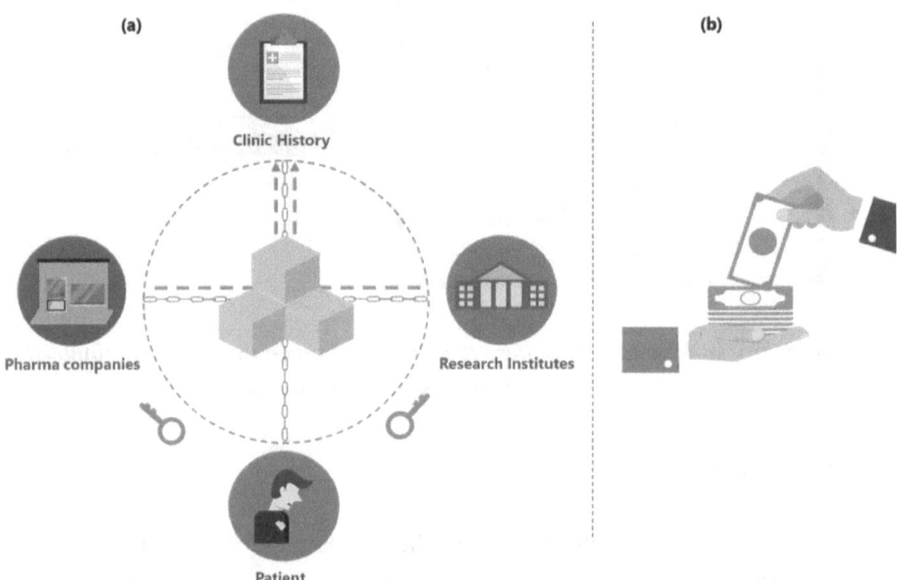

Fig 40-9: (a) Research institutes and pharma companies are permitted on Blockchain to use patient's data and (b) share of revenue given to the patient

Chapter 41: Blockchain in Blood Donation

Blood is the most precious gift one human being can give to another - it is indeed the gift of life. Since there is no synthetic blood available so far, somebody has to give his own blood to make it available for needy patients. Hence it is not incorrect to assume that blood transfusion is an essential component of healthcare. It contributes to saving millions of lives each year in both emergency and routine situations.

Blood transfusion makes it feasible to conduct increasingly complex medical and surgical procedures like organ transplants, chemotherapy, etc., which in turn, dramatically improves the expectancy and quality of life of patients suffering from a variety of acute and chronic conditions. Unfortunately, many patients still die or suffer because they don't have access to safe blood transfusions.

41.1. Challenges in blood transfusion

The timely availability of safe blood is essential in all health facilities where blood transfusion is performed, but in many developing countries, there is a big mismatch between the demand and the availability of blood, and this shortage of blood forces the cancellation of many critical surgeries, risking the lives of many patients. Some of the key issues contributing to this problem are as follows:

(i) The primary reason for this issue is the lack of blood donors who regularly participate in the blood donation process. One of the reasons that many people don't donate their blood regularly is the lack of transparency in how their donated blood is used later on. Imagine a scenario where a donor knows that his blood saved the life of a person; he would be more willing to donate his blood regularly versus a scenario where he doesn't know what happened to his blood once he donated it.

(ii) On one hand, we have a shortage of blood donations, while on the other hand, a considerable number of the donations made go straight to the bin and are never used. The reason behind this is the short shelf life of blood. Blood has a shelf life period of 42 days. Hence the donated blood must be transfused within 42 days of its donation. In simple words, there is a need for an efficient system that can help to map the donations with the needy recipients so that the donations don't go waste and people don't lose their lives unnecessarily.

(iii) Apart from this, unsafe blood transfusions or contaminated blood transfusions account for HIV infections, other viral infections, and Syphilis infections in the patients receiving this contaminated blood. Moreover, this problem is highly prevalent in developing nations where there is less accountability and traceability of blood.

All of these problems in the current blood donation ecosystem exist because of the complex journey of blood from a donor to a receiver, which in turn, makes it difficult to track the blood.

41.2. Blockchain-based blood donation system

Blockchain can be a great solution for these issues existing in the current blood donation ecosystem. Now let's understand how Blockchain can be implemented in the blood donation and transfusion process to make it more robust and transparent.

(i) In a Blockchain-powered blood donation ecosystem, when a donor goes for blood donation, his essential details, like age, identity proof, weight, medical history, etc., will be recorded on the distributed ledger. The blood collected from the donor will then be labeled with a unique identification number. This number can be scanned and tracked to find the donor.

(ii) In the next step, all of the blood collected from the donation venue will be transported to the blood center, where the donations will be sorted and registered on the Blockchain.

(iii) The donations will then be sent to the manufacturing area. In the manufacturing area, the donated blood is spun in a device known as a centrifuge, which separates the blood into transfusable components like red cells, platelets, and plasma. Each component is packaged as a "unit," – which is a standard amount that doctors use while transfusing a patient. And each of these components has its own functions and advantages. For example

- A patient suffering from anemia or iron deficiency may receive red blood cells to increase his hemoglobin and iron levels, which in turn helps to increase the amount of oxygen in his body.
- A patient whose body can not make enough platelets due to chemotherapy or illness may get platelet transfusions to stay healthy.
- And plasma transfusions are used for patients with liver failure, severe infections, and serious burns.

(iv) Before blood transfusion to a patient, nearly a dozen tests are performed on donated blood to establish the blood type and presence of any infectious disease like hepatitis, HIV, syphilis, Zika Virus, etc. Under the law, no blood can be released for transfusion without passing the required tests. But currently, in many developing countries, this is not practiced properly, and blood is released for transfusion without all the necessary tests done. Sadly, in the current system, there is no full-proof way for a doctor or a patient to know whether the blood has passed all the required tests. But once Blockchain is implemented, all of this data will be recorded on the digital ledger and will be linked back to the individual donor's identification number labeled with at the donation center. This data will also be accessible to medical professionals looking for a specific blood type. With this system in place, the required blood type can be found quickly and almost in real-time, thus, saving lives by preventing delays in the critical treatments.

(v) Currently, once the blood has been tested and is deemed suitable for transfusion, it is stored as per the recommended conditions, which are as follows:

- Red blood cells are stored in refrigerators at a temperature of 6°C for up to 42 days.
- Platelets are stored at room temperature in agitators, required for stirring platelets for up to five days.
- Plasma is frozen and stored in freezers for up to one year.

Because different blood components have different shelf lives, it's imperative that the labels on them match the individual donor and can be linked back to the donor at any given time. The blood is now ready for distribution to hospitals and to patients whose lives will be saved or sustained by this generous gift.

(vi) The donated blood meets its purpose when it finally reaches the right patient typically within the valid shelf life of the blood. Patients who require transfusion as part of their clinical management have the right to know that they are receiving safe blood. Blockchain technology, once implemented, can provide complete transaction history of every bottle of blood and can empower the patient to verify details of the blood being transfused to him/her.

(vii) The blood transfusion information of a specific unit of blood to a particular patient will also be recorded on the Blockchain in an immutable manner. With this complete end-to-end visibility, an automatic push notification can be sent to the donor when his blood is used to save another human's life. Thus motivating more volunteers to donate blood more frequently as they will have the assurance that their donated blood is saving many precious lives.

41.3. Scalability concerns

(i) Blockchain used will be permissioned Blockchain. The entire information of the donor, blood group, components of blood, tests conducted, storage and transportation, doctors, etc., will be stored on IPFS, and its hash will be stored on the smart contract. All the stakeholders in the network can access the data based on the permissions they have been granted. IPFS has been explained in detail in Chapter 15.

(ii) To make the Blockchain scalable for its use in blood donation and other healthcare applications, layer 1 (discussed in Chapter 12) and layer 2 (discussed in Chapter 13) scaling solutions will be required to be implemented.

Chapter 42: Blockchain in Clinical Trials

Behind every new drug discovery, there are an enormous number of researchers who conduct clinical trials and a vast number of people who volunteer to be a part of these clinical trials to prove the safety and efficacy of the drug. And After going through such rigorous processes and approvals, a drug gets approval from FDA.

42.1. Phases of clinical trials

There are 4 phases of every clinical trial:

Phase 1: Phase 1 clinical trials assess the safety of the drug in a small group of healthy volunteers, say 20-100.

Phase 2: Phase 2 clinical trials involve around 300 patients. These patients are evenly divided into 2 groups. One group of the population of volunteers receives an experimental drug, and the other group receives a placebo. This helps investigators, pharma companies, and FDA to understand the effectiveness of the new drug. Around one-third of the experimental drugs successfully complete both phase 1 and phase 2 trials.

Phase 3: Phase 3 clinical trials is a large-scale testing that involves several thousand patients. This phase of testing provides a more thorough understanding of the drug and its adverse side effects. Around 50% of the drugs that enter this phase 3 clinical trials are able to successfully complete it. Once the phase is completed, the pharma company can request FDA approval for marketing the drug

Phase 4: Phase 4 studies are done after the drug has been approved for consumer sale. Phase 4 clinical trial studies suggest how well the drug works when used with other treatments. Some rare side effects of the drug may only be found in large groups of people.

Phase IV studies can also result in a drug or device being taken off the market or restrictions of use being imposed on it if it is found to be ineffective and impacting the quality of life of patients.

42.2. Challenges in conducting clinical research and clinical trials

(i) The biggest challenge is data reproducibility. This may be due to several errors, research misconduct, or fraud that undermines the research quality. Inefficiencies in clinical trial data management is another major pain point. This leads to treatment delays, less conducive results, and sometimes even in the complete failure of a trial that could have succeeded had it been managed more efficiently.

(ii) The interval between initial clinical testing and product approval has been estimated to an average of 8 years, with only 1 in 6 drugs ultimately obtaining approval. The average cost of successfully developing a single drug is about 2 billion USD. Many drugs do not receive approval not only because they are unsafe or ineffective, but sometimes because the information supplied is unsatisfactory to prove the efficacy of a drug.

42.3. Blockchain Technology- The Solution

Blockchain technology can have a greater impact on sharing and tracking of data. The shared distributed ledger can help to keep a record of all the data interactions that occurred during a clinical study. This will lead to an increased credibility in clinical research as, in many cases, the efforts are undermined because of several frauds. Implementation of Blockchain would be a step towards transparency. This would help to improve trust within the research communities and between research institutions and patients.

(i) First and foremost, all the events in clinical research can be tracked through Blockchain. This will eliminate data falsification or data beautification cases. The Blockchain will record and time stamp all the information like researchers involved in the study, designed protocols, sample size, way of administering the drug to patients, way of data collection, and data analysis. And in the case at a later phase during the study, the researcher wants to change the sample size or wants to revise the protocol, all this information will be fully documented and easily accessible on the Blockchain. Each and every transaction related to clinical research will be time-stamped on the Blockchain. It will also enable the researchers to manage their data more efficiently.

(ii) Before clinical trials begin, it is mandatory to take the consent of a patient. The research protocols should also be in accordance with the guidelines of the regulatory bodies. According to FDA, around 10% of clinical research trials have issues related to consent collection from patients, failure to obtain written consent, unapproved forms, expired consent, consent form without date, and failure to get re-consent to a revised protocol.

Even document frauds are also reported, for example, backdating the consent forms. Taking consent is crucial for the safety of patients. According to a report, in 2016, an analgesic killed a patient. The investigation proved that re-consent was not sought from the patient before administering the drug to him when the major neurological side effects of the drug were reported in some patients. Even the re-consent has to be taken from a patient if the protocol has been redesigned.

In a **permissioned Blockchain-based system**, all the information about the drugs, designed protocols, revised protocols, as well as consent and re-consent forms will be stored on the Blockchain. The devices of patients registered for clinical trials will also be nodes in this system and will be given permission to access all the required information related to protocols and consent forms. Besides, this will ensure patients' safety and the protection of their rights. A smart contract will be executed whenever any change in the protocol occurs, and a consent form will be sent to the patient for his re-consent. After getting the re-consent, the patient will get automatically enrolled for the clinical trial. Now the proof of the existence of consent and re-consent will be available to all the stakeholders, including investors, pharmaceutical companies, research organizations, and regulatory bodies involved in clinical trials.

(iii) Blockchain can make it possible to track all patient-doctor encounters. Till date, all the clinical trial results are not reported, but with the implementation of Blockchain, any such data will be recorded on the shared ledger and can also be reviewed by other researchers.

(iv) Recruiting people for clinical trials is a major task which accounts for nearly one-third of the total timeline of a clinical trial. The patient data is largely secured in siloed individual databases with limited interoperability and transferability. This makes the recruitment of patients very difficult.

Pharma companies have to reach out to physician offices individually and attempt to recruit patients. It is also very difficult to find a sufficient no of patients. Many clinical trials get delayed because of insufficient no of patients.

(v) Patients who may be interested in going for clinical trials are largely unaware of such opportunities. According to a study by The Journal of Community Oncology, only 16% of cancer patients knew that clinical trials were an option for them at the time they were considering treatment options. It means that around 85% of the patients had no idea that they can explore the treatment options offered by these clinical trials. This dichotomy results in financial losses for the clinical trial administrators and missed opportunities for patients to try these new therapies.

Blockchain-based distributed ledgers can address this issue of patient recruitment.

Patients who are willing to go for clinical trials will be listed on a distributed database, and drug companies can directly reach them and recruit them for the clinical trials. Thus, skipping the hassle of visiting physicians personally. They can reach large numbers of potential participants and can get enough information about them to contact and recruit them. This can speed up the recruitment time.

(vi) The distributed ledger technology can be a proactive way for drug companies to prove that they comply with all legal and human rights issues. Because the complete time-stamped procedure of performing clinical trials will be available on the Blockchain. The respective organizations can easily verify that no unethical or illegal means are being used by pharma companies for these trials, thus bringing trust and transparency to the system.

42.4. Scalability concerns

(i) Storing vast amounts of clinical trial data, including consent forms, protocols, and information about the drug, patients, researchers, hospitals, patient-doctor interaction, FDA approvals, etc., on Blockchain is expensive and energy-draining. Thus, distributed file storage IPFS can provide low-cost off-chain decentralized storage to store data. A unique hash is generated for every uploaded file on the IPFS server, which is then stored on the Blockchain and accessed through the smart contract. Any change in the uploaded file would change its hash. IPFS has been explained in detail in Chapter 15.

(ii) To make the Blockchain scalable for its use in clinical trials, layer 1 (discussed in Chapter 12) and layer 2 (discussed in Chapter 13) scaling solutions will be required to be implemented.

Chapter 43: Blockchain in Health Insurance

In the current scenario, getting payment from insurance companies is a big pain point for the patients and healthcare providers. At the same time, it is also difficult for an insurance company to evaluate the verity of the claims submitted because of the rising medical insurance fraud.

The culprit for all of these issues is today's complicated, inefficient and outdated medical and payment system. Millions of dollars are wasted due to claim errors and unsettled disputes owing to the lack of transparency in the system.

43.1. Challenges for health insurance providers

(i) Time delays: Whenever the medical claim is submitted to any health insurance provider, he is required to inspect and analyze a lot of information to evaluate the authenticity of the claim. And the reason for this is the increasing number of fraudulent claims.

The whole process of claim submission and approval is very exhaustive and takes a lot of time.

(ii) Error-prone due to lengthy paperwork: The healthcare providers have to do a lot of paperwork before submitting a claim to the insurer. This leads to an increased probability of human errors, because of which there is a good chance that some fields may not be correctly filled in the claim form and some might even be completely missing.

In case of incomplete submission, some of the claim gets rejected by the insurance company and the healthcare provider has to reinitiate the whole process. Thus leading to a delayed payment cycle and an increased overhead cost.

(iii) Outdated Insurance Policy: It may happen that a patient has an expired or outdated insurance. The current system is quite complex and the information is not readily available. Because of which it is not always feasible for a health service to verify a patient's insurance status before rendering the services.

Let's understand it through a real-life scenario. Steve met with an accident and got admitted to a hospital. The hospital takes good care of Steve, and within a couple of days he gets discharged from the hospital. Now the insurance claim is prepared and submitted by the hospital to Steve's health insurer. After receiving the claim request the insurer verifies the patient's details in its database. Upon processing the request, it finds out that the policy is outdated and therefore rejects the claim and notifies the same to the hospital.

In such a scenario, the hospital contacts the patient to know about the latest health insurance company as it is required to resubmit the claim to the new insurer, which again is a lengthy process.

(iv) In many cases healthcare providers and patients both are not aware of all the conditions and situations that are covered in the insurance policy of the patient. This becomes a major pain point for both the parties involved.

For hospitals, it leads to a wasted time and effort on filling and submitting the claim and for a patient it leads to an extra burden as he is liable to pay the medical bills out of his own pocket.

43.2. Blockchain - The solution

Blockchain technology is the link that can provide the required solution for this. With the implementation of this technology, all the stakeholders involved will have access to the same information or in other words, there would be a single version of the truth without any discrepancies.

The shared and distributed ledger allows all the parties to monitor and analyze the submitted claim and the services rendered against that claim.

43.2.1. Pre-authorization Process in Health Insurance

(i) Through Blockchain, a single ledger is shared among the healthcare stakeholders and smart contracts are issued that encode all the conditions and situations in which health insurer provides medical coverage. These smart contracts get executed when the defined conditions are fulfilled. This leads to:

- an improved cash flow due to faster transaction settlements
- timely treatment of patients
- accurate payment to the service provider
- Reduction in the overhead costs for both healthcare providers and health insurance companies.

(ii) When information about a patient's health insurance is readily available on the shared ledger, it becomes easier for healthcare providers to check the patient's current insurance status and validate the conditions and situations that companies provide coverage for.

This would even cut down the unnecessary hassle of filling and submitting claims for an uninsured patient or condition, and a patient can be directly asked to pay for the medical bills out of his own pocket.

(iii) If a patient changes his medical insurer between visits, the healthcare provider can easily access this information via Blockchain. This in turn will help the healthcare provider to submit the medical claim for that patient to the right insurance provider, thus eliminating the need to resubmit the claim.

(iv) The smart contract shared on the Blockchain provides the claim and reimbursement rules of the medical insurance. Proper data format requirements are also provided so as to ensure that the claim form is correctly filled before submitting to the insurer. The healthcare provider, therefore, exactly knows what information is required to be filled prior to submitting the claims. Thus eliminating the chances of claims to be returned due to missing information or non adherence to the required format. This in turn will save time and effort for both healthcare providers and insurance companies.

(v) Lets us understand it through an example - A patient gets admitted to a hospital for his heart surgery. As the patient gets admitted, an online entry on the Blockchain is initiated by the hospital for that patient. After the surgery is done, the healthcare provider submits the claim to the insurer on the Blockchain. And simultaneously, the patient gives access of the required information to the insurer.

Insurer validates the identity of the patient and the information provided to him. If all the predetermined conditions are met and the claim is submitted in the correct format, a smart contract gets executed which initiates the cash flow thus settling the claim readily.

(vi) The patient's data stored with various healthcare providers and insurance companies makes it vulnerable to leaks and theft. Through Blockchain technology, the patient's data will be stored on the decentralized database where the patient will own his data. The tampering and stealing of data is very difficult thus making it safe and secure.

43.2.2. Countering fraud and false claims

Fraud and false claims are one of the biggest challenges that this industry faces. Though insurance companies have devised various tools and techniques to avoid such situations but fraudsters still find a way to dupe these insurers. This, in turn, leads to an extra due diligence by the insurer while validating a real claim as well.

But with the implementation of Blockchain, a single version of the truth will be accessible to all the stakeholders involved, and as a result verifying these claims will be a much easier task for the insurer.

Blockchain technology with its innate property of being transparent and tamper proof makes it nearly impossible for fraudsters to dupe the insurance companies.

43.2.3. Better customer experience through smart contracts

Blockchain is going to empower and make life easier. A key role in making this a reality will be played by the smart contracts. These contracts won't require any manual intervention and will be completely managed through rule based operations defined in the code.

Let us understand it through a real life scenario - A person met with an accident and died on the spot. In the current scenario, to claim the insurance money his nominee needs to go through lengthy and time consuming procedures.

The nominee is required to present copies of various documents to get the claim, which takes several weeks and sometimes even months. The person is already in pain due to loss of the dear one and on top of that these insurance procedures and processes, further aggravates his agony instead of supporting and helping him. A customer enrolls himself in the insurance plan in order to alleviate this pain.

But with such a complex system in place, the whole point of insuring life and health becomes useless and ironic. But with the power of smart contracts situations like these can really be simplified.

Smart contracts can easily be implemented for low dispute claim settlements like in case of death of a policyholder, these contracts will ensure an automated payout to the registered nominee. This automated processing will reduce the effort involved in filing a claim and in turn will lead to a world class customer experience.

43.2.4. Easy Registration of new clients

When new clients apply for health insurance, the providers must collect and validate the concerned patient's data like his name, date of birth, address, health and economic status to meet the compliance requirements such as KYC. This collection of data is a time-consuming process. The person has to submit all the documents and providers must review the data to complete the verification process. Sometimes the exchange of documents and information has to be done multiple times in case any required information is missing.

Through Blockchain technology the whole process can be simplified.

With the implementation of Blockchain, his entire details like personal identity, medical records, and financial records will be available on the shared ledger. The patient can give permissioned access to the insurer so that the necessary documentation required for verification can be easily accessed by the insurer. Thus the insurer can efficiently verify the eligibility of a new client for a particular insurance policy in a reduced time frame.

Section 6

Blockchain in Finance

Chapter 44: Blockchain in KYC verification

Fig 44-1: Blockchain in KYC verification

44.1. How is the KYC verification process currently done?

Knowing with whom they are trading is one of the most important jobs of banks and other financial institutions like an insurance company, stock exchange, etc. Because of this very reason, these financial institutions conduct KYC or Know your customer process as this process provides them with a sense of security. KYC verification ensures the authenticity of the other party involved.

The KYC process is initiated when a customer intends to work with a financial institution like a bank. Initially, the financial institution and the customer agree on certain terms of a relationship. Then, the customer sends the required documents like ID proofs, credit card information, utility bills, etc., to that institution to conduct the KYC verification process.

After receiving these documents, the institution analyses them and generates certification, where the customer is either validated or rejected to avail the services. Every time a customer initiates a relationship with any financial institution, the process is repeated. For example, if a customer wants to open an account in bank A, he has to exchange his documents with Bank A and go through their KYC process. After receiving his documents, Bank A will verify them, and after that, he is allowed to open an account in bank A *(Fig 44-2)*.

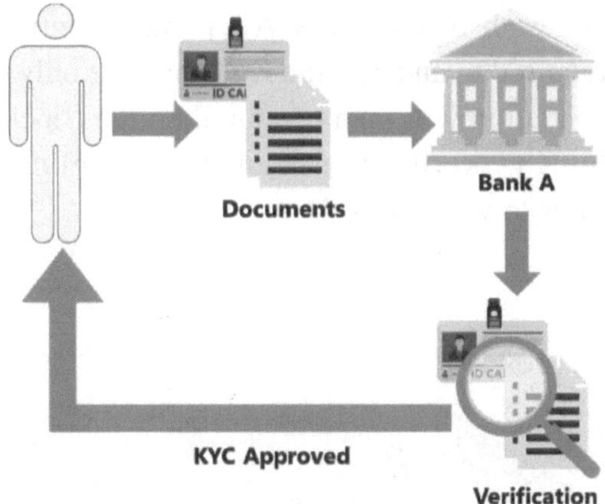

Fig 44-2: KYC verification by Bank A

But when he intends to work with other banks, let's say bank B and bank C, he has to exchange his documents again and go through the KYC verification process with the respective banks B and C *(Fig 44-3)*. These multiple validations are time-consuming and, at the same time, lead to an unnecessary increase in the cost of KYC validation.

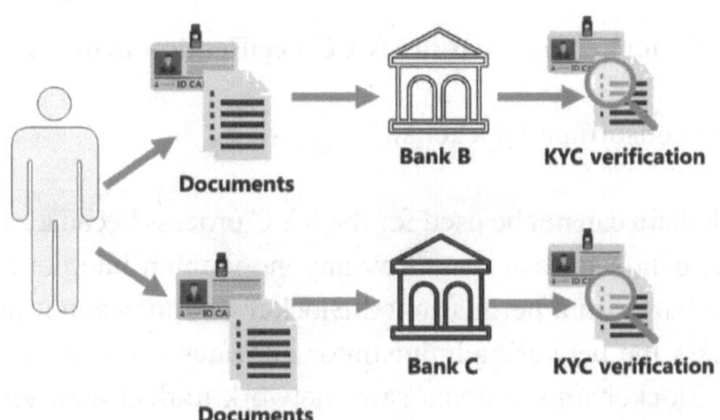

Fig 44-3: KYC verification by Banks B and C

Blockchain-The solution

So quite naturally, there is a need for a solution to make the KYC process easier. Blockchain technology can provide the required solution and can act as a single point of truth in this case. After implementing Blockchain, a customer will be required to undergo the KYC process only once. This KYC information and validation will then be stored on the Blockchain, and later on, he can share this KYC verification result with other financial institutions with which he intends to work *(Fig 44-4)*.

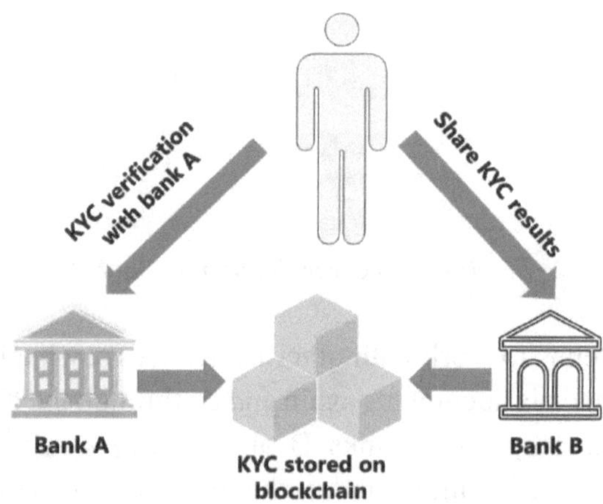

Fig 44-4: KYC verification stored on Blockchain

44.2. Type of Blockchain used for KYC verification process

Permissioned consortium Blockchain.

Public Blockchain can not be used for the KYC process because, as the name suggests, the data can be accessed by anyone with an internet connection. On the other hand, on a permissioned Blockchain, one cannot just join the network unless the network administrator allocates permission. Therefore, this type of Blockchain ensures a safer network to deal with sensitive and confidential data of the customer. For KYC verification, permissioned consortium/federated Blockchain is used. In the consortium Blockchain, a group of companies or representative individuals make decisions in the best interest of the whole network. For KYC verification, there is a consortium of financial institutes on the Blockchain network. The nodes will be pre-selected from these financial institutes to make changes on the network. These nodes have the authority to read or write transactions, and they can also allow or restrict participants on the network.

44.3. How can KYC verification be done on Blockchain?

Let's discuss in detail how KYC verification can happen on the Blockchain.

Step 1: Customer creates a profile

When a customer approaches bank A for the first time, he will be required to complete a one-time set-up of their digital profile, also called a Client Profile, where the documents and information like proof of the customer's identity (i.e., driver's license/passport information), address proof, and other documents required by the bank are required to be uploaded. Once the documents are uploaded, they will be accessible by the applicable bank for verification.

(a) The bank will verify the documents and perform due diligence according to the bank regulations.

(b) Once the documents are verified, the bank official will hash the documents using the Hash Function. Hash functions generate a fixed-length output for any input data irrespective of its size and length. Additionally, they work as one-way functions; in simple words, if you have a hash, you can not decrypt it to find the corresponding input, i.e., information in the documents.

(c) The hashes of each verified document will then be stored on the unique ID of the customer created on the Blockchain by the bank official *(Fig 44-5)*. The bank will be responsible for entering the data about the customer on the Blockchain platform, to which other banks and financial institutions have access. The copy of the KYC documents will be stored on the bank's centralized database and IPFS (not on the Blockchain platform – which means the KYC data is deemed to be stored "off-chain"). Only the hashed documents will be stored on Blockchain. It is important to note that the hash will not contain the contents of the KYC data; it only represents the code name of a specific file. This will be done to prevent the customer's sensitive information from being accessed by other members on the Blockchain network.

(d) The bank official will then generate a QR code for the customer that contains the address to the unique ID and hashed documents of the customer stored on the Blockchain.

(e) Finally, bank A will upload the QR code on the Client Profile.

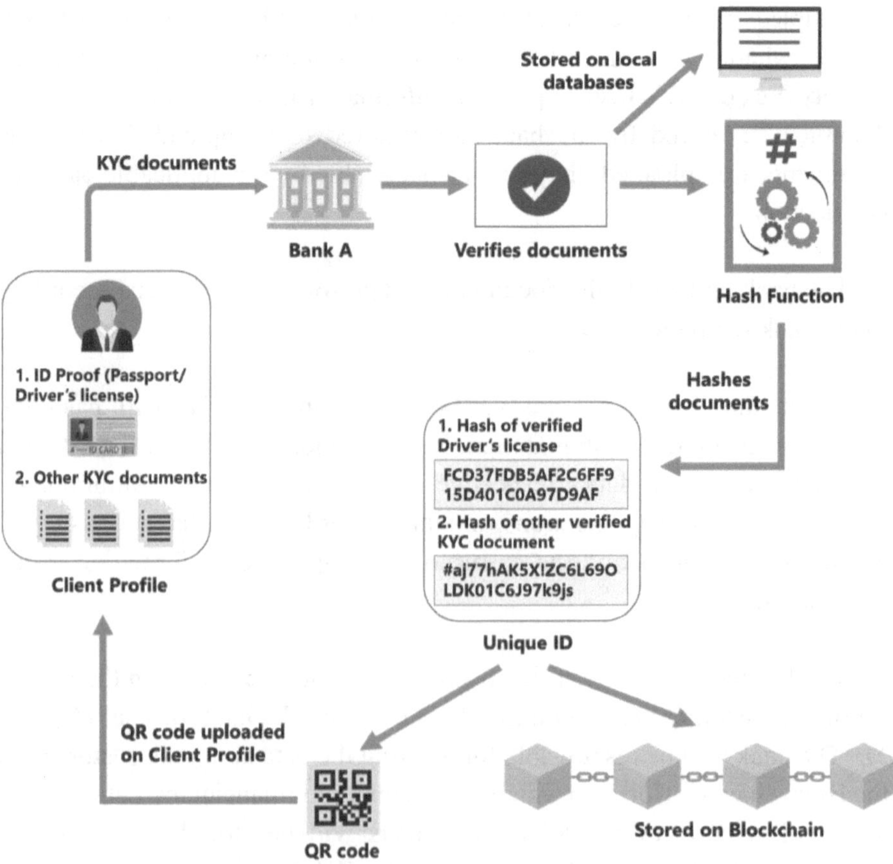

Fig 44-5: KYC verification (by bank A) stored on Blockchain

If KYC data is altered or modified by the customer, the corresponding hash would immediately change. Therefore, the hash will not match to hash function posted on the Blockchain platform, causing the system to automatically alert bank A about such change.

Step 2: Customer intends to work with bank B

Now, if the customer intends to work with another bank, say bank B. Bank B also requires the client to complete the same KYC documentation required by Bank A.

(a) Bank B will send a request to the customer to access his Client Profile *(Fig 44-6)*. To grant access, the customer will log in to his Client Profile through a one-time password (OTP). The OTP will be sent to the customer on email or SMS registered with the bank. Sending OTP proves that the user is who he claims to be. It also prevents data theft on loss or unauthorized scan of the QR code present on the client profile. Although the data can now be accessed by a third party (bank B), ownership of the data remains with the customer. It means the bank B official can not modify or alter the customer's data.

(b) After getting access to the client profile, the bank B official can scan the QR code to extract the unique ID of the customer present on the Blockchain platform. He would then hash the uploaded KYC documents and compare them with the hashes uploaded on the Blockchain platform by bank A. If the two Hashes match, then bank B will know that it has received the same unaltered KYC Data already validated by Bank A.

(c) On the other hand, if the two Hashes do not match, then bank B would need to manually validate the KYC documents according to its standard KYC processes. This could occur if the client has modified the KYC data initially uploaded to the Client Profile or has uploaded additional KYC Data to the Client Profile.

(d) After verification, bank B will then store the copy of the client's documents on the bank's centralized database.

44.4. Smart contracts and KYC

Smart contracts also play a crucial role in the KYC verification process. For example, suppose the customer obtains a new driver's license or passport; these documents must be updated and uploaded on the Blockchain. In this case, it is not possible for each financial institution to individually validate the new documents and update their systems accordingly.

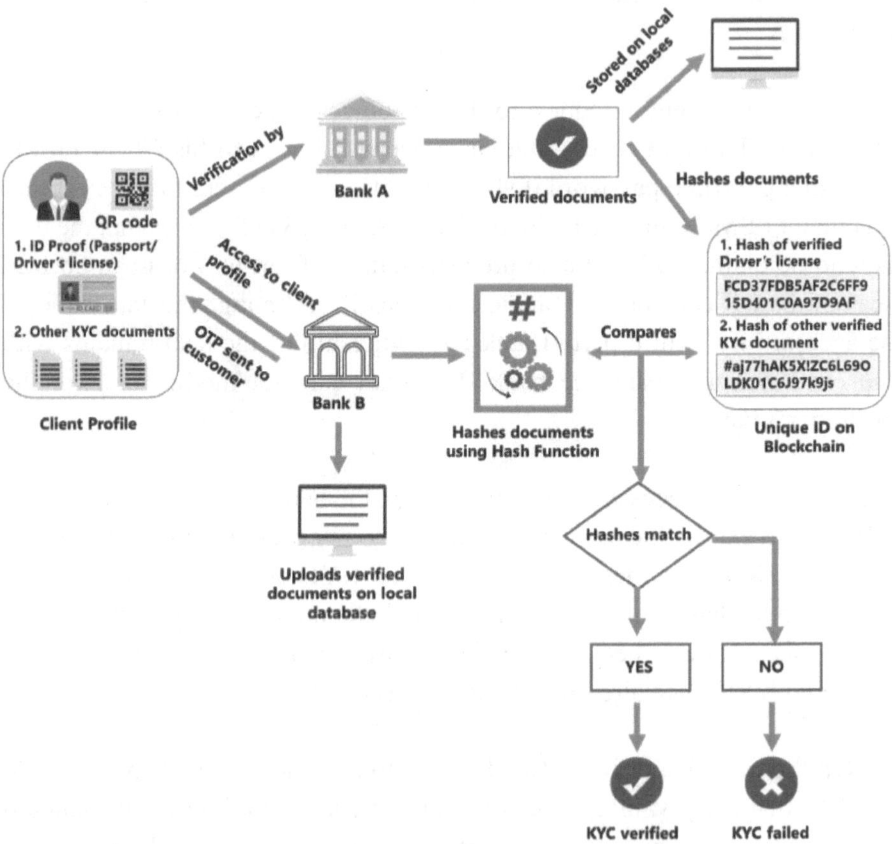

Fig 44-6: KYC verification by bank B

To avoid this, smart contracts can be used to automatically update the systems of financial institutions when the client provides new/updated documents. Specifically, the client submits the updated documents to only one financial institution who then validates and attests to its authenticity.

The financial institution then broadcasts this change in the form of a new hash on the Blockchain to the other participating financial institutions.

Additionally, the smart contract will also include the result of the core KYC verification done by the bank for that customer (can be either accepted or rejected). Thus, the customer's smart contract will contain complete information about the financial institutions he has worked with.

44.5. Blockchain in preventing money laundering

Curbing money laundering is a big challenge for banks. The criminals earn large amounts of money from illegal activities, such as drug trafficking, terrorist activity, tax evasion, bribes, kidnapping, etc.

To avoid detection from legal authorities, these criminals perform money laundering to create an illusion that the money they obtained from illegal activities originated from a legitimate source. **A Bank or a financial institution is used at some point of these money laundering procedures for converting the Black money into White.** One of the ways that they perform money laundering is by first dividing the accumulated sum of illegal money into smaller chunks and then depositing these smaller chunks into the accounts of unconnected depositors *(Fig 44-7)*.

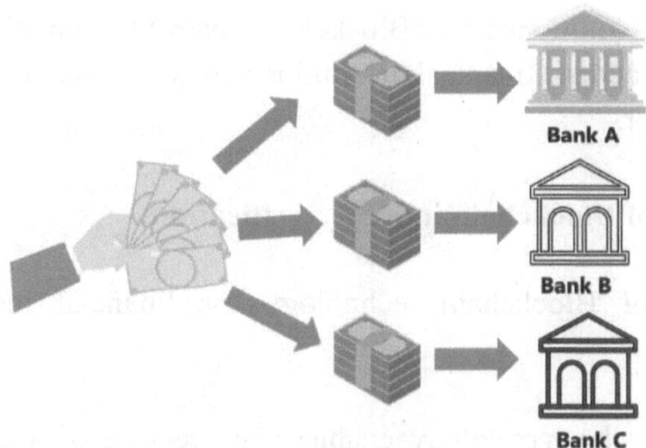

Fig 44-7: Money laundering process

Therefore, any government or financial institution must create a regulatory framework that makes it difficult for individuals to convert money obtained from illegal activities into legitimate assets.

The mainstream financial ecosystem has been developed in such a way that there are numerous checks and balances that can prevent money laundering. And Know your customer or KYC verification process is one of the most essential checks implemented by these institutions in this direction.
But the biggest challenge with the KYC verification process is the increased regulatory cost that these financial institutions bear.

- In fact, it is estimated that the yearly cost that financial institutions spend on KYC verification is around 60 million USD.
- Moreover, these costs are augmented by the fines levied on financial institutions due to their misconduct with regard to anti-money laundering (AML) and KYC regulations.
- These costs are approximated to be about 10 billion USD.
- Additionally, KYC verification is a time-consuming and painful experience for the customers too.

Thankfully, Blockchain technology has the potential to solve this issue related to KYC verification.

If all financial institutions adopt Blockchain, the KYC data of the customers can be shared across financial institutions in a secure, transparent, and seamless manner.

44.6. Benefits of Blockchain in KYC verification

The benefits of Blockchain technology for financial institutions are enormous:

(i) Specifically, the technology enables the creation of a chronological, decentralized interbank ledger using which financial institutions can verify the result of the KYC verification process that has already been conducted for a customer, thus avoiding the need for conducting redundant KYC verifications.

(ii) Moreover, the cost of the KYC process can be minimized and can be shared proportionally among the financial institutions that work with a specific customer.

(iii) This technology will be very helpful for the regulatory bodies since the distributed ledger provides a transparent record of the KYC process that financial institutions had undergone prior to working with their customers.

44.7. Challenges faced while implementing Blockchain

Before implementing Blockchain-based KYC systems, financial institutions must identify and address the following challenges:

(i) Currently, the KYC verification processes vary for different financial institutions, and they have their own internal risk profile and procedures that they are comfortable with.

(ii) To develop a KYC verification system on Blockchain that can be used and shared by multiple financial institutions, the participating institutions must agree upon certain standard KYC regulations and processes.

Chapter 45: Blockchain in the mortgage industry

A mortgage is a loan in which real estate or property is used as the collateral. The borrower enters into an agreement with lender, usually a bank, wherein the borrower receives the cash upfront. Then the borrower makes payments over a defined time-span until he pays back the lender in full. Failure to repay the loan allows the bank to legally take possession and auction off the property used as collateral to cover its losses. A mortgage is often referred to as a home loan when it's used to purchase a home. Mortgages play an essential role as they can make larger purchases possible for individuals lacking enough cash to buy an asset, like a house, up front.

45.1. Steps to getting mortgage approval

However, the process of obtaining a mortgage can be a little challenging. It is heavily paper-based, labor-intensive, time-consuming, and expensive. It is because of a long line of intermediaries that all have a role in the process, such as surveyors, credit agencies, escrow agents, lawyers, title deed offices, etc. Before discussing how Blockchain can simplify the process of obtaining a mortgage, let's discuss how the process works in the current scenario. One has to go through a series of steps to get mortgage approval:

(i) The first step is **mortgage pre-approval.** Pre-approval is when a mortgage lender or your bank reviews your financial situation and credit to determine how much they can lend you. Usually, you would do this before buying a home. It is done to get a rough idea of how much loan you can get and then buy within those parameters. Later, after you've made a deal to buy a house, you would go back to your bank for final approval. Through the pre-approval process, the lender/bank will determine whether you're qualified for a home loan. You must meet their minimum criteria like credit score, debt ratios, income, etc. The lender will offer you a maximum loan if you meet these requirements and will also give a pre-approval letter to use during the house-hunting process.

(ii) The second step is **house hunting and purchase agreement**. Once your lender has pre-approved a certain loan amount, you can confidently shop within that price range. The lender isn't majorly involved in house hunting work. It is primarily done by you and your real estate agents. After making a purchase agreement with the home seller, the next step is the mortgage approval process, which is filling out an application for a loan.

(iii) After filling application for a loan, **mortgage processing initiates**. During this phase, loan processors collect various documents related to you, the borrower, and the property being purchased. They will review your file to ensure it contains all the documents needed for the underwriting process. These documents include your bank statements, employment letters, the purchase agreement, tax records, and more. The loan processor may also:

- Ask for the credit reports,
- verify income, assets, employment,
- and ask for a home appraisal to determine the property's value.

After this, you'll enter into one of the most important steps during the mortgage approval process, i.e., underwriting.

(iv) **Mortgage underwriting**: It is the underwriter's job to examine all of the loan documentation prepared by loan processor to ensure it complies with the lending requirements and guidelines of the bank.

The underwriter (individual or team of individuals) is the key decision-maker during the process of mortgage approval, who has the authority to reject the loan if it doesn't meet a certain pre-determined criteria. It is done to evaluate the level of risk associated with the loan. In addition, the underwriter will double-ensure that both the property and the borrower match the eligibility requirements for obtaining loan.

The underwriter will review the following things:

- Do you have the means and financial resources to repay your mortgage loan? To know this, they'll look at your income history, credit history, overall savings, and your total debts.
- Do you have a good history of repaying your debts that can be known by your credit reports and credit scores?
- And what is the current market value of the property and can it serve as a sufficient collateral for the loan? The underwriter will use the home appraisal document to determine this.

If the underwriter discovers any issue that is outside the eligibility parameters for the loan, then the loan might be rejected. Thus underwriting is definitely the most critical step in the mortgage approval process as it decides whether or not the loan will be ultimately approved.

(v) The next step is a **Title search and title insurance**. The title is a legal term that means the ownership right to property. The title of the property is the prime concern of everyone at the time of purchasing a property. Every property has a title. A lender doesn't want to lend money for a property with legal claims. That's why a title company performs the title search to ensure that the property can be transferred. The title company will research the property's history, claims, pending legal action, unpaid taxes, purchase and sales history, etc. Based on this research, the title insurance is issued to:

- lenders who rely on title insurance to ensure that the property is clear of any disputes before they approve a loan on the property,
- and the buyer who relies on title insurance to safeguard themselves.

(vi) The final step is then **Mortgage Loan Approval and Closing**. If the mortgage underwriter is completely satisfied that the borrower and the purchased property meet all guidelines and requirements, he will mark the deal "clear to close," and the loan can be funded. The home buyers and sellers must then review and sign all of the pertinent documents, so the funds can be disbursed. This happens at the "closing" or settlement. The closing Disclosure gives you finalized details about the mortgage loan. It includes the loan terms, your projected monthly payments, the amount you will need to pay in fees, and other closing costs. Once all the documents are signed, the bank can initiate the disbursement of funds, and the land registry offices can be informed to update the property's title deeds.

45.2. Bottlenecks in the mortgage application process

But this traditional mortgage application process leads to 2 main problems: increased costs and extended processing times.

(i) Current mortgage approval process requires the involvement of a number of intermediaries, including loan processors to assess loan eligibility, underwriters to ensure the accuracy of mortgage down payments, surveyors to provide up-to-date property valuations, lawyers to draw up legal documentation, and title offices to confirm and update ownership.

(ii) With every intermediary the transaction goes through will add 1% to 2% of the property's value in their own fees to the overall cost. But it's not only fees they add; each of them also adds additional days of their own processing time, leading to a long, drawn-out process. The application process can take anywhere from 30 to 60 days to complete.

45.3. Blockchain-The solution

Blockchain has the potential to revolutionize the mortgage industry. Some of the key areas that can be targeted by Blockchain are as follows:

(i) The first one is in mortgage leads. Blockchain can enable customers to get good deals on mortgage on the Blockchain platform without visiting multiple banks. Once any financial institution collects information about the customer, the data can be published on the distributed ledger, which can be shared by various banks to offer the best product or deal as per the customer's need. Thus the customer can choose a bank depending upon the loan interests and the other suitable services that the bank offers on the Blockchain platform without visiting multiple banks to know about their services and then deciding with which bank he wants to work with.

(ii) The customer's identification can be made by banks on the Blockchain platform itself. Borrower's identity and Financial Institution's identity will be present on Blockchain. In such a scenario, a lender can put a request to the borrower on the Blockchain to get permission to access the borrower's financial data. As soon as the request is placed, a smart contract could notify the borrowers about such a request. The borrower could then approve such a claim on Blockchain. As soon as borrower approves the access, another smart contract could notify the lender about the approval along with the details of the financial institutions for which the request was granted. The lender could then reach out to the financial institution asking for the data. The financial institution, in turn, could refer back to the borrower's identity to check if such access was authorized. Once verified, the financial institution can hand over the data to the lender. The lender can get information regarding the borrower's bank statements, employment letters, credit reports, overall savings, total debt, etc., on the Blockchain platform. Automation of the verification process on the Blockchain platform can reduce the time of mortgage approval.

(iii) As we have already discussed earlier, to approve the mortgage application process, banks rely on accurate information from surveyors, law firms, credit agencies, title companies, etc. Suppose all of these agents update their part of the information on a distributed network; then underwriters can easily retrieve the various pieces of information they need from this network without having to rely on individual, paper-based communications from each of these intermediaries. Additionally, digitized copies of legal documents, property valuations, and title deeds can also be updated on the Blockchain network. All of this information can help underwriters to easily evaluate if the person is eligible for the loan.

(iv) Title search becomes essential to check the legal history of the property for which the borrower wants to get a loan. Currently, lenders rely on title insurance to make sure that the property is clear of any disputes before they approve a loan on the property. This process is time-consuming and is also costly. Blockchain can be used to create a digital ID for each property, therefore making the property trackable on the network. Information regarding property address, property type, owner information, sale and purchase transaction records, rent history, the current market valuation of the property, etc. will be recorded on the Blockchain that will allow banks and title deeds to quickly verify the current ownership status or confirm the market price of the property.

(v) Smart contracts can also automate the release of funds to the seller's account only once the mortgage documentation has been digitally signed and the borrowing bank has approved the mortgage. Thus through Blockchain, the whole mortgage approval process gets simplified.

45.4. Scalability concerns

(i) Blockchain used will be permissioned Blockchain. The stakeholders involved will be assigned specific functions on the smart contracts based on their role in the mortgage approval process. Storing the entire data on Blockchain is very costly; thus, distributed file storage IPFS can provide low-cost off-chain storage to store mortgage transactions data. A unique hash is generated for every uploaded file on the IPFS server, which is then stored on the Blockchain and accessed through the smart contract. Any change in the uploaded file would change its hash. IPFS has been explained in detail in Chapter 15.

(ii) To make the Blockchain scalable for its use in mortgage industry, layer 1 (discussed in Chapter 12) and layer 2 (discussed in Chapter 13) scaling solutions will be required to be implemented.

Chapter 46: Blockchain in P2P or peer-to-peer lending

Peer-to-peer or P2P lending is a method that enables individuals and businesses to lend or borrow directly from each other through an internet-based platform without the involvement of a bank or other traditional financial institution.

You might wonder why we need peer-to-peer lending when we have banks and other financial institutions for lending or borrowing. The reason why P2P lending came into existence is because of the fact that traditional bank loans currently available for start-ups, small enterprises, entrepreneurs, and students are often expensive and, in many cases, difficult to avail because of the lack of credit history or lack of tangible collateral.

P2P lending platforms facilitate access to new funding sources by acting as an intermediary between investors and the groups that require funding. On such platforms, borrowers usually obtain loans at lower interest rates than those offered by banks, and at the same time, the lenders receive higher rates of interest relative to other types of investments like in the savings account.

46.1. Steps involved in the P2P lending process

Peer-to-peer lending is a straightforward process. The steps involved in a P2P lending process are as following:

- A potential borrower interested in obtaining loan completes an online application on the P2P lending platform.
- Then the platform assesses the application and determines the risk and credit rating of the applicant. Post analysis, the applicant is assigned and aligned with the appropriate interest rates.
- When his application is approved, the applicant receives the available options from various investors based on his credit rating and assigned interest rates.
- The applicant then evaluates the suggested options and chooses one of them.
- And once the deal gets closed, the loan is disbursed to the borrower.

- After the loan disbursement, the borrower is responsible for paying periodic installments along with the applicable interest.

46.2. Challenges faced by P2P lending platforms

However, there are several challenges that these P2P lending platforms face:

(i) **Credit risk:** Peer-to-peer lending platforms are exposed to high credit risks. Credit risk is the possibility of a loss of the lender that results from a borrower's failure to repay the loan or meet contractual obligations. In other words, it refers to the risk that the lender may not receive the owed principal and interest from the borrower.

Many borrowers who apply for loans on P2P platforms possess low credit ratings, which don't allow them to obtain a conventional loan from a bank. Additionally, there is also a possibility that an online lender can be cheated if any fraudster submits his loan application with a fake identity and creates a profile with a fake IP address.

The geographical separation between borrowers and lenders may prohibit lenders from physically overseeing the business project they are investing in.

(ii) Moreover, as the entire P2P industry is based online, a severe cyber security breach is a real risk.

(iii) Apart from this, P2P lending platforms can also become a hub for money laundering. To avoid detection by legal authorities, the criminals perform money laundering to create an illusion that the money they obtained from illegal activities originated from a legitimate source.

It is quite feasible that an investor or a borrower may be involved in money laundering on these P2P platforms.

(iv) **No insurance/government protection:** Another disadvantage of P2P lending is that the government doesn't provide insurance or any form of protection to the lenders in case the borrower defaults.

46.3. Blockchain- The Solution

Therefore, it is evident that lenders and borrowers on P2P lending platforms are not immune to frauds or scandals. To mitigate these risks, it is essential that the lenders and borrowers on these platforms are properly evaluated.

(i) Blockchain technology can provide the required solution to mitigate credit and other risks involved in lending on today's P2P platforms. Blockchain can reduce these risks by improving credit risk assessments so that it becomes less probable for lenders to be matched with an uncreditworthy borrower.

P2P lending platforms are required to evaluate the historical financial and transactional data of a borrower to assess his creditworthiness. In the current scenario, these data points can be faked to get the desired funding, thus, creating mistrust and insecurity in this P2P lending ecosystem. Once implemented, Blockchain will create an immutable and permanent record of every transaction performed. Moreover, these transaction records can't be forged or faked, thus bringing trust in this ecosystem. Therefore, a Blockchain-based creditworthiness assessment will be more reliable as it will automatically assess the creditworthiness of borrowers based on their historical financial and transactional data available on the Blockchain.

Finally, Blockchain accounting guarantees that the data taken into account for credit risk assessment is accurate because all the transactions on Blockchain are time stamped and tamper-proof.

Another way Blockchain reduces credit risk is by allowing fast, and effective execution of collateral in case credit risk materializes. Cryptocurrency or tokens representing real-world assets can be used as collateral. For example, tokens can be used to represent company shares, bonds, intellectual property, art, and commodities. If in case the borrower fails to make the required loan repayments, the smart contract automatically transfers the tokens to the lender, who can then sell these tokens and monetize them. But it is very crucial to understand that tokens representing assets are worthless without a legal contract that gives the lender the legal right over the underlying asset. Therefore, the legal certificate to use these tokens, in case the borrower fails to make a loan repayment, is also required to be stored on the smart contract.

(ii) As already discussed, P2P lending platforms are not immune to frauds. In the context of P2P lending, fraud mainly refers to providing false financial or personal information while applying for a loan. For example, P2P borrowers may falsify their repayment history to obtain a higher credit score and lower rates of interest. However, Blockchain technology can be a great tool to prevent these frauds related to falsification of financial and personal information as the information about the history of repayment of a loan taken by a borrower during his lifetime will be recorded on the Blockchain. The immutability of records on a Blockchain enables the P2P lending Blockchain platform to identify such fraudsters.

(iii) Additionally, blockchain can also help to keep a check on money laundering. Know your customer or KYC verification process is one of the most crucial checks implemented to prevent money laundering in the current system. This verification aims to establish whether their names are on the defaulter list of financial institutions, what kind of credit history they have, and what their address is or, in simple words, where do they stay, etc.

Currently, the KYC verification needs to be done by the P2P Lending platform, even if the lenders and buyers have already undergone KYC verification with some other financial institution.

But in a Blockchain-based system, the KYC data of a lender or a borrower verified by financial institutions will be stored on the Blockchain, and during any P2P lending activity, the KYC data of the parties involved can easily be checked on the Blockchain without giving any trouble to them.

Additionally, the P2P lending platform is also not required to again conduct a complete KYC verification process of a customer. Every single transaction performed on a Blockchain platform is immutable, which allows for easy traceback of each and every loan transaction taking place on a P2P Lending platform, thus, controlling money laundering activities. To get a better understanding of how Blockchain can be implemented for streamlining the whole KYC process, *please refer the chapter 44 "Blockchain in KYC verification"*.

(iv) With the implementation of Blockchain technology, the P2P lending platforms can become resistant to hacking and identity theft.

46.4. P2P lending on the Blockchain platform

Now let's understand the process of how Blockchain can connect borrowers and lenders from all over the world through a decentralized platform. And also, how P2P lending will happen on a Blockchain-based platform.

In the first step-lenders and borrowers will be required to create their profiles on this Blockchain platform.

A lender can create his profile on the Blockchain platform by providing the following information:

- Personal Information like name, address, and ID number
- Bank account information
- Type of investments, he wants to make. For example, a lender may wish to lend money only to those borrowers who want it for business purposes
- Criteria for lending to borrowers, that is, setting up the rate of interests according to the borrower worthiness.

Once created, the lender's profile will then be submitted to the decentralized marketplace, where lenders and borrowers can find each other.

Borrowers can set up an account on the Blockchain platform with the following information:

- Personal Information, including name, address, and government-approved ID
- Collateral, which can be in the form of Crypto-coins or tokens or legal documents of some physical asset like real estate

After the successful creation of the account, a borrower can send a loan request to lenders around the world. In this proposed system, the smart contract will allow borrowers to send loan requests to lenders who are interested in the type of investment a borrower wants to make.

When a loan request is received by a lender, he will go through the borrower's profile and his investment plan. If the lender likes the investment plan and the borrower's profile, he will schedule an interview with the borrower. And once the interview is done, the lender can either approve or reject the loan application based on the interview.

In this system, borrowers will be categorized as high-risk, medium-risk, or low-risk borrowers based on their profile verification. Once the lender approves the loan request, the smart contract will capture the rate of interest agreed by the lender and the borrower based on the borrower's creditworthiness. For example, lenders can set a low rate of interest for a low-risk borrower having a good repayment rate. Through this Blockchain based P2P Lending Platform, the rate of interests remains fixed all over the world.

After getting the required loan, borrowers can make the repayments using smart contracts embedded with a crypto wallet. If in case, a borrower does not pay his installments on time, the smart contract will add late fees to the actual amount and will upgrade it on the ledger.

So, if a borrower doesn't abide by the terms of the loan, the smart contract would automatically deduct penalties without any manual intervention.

Thus, we can say that a Blockchain-based P2P lending platform will help in reducing time delays, getting quick approvals, will eliminate the need for middlemen, and will bring transparency to the system.

46.5. Scalability concerns

(i) Blockchain used will be permissioned Blockchain. The stakeholders involved will be assigned specific functions on the smart contracts. Storing the entire data like profiles of lenders and borrowers, details about collateral, lending deals, etc., on Blockchain is very costly; thus, distributed file storage IPFS can provide low-cost off-chain storage to store data. A unique hash is generated for every uploaded file on the IPFS server, which is then stored on the Blockchain and accessed through the smart contract. Any modification in the uploaded file would change its hash. IPFS has been explained in detail in Chapter 15.

(ii) To make the Blockchain scalable and increase the speed of transactions on P2P lending platforms, layer 1 (discussed in Chapter 12) and layer 2 (discussed in Chapter 13) scaling solutions will be required to be implemented.

Chapter 47: Blockchain in crowdfunding and ICOs

Most traditional business funding takes one of these three forms: self-funding, bank funding, or venture capital.

47.1. Need for crowdfunding

The problem is that for most people, self-funding is incredibly limited. Bank funding requires having an existing business that has good revenues and cash flow. And venture fund capital nearly always requires a product or service that has mass appeal. Traditionally, if you want to raise capital to start a business or launch a new product, you would need to pack up your business plan, market research, and prototypes, and then shop your idea around to a limited pool of wealthy individuals or institutions: banks, angel investors, and venture capital firms, thus, limiting your options to a few key players. This makes traditional funding either very limited or very hard to get for businesses and can inhibit growth even for products and services that have huge potential.

Crowdsourcing business funding has been one of the miracles of the modern Internet age. Crowdfunding allows businesses with really great products and service ideas to raise funds from a large number of people in small investment amounts. When it works, it can really give your business a big boost. By using crowdfunding platforms like Kickstarter or Indiegogo, you can access thousands of accredited investors who can see, interact with, and share your fundraising campaign. The 3 primary types of crowdfunding are donation-based, rewards-based, and equity crowdfunding.

Donation-Based Crowdfunding is a type of crowdfunding campaign in which there is no financial return to the investors or contributors. Common donation-based crowdfunding initiatives include fundraising for disaster relief, charities, nonprofits, and medical bills.

Rewards-Based Crowdfunding involves individuals contributing to your business in exchange for a “reward,” typically a form of the product or service your company offers. Even though this method offers investors a reward, it’s still generally considered a subset of donation-based crowdfunding since there is no financial or equity return. For instance, the maker of a new soap made out of bacon fat may send a free bar to each of its investors. Video games are a popular crowdfunding investment for gamers, who often receive advance copies of the game as a reward.

Equity-Based Crowdfunding: Unlike the donation-based and rewards-based methods, equity-based crowdfunding allows contributors to become part-owners of your company by trading capital for equity shares. As equity owners, your contributors receive a financial return on their investment and ultimately receive a share of the profits in the form of a dividend or distribution. Equity-based crowdfunding is growing in popularity because it allows start-up companies to raise money without giving up a significant level of control to venture capital investors. And on the other hand, offers its investors the opportunity to earn an equity position in the venture. As the organization grows, investors get more returns.

47.2. Risks associated with crowdfunding

But there are a few risks associated with crowdfunding through today's online platforms or social media, which are as follows:

(i) Fraud is perhaps the worst of the problems crowdfunding faces. Overly ambitious or inexperienced investors may not only channel support to the wrong projects but also expose themselves to unconditional fraud. Fraudsters use adulterated information that is hard to distinguish from authentic projects to conduct illegitimate fundraising. Despite the efforts of platform creators to filter out such fraudulent information, the concept of crowdfunding is an appealing target for expert and organized criminals. Online forums and social media are ideally suited for equity crowdfunding because they offer wide reach, scalability, convenience, and ease of recordkeeping. But these very features also make it easy for fraudsters to set up dubious attractive ventures to attract equity crowdfunding from investors. Investors who do not conduct due diligence on fundraisers before investing may end up losing their entire investment to fraudulent crowdfunded schemes.

(ii) Crowdfunding platforms can also be a safe haven for money launderers behind the facade of investors. In order to avoid detection from legal authorities, the criminals perform money laundering to create an illusion that the money they obtained from illegal activities originated from a legitimate source.

(iii) Some entrepreneurs even see their entire business model collapse before they even get a chance to start production. When their idea becomes popular on the crowdfunding platform, other experienced entrepreneurs get inspired and enter the market early with all the resources they have and rush to beat them to market with a nearly similar product. Even with copyright in place, you might only be giving more ideas and more inspiration to your top competition.

(iv) The other problem with crowdfunding platforms is empty promises. Modern crowdfunders typically contribute money in exchange for a promise. Depending on the contribution level, this could be a copy of the new product when it comes out or something more exciting. Unfortunately, those promises can be broken. Multiple highly popular crowdfunding campaigns have turned out to be scams. People never get the products they paid for months ago.

(v) Crowdfunding platforms are also vulnerable to attacks from hackers and cyber-criminals. There can be credit card or identity theft risks from a crowdfunding portal.

47.3. Blockchain- The solution

Blockchain technology can support and improve crowdfunding in several distinct areas:

(i) The distributed ledger in a Blockchain system would allow for accurate record keeping of all campaign activity: before the campaign starts, during the donation period, and after the campaign is funded. This level of visibility into a project helps all parties involved, including the fundraisers, investors, and platform administrators. Smart contracts can lock a part of the funds in an escrow. These funds will be released to the fundraisers only if they meet specific goals and milestones. This will ensure that investors can trust the fundraisers to deliver on their promises.

(ii) Blockchain technology also ensure digital identity verification to keep a check on fraud and money laundering. Know your customer or KYC verification process is one of the most important checks implemented to prevent fraud and money laundering activities. The KYC data of a lender or a borrower verified by financial institutions will be stored on the Blockchain platform. This verification aims to find out where a fundraiser or entrepreneur is from, whether their names are on defaulter lists of financial institutions, what kind of credit history they have etc. Blockchain technology creates an immutable, permanent record of every single transaction performed, which allows all transactions can be traced back and thus controlling fraud and money laundering activities.

(iii) Asset tokenization can mitigate the problem of empty promises made by fundraisers. Instead of crowdfunding to enable pre-orders of upcoming tangible products and waiting for weeks or months to receive the promised product, Blockchain could rely on providing utility tokens to provide investors with equity or some similar concept of ownership in the product. The utility tokens may offer investors several benefits, like a free product or discount, and these can be redeemed automatically in the future once the product is launched.

(iv) One of the drawbacks of a Crowdfunding investment is the lack of a proper and well-established secondary market, making it very difficult not just to early liquidate your investment if the funds are needed but also to have transparent and reliable pricing. But the Blockchain platform enables early liquidation of money and makes the funding process safe and completely transparent.

47.4. ICOs or Initial Coin Offerings

Blockchain crowdfunding is similar to other online crowdfunding platforms like Kickstarter, with the fundraisers posting their projects and then soliciting funds from a community of interested people who are interested in backing them. The fundraising organization can raise funds through Initial coin offerings or ICO. It differs from other online platforms in a way that the potential startups who are raising funds will make their own cryptocurrency to sell to potential investors. Initial coin offerings are offerings of this cryptocurrency in the form of tokens to the potential investors on a Blockchain platform in return for legal currencies or other cryptocurrencies like Bitcoin. These cryptocurrency tokens will be accounted for and kept track of by the Blockchain, which makes them immutable and impossible to forge. The tokens represent shares in the project, and these shares have the potential to increase in value over time if the company performs well. This is referred to as crypto-equity. The investors have the advantage of buying, selling, and trading of crypto-equity.

OpenLedger is one of the numerous projects that are popping up to apply Blockchain technology to the field of crowdfunding. When an organization wants to begin crowdfunding, it will release Initial Coin Offering (ICO) assets, which are the crypto equity. If the organization does well, these tokens can increase in value, as well as be traded on OpenLedger according to the desires and speculation of investors. The funds raised on the Blockchain crowdfunding platform are stored in a multi-sig account, but only one of three keys is held by the fundraiser. This ensures that a fundraiser can't run off with the money, and it protects the investors. Also, this Blockchain crowdfunding platform aims to provide greater liquidity. Collected funds are held in escrow, allowing fundraisers to access them as needed and allowing investors to trade their shares back in exchange for fiat currency if they need it. This represents a more equitable blueprint than many current crowdfunding exchanges where the fundraiser holds the funds, and the investor is ultimately at their mercy once the money is handed over.

Many existing platforms are also planning to move their crowdfunding operations on Blockchain, including Kickstarter.

47.5. How does an Initial Coin Offering (ICO) work?

When an organization wants to raise money for the project through ICO, the first step is determining how it will structure the token.

Static supply and static price: An organization can set a specific funding goal or limit, which means that each token sold in the ICO has a preset price, and the total token supply is also fixed.

Static supply and dynamic price: An ICO can have a static supply of tokens and a dynamic funding goal. It means that the amount of funds received in the ICO determines the overall price per token.

Dynamic supply and static price: Some ICOs have a dynamic token supply but a static price, meaning that the amount of funding received determines the supply.

When an organization is ready to offer an ICO, it announces the initial coin offering list, the date of launch, rules to follow, and specifics well in advance in a whitepaper. This helps investors to decide and be ready to buy the tokens in exchange for cryptocurrencies or other legal currencies on the said date. As soon as the investor buys the ICO, the money paid goes to a specific compatible crypto wallet address, and investors receive the tokens purchased in return.

If the money raised in an ICO is less than the minimum amount defined on the smart contract by the organization, the funds may be returned to the project's investors. The ICO would then be deemed unsuccessful. If the funding requirements are met within the specified period pre-defined on the smart contracts, the funds become accessible to the fundraiser organization and is spent in pursuit of the project's goals.

47.6. Difference between ICO and IPO

An IPO is used to describe the launch of a company on a stock exchange, also referred to as "going public." The purpose of the IPO is to raise capital for the company by selling its company stocks to the public. On the other hand, ICOs sell coins known as tokens as a way to fund a specific project. The general idea is, that if the project is believed to succeed, the investor buys the tokens to fund the project beforehand at a discount, and he will be able to sell them later at a profit when the project succeeds *(Fig 47-1)*.

In other words, unlike stocks, the tokens generally do not provide an equity stake in a company. Instead, most of the tokens provide their investors some stake in a product or service created by the fundraiser company.

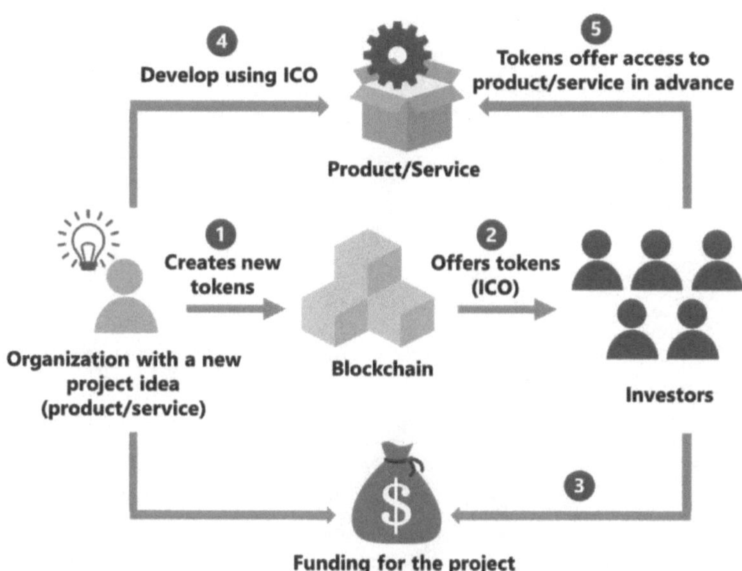

Fig 47-1: Initial Coin Offering or ICO

47.7. Risks of buying or investing in ICOs

The potential earnings from investing in a successful ICO can be enormous. But the investors should also consider the following risks before deciding to buy or invest in an ICO.

(i) The cryptocurrency market is still under-regulated. Investors may provide false and misleading information to investors to raise funds from them. If the project fails, the fundraisers may run away with the investors' money.

(ii) It can be challenging to get the full picture of the ICO returns before you invest. Many investors let themselves be tempted by the promise of tremendous returns by the fundraisers. Also, there can be a high risk that the ultimate value of the product/service will be far too low compared to the amount you invested.

(iii) The value of ICO tokens can be purely uncertain and subject to wide fluctuations. The hype of an ICO may also contribute to exceeding its actual value.

Section 7

Blockchain for Government

Chapter 48: Blockchain in Voting

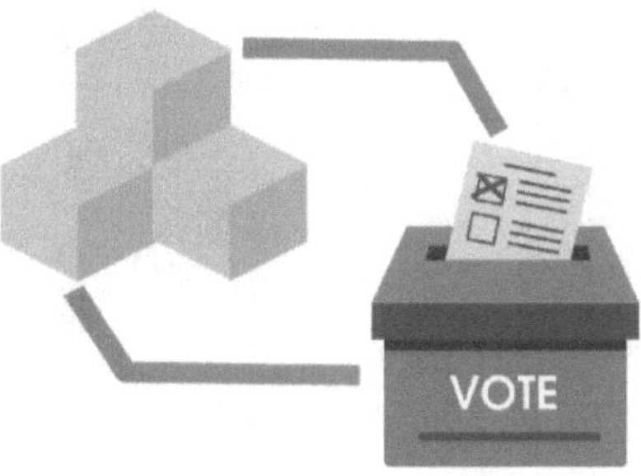

Fig 48-1: Blockchain in Voting

In any country, Democratic voting is the most important event that allows its citizens to exercise their power by voting and electing their representatives. And to protect this right of the citizens, conducting fair elections is the basic prerequisite for any country.

48.1. Challenges

In a democratic system, every vote counts. But still, many adult citizens don't go to cast their votes on the Election Day. They may be out of town or maybe they feel that the voting center is too far. Some might not go because they feel and believe that their vote doesn't count because of the unfair election results. Even the responsible citizens who go to vote have to stand in long queues to cast their votes.

(i) In the current system, voting is generally done either by writing your opinion on paper or by electronic voting machines *(Fig 48-2)*.

Replacement of this traditional system is necessary to limit voting frauds and to make the voting as well as the counting process more transparent.

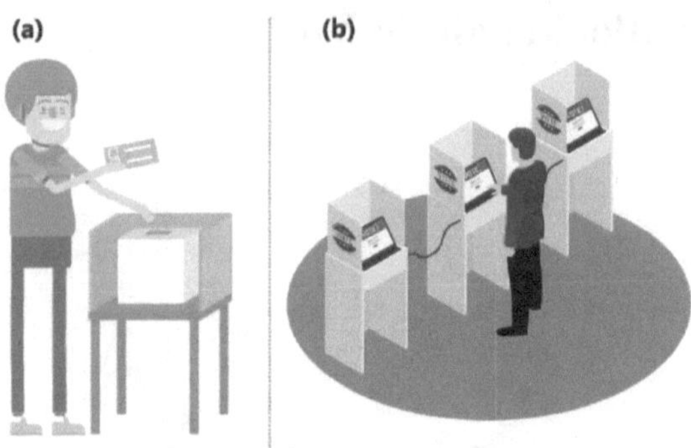

Fig 48-2: Voting (a) on paper and (b) by electronic voting machine

(ii) Further, a system is required that makes voting convenient for the voters. A system that minimizes the cost of conducting elections as money spent on the national elections is huge. And a system that allows us to vote even when we are traveling abroad or are not present in our home state.

We are a society that prefers to live online right from ordering food, to booking cabs, to shopping for our daily groceries and even finding our life partners. Then why can't we cast our votes and select our representatives with a few taps or clicks on a screen? Why can't there be a system where we can vote online from the comfort of our homes?

Though many online voting solutions have been proposed in the past we don't see them in reality. There are a number of challenges that such online e-voting or remote voting system faces:

- Remote electronic voting requires stringent security measures for the voting process because in this case, the risk of large-scale manipulation is simply too high.
- There is a risk of hacking activities by hackers who could directly infect and hack the servers.
- Even the cases of coerced or influenced voting can be in large numbers.
- There is no way till date to verify if your vote has been counted in this online voting system

48.2. How would voting be done on Blockchain?

Blockchain can help to implement an electronic voting system that is immutable, transparent, and cannot be hacked into in order to change the results. Blockchain Voting is an effective means to conduct fair elections.

(i) The first and foremost step in this Blockchain-based voting system is to validate the identity of the voter. It is very important to ensure that someone's identity is not being faked because every vote counts and is equally important. To keep a check on this the voter needs to download the remote voting booth on his mobile, laptop, or any other smart device.

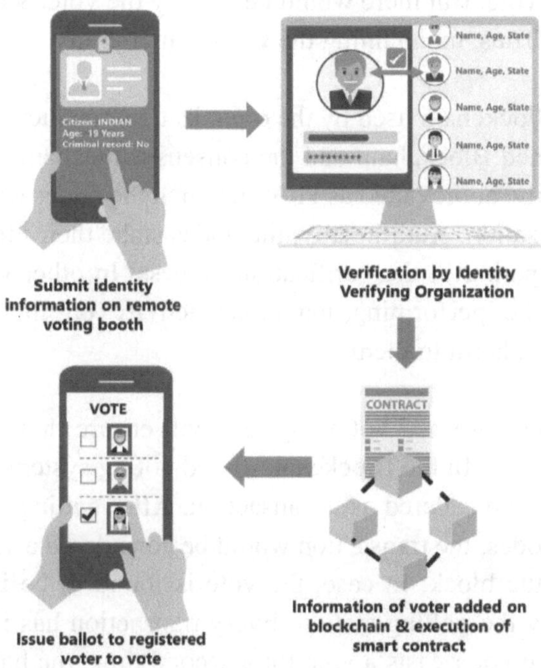

Fig 48-3: Blockchain-based voting system

(ii) After that he needs to submit his identity information which gets verified by the organization conducting these elections. The organization will refer to their database of registered voters and verify if the person is registered on their database and is eligible to vote. Then all the information of the voter will become a transaction and will be securely added to the block in the voter

Blockchain *(Fig 48-3)*. Thus, the voter's list will be updated with all the polling stations.

(iii) After his identity is verified, a smart contract will be executed that will issue a ballot so that he can vote and submit it to the ballot box. Also, the private and public keys will be generated for each voter. The vote will be digitally signed by the private key. The digital signature + the public key of the voter are enough for nodes to verify that the private key associated with the voter has been used to make such a signature. Hence, it can be proved that the vote is authenticated, and the vote has been cast by the intended voter. Since the hash function is one-way, it will only tell the registered voter has cast a vote. But there would be no way the voter's information could be retrieved. Thus, maintaining the voter's anonymity.

(iv) The Blockchain used by the organization conducting elections will be a permissioned Blockchain and the consensus mechanism used can be Proof of Authority, abbreviated as PoA, in which the nodes will be pre-selected by the organization. Additionally, the nodes stake their identity and reputation for participating in the verification process. In other words, if the node is found to be performing malicious activity on the network, it causes reputational harm to them.

(v) Blockchain-based voting system will ensure that a user does not vote multiple times. In the Blockchain-based voting system, when a voter votes, it would be considered as a transaction. After getting validated by the pre-selected nodes, the transaction would be considered a valid vote and will be added to the block. In case, the vote is found to be invalid his vote gets rejected by the polling station. Every transaction has its own unique hash. Thus, if the voter casts a vote for a second time, the hash generated will be the same. Therefore, this vote would be considered invalid and will get rejected by the nodes of the network. Thus, tackling the issue of multiple voting by a single person.

(v) And once the vote is cast, it cannot be modified because of the innate immutable characteristic of Blockchain.

(vi) The voter will be even provided with the option to print the receipt as proof of casting the vote.
(vii) Through Blockchain the voter will be able to verify that his vote has been cast and counted.

(viii) The voter can even audit each ballot in the ballot box and confirm if the election results are accurate while retaining the privacy of other voters *(Fig 48-4)*.

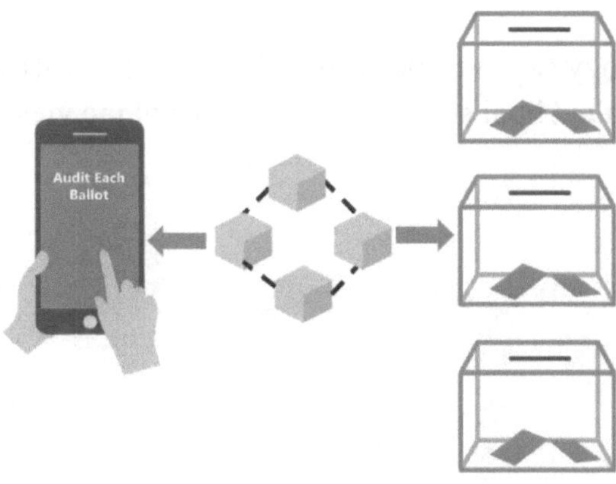

Fig 48-4: Auditing each ballot in the ballot box on Blockchain to confirm election results

(ix) In the current scenario, it takes days for the election results to come out. Further, the declared election results are prone to human error. But with Blockchain, the election results can be declared immediately after the voting is over without any chances of human error.

(x) Blockchain technology will provide the required flexibility to a voter to log in and vote from any part of the world. He just needs a phone and an active internet connection. This would encourage more and more people to vote and become a part of the democratic world where the opinion of every person matters. With this system, the valuable votes won't get wasted.

(xi) And last but not least, this is definitely a cheaper method as compared to the current way of conducting elections.
Many countries and states are running a pilot to adopt Blockchain technology for a secure voting system for example West Virginia, Sierra Leone tested mobile voting through Blockchain in 2018.

Apart from state elections, this Blockchain-based voting system could also facilitate voting processes inside private companies, organizations, and college elections.

The technology can even be used to facilitate the process of voting in reality shows like talent hunt shows where the vote of the viewers matters the most.

Chapter 49: Blockchain in Land Registration

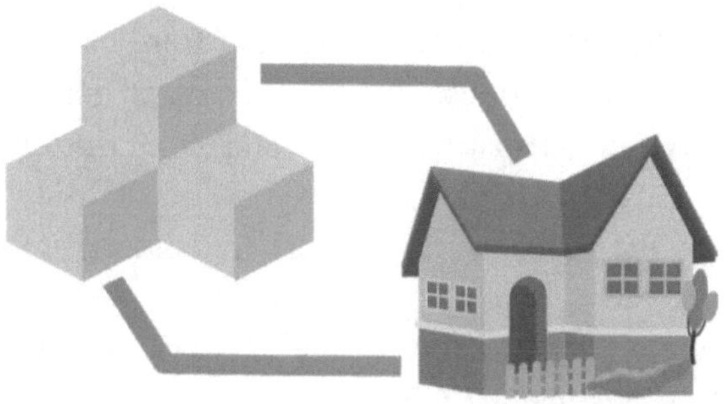

Fig 49-1: Blockchain in land registration

Real estate has always been a lucrative sector for the purpose of investment around the globe. And the land being the most expensive asset in this class has often been the focal point for various frauds, crimes, and fights.

49.1. Challenges in land registration

Titles and deeds are an integral part of the land registration process and provide the required safety net for the buyers. But in many countries, even these land titles are not a foolproof method to prove one's ownership of the property. And this is because of the opaque, ineffective, and inefficient land record maintenance system.

In the current scenario, the land registration process in many developing countries is highly manual and paper-intensive. Thus, making it inefficient and vulnerable to tampering.

And on top of that land registration process involves multiple government bodies for authentication and verification. Transfer of land title requires the same processes and paperwork to be repeated and duplicated several times, thus leading to extended processing time and cost.

49.2. Blockchain — The Solution

With Blockchain, the whole process of land registration can be streamlined. And that's why it has been garnering attention from many governments for its capability to record land titles, mutations, digitized maps, spatial data, and settlement records in a transparent, secure, and tamper-proof manner.

Now let's see how the Blockchain will work for land registrations:

(i) First of all, the geo-coordinates of the land will be uniquely coded and recorded into the Blockchain *(Fig 49-2)*.

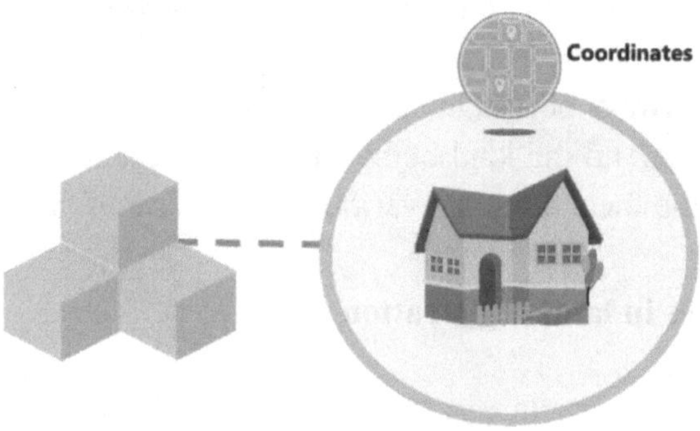

Fig 49-2: Geo-coordinates of land recorded into the Blockchain

(ii) Each property would also be linked to a smart key that would be held by the owner of that piece of land *(Fig 49-3)*.

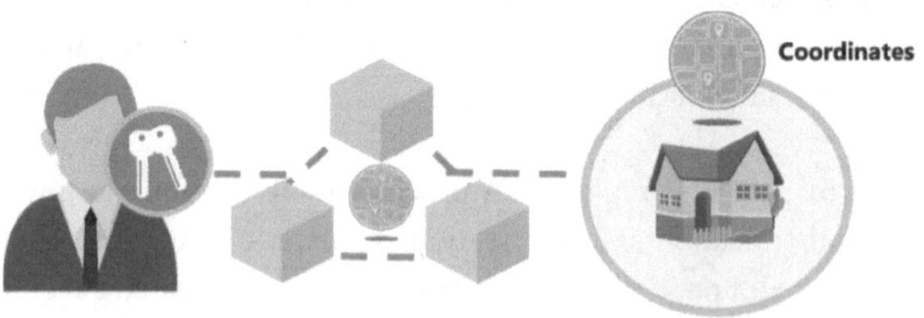

Fig 49-3: Smart key of the property held by the owner

(iii) Further **smart contracts, when combined with Blockchain**, can be used to fasten the transfer of land entitlement and other related transactions. Let's understand it through a real-life scenario. Mr. X wants to buy a property from Mr. Y. A smart contract will be agreed upon by Mr. X & Mr. Y *(Fig 49-4)*,

Fig 49-4: The smart contract between Mr. X and Mr. Y

where the title of the property would be transferred to Mr. X automatically on receipt of the agreed fund into Mr. Y's account *(Fig 49-5)*.

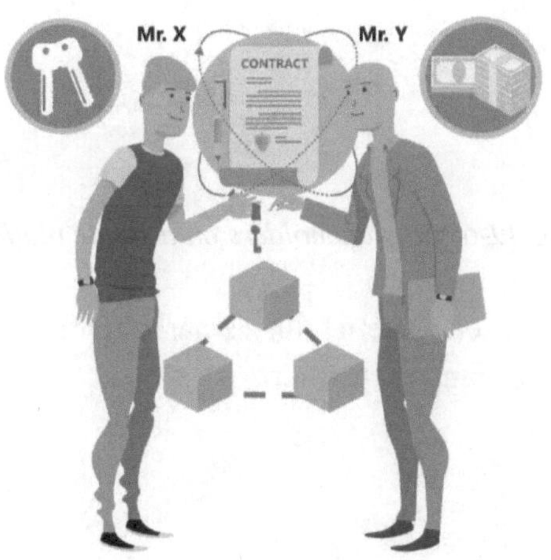

Fig 49-5: Transfer of property title to Mr. X

This transparent and immediate change of land title in the ledger will also speed up the property registration process. And as a result, this would lead to cost savings and greater efficiencies for land registrations.

Implementing Blockchain to record property transactions will also help in better and effective property management as the transactions, and other related information would be updated in almost real-time.

A blockchain-based system will bring all the stakeholders, including the concerned government bodies, sellers, and buyers on a single platform *(Fig 49-6)*. And whenever a land registration or title transfer process is initiated on the Blockchain — all the stakeholders can view the transaction with distributed owner rights.

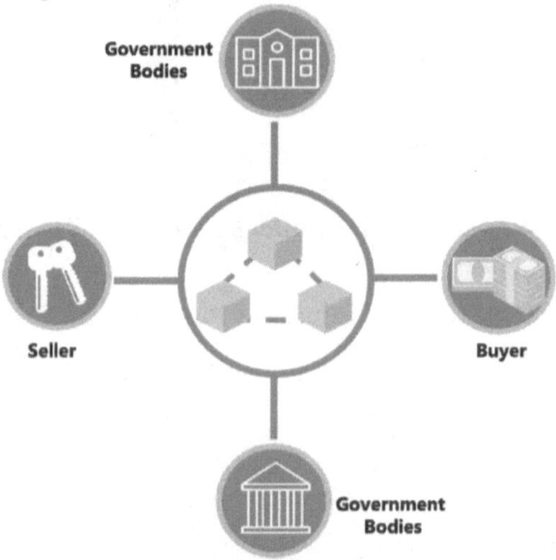

Fig 49-6: All stakeholders on a single platform

Thus, a Blockchain-based system with a smart contract provides a transparent and immutable trail of land ownership.

Chapter 50: Blockchain in Vehicle registration

The process of vehicle registration has always been an arduous and time-consuming task.

50.1. Current vehicle registration process

Various stakeholders are involved from buying a vehicle until the final registration is done *(Fig 50-1)*. In the current scenario, when you buy a vehicle from a dealer, you need to take it to the registration authority to get the permanent registration number. It takes approximately 3-4 days for this request to get processed. Then you have to approach an insurance company to get the required insurance for your vehicle. Further, you have to approach the concerned authorities to obtain NOC and clearance for your vehicle.

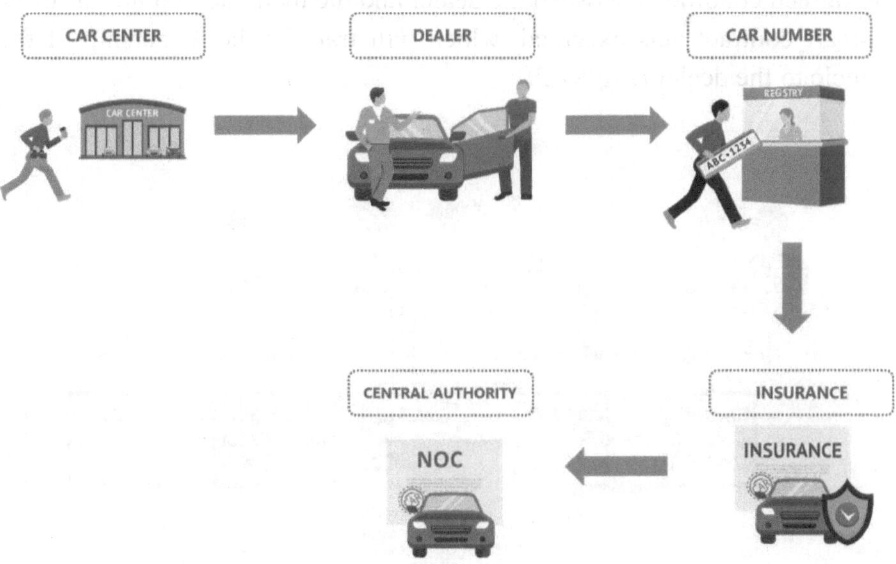

Fig 50-1: Stakeholders involved in the vehicle registration process

The whole process is tedious and takes not less than seven days. Moreover, the customer's information lies on several central databases of these stakeholders involved, which can even lead to fraud and misuse of the information in some cases. The whole process of vehicle registration can be simplified if all the information about the vehicle and the customer is stored on the Blockchain, and all the stakeholders have access to this information.

50.2. Vehicle registration with Blockchain

Let's look at the various stakeholders involved and how Blockchain can make this complete process a seamless experience for the customer.

Manufacturer to Dealer

The manufacturer is the first stakeholder in the Blockchain network. He will be responsible for adding all the information of a manufactured vehicle, like manufacturing date, model no, engine, etc., to the Blockchain. He can then execute the sale of a vehicle to a dealer through a smart contract. Once the pre-agreed conditions between the dealer and the manufacturer are fulfilled, a smart contract gets executed, which will transfer the ownership of the vehicle to the dealer *(Fig 50-2)*.

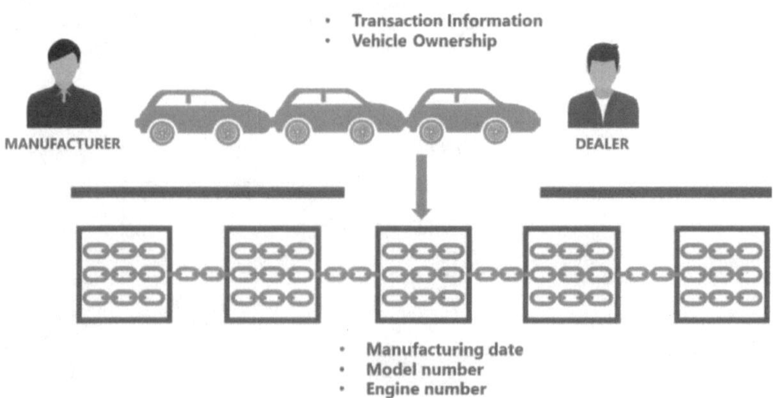

Fig 50-2: Information stored by the manufacturer on Blockchain

Dealer to customer

Through the smart contract, the dealer then executes the sale of the vehicle to the customer.

Registration of vehicle

And after the customer gets ownership of the vehicle, the smart contract is again executed, which will send requests to the concerned authorities for insurance and registration of the vehicle *(Fig 50-3)*.

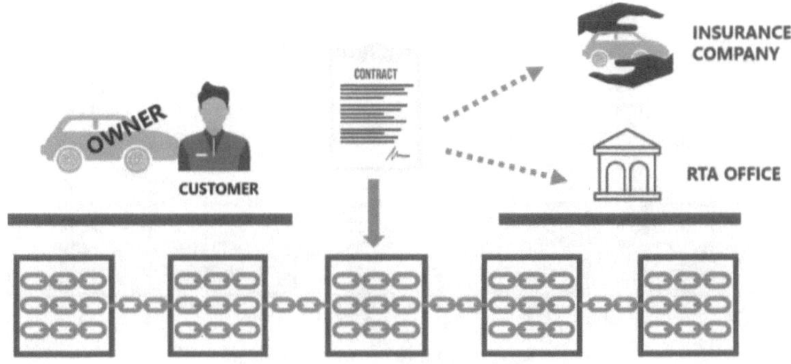

Fig 50-3: Requests for insurance and registration of the vehicle are sent through Blockchain

(i) The Insurance agency and the concerned Regional Transport Authority can validate the information about the vehicle and the customer through Blockchain. After the verification is done, they can provide the insurance and the registration certificate respectively for the vehicle *(Fig 50-4)*.

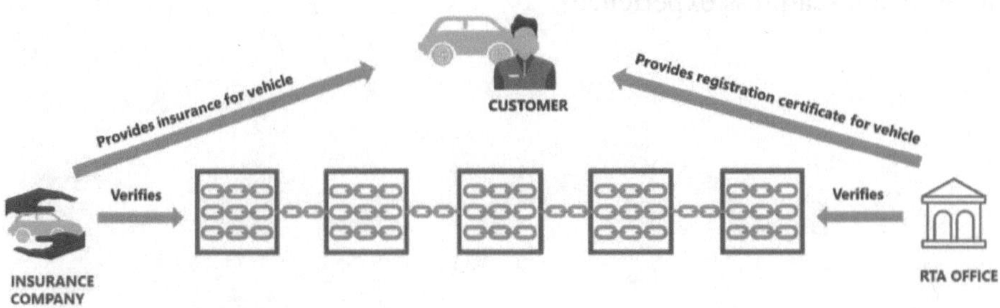

Fig 50-4: Issue of insurance and registration certificate on Blockchain

Under this technology, there will be no need to take your vehicle to RTA for registration. The dealer can issue you the vehicle registration certificate once the RTA validates the information on the Blockchain.

(ii) Further, the customer can request the concerned authorities for NOC and clearance through Blockchain. The authorities will validate the information on Blockchain, and if all conditions are fulfilled, the NOC and clearance will be issued to the customer *(Fig 50-5)*.

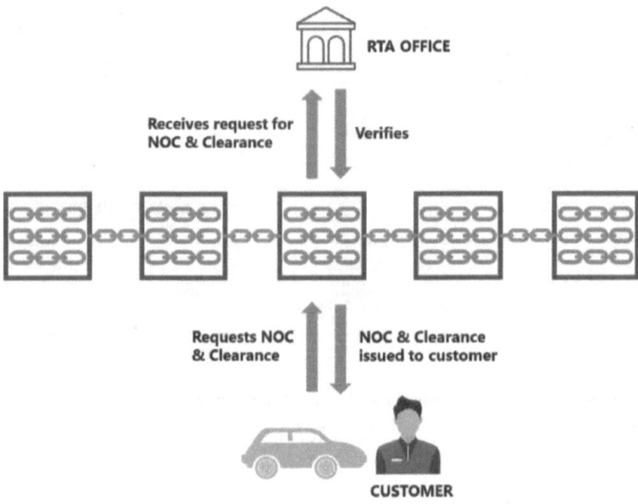

Fig 50-5: Requesting and issuing NOC and clearance on Blockchain

Thus, saving a lot of time and hassle for the customer. And who wouldn't love such a seamless experience?

Chapter 51: Blockchain in the Implementation of Government schemes

The efficient flow and storage of citizens' data for providing services to them is of paramount importance for any government organization. In the current scenario, centralized Database Management systems represent the majority of the databases for storing this information about people in the world.

51.1. Challenges in the implementation of government schemes

In every country, there are a lot of government schemes. But many challenges arise in the implementation of these schemes:

(i) Many needy people cannot avail the schemes because of the corruption involved in the process. A lot of money disbursed by the government under such schemes gets siphoned off by middlemen, thus leaving many needy people either with unpaid wages or less than standard wages.

(ii) The second challenge is data manipulation. This situation arises when user data entry is first done in manual registers at one location of the users, and then the copy of this register is transported to another location for entry in the database. Because of this process of data entry at multiple points and storage of data in different central databases, third-party manipulation is highly possible before data entry in centralized databases. These manipulations pertain to changing, faking, or delaying user data intentionally.

(iii) Even if the data manipulations are not done, delays in availing services might occur due to labor-intensive paperwork and slow inter-bureaucratic communications.

Let's understand how Blockchain can help in the efficient implementation of government funds through a real-world example. A social welfare scheme was started by the Indian government for laborers in India. The scheme aimed at providing 100 days of guaranteed employment to laborers from the

rural parts of India. If employment cannot be provided, an unemployment allowance must be delivered to those laborers.
In implementation of such schemes, an effective communication between the needy people and the government that will arrange funds for them is crucial for the smooth implementation of the scheme. For this communication, there come third-party intermediaries that handle the data of laborers and subsequently ensure funds are disbursed to the laborers. However, there are various challenges in the effective implementation of the scheme. The money provided by the government for the scheme can be exploited.

- Firstly, a huge number of applications received by the Government to provide money and job to laborers are not always correct.
- Local authorities issue more job cards than the number of workers employed to acquire a larger amount of funding from the government. These local officers then pocket the excess money.
- There have also been instances of local people paying bribes to the authorities to acquire a job card to receive the funds.

51.2. Blockchain - The solution

In such situations, Blockchain can help effectively implement government schemes. The data entry would be done on a distributed shared ledger rather than a centralized database. In the case of such schemes, the data entry of laborers applying for work along with their information on their identity cards should be done directly on the Blockchain. It could mitigate the risk of data manipulation, as data once entered, becomes tamper-proof and immutable. The smart contracts on Blockchain contain predefined terms and conditions to decide if the laborers are eligible for the scheme.

After entering the information of laborers, the smart contracts get executed and decide if the laborer is eligible for the scheme, and the result will be stored on the Blockchain. If the laborer is found eligible for the scheme, a notification will be sent to the central government, and the work will be allocated to the laborer. If work has been allocated to the laborer, then the smart contracts will release funds in the form of wages to the laborer's account on the stipulated time based on the work completed by the laborer. As per the scheme rules, if such employment cannot be provided to the laborer within 15 days of applying for work, the smart contracts will again be executed, and an unemployment allowance will be initiated to the bank account of these laborers. The higher authorities would be able to view the related information, for example, the number of days for which work is allocated for the laborers, the total budget of the work, funds allocated to the laborers, etc. Thus enabling a transparent flow of funds.

Even the social audit agencies, whose job is to scrutinize government operations, will be an essential part of this platform as they will have the authority to view the information updated on Blockchain by any authority at any level.

Further, the Blockchain technology will also ensure that people who are not in need should not avail such schemes by forging the documents. Similarly, government issues subsidies to people of its country—for instance, subsidies to farmers to purchase fertilizers for agricultural purposes. But because of the corruption involved, these subsidies are misused and sometimes do not reach the intended farmers at all.

Introducing Blockchain technology can provide transparency in issuing subsidies as well. It would ensure that the farmers or the targeted group of people are getting the appropriate and planned benefits.

51.3. Scalability concerns

(i) Blockchain used will be permissioned Blockchain. The stakeholders involved will be assigned specific functions on the smart contracts. Storing the entire data about the scheme, laborers, funds, authorities responsible for disbursing funds, etc., on Blockchain is very costly; thus, distributed file storage IPFS can provide low-cost off-chain storage to store this data. A unique hash is generated for every uploaded file on the IPFS server, which is then stored on the Blockchain and accessed through the smart contract.

Any change in the uploaded file would change its hash. IPFS has been explained in detail in Chapter 15.

(ii) To make the Blockchain scalable and increase the speed of transactions, layer 1 (discussed in Chapter 12) and layer 2 (discussed in Chapter 13) scaling solutions will be required to be implemented.

Section 8

Tokenization and Blockchain

Chapter 52: Asset tokenization on Blockchain

Asset tokenization refers to converting an asset into a digital token and recording it on a Blockchain network. In other words, digital tokens on the Blockchain represent ownership of the digital or physical assets. Once you buy tokens representing an asset, no single authority can erase or change your ownership; simply put, your ownership of that asset remains entirely immutable on Blockchain.

The term "token" in data science is defined as a value (a randomly generated number) assigned to sensitive data to mask the original information. So, in a Blockchain, a token is a number assigned to data stored within the Blockchain. Giving an asset a token is called "tokenization." Thus, each digital token on the Blockchain has a unique token ID that distinguishes it from any other token.

52.1. Types of tokens

Whether it be paintings, digital media platforms, company shares, venture capital funds, collectibles, or real estate property, everything can be tokenized on a distributed ledger.

Basically, there are two types of tokens:

(i) Utility tokens: They are also known as user tokens or app coins. Utility tokens represent a form of value that can be redeemed in the future. Organizations create them for a specific purpose. They offer token holders several benefits, often access to products and services, like, a discount, ticket, coupon, or access to unique features in a DApp or in a game. A few examples of utility coins are as follows:

- Smooth Love Potion or SLP token is an ERC-20 utility token featured by Axie Infinity metaverse game built on Ethereum. By earning or purchasing SLP, players can perform exclusive in-game tasks, like collecting unique digital pets called Axies which they can breed, sell, or deploy in the battle against other players.
- Filecoin network is a peer-peer system (built on IPFS) facilitating secure data storage on the internet and retrieval through a

Blockchain-based decentralized network. The users are rewarded who wish to store data online and who wish to rent out unused hard drive space. The users having the utility token FIL can gain access to the platform's network and storage space.

(ii) Security tokens: They are digital assets representing legal ownership of an asset, like shares of ownership in a company, intellectual property, land, or any other kind of asset. The name security tokens are often tied to the securities offering. Security tokens could represent a share in a company or an investment in real estate, or a film project.

Simply put, a utility token can buy access to a company's product or service, while a security token can buy you a stake in the company itself. Additionally, security tokens are regulated by the US and many other governments like any other security, while utility tokens are not.

52.2. Difference between tokens and crypto coins

A token is built for a decentralized project on an existing Blockchain and is used to represent some kind of noncash asset, like an ownership stake; special rights within a project, like voting rights; or early access to a product developed by the company that's issuing the token.

Crypto coins, on the other hand, represent digital currency created for making payments. Coins are created to act like money: they always have a given cash equivalent based on demand and market pressures like Bitcoin (BTC), Bitcoin Cash (BCH), Litecoin (LTC), and Ether (ETH).

Crypto coins are native to their own Blockchain. For instance, the Bitcoin blockchain coin is BTC. The Ethereum blockchain has an ETH coin. And the Litecoin blockchain uses an LTC coin. These crypto coins are primarily designed to store value and work as a medium of exchange, like paying for goods or services, transferring to others, etc., similar to traditional currencies. This is why crypto coins are also referred to as cryptocurrencies.

Tokens can have value, but they don't exist solely as a way of transferring that value. Typically, they're designed for something more complicated than a simple monetary transaction.

52.3. Steps to create a token

If you want to create a token, you would be required to follow these 4 steps:

Step 1: First of all, define the properties of your token

(i) Select an asset that you want to tokenize, for example, real estate, a physical commodity (e.g., a precious stone), an artwork, a collectible, a piece of intellectual property, a medicine, etc.

(ii) Specify total token supply, token's name, symbol, and value. Also, describe the rights associated with assets.

(iii) Analyze global, country- and industry-specific legal regulations relevant to asset tokenization. For instance, SEC regulations for financial securities, HIPAA for healthcare assets, etc.

Step 2: Develop a smart contract

(i) Choose the optimal Blockchain platform that supports smart contracts for asset tokenization. Ethereum is the most commonly used Blockchain for creating tokens, and the ERC-20 standard is the universal language that all tokens created on the Ethereum network must follow.

(ii) Assigning unique IDs to the tokens and developing smart contracts to program the behavior of the tokenized asset is essential.

(iii) Then, it is required to integrate the tokenized asset with required systems, e.g., a crypto wallet (MetaMask), payment gateways, KYC/AML verification services, and more.

Step 3: Run on a Test chain

If you deploy the smart contract of the token on the Blockchain, it will be immutable and would be impossible to replace it in case there's a bug. Therefore it is always a good idea to test your smart contract code by running it on a test Blockchain like Rinkeby or Ropsten.

Step 4: Deploy to main net Blockchain

After you have confirmed your smart contract code, you are all set to deploy it on Blockchain. It's just a matter of few clicks, and your token is there on Blockchain.

Thus, the tokens represent a set of rules encoded in a smart contract. Every token belongs to a Blockchain address. These tokens are accessible with a dedicated wallet like MetaMask that communicates with the Blockchain and manages the public-private key pair related to the address. Only the person who has the private key for that address can access the tokens. He can, therefore, be regarded as the owner of that token. If the token represents an asset, the owner can initiate the transfer of the tokens by signing with their private key, which in turn generates a digital signature. If the token represents an access right to something, the owner of that token can initiate access by signing with his private key. If the token represents voting, the owner of that token can vote by signing with their private key.

52.4. Benefits and challenges of asset tokenization

(i) Fractional asset ownership: Tokenization enables Fractional ownership, which means splitting and converting a physical asset such as real estate into several digital tokens, like stocks of a company. Every token represents direct ownership of an asset and will have a unique ID. Therefore, those who buy the tokens own a portion of the equity in that asset. Additionally, tokenization democratizes the investment space by opening it up to allow more people, specifically those who aren't in a place, to invest a large amount of money at a time in expensive assets like real estate. Tokenization of land breaks large, expensive investments into fractional slices, creating a security token for each piece of land. With fractional ownership, if the asset increases in value, the value of the shares in the investment does as well.

(ii) Increased liquidity: Tokenizing assets would also increase an asset's liquidity, as it facilitates fractional ownership. Let's use the example of an individual requiring $50,000 taken out of a property valued at $500,000. This individual may have tokenized their property into 500,000 security tokens, each worth 0.0002%. They might sell 50,000 tokens on the

Blockchain instead of selling the entire property, thus ensuring a more liquid asset.

(iii) Peer-to-peer asset trading: The ownership of tokenized assets can be transferred directly between asset owners and investors. But the transfer of securities follows regulations. All transactions on tokenized assets are automatically validated, timestamped, cryptographically encrypted, and recorded in the immutable distributed ledger available to asset owners and investors.

(iv) End-to-end asset traceability: Asset owners and investors can trace the whole history of activities performed over tokenized assets on Blockchain. It helps verify asset origin and provenance and prevent fraud and counterfeiting.

(v) Smart contract-based automation: Self-executing protocols on smart contracts automatically enforce actions related to tokenized assets upon particular events pre-defined by token issuers. For example, asset ownership is automatically transferred to the investor upon payment for the asset.

Various industries, including healthcare, finance, real estate, sports, banking, entertainment, gaming, etc., are embracing the concept of tokenization of their assets.

52.5. Challenges in asset tokenization

(i) There are no universal regulations that would apply in different countries and different jurisdictions.

(ii) Regulators, developers, and governments need to work together to define the legal framework regarding tokenized assets.

Chapter 53: Blockchain in Real Estate

The real estate market business is one of the most lucrative and important businesses in the world. Real estate is a valuable distributed resource that solves different tasks. It satisfies the basic human need for living space and security, and it is also the basis of many types of business, a part of the national wealth, and a source of budget revenues. Real Estate is a $217 trillion global industry, and residential property makes up about 75% of the total value. In this article, we will understand the problems that are currently haunting the real estate industry and how Blockchain technology offers solutions to these problems.

Before talking about problems that the real estate industry is facing, let's try to understand a typical property buying process:

- An individual looking to buy property either visits a property listing website or booking website or a real estate broker in person.
- Based on the individual's requirements, these intermediaries suggest some sellers who are selling properties matching the buyer's criteria.
- These intermediaries then contact the seller to discuss the deal's details and negotiate.

53.1. Challenges faced by the real estate sector

These intermediaries promise to get the buyers the best deals based on their criteria. No matter how reliable and honest these intermediaries claim to be, there are some issues that hamper the real estate industry from functioning optimally:

(i) The first one is lack of transparency. All these intermediaries are in the market to make a profit. They all have a business model, which makes them biased towards the deals that earn them more profit. Such deals are not always in favor of buyers. These intermediaries can choose to limit the options visible to the seller or give priority to the ones that are more lucrative to them. Hence, there is a good chance that the buyers would lose out on the property, which might be the best fit, but rather get the property that might provide more profits to the intermediaries.

(ii) Second issue in the real estate industry is fraud. Both low-level petty renter fraud and high-level wire fraud are prevalent in the real estate industry. Fraud is responsible for millions lost annually. With an impressive website and alluring claims, buyers can be deceived into buying a property that is unavailable or suitable for sale. Not all buyers are well educated or vigilant enough to do background checks on these intermediaries. The result is a lot of legal suites and loss of a significant chunk of money. Even the forged documents also play a crucial role in fooling buyers and making them buy illegal/not for sale/unsuitable property. With many softwares, editing text in physical documents like property papers or bank statements and reproducing it is an easy task and can easily prove that the fake documents are legitimate.

(iii) The third issue in the real estate industry is the high fees of intermediaries. The property owner wants to sell the property, and the buyer wants to own it. And the intermediaries which connect these buyers and sellers charge exorbitant fees. Many times, the amount of money they charge doesn't justify the services they deliver. And instead of getting better deals and making the whole experience smooth for the buyer, they end up doing more harm than good for instance, the buyer ends up in getting an unsuitable property. And in many cases, the broker partners with the seller to sell a property at a higher price than the market standard.

(iv) The fourth issue in the real estate industry is that closing deals are time intensive process. To close a deal in the real estate industry, there are many moving pieces that all rely on paper processes. Between inspections, releasing contingencies, loan approval, unexpected repairs, completing cash transactions for closing, and completing all the other necessary paperwork for closing a deal is an incredibly time-intensive headache for buyers, sellers, and third parties. Anyone who has bought or sold property can agree that it is a bureaucratic nightmare and a complex event.

(v) The other challenge that arises in the real estate industry is record keeping and security. With so many transactions happening while closing a deal, recording each transaction is challenging. It's not about ensuring everything gets recorded but also guaranteeing that the records can't be tampered with and are only accessible to authorized people. To purchase or sell property, clients as well as sellers need to disclose an alarming amount of personal information to various parties, leaving them vulnerable to identity theft.

53.2. Blockchain- The Solution

Blockchain technology can have a major effect on the real estate industry. Following are the areas of the real estate industry that can be benefitted from blockchain technology.

(i) The first benefit of Blockchain can be in due diligence and the financial evaluation process. Physical paper documents for proof of identity are still the norm today. This manual verification process also increases the likelihood of errors, and multiple third-party service providers are involved in this verification process. These factors can be a costly and time-consuming process that slows down the closing of a deal.

But on the Blockchain platform digital identities of all the parties involved, including buyer, seller, and real estate agent, will be registered; thus, the entire process of verifying identity can be done very efficiently on Blockchain by the verification companies, government agencies, banks, and investors. Hence, lowering costs of due diligence, enhancing data security, and reducing the chance of manual errors. The leasing and sale process in commercial real estate transactions is also flooded with tasks that require verification of other physical documents such as supporting the history of ownership, a tenant or buyer's income, occupancy history, and repairs and maintenance records. Blockchain-based verification processes could also expedite sales and pre-transaction activities such as financial evaluation, obtaining a mortgage commitment, and others.

(ii) Smart Contracts can streamline the Payouts. Smart contracts are the lines of code written to get executed autonomously when the pre-defined conditions or rules are fulfilled. These rules can't be edited once coded. For example, If a code is written on a smart contract that if the deal gets closed, then transfer the amount in the ratio 20:30:50 to A, B, and C people, and the smart contracts will transfer the predefined amount to the respective people when the deal gets closed. Smart contracts can streamline extremely complex payout contracts. And the other benefit is that it will cut off all the middlemen imagine how much money you can save by cutting out all the brokers' fees. Real estate transactions can take months, and that is mainly because of the vast amount of bureaucracy, middlemen, and lack of transparency that you need to go through. But, smart contracts can expedite the transactions. Since each transaction is time-stamped and recorded, there is no need to keep track of everything on paper. As a result, the whole process gets automated, saving time, effort, and money.

(iii) Smart contracts can also streamline rental payments. Smart contracts can be converted into rental contracts. A smart contract will have all the agreements made between two parties, the rent terms decided, the monthly rental amount, the security amount, etc. A smart contract can automate the rental process between the two parties. A rental amount can be automatically deducted from the tenant's account after a pre-defined time and then get transferred to the landlord's account. Smart contracts can also automate the lease agreement such that little or no monitoring is required by either of the parties. Upon the termination of the lease, the rental terms expire, and the security amount is transferred back to the tenant's account.

(iv) Blockchain can also help to combat property fraud and missing property records. Despite the advancements in the technological era, land records are still stored on paper in most nations, even today, and are kept in centralized siloed locations. The paper-based land records are very easily prone to natural or man-made disasters. The classic example of what happens when you store land records in a centralized location is the case of 'Haiti city.' In 2010, in a catastrophic earthquake, most of the land records of the city were either damaged or destroyed. The city still faces disputes on land with the lack of clear land titles.

Additionally, the paper-based system is not only hard to maintain but also vulnerable towards corruption of land titles. It reduces the authenticity and security of land records. Moreover, the pen and paper system makes the whole land registry process more complex and tedious. Storing digital records on the decentralized, immutable Blockchain ledger can be the first step to having a robust land registration system. This immediately removes the threat of losing, destroying, or damaging records. Because if the records are lost or destroyed from one server/location, can always be retrieved from another location.

The shared platform of Blockchain also makes digital records less susceptible to fraud and manipulation. Since the information once entered on a Blockchain is impossible to edit or delete, it becomes difficult to exploit it. Hence, the disruptive technology ensures that documents remain tamper-proof. The transparent nature of a public ledger also allows a person to trace the data origins of the property. Property history databases are never up-to-date and are certainly not transparent in their origins or motives. Using Blockchain to track the construction of the property, the history of repairs, issues property experiences, and the improvements done can make buyers aware of the property's troubled past. This would help buyers feel more confident in their purchases knowing the full history of the property. And thus, better data about property provides a basis for improved decision-making, and people can truly know what they are buying.

53.3. Real estate Tokenization

The real estate market is considered to be one of the most prominent investment markets. However, in order to make an investment in real estate, you need to have a sizable chunk of money. This creates a barrier for a lot of people. In the present scenario, the seller cannot sell fractions of the property. Even if he wants to, the buyer needs to trust the seller that he or she has the equity they claim to have. Hence such a financial model is unsustainable with the present tools at hand. Blockchain-driven real estate has the power to incorporate a new business model of "**Tokenization ownership**." Tokenizing ownership means fragmenting and converting a physical asset such as real estate into several digital tokens; much like stocks on exchanges. One property can be divided into several tokens. Every real estate token represents direct ownership of an asset. Therefore, those who buy the tokens then own a portion of the equity in that asset.

To understand how this will work, let's take a hypothetical example.

Suppose a property at the beachside costs ~$650,000, which is out of the budget for most people. However, suppose the seller tokenizes the property. After that, five people each $130,000 worth of these tokens and jointly own the property. When the transaction is complete, these five enter a multi-signature smart contract based on the ownership of the property. A multi-signature smart contract will ensure that whatever decision is taken with respect to the property is agreed upon by a majority of the owners. Since the contract is self-executing and enforceable, it will not require any supervision and will force the joint owners to be honest.

Thus, tokenization enables **Fractional ownership**, which creates a win-win situation for buyers and sellers. Buyers don't need to have a bulk chunk of money pooled in order to make an investment in real estate. Instead of saving up and taking loans to buy one expensive asset, you can simply buy one-fifth of that expensive and out-of-budget asset. So this lowers the barrier to entry for real estate investments with Blockchain. Additionally, the property shares can be used as security against which they can get a loan. And sellers can sell the shares that they are comfortable with. This allows them to create an additional source of income as well as not give up the whole piece of land. The idea of tokenizing the real estate shares is to create a new business model which is more open, accessible, and easy.

Once the real estate is tokenized, it is recorded digitally on a Blockchain. The information of shareholders, their token ownership status, and trading of the tokens are also immutably recorded as transactions. The contract details of buying and selling tokens are pre-defined in "smart contracts." Once the conditions are fulfilled, transactions happen, which are permanently recorded on Blockchain.

53.4. Challenges in real estate tokenization

(i) Tokenization of assets will probably take years or decades to develop completely. Indeed, as we know from previous trends, technology evolves and changes quickly, but regulation usually follows a long and slow path to adapt. Thus, asset tokenization may probably represent one of the greatest challenges for global regulatory agencies.

(ii) Since the tokenization of a real estate asset leads to splitting asset property, it makes property management and maintenance monitoring a challenging task. Each owner with a smaller share may not have incentives due to the higher costs of monitoring with respect to their investment compared to a single owner with a bigger share. The market needs to make strategies to motivate all shareholders to maintain and manage the property.

53.5. Scalability concerns

(i) Blockchain used will be permissioned Blockchain. The stakeholders involved will be assigned specific functions on the smart contracts. Storing the entire data on Blockchain is very costly; thus, distributed file storage IPFS can provide low-cost off-chain storage to store data about the real estate, buyers, sellers, etc. A unique hash is generated for every uploaded file on the IPFS server, which is then stored on the Blockchain and accessed through the smart contract. Any change in the uploaded file would change its hash. IPFS has been explained in detail in Chapter 15.

(ii) To make the Blockchain scalable and increase the speed of transactions, layer 1 (discussed in Chapter 12) and layer 2 (discussed in Chapter 13) scaling solutions will be required to be implemented.

Section 9

Non-Fungible Tokens or NFTs

Chapter 54: Non-Fungible Tokens or NFTs and Blockchain

NFT stands for "Non-Fungible Token." To understand NFTs, firstly, it is important to understand the difference between non-fungible and fungible.

54.1. What do fungible and non-fungible mean?

You can think of something that is fungible as interchangeable while still maintaining the same value because its value defines them rather than its unique properties. For example, in fiat currencies like US dollars, a 10$ note can be exchanged with another 10$ note or even can be swapped for two 5$ notes. Cryptocurrency coins like Bitcoin, Ethereum, etc are also fungible because one coin can be exchanged for any other coin. They hold the same market value. It doesn't matter from whom a BTC was purchased since all BTC units have the same functionality and are part of the same network. The only thing that changes is a record on the Blockchain registering the transaction.

On the other hand, non-fungible items are not interchangeable because they have unique attributes attached to them. You can't trade one non-fungible item for a different item; otherwise, you would have something completely different. For example, a painting like the Mona Lisa.

54.2. What are NFTs, and how are they created?

Non-fungible tokens or NFTs are digital tokens that can be thought of as certificates that represent ownership of unique digital non-fungible items. You can't trade one token for a different token, as you'd have something completely different. An NFT is created or "minted" from digital objects that represent both tangible and intangible items, including art, GIFs, videos, tweets, collectibles, music, and even real estate. NFTs are created to protect digital files from getting replicated and used without the permission of the original creator.

How are NFTs created?

To create an NFT, a creator first creates a digital asset, which could be an image, a video, a tweet, a domain name, a game, a digital trading card/collectible, artwork, a meme, or anything else that lives in the online world. The creator then creates a token or NFT using smart contracts on the Blockchain platform like Ethereum, Cardano, or Solana that supports smart contracts. The smart contracts on Blockchain are written using different standards, such as the ERC-721 standard for NFTs.

When you create an NFT, it is known as **minting**. You are basically writing the underlying smart contract code. Each token is unique and contains information about the digital assets, including the token name, the token symbol, and a unique token ID/hash that proves the authenticity of the NFT.

Additionally, these tokens cannot be traded or exchanged equivalently like cryptocurrencies. NFTs give exclusive ownership rights, which means they can have only one owner at a time.

54.3. How are NFTs stored?

It is very difficult to use encryption to store something as complex as a digital photograph, a digital painting, or a music album inside one of the smart contracts or blocks of data on Blockchain itself. Because the common media files such as JPG, PNG, GIF, MP3, etc. associated with NFTs are so large, the cost of encrypting and storing them on the Blockchain is exorbitantly expensive and consumes a lot of electricity.

NFTs exist in two parts-the smart contract and the metadata. The smart contract exists on a Blockchain, typically Ethereum (although that is changing rapidly), and contains a set of rules or standards that facilitates the transaction and serves as a digital description of the content. The smart contract also includes a link that points to the server that stores the digital asset somewhere else on the internet. Metadata is data that describes other data of the digital asset. Metadata helps servers find, process, and store data more efficiently. But the actual digital asset is what people value. It's what you see and hear, like a profile picture, digital art, or a song. The metadata also describes characteristics of an NFT like its name, color, size, shape, etc. The smart contracts also specify certain rules about trading the NFTs. This could, for example, be the percentage of royalties they receive for every subsequent sale. Basically, smart contracts are what make each NFT unique and valuable.

The common misconception is this media is stored on the Blockchain, which typically isn't the case. Sometimes, the media is stored on a centralized server or computer. For example, the image associated with an NFT may be stored on an Amazon Web Services (AWS) cloud storage solution. The problem with centralized storage is in any case if the servers shut down at any time, then the files stored would be lost and become inaccessible. In this scenario, the link contained within the smart contract of your NFT would point to nothing. Also, the files stored on centralized servers are susceptible to hacking. If somebody alters that URL, your precious digital asset JPEG, or song, is gone forever. This is in direct conflict with the immutable nature of the Blockchain. Collectors and owners of NFTs generally buy them, believing that what they're getting will last forever and cannot be altered.

To help solve this issue, there are popular alternatives to centralized storage for storing NFT media like InterPlanetary File System or IPFS. IPFS is a protocol and peer-to-peer network for storing and sharing data in a distributed file system. A unique hash is generated for every uploaded file on the IPFS server, which is then stored on the smart contract. Decentralizing file storage helps guarantee that digital assets such as artwork, songs, etc., associated with your NFTs will be as immutable as the smart contracts that live on the blockchain.

In simple words, the content of NFTs, such as the physical art or image file, isn't actually stored on the Blockchain; only the smart contract stating that the NFT exists is recorded on the Blockchain. The content is stored elsewhere, such as a centralized server or decentralized IPFS.

54.4. Where are NFTs stored after purchase?

So if an NFT is stored on the Blockchain, where does it go after you purchase it? Technically speaking, once you purchase an NFT, it doesn't go anywhere; it simply remains on the Blockchain indefinitely. However, the change of ownership is recorded on the Blockchain. **Your wallet address will be the new owner in the smart contract of that NFT.** It means that ownership of NFT with the old owner's wallet address is replaced by your wallet address.

The smart contract is also transferred to your wallet like MetaMask, and you become the new owner. To understand it better, let's take the example of land. A land deed exists as a paper document that represents ownership of physical land. So, what happens if the landowner decides to sell their land to someone else? The land deed, which is a legal document, is used to transfer ownership of real estate from the seller to the buyer. The document still exists as a document, it is simply signed over to the new owner. So legally, the buyer becomes the legal owner of the land.

An NFT isn't much different, the main difference is that the contract is digital and lives on a decentralized public ledger, i.e., the Blockchain as opposed to a piece of paper.

The smart contract stored in your wallet points towards the link where the digital assets associated with your NFT are stored. The wallet is secured by a private key, and to access your NFTs, you must access your wallet through the private key. Thus, you are solely responsible for controlling your wallet address via your private key.

Also, an NFT can be purchased, sold, or traded by having access to the wallet address.

Chapter 55: Blockchain and NFTs in the Education sector

Education is an amazing tool that can be used to change the world and facilitate one's purpose in life. Blockchain technology and NFTs have the potential to revolutionize this field as well.

55.1. NFTs in replacing paper documents

The biggest advantage of blockchain in education is storing the education credentials in digital format in a safe and secure way. In the traditional education system, all the education qualification certificates, including school certificates, higher education certificates, and other skills certificates, are kept on paper. Having all of these documents on paper poses many challenges. Imagine a scenario where your file containing all these certificates gets lost or stolen. In such a scenario, the first risk you may face is unauthorized use of your documents. The second biggest challenge will be running from one department to another to get another copy of your documents. Won't it be great if you could store your documents online safely and securely? This can be done by **document tokenization**, which means converting documents into digital tokens known as NFTs and recording them on a Blockchain network. However, storing all the credentials on Blockchain is very expensive and consumes a large amount of electricity. Therefore, the certificates are stored on decentralized IPFS, and their ownership provided in the form of NFTs, is stored on the Blockchain. The smart contract of NFTs contains a link to the education qualification certificates stored on IPFS. The NFT awarded to each student will be unique and different from others. Once stored on Blockchain, NFTs become immutable and can never be lost or replaced.

Duke University is among the first institutions that has provided educational credentials as NFTs to the students who have completed their Blockchain course on Coursera in 2022.

The NFTs representing credentials like diplomas, degrees, etc., are stored in a digital wallet that serves as a person's educational profile.

55.2. NFTs in verifying documents

Getting proper education is obligatory for obtaining a job. Each employer has specific qualification criteria for each job that they float into the market. As a job candidate, you have to show your credentials and certificates to prove your qualifications. And these days, frauds and forgery of education credentials to match one's qualifications are on the rise. These cases of frauds and forgeries can easily be mitigated with the help of Blockchain technology as the data stored on the Blockchain is immutable and can easily be verified. The candidate can share NFTs (representing the education credentials) with the employer by encrypting some, or all, of the data held within the NFTs to provide privacy-preserving features. To view data within the token, the employer requires a code to decrypt the NFT, which could allow read-only and single-use access rather than allowing him to edit or grant indefinite access. In this way, the employer can verify the legitimacy of a candidate before hiring him or even before considering him for an interview. An additional advantage is that it stops anyone from falsifying their academic certifications. The NFT token would act as a unique digital fingerprint.

55.3. NFTs in Online learning

Blockchain technology can revolutionize the whole education system. Today students not only receive education in formal settings of schools and university lecture halls, but the informal educational settings have been widely adopted by the student community. There are a plethora of online courses, workshops, conferences, boot camps, and a lot more to enhance one's skills. The platforms offer certificates in printed form or as a digital badge; the biggest challenge has always been verification, as well as assessing the value of the credential. But what if online platforms and universities offer course completion certificates in the form of NFTs? These educational NFTs do not have a monetary value, but they prove the student has passed the course and contain unique details about the course syllabus and the performance of the student.

Chapter 56: Utility NFTs or NFT 2.0

Utility NFTs or NFT 2.0 are a class of non-fungible tokens designed not just for collecting but also for utility, i.e., these NFTs have underlying valuable and practical applications.

56.1. What are utility NFTs and how do they work?

Utility NFTs are NFTs with use cases beyond just being the representation of unique digital assets. Now nobody wants to buy your NFT because they look fantastic, but the expectation is what actual value your NFT will bring to others. Just like any other NFT, utility NFTs are created with smart contracts and are unique. But the core focus is to grant their NFT-holders rights, privileges, exclusive experiences, or rewards that they would not otherwise be able to access.

Like any other NFT, a utility NFT is also cryptographically secure and represents unique digital assets stored on a Blockchain. The immutability and transparency of blockchain technology make it easy for NFT holders to prove their ownership and help them verify the provenance of their NFTs.

56.2. How to add utility to an NFT?

Utility refers to how you add or create value, specifically in being helpful, profitable, or beneficial to others. There are several different ways by which one can add utility to their NFTs:

(i) Make your NFTs redeemable: Making NFTs redeemable will allow the NFT-holders to claim for either a physical or digital good, for example, allowing NFT owners to claim a T-shirt or hoodie at the event. Since authentication is tighter with NFTs, you can also weed out any scammers that go after the free items you offer. As an artist, you may conduct a competition where the person holding the highest number of your NFTs receives a valuable product like an original hand-drawn art from you. People always love having access to original and rare art, therefore turning your NFTs into utility-based NFTs.

(ii) NFT utility linked with exclusivity: You can provide your NFT holders with a certain type of exclusivity. For instance,

- NFT holders can be rewarded with tickets to exclusive events, show passes, membership cards, etc. For example, motivational speakers have started to sell NFTs that give the holders limited or lifetime access to their events and provide access to them either for video calls or in-person meetings for breakfast, lunch, or dinner.
- NFT buyers can also be provided VIP access to events and shows.
- Special discounts on tickets or products can be given, especially if they can't be offered for free. For example, suppose if you are a gaming company, provide NFT holder-only discount coupons on the early release of your next game.
- Another example of exclusivity to NFT owners is playing as a unique character in the video game.
- You can also give early access to merchandise sales to NFT holders first.
- Or you can also host events in the metaverse for NFT holders only.

(iii) NFTs With Passive Income Utility: Passive income can be provided to the NFT owners.

- In the stock market, when investors buy and hold shares, they get dividends according to the percentage of shares they are having. In the same way, you can offer a percentage of dividends to be paid to the holders of your NFTs after a set length of time.
- Additionally, you can share a certain amount of profit with your NFT holders. This provides a consistent passive income stream to your NFT buyers and helps turn your NFTs into utility NFTs.
- The other example of NFTs that provide an opportunity to earn is in play-to-earn games. Utility NFTs can represent in-game assets, weapons, or virtual goods that players can purchase and use within a game. With NFTs, players hold a certificate of ownership of online assets, allowing them to sell their NFTs to other players within the game and on other NFT marketplaces to earn additional income.

With NFTs, play-to-earn games are not only exciting but also potentially rewarding. One such game that incorporates utility NFTs as its in-game assets is Blockchain Cuties. In this game, players can play with puppies, lizards, bear cubs, cats, and other real and fantasy creatures. Each cutie/creature is a unique NFT that 100% belongs to the owners. The players can collect their creatures, breed them, test their skills in battle, arm them, and level them up, meaning that they can increase their creature's value within the game's ecosystem. Within the game, the smart contracts allow users to trade their creature with other players for another creature. In traditional games, the assets belong to the game itself, and a player can not do anything with these assets outside of the game. But with Blockchain, the players can sell or transfer their creature NFTs to other players like regular cryptocurrencies.

(iv) Special Content Access: Providing access to unique content also adds utility to the NFT. Your NFT project could come up with premium content that would be of value to your NFT holders. It can be in the form of

- Research PDF
- Video reports
- Online education course
- eBook
- High-value cheatsheets and guides
- Bonus and additional content that buyers of your NFT can only access. Whether you're a YouTuber releasing extra videos, or a music artist releasing bonus tracks that your NFT-holders can access, it also creates a sense of exclusivity.

(v) Make your NFTs usable in the metaverse: A metaverse is a limitless virtual reality space within which people can live, work, shop, and interact with others. You can add qualities to your NFTs that make them possible to be uniquely identifiable, purchasable, and exchangeable on NFT marketplaces in the metaverse.

- For instance, an NFT could represent a piece of virtual real estate in the metaverse. By buying an NFT, you would own that piece of property and would be able to sell it or rent it out to other users in the metaverse. For example, Decentraland is a virtual world that uses NFTs to represent ownership of virtual land. Users can buy, sell, or rent their land on Decentraland's decentralized marketplace.

- Another example may be of NFT sneakers so that the user character can wear them in the metaverse.

The options are limitless, depending on how much value you want to add to your NFT.

Chapter 57: NFT ticketing for events

NFT tickets are digital assets that hold your access credentials to an event.

Before the advent of digital ticketing, people used to buy and collect old-school tickets. Each of those tickets was unique, reviving memories, whether the World Cup in England or a music festival in New York. But there are good chances of misplacing the paper tickets.

Now that digitization has streamlined ticketing; ticketing systems have also become more efficient with a QR code embedded on the tickets. One doesn't have to carry the paper tickets; scanning the QR code on the mobile tickets is sufficient to get access to the event. However, these tickets cannot be used as memorabilia that people want to keep and have to reminisce about. Undoubtedly, getting a digitized ticket can lower your chances of misplacing your ticket, but QR Codes can be easily forged.

57.1. What are NFT tickets?

NFT tickets have the potential to address the shortcomings of the traditional ticketing system and can combine physical and digital ticketing. NFT tickets are digital assets stored on a Blockchain, so the risk of your ticket getting lost, stolen, or damaged is relatively low. Additionally, NFT tickets can become valuable collectibles and act as lasting memorabilia.

NFTs and the ticketing industry have a natural fit because of the following reasons:

(i) Both tickets and NFTs are non-fungible. Just like every NFT, tickets are also unique because only one person can use their ticket to occupy their seat for an event.

(ii) Both tickets and NFTs are limited in supply; just as NFTs are released in limited quantity, all live events offer a limited number of tickets to customers according to the seating capacity.

Ticketmaster, Coachella, the NBA, the Olympics, and more have all embraced NFTs.

57.2. How does NFT ticketing work?

For creating NFT tickets,

(i) Event organizers can mint the required number of NFT tickets on their choice of a Blockchain platform like Ethereum that supports smart contracts.

(ii) The smart contracts are programmed, where the rules for sale price, auction rules, resale rules, royalty fees, etc., are pre-defined.

(iii) The next step is to link an IPFS system to the ticketing system because storing tickets on the Blockchain itself will be costly. The ticket itself is stored on the IPFS, but the hash of the ticket, along with its address, is stored on the smart contract of the NFT ticket. The smart contract is recorded on the Blockchain.

(iv) A buyer purchases NFT tickets directly from the ticketing company. On receiving payment, a smart contract triggers, and a ticketing database sends an NFT ticket to the buyer's digital wallet. Now, the buyer can access the ticket anytime via their phone.

57.3. Benefits of NFT tickets

(i) Tickets go through distribution channels with limited regulation or control. For example, resellers in the secondary ticket market can inflate prices, and ticket bots can buy up most tickets online to resell at a higher price. With NFT tickets, the event organizers can track the transactions on a Blockchain ledger, making it easier for everyone to see when and where the ticket was bought and sold. Thus, event organizers have full control and visibility over primary and secondary ticket sales.

(ii) Also, organizers can write a code in the smart contract of NFT tickets to set a maximum price they can be resold for.

(iii) Through smart contracts, organizers can also determine how royalties are split on secondary ticket sales. The smart contract will automatically execute and trigger a royalty payment to the organizer whenever the ticket is sold to a new customer.

(iv) The organizers can write a code in the smart contract to block the resale of tickets if they want to do. Through Blockchain, both ticket holders and organizers have access to a single version of the information. As a result, when transitioning from initial sale to resale, all parties can check the legitimacy and authenticity of an NFT. If they want to prevent resale, they can make NFTs non-transferable, which means tickets can't be sold to someone else.

57.4. NFTs hold enormous potential for the event industry

(i) Turning tickets into collectibles: People have collected tickets for a long time. They're souvenirs of an experience. While people will probably not save their used bus tickets to remember the trip to work, they save tickets from significant moments they want to preserve and remember. Their first sporting event. The first time they saw their favorite artist live. Their once-in-a-lifetime music festival experience etc. etc.

NFT tickets let fans fill their digital wallets with NFTs of memories, events, and experiences. Thus, making preserving tickets easier.

(ii) Fan engagement and creating unique experiences: NFTs can have many utility benefits beyond the event to which it grants access. NFTs can be a rewards system for your loyal fans and valuable customers. NFTs can allow the event organizers to not only buy and sell event tickets but the event moments as well. Events are all about creating unforgettable experiences, and NFTs can help keep those moments alive for attendees. For example, an NFT ticket holder will get an event video highlighting the best moments to relive again.

Letting people own experiences this way strengthens your fan base and tightens the community around your brand. You can also sell experiences as NFTs to those people who missed the event, thus reaching an even wider audience and making your event more inclusive.

NFT tickets can also be a membership to an exclusive community. You could offer your fans who bought NFT tickets, invite-only access to future events. You could offer them lifetime passes to your events, VIP access, or discounts on tickets to your future events.

You can also set NFTs to unlock your exclusive physical products, thus allowing NFT-ticket buyers to claim a T-shirt or keychain with a photo of the event artist at the event. Since authentication is tighter with NFTs, you can weed out any scammers that go after the free items you offer.

These things not only enhance the fan experience but will also strengthen your bond with your fans.

(iii) Build communities: NFTs are a powerful tool for generating communities. Creating loyal customers has always been one of the toughest challenges for any organization. With NFTs, any organization can make lifetime relationships with their customers. If they are getting benefits from your NFTs, they will automatically promote your NFT. On Twitter, you'll see NFT buyers are among the most vocal and community-oriented customers. Thousands of Twitter users make their NFTs their profile pictures. They connect and follow one another. If they find utility in the NFTs, they retweet and like announcements from creators and community members. Thus your NFT customers sometimes do wonders and do the same thing that the marketing teams spend millions on boosting the visibility and level of engagement with the brand.

57.5. Real-world examples of NFT tickets

(i) In March 2021, the band Kings of Leon released their new album 'When You See Yourself. They released their album as an NFT but also offered two different types of tokens. One included perks for their live show, and another offered 18 "golden NFT tickets" for front-row seats for every Kings of Leon concert for life. In addition, the NFT ticket holder will also receive a VIP experience at their concert, including a personal driver to and from the concert, concierge services at the show, time for personal interaction with the band, exclusive lounge access, and branded bags, t-shirts, etc.

(ii) The football club 'Dynamo Kyiv' is the first major club in the world to sell NFT tickets in July 2021. Once someone buys NFT tickets, he unlocks game tickets and gets exclusive rewards and experiences.

Chapter 58: Physical NFTs and their importance

NFTs are most commonly associated with digital assets, but they can also be used as a digital representation for physical assets like jewelry, property, antiques, or even consumer goods. In fact, they act as a guarantee of ownership over a real-life, physical asset. So, in short, a physical NFT is a non-fungible token that is linked to a physical asset. Physical NFTs are also called phygital NFTs.

So you can say phygital assets have two distinct parts. One of the parts refers to the actual physical asset, such as the tickets, property, jewelry, etc., and the other part is in the form of metadata, present in the smart contracts (on Blockchain) that contains the link to documents/certificates, indicating the ownership of the physical asset. Storing documents on the Blockchain itself will be costly; therefore, they are stored on the decentralized IPFS. But the hash of the documents, along with their address, is stored on the smart contract of the physical NFT. The smart contract is recorded on the Blockchain.

Thus, through physical/phygital NFTs, every physical object can be digitally connected to the Blockchain.

58.1. Benefits of physical/phygital NFTs

(i) Traceability for products to increase consumer trust: Physical assets, as they are today, are largely untrustworthy. We often do not know whether the product we are buying is genuine or counterfeit. We trust that the retailer or brand is selling authentic products as they are advertised. In reality, not even the retailers know whether these products are authentic. This applies to both high-priced items, like designer jewelry, and low-cost items, like oil. Another important example of physical assets being inherently untrustworthy comes from the art world. Phygital NFT provides proof of authenticity of a physical product. The product data can be about where the raw material was sourced from, the manufacturing process, and how the shipment was handled. All this product information is stored on Blockchain, which acts like an immutable database, and the NFT acts as a certificate of quality and trust. For example, precious stones like diamond are valuable only when they contain proof of authenticity, such as a certificate from professionals. Here the NFT attached to the diamond provides this proof. The whole information about the origin, provenance, and history of the physical asset will be present on the Blockchain, which can be accessed by the NFTs. The other example of phygital NFTs can be in the wine industry.

(ii) Fraud Prevention: Anyone imitating a product of a high-value luxury brand with a limited edition would earn huge profits but spoil the reputation of the original brand. Brands have been using the certificate of authenticity for years, but these can also be easily counterfeited. An NFT gives the physical products a certificate of authenticity that cannot be tampered with. As the information is stored on Blockchain, the brands can easily use it to maintain the proof of authenticity to prevent any kind of fraud.

(iii) Secondary sales royalties: NFTs are powered by smart contracts which handle the transferability and verify the ownership. Once you have an NFT for your physical product, you can write a code in a smart contract to include pre-defined royalties on every resale. Then, on the resale of your product, the smart contract will automatically execute and trigger a royalty payment to you as defined on the smart contract.

58.2. How to add a QR code to access physical NFTs?

The physical assets will be tagged with an NFT and stored on a Blockchain. NFTs let you give your products a unique digital identity by serializing every item. This works just like any other serial number, but the difference is that the information is stored on the Blockchain. Additionally, each physical item tagged with an NFT can be tracked independently from all the others. So the Blockchain will also contain the information of who owns each item and whether or not it has been sold. Thus the NFTs act as unique identifiers for each of the products. You could have hundreds of NFTs on the Blockchain, with a different signature for each.

The NFT present on the Blockchain can be accessed by scanning the QR code present on the product. You might wonder, “Can’t the QR codes be faked or copied?” The answer is simple: No. It is because each certified document stored on the Blockchain has a unique hash. While minting NFT for the product, a QR code is generated by encrypting it with the hash of the product's documents. The QR code can be scanned only by a specific dApp. The dApp will not scan any other QR code unless it is Blockchain-based and has a hash value. The dApp cross-checks the hash value in the QR code and compares it with the hash value on the Blockchain network. If the hash value matches, then only the customer gets access to the content associated with the NFT.

If the product is sold, then the ownership status will be updated on the Blockchain. Suppose the encrypted QR code is copied on the fake product. If you scan the QR code, you will see that this product has already been sold. Thus, preventing counterfeiters from introducing fake products into the market.

Additionally, if the hash value doesn't match or the QR code points to the malicious link, the dApp will not open the malicious link. This is how encrypted QR codes also prevent hacking and attacks such as malware attacks, phishing attacks, etc.

58.3. Few applications of physical NFTs

(i) In art: The physical NFTs can be used to represent the authenticity of the physical fine art. This would ensure safeguards against counterfeiting, fraud, or plagiarism. Another significant benefit in physical versions of NFTs is the generation of royalties with each secondary sale of the art. The rules of royalties on secondary sales can be indicated on the smart contract associated with the NFT.

(ii) In supply chain: The end consumers in the supply chain can personally verify if a product is authentic by simply scanning the smart label or QR code attached to each product's packaging. After scanning, the customer gets full access to the unique content that comes with the NFT, like raw material used for the specific product, its origin, current location, shipment conditions, etc. If the customer buys the product, the status and ownership will be updated on the Blockchain.

NFTs can also help in managing the complex returns process. For example, through the NFTs, the companies can determine whether the returned item should be recycled, repaired, sold to discounters, or destroyed.

(iii) In metaverse: In the future, physical NFTs can act as a digital twin, which are 3D models of your physical products. You can easily bring these products to the Metaverse and interact with them digitally. For instance, if your avatar can travel in the same car you own physically, and can use the same laptop you own physically. As more and more physical goods we own are available in the metaverse, the Metaverse will become more and more an extension of our physical reality.

Not only this, online shopping in the metaverse will become more convenient for users. Your avatar can shop for phygital NFTs with other digital avatars in a shared space. The physical products associated with phygital NFTs we purchase in the Metaverse will be delivered to our physical homes. For instance, on an online store in the metaverse, you purchased physical NFT for a shirt after trying on your avatar. After buying NFT, the shirt associated will be delivered by the physical store to your physical home. In this way, shopping in the metaverse will provide a lot of opportunities for businesses to increase customer satisfaction and decrease return rates.

Chapter 59: NFTs and Blockchain in genomics

59.1. Blockchain in managing and storing genetic information

Human DNA contains a lot of information. Like in the case of computers, where the data is stored in 0 and 1 binary digits, in human DNA, the code of life is stored in 4 letters A, T, G, and C. The total amount of DNA found in a cell is referred to as the genome. The sequencing of this genome can be helpful in enormous ways. For example,

- It can help in designing personalized medicines for individuals.
- It can be useful in treating genetic diseases and even can be used for designing personalized diet plans for individuals.

In recent years, the cost of genome sequencing has come down significantly, which has led to advancements in the genetics industry, and the cost is further expected to drop to as little as $100 within the next few years.

Today genome sequencing is so efficient that it can sequence significant amounts of DNA in parallel. But there is a

- challenge of managing, storing, and transmission of this huge amount of information encoded in the DNA.
- Another pain point for researchers is the security and reliability of this DNA information that is stored in public databases.

The security to genetic data can be provided by **genome tokenization**, which means converting an individual's genome into a digital token known as NFT and recording it on a Blockchain network. However, storing all the genome sequencing data on Blockchain is very expensive and consumes a large amount of electricity. Therefore, it is stored on off-chain decentralized IPFS, and its ownership, provided in the form of NFT, is stored on the Blockchain. The smart contract of NFT contains a link to the genetic data stored on IPFS. The genome NFT of each individual will be unique and different from others. Once stored on Blockchain, NFTs become immutable and can never be lost or replaced. Hence, using Blockchain and NFT can make genetic information resistant to fraud or fabrication. Thus, helping researchers and companies in transmission and storing this massive amount of data obtained from DNA Sequencing with high security.

59.2. The genetic material contributors will be owners of their DNA

Another matter of concern is preserving the privacy of the individual who contributes his genetic material. And another very important question to be answered here is who controls this data? Ideally, the individual should be able to control his data directly or through trusted parties such as doctors or research groups with the necessary permissions. But in the current scenario, an individual's genetic information is sold to other research companies without his knowledge. By selling this genetic data, companies are earning huge profits, and that too without the permission of the individuals.

Through Blockchain technology and NFT, an individual will be the owner of his DNA or genetic information, and he will decide who can access his genetic information and for what purpose. If a research company, for instance, wants to run a genetic study, it must send a proposal for access. A user can then sign the proposal to approve access to his genetic data. Tokenization data in the form of NFT also allows the users, healthcare providers, and companies to share genetic data without revealing the identity of the patient by encrypting the patient's private information, which can't be decrypted to reveal the original information. But the data buyer needs to be transparent and will be required to reveal his identity on the Blockchain network. Through NFTs, it is also possible to grant read-only and single-use access rather than allowing editing or granting indefinite access.

59.3. Blockchain in reducing the cost of genome sequencing

The current fees for sequencing of genome is around $1000. The genome sequencing companies generally store this data with themselves and sell the genetic data of individuals to other pharma and biotech companies for the purpose of research and development. But with the implementation of Blockchain, the data of an individual will be stored securely on the Blockchain network. The data buyers, including researchers, drug design companies, and healthcare organizations, who are in need of this genomic data for their research, can directly obtain an individual's genetic data from him. The individual will get paid by the data buyers for sharing his data. Thus reducing the overall cost of getting DNA sequenced and also enhancing the security of the genomic data. Many companies like Nebula Genomics and Genetica are working in this direction. For this, smart contracts will be executed. As soon as data buyers receive genetic information, the data owners will automatically be paid.

59.4. Benefits to researchers and companies

In the current scenario, the availability of genome data is low because very few people have their genomes sequenced. This remains a major roadblock for researchers, pharma, and biotech companies as they require a huge volume of genetic data for conducting their research on genetic diseases. The researchers are usually not interested in random datasets, but instead, they seek to acquire genomic data from individuals with specific phenotypes, such as particular medical conditions, because genomic data without phenotypic data is not particularly useful.

Another challenge that they face is regarding the quality of the data. The quality of collected data is often uncertain because it is typically collected through intermediaries, and personal genomics companies, which rely on self-reported data. The data bought from different sources is often encoded in different formats, which makes it time-consuming for data buyers to convert it into a consumable format. But through Blockchain, the data buyers will get directly connected to individuals; therefore, it would be easy for them to acquire phenotypic information along with genotypic information from individuals. And on the Blockchain, the genomic data will be stored in standard formats that will save time and money of researchers.

59.5. Scalability concerns

(i) To make the Blockchain scalable for its use in genomics and increase its transaction speed, layer 1 (discussed in Chapter 12) and layer 2 (discussed in Chapter 13) scaling solutions will be required to be implemented.

(ii) Blockchain used will be permissioned Blockchain. The stakeholders involved will be assigned specific functions on the smart contracts and granted limited access based on their roles.

Section 10

Metaverse

Chapter 60: What is metaverse?

Meta is a prefix that means 'beyond,' and 'verse' comes from 'universe,' making the word Metaverse.

The term "metaverse" originated from the science-fiction novel 'Snow Crash' by Neal Stephenson, where humans interact with each other and with computer-generated characters in the 3D virtual world. While the idea of a metaverse was once fiction, it now looks like it could be a reality in the future. Now, the metaverse is a major buzzword that's garnering significant attention. Many are even considering it to be the next big thing that has the potential to revolutionize the way we interact with each other and with digital content. Considering its vast potential in benefitting the digital world, many big tech giants are already taking a leap and entering the world of Metaverse. Like, on 28 October 2021, Facebook changed its name to Meta.

The Metaverse is the idea that there will be one single 3D universe that combines multiple different virtual spaces. You can think of it as a future iteration of the internet. The metaverse would connect multiple virtual platforms, similar to the internet containing different websites accessible through a single browser. The metaverse would allow users to engage in this shared virtual space, talk, hang out, play games, watch movies, visit virtual museums, shop, and even work together. So you can say it is supposed to be the new, more interactive internet.

60.1. Metaverse Avatars

People interact in this virtual world via an avatar. In other words, an avatar is an online representation of a user in the metaverse. On websites or social media networks, you are represented by your username or thumbnail picture. But in the metaverse, you will be represented by your avatar. Your avatar can be customized to look like you or any other character you choose to represent yourself. Metaverse avatars are entirely customizable. You can shape it according to how you exactly are, customize its hairstyle, apparel, accessories, and much more. Metaverse avatars aren't stuck in any one experience in the universe metaverse. A Metaverse avatar can cross through numerous experiences in the entire Metaverse. So whatever avatar you create, along with its appearance, will easily be carried over to different virtual worlds you will visit. The avatar thus becomes your identity in the Metaverse.

60.2. Technologies that power metaverse

To make the metaverse experience more immersive, cutting-edge technologies like Blockchain, augmented reality (AR), virtual reality (VR), MR, XR, artificial intelligence (AI), and the Internet of things (IoT) are required to power the 3D world.

Immersive technologies: They create experiences by merging the physical world with digital or simulated reality. They comprise VR, AR, MR, and XR technologies.

(i) Virtual reality (VR): VR refers to an entirely computer-generated virtual environment either to replicate a real environment or an imaginary world. Users can explore it using VR headsets. In VR worlds, you can also use body sensors in addition to the VR headset to control your avatar with your entire body, taking VR to the next level of immersion. Some of the popular VR devices available in the market are Oculus Quest 2, HTC Vive, Meta Quest, Samsung gear VR, etc.

Virtual reality will let customers enter the metaverse, bridging the perceived gaps between digital and physical realities. It is a virtual reality world wherein you may visit virtual schools, virtual workplaces, play games, watch concerts, browse store shelves, and plenty more without traveling physically and leaving your physical home.

(ii) Augmented reality (AR): As the name suggests, Augmented Reality is a technology that augments reality. Unlike VR, where we explore virtual spaces, AR exposes us to an ecosystem that integrates digital components with the existing environment. Through the cameras of phones/ tablets or AR smart glasses, the AR apps can put an overlay of the digital content into our actual environment. For example, in the mobile game Pokemon GO, when players open the camera on their phones, they can see Pokemons in the real-world environment. IKEA has developed a smartphone app called "Ikea Place," which allows the customers to use AR through their smartphone camera to place the furniture items into their own homes, so they can visualize how the products will look exactly in their setting. Snapchat also provides users with many exciting and trendy filters with AR technology by imposing these filters on users' faces. The filters are digitally overlaid on the users' faces after detecting them with the help of artificial intelligence. The filters can turn users into numerous characters like a cat, cartoon, etc.

AR has a use case in the metaverse as well. It is AR that helps to bring Metaverse closer to the original environment. It enhances the overall digital experience for users by offering the perfect combination of physical and virtual components.

(iii) Mixed reality: MR is referred to as hybrid reality; it is the merging of the virtual and physical worlds to produce a new environment in which the physical environment interacts in real-time with the projected digital data. For instance, a character in an MR game would recognize the physical surroundings and hide behind under a table or behind a sofa.

(iv) Extended reality (XR): XR systems allow active interaction with virtual elements through controllers. Using the controllers, users can touch, hold, manipulate and operate virtual objects. Interaction in XR environments does not require users to be stationary. Users can activate their entire bodies. Physical movement is transferred into XR environments through positional and rotational tracking.

With the use of AR/VR, MR and XR technologies, metaverse users will be able to enjoy more immersive experiences, blurring the lines between reality and the virtual world. This will make concerts, performances, and professional or educational experiences seem more authentic.

Internet of Things (IoT): IoT sensors also play a crucial role in mapping data from real life and transforming it into virtual reality. As a result, the gap between the real world and the virtual world would be greatly diminished. For example, with the gaming interface, IoT sensors capture your elevated heart and breathing rates, which might trigger your avatar to start sweating or reduce its strength in the virtual environment and making it more susceptible to fatigue. Thus, trying your avatar to replicate you in real.

IoT sensors are also capable of enabling realistic responses to interactions done in the Metaverse. With haptic gloves, every time users interact with a virtual object, IoT sensors transform these interactions into data, and with haptic gloves, users will be able to feel these virtual objects. IoT sensors can be paired with devices like VR headsets, haptic gloves, speakers, voice recognition, etc.

Artificial Intelligence (AI): From Alexa and Siri to smart air conditioners, use Artificial Intelligence to operate effectively and perform better over time. So, it is pretty evident that the metaverse would also use Artificial Intelligence to improve its performance. After all, the core intent behind Metaverse is to deliver an immersive experience to its users.

Users would expect the same actions they do in real life to be available in the Metaverse. They would also like to have digital avatars that replicate them largely in the metaverse. This is possible through artificial intelligence tools, which analyze 2D and 3D images from the real world, study physical movements, and then train a model using those studies to create more realistic and accurate avatars.

Natural language recognition tools can also make the experience more intuitive and enable users to interact with the 3D world and other users. Users can use their voice to navigate the Metaverse. For example, you may be able to change the weather, the landscape, or any other tangible feature simply by requesting it.

AI-driven bots and other automated assistants can act as “helpers,” guiding users to navigate virtual premises for a better customer experience.

Blockchain: Blockchain technology is crucial to provide digital proof of ownership for assets and NFTs in the Metaverse. Security is paramount in the metaverse. Blockchain can secure your virtual avatar and other personal information.

IPFS: Hosting 3D environments requires sizeable computing and storage resources. IPFS provides a decentralized storage solution for this.

The importance of Blockchain technology, NFTs, and IPFS in the metaverse will be discussed in detail in the next chapter.

Chapter 61: Blockchain and NFTs in the metaverse

To realize the potential and benefits of virtual environments, metaverse applications have to overcome various challenges such as data security, avatars security, and privacy, interoperability, etc. Blockchain technology has been considered to be a promising solution to address these challenges.

61.1. Blockchain in securing avatars

Avatars are the virtual embodiments of the users and has the same legal authority in the metaverse as one's legal rights in the real world. Your avatars are responsible for performing all the financial and other activities in the metaverse. So obviously, there is a need to protect your digital identity to protect it from getting compromised in some way; criminals may use your digital avatar to perform illegal activities in the metaverse. Your avatars would be protected by creating an NFT of your avatar that is recorded on Blockchain and represents your ownership of your avatar in the Metaverse. An NFT avatar is inherently unique, and whoever owns it is the only one on the Earth. The NFT, a digital property certificate, will certify that the NFT avatar belongs to its sole holder. It will also prevent anyone to use or clone your avatar.

Protecting avatars' rights in the metaverse: It would be a challenge in Metaverse to protect the rights of avatars and impose liability using existing legal concepts. For example, if an avatar steals a digital 'Gucci bag' or threatens another avatar in the 'metaverse,' this would involve issues relating to property rights, theft, and intellectual property law, like in a real court of law. That avatar could be punished using Blockchain. Every activity of the avatar would be recorded as a transaction on Blockchain. The smart contract would contain all the legal rules. If the avatar is found to be performing an illegal activity, the smart contract will trigger, and action will be taken against it based on the conditions pre-defined in the smart contract.

Similarly, disputes may arise among avatars when they interact with each other on the metaverse. Again, these would also be solved through smart contracts on Blockchain.

61.2. Blockchain in ensuring data security, privacy, and quality

The metaverse collects vast volumes of sensitive information in order to present the user with personalized experiences. Organizations or applications need this data for the successful development of targeting systems. If the information is leaked into the hands of the wrong people, they might also target users in the real world. Blockchain, with its authentication, access control, and consensus mechanisms, provide the users complete control of their data, thereby securing data privacy of the users. The Blockchain uses asymmetric-key encryption and hash functions which ensure data security in the metaverse. Ensuring your wearable hardware is highly updated and free of all malware is also a step to protect your digital identity and information.

Ensuring the Quality of the Data: The metaverse receives data from multiple applications ranging from healthcare to entertainment. The AI models in the metaverse rely on this data for making key decisions for its users. Creating the objects in the metaverse depends highly on the quality of data shared by the users from the real world. Blockchain provides complete audit trails of transactions, allowing individuals and organizations to validate all transactions. Furthermore, the data collected is secured in the blocks; each block containing a cryptographic hash of the previous block along with a timestamp and the metadata so that they are resistant to attack. Thus Blockchain technology will prevent manipulating and duplication of the in-process data. Thus, the data acquired with the help of Blockchain-enabled systems in the Metaverse will be 100% reliable.

61.3. NFTs and metaverse

NFTs serve as a key concept in the metaverse ecosystem, allowing people to own virtual goods in the form of real estate, items like cars, clothes, fashion accessories, in-game assets, etc., and even digital paintings. This is because NFTs are proofs/certificates of ownership given to their holders and are stored on Blockchain technology. For instance, if you own land in the metaverse, you get an NFT as the deed to the virtual property. This means you are the rightful owner, and only you have exclusive access to enter the location in metaverse alongside allowing access to others. NFT-controlled access could also help in ensuring VIP access to the events in the metaverse. Cryptocurrencies and NFTs have also made it possible to build a fully functioning economy inside the virtual world where you can buy and sell virtual assets, including virtual real estate, digital art objects, and so on.

Additionally, since NFTs are immutable, they are only owned by their holders, and nobody else can destroy, duplicate, or edit them. So, it is quite clear that the metaverse and NFTs are made for each other.

61.4. Blockchain in providing Interoperability in the metaverse

Metaverse interoperability is the ability for different virtual worlds and platforms to interact with each other. It would allow taking their digital identities or avatars, NFTs, and currencies across different virtual platforms. This means the avatar on one platform can communicate and interact with avatars on another platform, as well as share data and content.

Interoperability is essential as it allows individuals to be unconstrained and have a more unified experience in the metaverse, just like in the real world. Like the modern-day internet browsers, which can access any website, and several links are often linked to a single page. The creation of this globally interconnected and interoperable system is similar to the real world – we move from one place to another with our identity intact. Similarly, interoperability in the metaverse would authorize avatars to voluntarily switch from one virtual world to another, just like humans do in the real world. Avatars can also take their assets from one platform to another for different purposes, including gaming. One can use their in-game NFTs to play games hosted on different platforms.

For the Metaverse to be interoperable, you must choose to build it on an interoperable Blockchain ecosystem. Suppose two gaming platforms are build on different Blockchain ecosystems. If Blockchains exist in silos, they will not be able to communicate with each other. It means avatars on one platform can not communicate with avatars on another platform and can't even have the gaming experience on another platform. But for both platforms to interact with each other, cross-chain technology comes in that facilitates interoperability. This is possible by special smart contracts that record and verify the events taking place in virtual world A, then mediate the communication with virtual world B and record these events.

Blockchain Interoperability has been explained in detail in Chapter 16.

Chapter 62: Virtual concerts in the metaverse

During the COVID-19 pandemic that canceled and delayed many real-life concerts, many artists saw an opportunity to organize virtual live or pre-recorded concerts over the platforms like YouTube, Zoom, Instagram, and Facebook, but they were far from what we used to experience live concert experiences at real-world concert venues.

On the contrary, virtual concerts in the metaverse are much more immersive, and participants feel connected to the artists beyond just merely watching a live video.

62.1. What exactly is a virtual concert in metaverse?

A Virtual Concert is a performance that takes place in the metaverse in which a performer is represented by a virtual avatar and is projected onto a virtual stage, synced to pre-recorded music. If the artist wishes to have a live performance in the metaverse, he can perform live in a motion capture suit equipped with various sensors to create a more realistic artist's avatar to have their virtual avatar replicate their movements beat for beat. Either way, the performances are genuine, and fans attend, and experience concerts live. The virtual concert is also different from a hologram concert which is a live musical performance that takes place in the "real" or physical world that uses lasers to project a 3D hologram of an artist onto a glass panel. On the other hand, metaverse concerts occur on virtual land and are attended by the audiences in the form of avatars. A person can access the metaverse concert through VR headsets like Oculus Quest 2, Valve Index, HTC Vive Pro 2, Samsung Gear VR, Meta Quest, etc., from the comfort of their homes.

In 2022, the 64th Grammy Awards were presented in Roblox, and the MTV Video Music Awards (VMAs) debuted a new award category for Best Metaverse Performance, further cementing the metaverse as a venue for artists to host concerts and release their music videos.

62.2. Benefits of hosting a Virtual Concert in the metaverse

(i) Being an artist, you can reach a larger audience in the virtual concert. For physical concerts, the venue is subjected to one place only; you cannot reach out to the global audience at the same time. But with virtual concerts, the event has endless opportunities to reach fans anywhere in the world.

(ii) You can create a Virtual Concert with the ease of a computer program. This means you can create your show in whatever format you want without worrying about the physical limitations of a live performance. A virtual concert provides you with more flexibility than a physical concert.

(iii) In the Metaverse, virtual artists are no longer bound by physical limitations. An artist can quickly change outfits in a virtual concert or create a new stage by changing the environment in the virtual world. While performing, he can fly, enter outer space, or even go underwater. Also, even the avatars of audiences can change their outfits and dance steps.

(iv) Metaverse concerts also keep the audience engaged and motivated to stay through the entire concert as they can dance, walk around the stage, and see the artist from a different point of view. For instance, **Epic games** organized the concert of Travis Scott in their popular game Fortnite. In the concert, Travis Scott's giant skyscraper 3D avatar walks around the virtual world with the audience avatars following behind him as he ventures through outer space and even underwater at one point. On the other hand, Ariana Grande's virtual event in Fortnite took place for several days, where her avatar interacted with the fans during her performance by lifting them and dancing with them.

62.3. NFTs in the metaverse concerts

(i) The artists can buy virtual lands to organize their concerts in the metaverse. NFTs represent certificates of virtual land ownership. For example, earlier in 2022, Music industry powerhouse Warner Music Group (WMG) purchased LAND on the decentralized platform The Sandbox (SAND). It is a beachfront property in the Metaverse, where WWG wants to build a musical theme park and open a concert venue. They have also signed major artists like Ed Sheeran, Madonna, Coldplay, and Red Hot Chili Peppers, just to name a few. Also, a popular Indian singer Daler Mehndi bought a piece of land on the metaverse platform PartyNite and named it Balle Balle Land, where he hosted his concert.

(ii) NFT tickets: The metaverse concert organizers can send an NFT "ticket" to the attendee's digital wallet. These unique NFT tickets provide access to the concert while keeping others out and also erase all possibilities of counterfeit ticket sales and resale. Additionally, NFT tickets can act as collectibles. For instance, the virtual concert organized by your favorite artist sold only 1000 NFT "tickets." Now that NFT "ticket" you own is 1 of 1000 tickets that will ever exist worldwide. Thus, the NFT ticket has value purely as a collectible.

62.4. Few examples of platforms hosting virtual concerts

(i) Decentraland is a virtual 3D world where users can buy land plots using the metaverse's crypto token MANA. It was launched in February 2020 and is managed by the nonprofit Decentraland Foundation. Music artists such as Grimes and Deadmau5 have held virtual concerts in Decentraland.

(ii) Warner music group (WMG) has partnered with The Sandbox to host its virtual concerts.

(iii) Ariana Grande, Marshmello, and Travis Scott did in-game live music concerts on the highly famous game Fortnite.

(iv) Music streaming application Spotify partnered with virtual gaming universe Roblox to enter the Metaverse with the first music-themed island, Spotify Island, allowing the players to create new sounds together, explore new music and exclusive merchandise alongside their favorite artists.

(v) There are many other artists and musicians who have embraced the metaverse, like Dolly Parton, Justin Bieber, Daler Mehndi, Li Nas X, Marshmello, Young Thug, etc. Dolly Parton partnered with FOX Entertainment's Blockchain Creative Labs (BCL) to launch Dollyverse. On November 18, 2021, Justin Bieber performed his first-ever live show as an avatar in collaboration with Wave, a virtual entertainment company.

(vi) Rapper Snoop Dogg partnered with The Sandbox to release the first-ever metaverse music video.

(vii) Decentraland and Roblox have also organized music festivals in the metaverse.

Chapter 63: Metaverse applications in various sectors

Some of the ways in which metaverse could bring innovation in various sector are as follows:

63.1. Metaverse in Real Estate

(i) House hunting: Metaverse can eliminate the hassle of house hunting. No more driving around and spending a lot of time looking at the houses that aren't a good fit. In the metaverse, you can explore a 360° view of the properties from the comfort of your home and make buying decisions. Virtual tours in the metaverse can help create a deeper emotional connection compared to looking at photos. This helps you gain a deeper understanding of the advantages and disadvantages of a particular property.

(ii) Saves realtors' effort and time: Meeting potential buyers, showing homes, and accompanying clients to close dealings are time-consuming and require a lot of effort. With a virtual tour on metaverse, clients can see the property on their smartphones or laptops. Those who are really interested in the property will call the realtor and ask for more information. This would save time and effort of the realtors.

(iii) Land and real estate in the metaverse: In the Metaverse, properties can also be constructed, purchased, and sold with ease, just like traditional real estate. Virtual land can also be rented out to other people. By buying land on the metaverse, brands and companies can open their stores on virtual property where customers can explore and purchase their commodities. Metaverse land can be used to build digital casinos, clubs, concert venues, museums, theme parks, NFT galleries, and much more.

A metaverse property is purchased in the form of a unique non-fungible token or NFT. Your deed of ownership in the form of NFT is a unique code on the smart contract of a Blockchain. This code certifies your ownership or rights over that piece of digital land. So to buy and keep your digital estate NFT, you'll need to have your own digital crypto wallet.

Major metaverse platforms for buying and selling virtual land include Decentraland, Sandbox, Somnium Space, and Cryptovoxels.

63.2. Metaverse in Gaming

The gaming industry is one of the leading industries that is making use of the Metaverse features to offer a next-generation gaming experience to gamers.

(i) Gaming together: Metaverse has the ability to engage gamers in ways that were never thought possible in the gaming world. They can have an immersive experience. Rather than focusing only on a flat screen, they can interact with other gamers from all over the globe and the virtual environment around them.

(ii) Flexibility: Gaming in the metaverse also brings flexibility. The gamers can also make an addition to the virtual gaming world like they can create their own content and even build sub-games within a game.

(iii) Earn while Playing: Game assets refer to NFTs' owned by gamers that provide them ownership over numerous virtual objects in games, like weapons, enhanced avatars, or anything that gamers can purchase and use within a game. Play-to-earn games allow gamers to sell their NFTs to other gamers within the game and on other NFT marketplaces to earn additional income.

(iv) Portable game assets: The interoperable nature of the metaverse could also allow for game asset portability. Weapons or avatar enhancements acquired in one game could be portable to a different game hosted on a different platform, keeping your identity intact, and NFTs govern ownership over your assets. Therefore, you can interact and sell NFTs to the gamers of other games, increasing the possibility of earning extra revenue.

(v) Hosting concerts: Even the concerts can be hosted in the metaverse games for gamers, where the avatars of gamers can interact with the artist, dance and walk around the stage. For instance, the popular game Fortnite of Epic Games has hosted concerts by musicians, including Travis Scott and Ariana Grande.

Some notable players in the Metaverse Gaming industry are Epic Games, The Sandbox, Roblox, Axie Infinity, etc.

63.3. Metaverse in Remote working

With more people working remotely, the metaverse has many potential uses in the modern workplace and beyond. Remote work refers to the practice of employees working from a location other than their centralized office(s). It could be an employee's home, a co-working space, or any other place other than a traditional corporate office building.

(i) Collaborations and meetings in the metaverse: Limited mobility and body language in online meetings and video conferences can make team meetings fatigue and unproductive. But, in the metaverse, employees can create 3D avatars with unique facial features and clothes. The avatars of remote employees can meet and even walk around between virtual offices and meeting rooms in the metaverse without leaving their physical homes. Thus, employees thousands of miles apart can discuss ideas and work on projects together in the same virtual 'room.'

(ii) Improve mental health: The Metaverse can potentially increase productivity and improve the mental health of professionals who work remotely by simulating office spaces, holding meetings in real-time with remote colleagues, conducting business presentations in dynamic environments, and having face-to-face conversations with people from all over the world.

The meditation and yoga sessions can be organized in a virtual garden or lakeside in the virtual world, which employees can attend and relax.

(iii) Workshops and events in the metaverse: Virtual workshops, conferences, and events can be organized in the metaverse that will replace the need for employees to attend them in person. The venues for conferences and events can be customized, which will make them more engaging. It can be on the Moon, in the forest, or on a virtual beach. No matter where they are located, remote participants can access live, interactive networking opportunities and content. Just log on through the conference portal, and you're good to enter the metaverse to attend events wherever you may be in the world.

In a virtual event, a virtual booth can also be set up where avatars of attendees can walk up in much the same way as they would with a physical event.

(iv) A Healthier Remote Work-Life Balance: With the lines between work and home life being so blurred, reports say remote workers have difficulty disconnecting and "turning off" at the end of the day. But saying goodbye to your team in the metaverse and physically taking off your VR headset may mark a clear line between work and home life. It gives off the same vibes as walking out of a physical office building and heading home to relax and spend time with family.

(v) Virtual training and onboarding process: 3D displays with step-by-step instructions also allow interactive employee training and upskilling. Employees can put themselves into virtual real-world scenarios, like a simulated cybersecurity breach or client meeting, and practice different solutions.

Virtual onboard processes can also be benefitted from the metaverse. Instead of having new recruiters read lengthy page documents about your company, they can explore a personalized, interactive 3D experience that gamifies learning. So it's much more fun and exciting to learn on the metaverse.

The two biggest players in the metaverse workspace so far are Microsoft Mesh and Meta's Horizon Workrooms.

63.4. Metaverse in Travel and Tourism

(i) Destination Window Shopping: The metaverse cannot replace physical travel but can enhance your traveling experience. Imagine how it would feel if you could virtually visit and check out a destination before you traveled there. You could compare destinations before deciding where to visit and evaluate whether an attraction is worth visiting by having virtual tours. The immersive experience provided by Metaverse will be a great leap from the current modes of vacation planning that include watching YouTube videos, reading blogs/magazines, etc.

(ii) Hotel booking on metaverse: Virtual reality tours can enhance the booking process of hotels, but the metaverse can take this a step further. For instance, using a digital avatar could make it possible for a potential customer to walk through a metaverse hotel, which has been designed to look exactly like a real physical hotel. This then gives them a 360° view of the hotel room, a clear picture of how big each room is, or what features they can expect if they upgrade. Thus the metaverse takes the hotel booking to a next level.

(iii) Virtual celebrations: People often prefer hotels for celebrations, including birthdays, weddings, and business events. With a metaverse hotel, you can celebrate with your friends and family and have a uniquely immersive experience without ever actually physically being there. Through your avatar, you can mingle with different online "guests" from all over the world, celebrate and attend events held in the hotel venue. Even the metaverse hotels will have avatar receptionists to greet you and your guests.

63.5. Metaverse in Education and Learning

(i) Virtual 3D classrooms: With the emergence of online classes, students have begun to experience a gap between physical classrooms and virtual ones. The metaverse has the ability to bridge this gap by creating 3D virtual classrooms for the students, where they can virtually interact and meet with their classmates and instructors. These immersive experiences can democratize education by enabling students from any geographical location to be a part of the metaverse-powered learning setup.

(ii) Enhanced learning: The smart classes added to school education curriculum enhance students' learning with video projection on various topics. The metaverse aims to make this learning experience a notch smarter by allowing students to fully immerse in such videos, helping them experience the content more closely. For instance, any specific historical era can be recreated in a metaverse, where students can enter and learn about it in an immersive way. Students can explore the solar system, different layers of the earth or the constellations in the virtual world and can do dissections to learn the anatomy of insects and animals. Also, a novel or a story can be recreated in the metaverse, where students can enter and watch the scenes as they unfold, helping them relate to the characters and understand the story better.

(iii) Improve accessibility for people with disabilities: The metaverse also holds promise to improve educational and social access for people with disabilities. In the metaverse, they can make friends, learn, and socialize without having to worry about their physical limitations. Even it can help young adults with special needs, autism, and social interaction issues in improving their interpersonal and job skills, such as visiting a mall or grocery, shelving products at a store, interacting with other customers, or using an ATM machine. Thus, through metaverse, they can practice the required skills and interact with others in a safe environment without feeling overwhelmed or anxious.

63.6. Metaverse in Healthcare

(i) Teleconsultation: While telemedicine has already seen adoption during the COVID-19 pandemic, its features and user experience can be further enhanced by the metaverse. It would allow patients to visit a virtual office and meet the physician at a 3D location, making the consultation more immersive, informative, and smarter than consulting through other virtual environments like websites, messaging applications, or social media.

(ii) Education and training: Metaverse can remove the limitation of physical barriers and ensure medical trainees/students receive education and training, even in the most remote places from skilled doctors. Furthermore, VR can help upskill healthcare workers in treatments by creating a simulated real-life environment without risking patients' life. They will be able to examine the human body in precise anatomical detail in 3D rather than 2D images. Metaverse provides a more immersive experience by allowing the digital avatars of healthcare workers to interact with their colleagues and trainers.

The avatars of physicians and surgeons worldwide can also meet in the metaverse and discuss complex surgeries. Such types of interactions are more immersive than discussing on the phone or via video calls.

(iii) Mental health: The global pandemic led to a rise in conditions such as depression, anxiety, and addictive behaviors due to forced isolation. The metaverse can be effective in counseling patients suffering from these conditions and encouraging follow-ups.

Section 11

Blockchain for Good

Chapter 64: Blockchain in tracking carbon emissions and carbon trading

Carbon emissions lead to a change in the environment, which results in serious health consequences for us. According to the U.S. Environmental Protection Agency, carbon emissions, in the form of carbon dioxide, make up more than 80% of the emitted greenhouse gases. These carbon emissions raise global temperature by trapping solar energy in the atmosphere. This, in turn, alters weather patterns and water supplies; further, it changes the growing season for food crops and threatens coastal communities as chances of floods increase with the rising sea level. Rising sea levels can also cause saltwater to infiltrate some freshwater systems, thus increasing the need for desalination and more vigorous drinking water treatment. To summarize, it is essential to fight against global warming and reduce these carbon emissions for a better and healthier tomorrow.

Sustainability initiatives are gaining momentum as organizations are becoming increasingly interested in monitoring their business practices, and many companies have even started recognizing that sustainability is beneficial for all. Sustainability initiatives are not only good for the planet but are also a great way to boost the brand image as these initiatives are getting noticed and appreciated by both consumers and investors. Research shows that supply chains are often responsible for a large share of a company's overall greenhouse gas emissions, with transport or shipping being the major culprit. In fact, the greenhouse gas emissions through the supply chain are four times higher than the company's direct operations.

64.1. Challenges faced while calculating carbon emissions

Let's understand how carbon emissions are calculated in the current scenario by these businesses and organizations:

(i) Organizations first need to identify all the carbon emission sources like transportation, electricity consumption, HVAC emissions, and other business operations.

(ii) Then, they are required to calculate the emissions from these sources. This is calculated by first noting down the energy consumption by every individual process of the company. Then this reading is multiplied by the standard conversion factor to calculate the carbon footprints *(Fig 64-1)*. For example, the electricity grid provides the emission factor taking the standard amount of CO_2 that would be released when you use one unit of the energy. This value would be different for different grids.

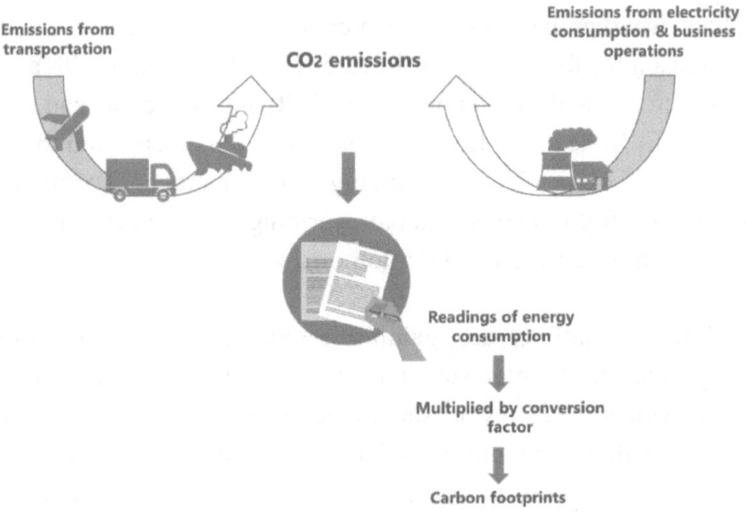

Fig 64-1: Calculation of CO_2 emissions by the organizations

(iii) Similarly, every fuel has its own emission factor, and you can use this value to calculate the carbon emissions from different modes of transport, business operations, etc. For example, there are fixed conversion factors for calculating emissions from 1 liter of petrol or using 1 liter of diesel as a fuel.

(iv) After calculating the emissions from all the sources, they are all added up to find out the total emissions.

But the problems that companies face in calculating the carbon emissions through these methods may be:

- Since calculating carbon footprints is a manual process and requires human intervention, chances of errors increase.
- Besides, this is a time-consuming process.
- Moreover, it is an approximate method as the real-time carbon emissions are not calculated but are calculated based on fuel, electricity, etc., consumed using the standard conversion factor for each different fuel or electricity used.

64.2. Blockchain & IoT- The solution

Blockchain and IoT sensors can solve this problem of calculating carbon emissions accurately.

64.2.1. Carbon emissions collection

There will be two types of IoT sensors to calculate carbon emissions *(Fig 64-2)*:

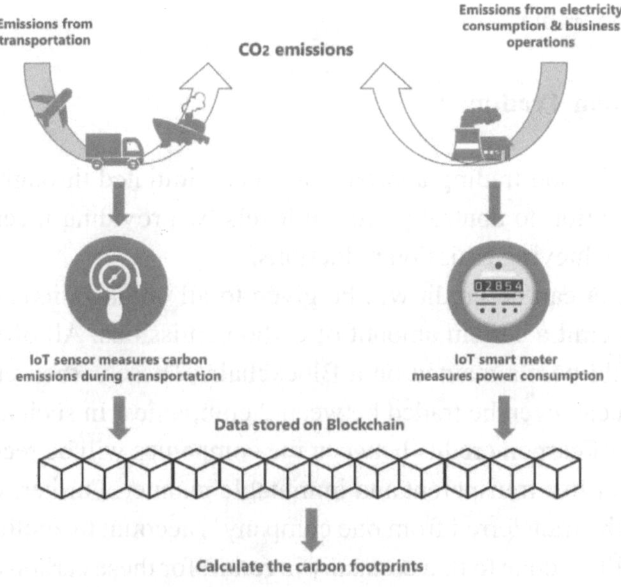

Fig 64-2: IoT sensors to calculate carbon emissions

- First, IoT smart meter that can measure power consumption by the companies. It will ease the pain of the company's manpower to take readings manually, which can be prone to manual errors.
- The second IoT sensor can directly exchange information with the environment and capture carbon emissions either by the company's operations or during transportation.

Data on blockchain: The data collected from IoT sensors will be stored on the blockchain. As soon as the platform receives the data, smart contracts will get executed and calculate the carbon footprints based on factors including the type of electricity generator and energy sources (diesel or coal), meters efficiency, conversion factor, company's total fuel consumption, etc. Thus smart contracts will help create a reliable and authenticated carbon footprint report for a company.

The company's carbon footprint report will be stored on the blockchain in a tamper-proof manner. Further, Blockchain can enable the companies to prepare their Carbon footprint report with more accuracy and that too in a reduced time frame.

64.2.2 Carbon Trading

In fact, the carbon trading approach has been initiated through Blockchain with an intention to control pollution levels by providing incentives to the companies achieving emission reductions.
In this case, a carbon credit will be given to all organizations that grants a business to emit a certain amount of carbon emissions. All of these carbon credits would be maintained on a Blockchain. These carbon credits on the Blockchain can even be traded between 2 companies. In such a system, any transaction of carbon credits between the companies will be recorded on the digital ledger in a transparent and immutable manner. Further, when carbon credits will be transferred from one company's account to another automatic payment will be done to that company in return for these carbon credits using smart contracts.

Say, for example, there are two companies A and B, which have their own carbon permits. Suppose company A is under its carbon cap and company B is over its carbon cap. In that case, company A can sell its surplus carbon credits to company B who seeks additional carbon credits for the carbon emissions *(Fig 64-3)*. This can be a way to incentivize companies with low carbon emissions, and it can become a second revenue stream for these companies.

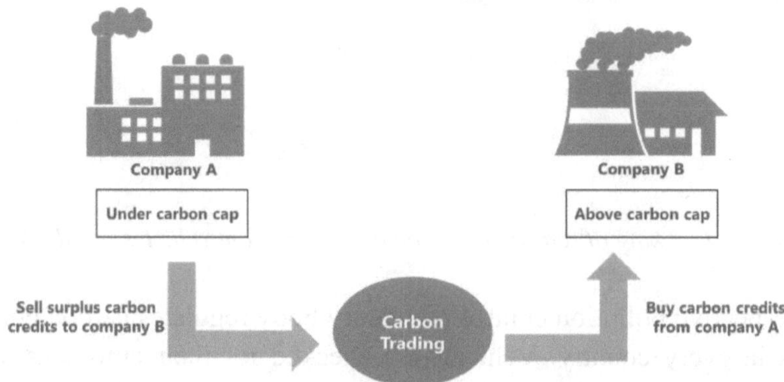

Fig 64-3: Carbon Trading on Blockchain

The second advantage of carbon trading is that it will encourage organizations to adopt carbon-friendly energy practices that can reduce their carbon footprint.

64.3. Tracking real-time carbon emissions from vehicles

IoT sensors can also be attached to vehicles that can track the real-time carbon emissions from these vehicles. This information can then be stored on the blockchain to ensure a better and safe environment. If carbon emissions exceed the stipulated limit, the smart contracts will get executed, and an alert will be sent to the respective person or department *(Fig 64-4)*.

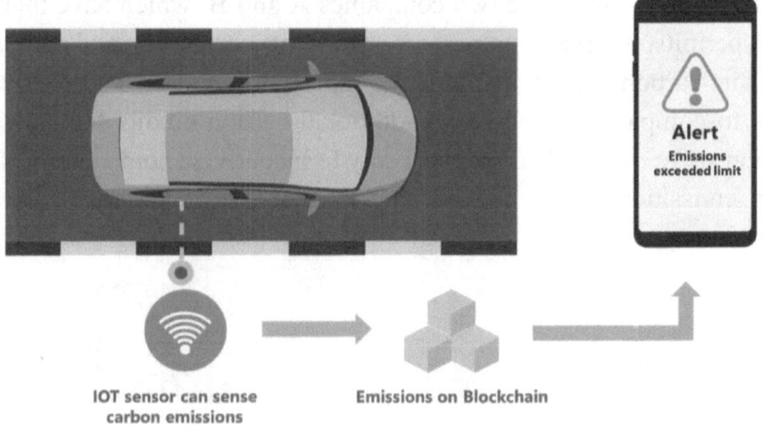

Fig 64-4: Tracking of real-time carbon emissions from vehicles on Blockchain

The respective pollution control regulatory body regulates carbon emission norms in every country. Vehicles are checked for their emissions, and if emissions are within the specified limit, a certificate is issued for the vehicle, which generally comes with an expiry date. However, this system has its own loopholes—the system only checks for the emissions on the date of the test.

Also, the emissions from the vehicle might change based on the age and condition of the vehicle. Other factors like adulteration of fuel, etc., might temporarily increase pollution to an unacceptable level.

Therefore, if IoT carbon sensors are attached to vehicles and the information about carbon emissions is stored on the shared ledger, it will help regulatory bodies to keep a better track of carbon emissions by vehicles. The regulatory body can even issue warnings to vehicle owners whose carbon emissions exceed the stipulated limits. In this way, a strict pollution check regime can be implemented, and a concrete step can be taken towards a healthier environment.

Chapter 65: Blockchain in Fighting Human Trafficking

Our I.D. cards, passports, driver's licenses, birth certificates, and social security cards are the documents that work as proof that we exist. These are the documents that allow us to attend a school, get medical insurance, get jobs, cross borders, and visit other countries.

65.1. Challenges

According to the World Bank, there are around 1 billion people in the world who live but don't exist in any system and don't have a valid ID to prove their existence. And shockingly, this number of 1 billion is only an understated estimate. The exact stats about this unregistered population is unknown even today.

Of these 1 billion, nearly half of the population is below the age of 18. These people are flesh and blood, living and breathing, but according to our global system, they don't even exist. Without an identity, these people are unable to travel legally, are unable to get an education, and are even robbed of their right to life and freedom.

Because of this very reason, human trafficking and prostitution have thrived primarily in the third-world and war-torn countries because of the weak legislative laws, unsecured borders, and deep-rooted corruption. In such scenarios, human traffickers can easily use fake identification documents to transport undocumented young people across borders for forced participation in illegal activities like sex trade, labor, illegal human organ trade, begging, drug supply, etc. Trafficking generates illegal profits of $150 billion a year, with about 40 million people estimated to be its victims.

65.2. Blockchain-The solution

Blockchain can provide a solution to curb this menace of human trafficking. In this proposed system, a person's identity needs to be created on the Blockchain platform using his/her biometric information such as fingerprint or iris scan. This information on Blockchain cannot be forged or tampered with. The distributed ledger of Blockchain aims to store the digital identity of every individual along with the information of their relatives. Identification of individuals is always at the heart of the solution. By digitally storing identities on a blockchain, it will significantly be easier for international law enforcement agencies and governments to catch traffickers.

Collected fingerprints or facial scans, which would be impossible to fake, would stop traffickers from making false documents of their victims. Blockchain will ensure that no human is taken out of his home country using fake ID documents produced by human traffickers.

United Nations (UN), in partnership with World Identity Network (WIN), has taken an initiative to end child trafficking using Blockchain technology. The goal is to maintain a digital database of children, which can not be tampered with or hacked into, and make all children visible by providing them with an identity. In this proposed system, the digital identity of every child will be linked to the information of his parents *(Fig 65-1)*. This secured data on a shared, immutable digital ledger will make trafficking attempts trackable.

Fig 65-1: Digital ID of every child is linked to his parents' information on the Blockchain

Under this Blockchain project, children trying to exit the country will have to have their eyes or fingerprints scanned, and then a phone alert will be sent to their legal guardians, who will have to approve their border crossing *(Fig 65-2)*. Additionally, when the criminals would try to move children abroad, the action will be recorded on the Blockchain, helping law enforcement agencies to spot patterns to catch these traffickers. Thus Blockchain can be a great tool to address this global issue of human trafficking and potentially save millions of children from becoming its victims.

Fig 65-2: After scanning the eyes or fingerprints of children, a phone alert will be sent to their legal guardians to approve their border crossing

Chapter 66: Blockchain for Philanthropy

Charity and non-profit sectors are always surrounded by dark clouds of inefficiency and corruption. The environment of mistrust and opaqueness has impacted people's faith in these charities and nonprofit organizations.

And in turn, this has impacted their will and wish to donate to these charities.

This decline in the inclination to donate, has lead to a situation where many genuine charities are underfunded and are struggling to match the demand of their services.

In the current scenario, donors don't have a reliable way to know how their funds are being used and whether they are being used for the intended purpose or not. They only have limited access to this information through annual reports and websites of these Charity organizations and NGOs, where these organizations report their updates on where and how these funds were used.

Additionally, there are many third-party organizations that report on these charities and also rank them based on their performance. But again, the reporting is done on the basis of the information which is made public by these charities.

Blockchain- The Solution

In such an opaque and fragmented system, there is no single place for a donor to know if his donations are really creating the impact that was promised to him when the funds were being raised. Blockchain is the solution that has the potential to transform this sector and make it more transparent, efficient, and accountable.

With this distributed ledger technology, donors can easily track how their funds are being used by these charities. For this purpose, a unique public address will be assigned to each charity registered on the Blockchain. This will help people to track the donations and to check where these funds are being redirected to. Thus, bringing accountability and transparency in the system.

Further, no record can be erased because of its innate characteristic of immutability.

Smart contracts, along with Blockchain, will further disrupt this sector. For example, say certain terms were promised to you when the funds were being raised. But how do you know if the conditions were fulfilled?

With smart contracts, an extra layer of security and effectiveness will be added to these donations. With the implementation of smart contracts, funds would be transferred only to the expected recipients, and that too, when the specific predetermined conditions are met.

In case the predetermined conditions are not met, then the donations made can be reversed back to the donor. The best use case of this can be the 2010 Haiti Earthquake, where Red Cross raised 500 million USD to build more than one hundred thousand homes. But only six homes could be constructed out of these proposed one hundred thousand plus homes. Imagine how useful this technology could have been in such a scenario. The unused money left could have been sent back to the respective donors or used to fund another cause with the permission of these respective donors.

With Blockchain, it would also be much easier to track the administrative cost of these charities. As in many cases, these costs are reported after inflating multiple times by some corrupt officials for their personal gains. Hence Blockchain undoubtedly has the potential to put a check, on the corruption that prevails in this sector.

Section 12

Other use cases of Blockchain

Chapter 67: Blockchain and IoT in Agriculture

Since the advent of agriculture, farmers have confronted unpredictable weather conditions. And there are times when their crops get destroyed because of natural calamities, and they are left with no source of income. This sometimes even leads to mass suicides by farmers in many developing countries.

The only way for farmers to protect themselves from these unfavorable weather conditions and crop loss is through crop insurance. It can cushion their loss of the destroyed crops.

There are multiple crop insurance policies for farmers that they can avail to cope with such difficult times. But the biggest problem with these policies is the processing of insurance claims, which is a tedious and time-consuming task. When the crops get destroyed, and farmers are in dire need of the financial assistance, what they get is lengthy and tedious processes instead of their due coverage amount. The processing of insurance claims sometimes even takes years.

The need of the hour is to help these farmers and make their life easier when they are going through such difficult times.

67.1. Smart contracts, IoT, and crop insurance

Blockchain technology and smart contracts can radically improve the whole insurance claim process and can make the whole experience seamless.

In the event of a natural disaster when the crops get destroyed, the smart contract will be triggered, and payouts for the victim farmers will be released automatically.

Let us understand it through a scenario:

A farmer bought a crop insurance in this new Blockchain-powered System. Under this insurance policy, a smart contract gets agreed upon by the farmer and the insurance company. In the smart contract, all the terms are clearly defined under which the farmer will be eligible for the claim amount. One of the terms is regarding the amount of rainfall. If it rained more than X cm and that too for more than a week the farmer will be eligible for the insurance claim.

During the rainy season, it rained heavily for more than 10 days, and there were floods, which destroyed the crops of the farmer. The meteorological station released the rainfall data for that region which was above X cm. As the rainfall was above the predefined threshold limit, the smart contract gets triggered, and an automatic payout to the victim farmer is initiated.

Thus the farmer gets the required resources and financial assistance without going through any hassle during such a bad time.

In fact, Blockchain technology and IoT can even help farmers to take preventive measures before the natural calamities strike. Pre-installed IoT sensors can predict the unfavorable weather conditions like drought or heavy rainfall. And as soon as the pre-decided conditions of the smart contract are met, it gets executed, and the preventive crop insurance payout is automatically released to the farmers. This in turn, would help farmers to take precautions before the natural disaster strikes. For example, in storing the harvested crops at appropriate places where these crops will not be affected by these natural calamities. Thus saving costs for the insurance company and avoiding damage to the farmer's crops.

IoT can also help farmers in improving the yield of their crops. IoT sensors can be installed on the fields that will monitor crop growth, harvesting, and crop yield. IoT sensors installed can also help farmers in providing real-time updates about the irrigation needs of the crops, seed quality, soil moisture, manure, fertilizer requirements, and also about diseased crops. This information would become an invaluable resource for farmers to maximize their crop yield.

67.2. Blockchain in providing a fair price to farmers

Another challenge faced by farmers is that they have to rely on the traders for selling their product, who dictate order prices and quantities. This directly results in low farmer income as farmers do not receive their due share, even though they are the most important part of the chain being the food producers. Blockchain will help establish a direct link between farmers and consumers/retailers. It will empower small farmers to organize themselves and get together to reach the market without taking any help from the middlemen.

Today, the agricultural sector's supply chain is notoriously complex and opaque, as the products change hands multiple times before reaching their final destination. It is difficult for farmers to know where and at what price their products are getting sold ultimately. This lack of information leaves them vulnerable and at the mercy of traders who dictate order prices and quantities. Through Blockchain, farmers will get transparency in the supply chain, thus enabling them to get a fair share of their produce.

In the current scenario, consumers are always skeptical while buying an organic food. There is no way to verify whether a product labeled as organic really organic. Blockchain would allow genuine organic food brands to stand out from the crowd. This is because the provenance of these products can be easily traced, giving consumers confidence that they are getting added value from a high-quality product and it is worth paying for such a high-quality product.

Further, in the current system, it often takes weeks for farmers to get paid for their goods. But through the implementation of Blockchain and smart contracts, payments will be triggered automatically as soon as the buyer confirms the acceptance of the product.

67.3. Blockchain in Land Registry

Secure and formal property rights are important for the economic development of humans worldwide. A lot of farmers worldwide lack access to land titling and land demarcation. Many farmers lack legal ownership of the land they live and work on. And this lack of secure land ownership is the biggest cause of poverty. Land registries are typically dependent on paper documents, handwritten signatures, and manual labor to register land titles. This land registry process is prone to frauds and corruption, and the poor farmers have to suffer a lot because of this. Few fraudsters use violence and bribery to falsely claim the ownership of the lands of poor farmers. The land records get corrupted because of which poor farmers get no land or less land, and less land results in less income for them.

Blockchain technology will be able to address many of these shortcomings in traditional land registries as it provides an immutable method to register land titles. Thus protecting the farmers from corruption and frauds. An immutable and transparent land record will also help farmers to resolve any land disputes that may arise in the future.

For the implementation of a Blockchain-based land registry process, the geo-coordinates of the land will be uniquely coded and recorded into the blockchain. Each property would also be linked to a smart key which would be held by the owner of that piece of land. Further smart contracts, when combined with Blockchain, can be used to fasten the transfer of land entitlement and other related transactions. It will also empower farmers to get quick loans as they can easily prove their ownership of the land, which is generally kept as collateral against the loan disbursed.

67.4. Blockchain in Subsidiary Disbursement

Across the globe, the agriculture sector is largely dependent on government subsidies for irrigation, electricity, seeds, fertilizers, etc., where farmers get these facilities at a lower rate. For instance, in India's 2020-2021 budget, more than 10 billion USD was allocated for agriculture-related subsidies to farmers.

But one question always remains unanswered how much of this amount actually reaches these intended beneficiaries? Through Blockchain, the distribution and delivery of subsidies can become more transparent as each transaction on the blockchain is recorded in a transparent and immutable way. Further, with the implementation of Blockchain, these subsidies can be targeted to the intended farmers.

Thus we can conclude that Blockchain along with smart contracts, can really work for the upliftment and betterment of our farmers.

67.5. Scalability concerns

(i) To make the Blockchain scalable for its use in the agriculture sector, layer 1 (discussed in Chapter 12) and layer 2 (discussed in Chapter 13) scaling solutions will be required to be implemented.

(ii) Blockchain used will be permissioned Blockchain. The farmers, supply chain stakeholders, insurance companies, etc., will be assigned specific functions on the smart contracts. Storing the entire IoT data, supply chain data, and data about insurance, subsidiary, land registry, etc., on Blockchain is very challenging as it is very costly and will significantly slow down the processing on Blockchain. Thus, distributed file storage IPFS can provide low-cost off-chain storage to store data, and the hash of the uploaded file is then stored on the Blockchain and accessed through the smart contract. Any modification in the uploaded file would change its hash. IPFS has been explained in detail in Chapter 15.

Chapter 68: Blockchain and Intellectual Property Rights

Intellectual property rights, abbreviated as IPRs, are the rights given by law to a person or a company to have exclusive rights to use their invention or creation without the worry of competition, at least for a specific period of time. Examples of intellectual property include music, literature, and other artistic works; discoveries and inventions; words, phrases, symbols, designs, etc. The intellectual property rights include copyrights, patents, trademarks, industrial design rights, and trade secrets. The reason for intellectual property is to encourage innovation without the fear that a competitor will steal the idea and/or take credit for it. This also gives economic incentives to the innovators for their creation because it allows people to profit from the information and intellectual goods they create. These economic incentives not only stimulate innovation but also contribute to the technological progress of countries.

68.1. Challenges to Intellectual property rights

(i) The intangible nature of intellectual property presents difficulties when compared with traditional property like land or goods. Unlike traditional property, intellectual property is indivisible, which means an unlimited number of people can consume an intellectual good without it being depleted. Thus, protecting intellectual rights is a challenge. Let's understand it through an example a landowner can surround his land with a robust fence and hire armed guards to protect it, but a producer of information or an intellectual good can usually do very little to stop their first buyer from replicating it and selling it at a lower price. Intellectual rights are strong enough to encourage the creation of intellectual goods but not so strong that they can prevent the unethical use of intellectual property rights.

(ii) On the other hand, electronic distribution of intellectual property on the internet poses numerous risks for content creators since it becomes difficult to maintain control of such property or monitor who is using it and for what purpose. Ownership can be hard to prove, and authors may be unable to stop infringements or monetize their works effectively.

Now the question arises how can Blockchain protect Intellectual Property Rights?

68.2. Blockchain in patent and trademark protection

In today's scenario, the only way to get patent rights is by filing an application with the Patent and Trademark Office and then having a patent issued in your name. That is the only way to get a legal monopoly. If you don't patent your rights, it will be free for anyone to copy once it is out in public and you have exceeded the timetable to get a patent. The IP offices that grant intellectual property rights can use Blockchain technology-based repository to create "smart IP registries," which would create an immutable record of events in the life of registered IPRs. It could include when a patent or a trademark was first applied for, registered, first used in trade; when a trademark or patent was licensed, assigned, and so on. The ability to track the entire life cycle of an intellectual property right would have many benefits, including smoother IPR audits.

Let's understand it through an example, collecting information on the use of a trademark in trade or commerce on a Blockchain-based official trademark register would allow the relevant IP office to be notified immediately. This would result in reliable and time-stamped evidence of actual use of a trademark in trade, both of which are relevant in proving first use, genuine use, acquired distinctiveness, or goodwill in a trademark. Similarly, distributed ledger technology could be used for defensive publication documents as prior art to prevent others from obtaining patents over such technologies.

68.3. Blockchain in copyright protection

(i) Copyright protection is a bit different. Copyrights may be registered, or they may be unregistered. At the moment of creation, when the artwork is "fixed" in some tangible form, it becomes automatically protected by copyright. For instance, a photographer, when he clicks the photo, gains copyright to that photo at the same time. Registration is not necessary to receive copyright protection. An unregistered copyright entitles you to reproduce, sell, and perform the copyrighted work. Beyond this, your rights are limited if your copyright is not registered. You cannot bring a suit for copyright infringement without first registering your copyright. In such a scenario, Blockchain technology can play an important role within the context of unregistered IP rights such as copyright since it can provide evidence of their authorship, creation, originality, and use. Uploading an original design or work and details of its designer or creator to a Blockchain will create a time-stamped record and solid evidence to prove these matters. Blockchain technology can be used to track the path of any single copyright product through the stream of commerce. This can let companies know what path their products have traveled to get to a seller, and whether their products are being diverted to unauthorized markets, and therefore know whether products showing up for sale by third parties are, in fact, authentic or whether the goods might be unlawful copies. Without Blockchain, this type of investigation can be much more painstaking and sometimes virtually impossible. Thus using Blockchain technology to track the root of every single product that a company produces will provide the promise of knowing, with certainty, if a product is truly a copy or whether it is a genuine product that has been sold.

(ii) The age of the internet has presented many challenges for intellectual property law. Most notable is the fact that digital products and content can be copied with extreme ease and can instantly be shared across the entire world. By this, intellectual property owners can lose control of their creations virtually overnight. Software piracy is a perfect example of the loss of revenue that can result from unauthorized copying. In the current scenario, it is very hard to prove the ownership of a creation. It can also be difficult for authors to see who is using their work and equally difficult for third parties who want to use the author's work to know who to seek a license from. Because of this opaqueness, authors are often unable to stop infringements or to make the most of monetizing their works.

(iii) Using Blockchain as an IP registry may help give clarity of the owners holding the copyright. By registering their works to a Blockchain, authors could end up with tamper-proof evidence of ownership. This is because a Blockchain transaction is immutable, so once a work has been registered to a Blockchain, that information can never be lost or changed. Thus the third parties who want to use an author's work could use the Blockchain to see the complete chain of ownership of a work, including any licences, sub-licences and assignments. Currently, once an author uploads his or her work to the internet, it becomes extremely difficult to maintain control of that work, and to monitor who is using it for what purpose. With Blockchain platforms such as Blockai and ascribe, once a work is registered and verified, authors can know who is using their work, thereby making it easier to identify and stop infringements and put in place licenses for any use they wish to authorize. Thus through Blockchain, an artist can find out who is using his/her art or photos on the internet in seconds. By putting their work on Blockai, such as digital art or photos, they create a timestamp in the Blockchain and receive a copyright certificate as proof.

68.4. Blockchain in obtaining IP license

An intellectual property can also be sold or licensed to generate revenues for you or your business. With copyright, in particular, it is difficult for people wishing to use to know who is the author or owner, and how to get a license. Often, people will end up using the work illegally rather than seeking a license because of the difficulty or high price of doing so. Blockchain may offer possibilities for licensing works by creating a direct link between authors and users. One useful feature of blockchain is smart contracts, which could assist in establishing and enforcing IP agreements such as licensing agreements and allow the transmission of payments in real-time to IP owners. A licensing agreement is a partnership between an intellectual property rights owner, i.e., licensor, and another who is authorized to use such rights, i.e., a licensee in exchange for an agreed payment in the form of fee or royalty. Such types of licensing agreements are also important in other circumstances, such as during a merger or acquisition, or in the course of negotiating a joint venture. As an intellectual property owner and a licensor, you expand your business to the other horizons of your country and the world by issuing license to other authorities to manufacture, sell, import, export, distribute and market various goods or services which otherwise may be prevented from doing so because of your monopoly on them.

68.5. Blockchain for micropayments

Smart contracts can also be tied into micropayments for the use of content by enabling a potential user to make a small payment to the author in return for this use. As a result, the author can be remunerated without having to pay the high transaction costs of existing financial networks. Let's take the example of tech business Ujo which has used Blockchain in its business model to rectify inefficiencies in the music industry. In one of its projects, Ujo worked with singer-songwriter Imogen Heap to release her song on Blockchain. Users were able to purchase licenses to download, remix and sync the songs via smart contracts, with each payment sent to Imogen Heap directly. Thus, artists can use Blockchain to better control and exploit their creative works, to improve collaboration, and achieve fair and efficient remuneration.

Layer 2 scaling solutions: Transaction fees on the Blockchain network is high. But by implementing the Layer 2 scaling solutions (channels, rollups, sidechains, and plasma), transaction fees would become significantly low, making micropayments feasible.

68.6. Scalability concerns

(i) Blockchain used will be permissioned Blockchain. Storing the entire data about the intellectual properties and their rights, IPR holders, etc., on Blockchain is very challenging as it is very costly and will significantly slow down the processing on Blockchain. Thus, distributed file storage IPFS can provide low-cost off-chain storage to store data, and the hash of the uploaded file is then stored on the Blockchain and accessed through the smart contract. Any modification in the uploaded file would change its hash. IPFS has been explained in detail in Chapter 15.

(ii) To make the Blockchain scalable, layer 1 (discussed in Chapter 12) and layer 2 (discussed in Chapter 13) scaling solutions will be required to be implemented.

Chapter 69: Blockchain in the sports industry

Blockchain is an exciting technology that has the potential to change the way in which a number of industries work within a span of a couple of years.

And the sports industry is no exception.

In this chapter, we are going to discuss how blockchain technology is going to provide solutions to the pressing issues in the sports industry and bring about a radical shift in how this industry works.

69.1. Funding for professional athletes

Budding athletes face a lot of hurdles when it comes to funding their training and participating in sporting events across the world. Basic requirements such as sports equipment, cost of registration in tournaments, and travel costs are just a few of the challenges that these rising stars have to face day in and day out. They are always looking for a solution that can help them to deal with these unwanted hassles so that they can focus completely on their sports.

Blockchain can be a potential solution to many of these issues that these budding sportspersons have to go through. A Blockchain-based platform can serve these athletes, by enabling them to raise funds for their activities. This platform can act as an intermediate between the athletes and the potential investors. In this blockchain-powered system, the athletes will be required to upload their profiles stating their current achievements and their future sporting plans *(Fig 69-1)*.

On the other side, sports fans and small investors can access these profiles of the athletes on this blockchain platform.

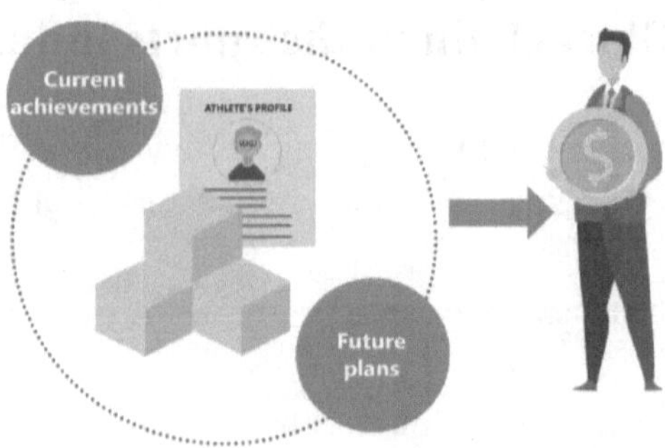

Fig 69-1: Profiles of athletes on Blockchain-powered system can be accessed by investors

On this platform, they will decide or select the player that they want to invest in and they can also define the conditions for their investment for each individual player as they also seek future returns from these investments. Once all the terms and conditions are agreed upon by both parties, a smart contract will be signed between them containing all of these terms and conditions. Additionally, through this platform, investors and fans can also contribute funds to teams or clubs who have an active need for funding for their projects.

69.2. Antidoping data of athletes

Doping scandals are undermining the integrity of many sports players. For instance, during the 2016 Olympic Games in Rio de Janeiro, hackers leaked the medical records of several athletes and made these files public. In such unwanted and unprecedented events, many of the athletes had to face reputational damage and many of them were forced to go through lengthy investigations. Their medical records were analyzed to discern what medications were administered to them and whether there was a legitimate reason for administering such medications. In such situations, even if an athlete is officially cleared of the doping charges, a whiff of doubt still hangs in the air, with reputational damaging effects on the athlete. Blockchain technology could provide the required cybersecurity and prevent cyber fraud by securing the medical records of these athletes *(Fig 69-2)*.

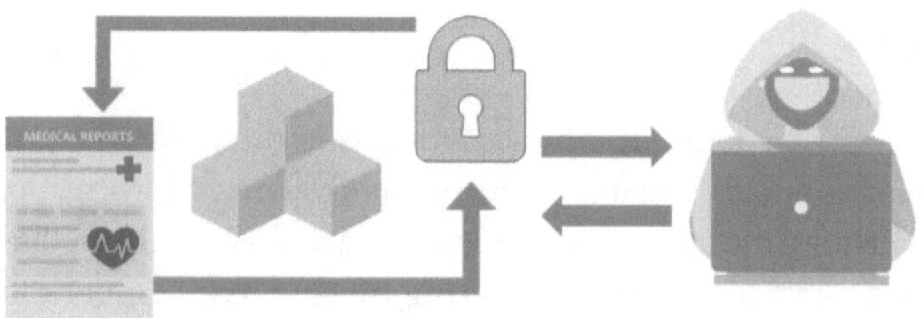

Fig 69-2: Blockchain secures medical records of athletes

The platform will also maintain fairness in the sports world, by ensuring that even the home federations don't manipulate the data of the athletes to hide doping cases. Thus, blockchain technology can ensure clean sports by helping in this fight against doping while respecting the privacy of the athletes.

69.3. Tracking counterfeit sports goods

Sports industry is grappling with the challenges posed by counterfeit sports goods. The online ecosystem provides a perfect breeding ground for counterfeiters to sell fake products. Blockchain technology has the potential to curb the entry of counterfeit sports goods into the market. The complete information from raw materials used for the manufacturing of sports goods until it reaches the retailer would be registered on the Blockchain. The customer can scan the unique ID present on the sports good through his smartphone and can trace its provenance and the complete journey it has taken before coming in his hands *(Fig 69-3)*.

Fig 69-3: Tracking counterfeit sports goods

69.4. IoT and Blockchain

IoT based smart sports activity sensors can become an athlete's personal coach, helping him thoroughly with both motivation and instructions. These sensors will store the athlete's data securely on the Blockchain, thus, making it resistant against hacking activities *(Fig 69-4)*. These sensors can measure factors that can help athletes improve their form. These sensors can analyze the movements of players in the right direction to improve their game. For instance, IoT sensors in connected basketball capture data about the spin rate or spiral efficiency. It also tracks distance threw and other statistics. This data will be stored on the Blockchain and the processed data will be presented to the athlete exactly pinpointing his improvement areas.

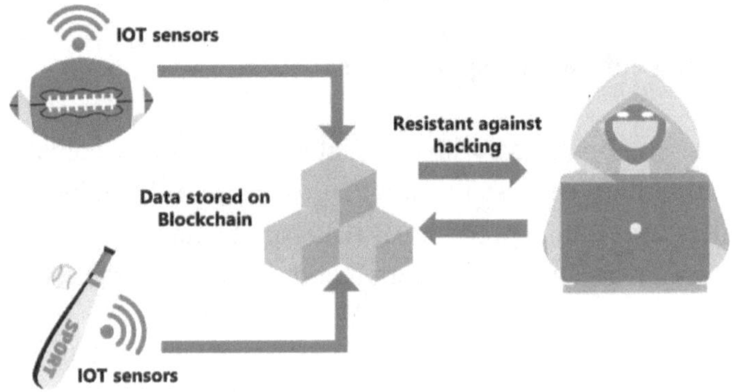

Fig 69-4: IOT sensors and Blockchain

69.5. Sports betting

Millions of people bet billions of dollars on sports every year. But there are challenges for bettors as well:

1. Currently, bettors have no way to establish the genuineness of the betting websites and in such a scenario these websites could easily take off their money.

2. And most importantly, there is a risk of the exploitation of their identity or information.

Blockchain can provide the required safety net for bettors and create a secure environment for betting. Let's understand how Blockchain will work for betting. Betting can be between two or multiple players that will be registered on the Blockchain. The players will bet against each other about the outcome of a sports event and this information will be stored in the smart contracts *(Fig 69-5).*

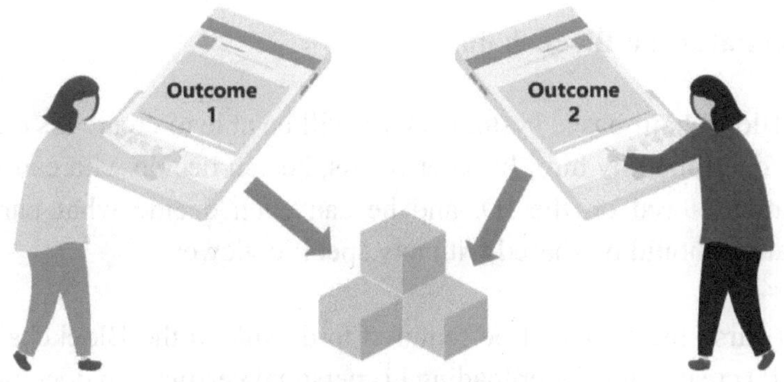

Fig 69-5: Sports betting on Blockchain

Chapter 70: Blockchain in Airlines

Currently, travelers are required to show their IDs at multiple checkpoints - from entering the airport to the luggage drop-off to buying stuff from the duty-free shops. Further, the long queues at security check-in and border control checkpoints are some of the other key pain points that travelers have to go through. Blockchain technology has the potential to simplify this process and eliminate the need to shuffle your bag repeatedly for taking out IDs and various other documents for verification.

70.1. Digital ID on Blockchain

With a Blockchain-based system, a user will be able to create his digital ID, entirely controlled by him. In other words, he can decide who can view his information stored on the ID, and he can even decide what part of the information should be shared with any specific viewer.

For this, first, the user will be required to download the Blockchain-based Digital ID creator app for uploading his personal verification documents like passport, visa, etc., and biometric data like fingerprints, eye scan, and voice *(Fig 70-1)*. This data will then be uploaded on the Blockchain, and a unique hash will be generated for the user's information.

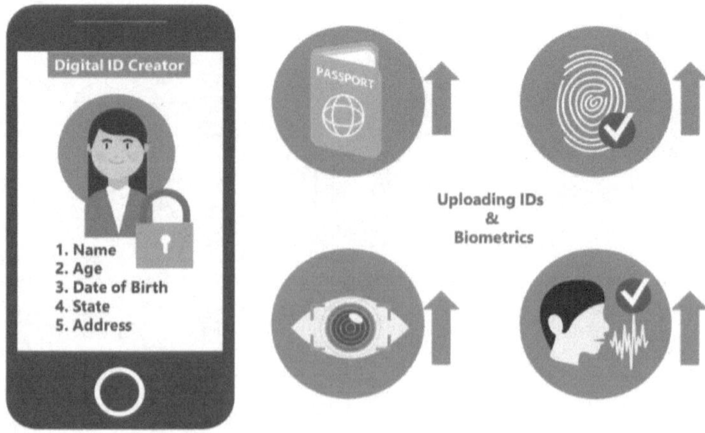

Fig 70-1: Creating digital ID on Blockchain

Now, this data will be sent to a government agency for verification. This agency will check and verify the user's data against the central database and will either approve it or disapprove it. The verification status of the uploaded documents and ID will get stored on the Blockchain.

When a user needs to take a flight, after reaching the airport, he can then simply go to a self-check-in security booth, where the user will be required to share his verified digital ID. After this, the user's biometrics like the fingerprint or facial recognition will be captured by the booth and will be verified against the verified digital ID provided by the user. On verification, a QR code will be generated, which can be scanned by the user through his mobile app and can be used in further rounds of verification done at the airport *(Fig 70-2)*. Thus, saving him a lot of precious time and unwanted hassle to take out his passport and other documents again and again to verify his credentials.

Fig 70-2: At the self-check-in booth, a QR code is generated after the verification of digital ID, which can be used for further verification done at the airport

In the case of international travel, the user can also share his verified digital ID with the border agencies well before his arrival dates. This will initiate the risk assessment in advance, and the actual process would be much faster and smoother when the user actually arrives at the border site. As the digital ID is government verified, the user can even be saved from the hassle of showing the passport.

70.2. Baggage Tracking through Blockchain

What comes to your mind when you think of travel. Packing your bags and leaving for that vacation you have been planning all month long. With your bags ready, you leave for the airport thinking about the wonderful beaches that you will hit or the unconquered mountains you will conquer. But as you leave your bags at the baggage drop-in counter, a slight sense of skepticism creeps in, and you become slightly worried about your luggage carrying all your important stuff and gears. You just wish that it gets loaded on the right plane, and in case you have a connecting flight, your concern reaches the next level. And all of this happens because you have no clear visibility of your luggage. In the current system, there is no way to track your luggage even at a single point during your whole journey.

Fig 70-3: When baggage changes hands, information is stored in local systems, which is not shared with other stakeholders

The main reason behind this is the lack of data exchange among the parties involved in the luggage transfer. The responsibility for every luggage item repeatedly changes during the journey *(Fig 70-3)*. And when the baggage changes hands, the relevant information is uploaded and stored in their respective local and private systems. This information stored in the local systems is not shared with other stakeholders. Thus, making the backtracking of any luggage difficult and complicated. This is especially applicable to multi-stop flights because an increased number of airports and authorities are involved in the luggage transfer, which in turn makes the data sharing complex and confusing.

But in a Blockchain-based system, the data stored will be secure, immutable, and accessible to all the stakeholders involved. Each bag will be marked with a unique code or number, and each traveler will be given a corresponding unique number to track their luggage.

When the bag moves through a security scanner or tracking system, the data will be uploaded and recorded on the blockchain. Every stakeholder on the Blockchain can track the entire journey of the baggage. Through this, every passenger can see the location of their bags in real-time *(Fig 70-4)*. This will give him the mental satisfaction that his bags have been loaded into the right plane, even during multi-stop flights. Further, it will also fasten the tracking of lost baggage as every stakeholder will have a clear picture of the luggage, its last tracking point, and the authority responsible for it. Thus, leading to a significant improvement in the customer experience for the flyers.

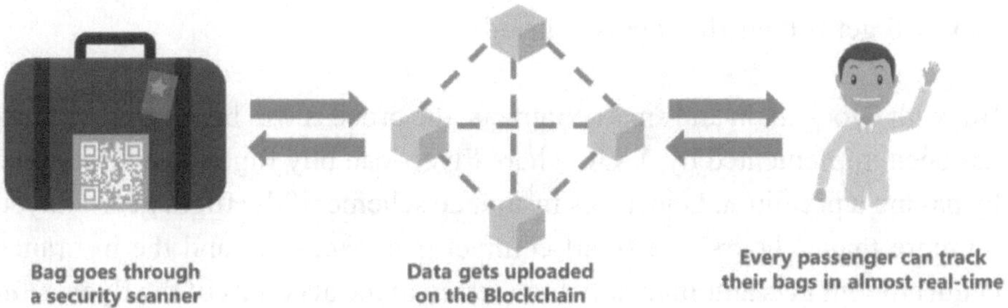

Fig 70-4: Tracking bags in real-time on the Blockchain

70.3. Redeeming Loyalty Points on Blockchain

Loyalty points and air miles are some of the very crucial ways through which airlines tap repeated customers. But in the current system, customers have to wait until they have substantial loyalty points accrued in their account. Further, the usage of these points is limited to very specific places, which leads to a lot of points being left unused or expired.

But with Blockchain-based royalty points, the points can be redeemed at various other partner outlets. Thus, increasing the usage and attractiveness of these points to the consumers. Very recently, a Blockchain-based loyalty program has been launched by Singapore Airlines for its flyers. They have developed a digital wallet named Krispay, in partnership with Microsoft and KPMG where their flyers can convert their air miles into units of payment that can be used at partner outlets in Singapore. Customers are provided with a mobile app. Using this app, the customers can convert their miles into units of payment and use these units to pay at registered outlets by simply scanning a QR code.

70.4. Flight Insurance Payout using smart contracts

Many airline carriers and their travel partners sell flight delay insurance along with flight tickets. But when the flight gets delayed, we don't know whom to approach to get our insurance claim. The whole claim process is opaque, and no one knows what steps are involved or what compensation they will get if their flight gets delayed.

But with Blockchain and smart contracts, the process will be simplified. This has been implemented by AXA, where Flyers can buy flight delay insurance by paying a premium. Under this insurance scheme, if the flight gets delayed by more than 2 hours, the smart contract gets executed, and the insurance claim amount gets automatically transferred in the accounts of the flyers *(Fig 70-5)*.

For buying this smart contract-based insurance, a person needs to first register their flight details on the service provider's platform and fill in their identity and account details. Then they can pay and buy the insurance plan. And if the flight gets delayed more than the stipulated time defined in the smart contract, an automatic payout is triggered by the smart contract into the flyer's bank account. This payout is done without any manual intervention from any of the stakeholders involved. Thus, making it swift and transparent.

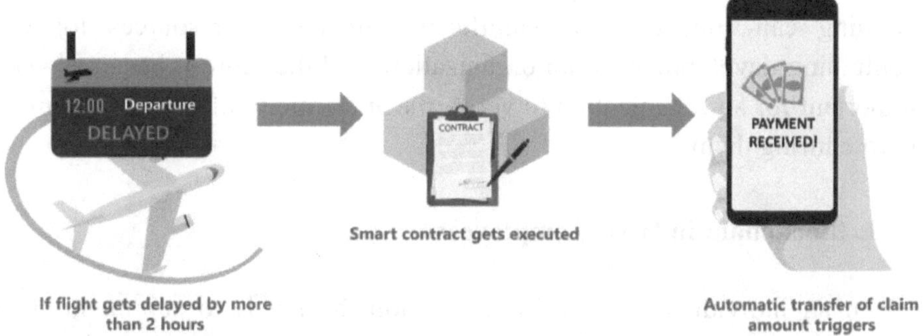

Fig 70-5: Flight Insurance payout on Blockchain

Chapter 71: Blockchain in Human Resources

Another important domain blockchain is going to disrupt is Human Resource Management. Employees being the crucial bearers of technology, knowledge, and service, represent the core component of any enterprise. Nothing can substitute the significance of human resources for the continuing development of an organization, and therefore it becomes very important for an organization to verify the authenticity of human resources before hiring them.

71.1. Blockchain in Hiring employees

When an individual applies for a new job, he needs to submit his CV describing his complete history, including personal details, education details, previous work experiences, etc. These details are then checked by the HR officials of the organization. This is quite a lengthy process, as the HR office needs to verify an individual's credentials mentioned in his CV.

But with Blockchain, the complete history of the applicant will be available on the shared ledger. This includes and is not limited to his education certificates, acquired skills, workshops or conferences attended, contact information, his previous work experience, all his promotions, appraisals, appreciations, and awards won in the previous organizations and even the reason for leaving the previous organizations. Before interviewing suitable candidates, organisations can pull all their history from the Blockchain as that will help them to take better decisions during the hiring process *(Fig 71-1)*.

71.2. Blockchain in Employee life cycle

The current procedure to onboard new recruits is quite a lengthy and tedious process. When an organization hires an individual, there is a lot of paperwork that he needs to complete, like submitting his previous records, signing job offer agreements, signing Non-disclosure agreements, etc. The paperwork and multistage approvals continue throughout his whole employment life cycle. For example, when he switches his role or department, or he gets promoted or when he quits the company for a better career opportunity, he must go through a multi-level approval process.

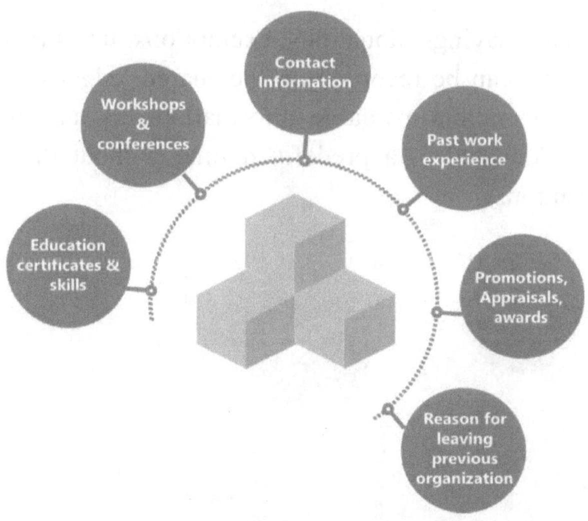

Fig 71-1: History of the applicant on Blockchain

Further, when he joins the new organization, he has to go through the entire process again. He has again to submit all his documents to his new employer.

But with the implementation of Blockchain, complete information of an individual will be available to the potential employer. Thus, reducing the time and energy spent on the validation and verification of an employee and therefore streamlining the whole HR process.

71.3. Blockchain in automating taxes

In the current scenario, estimating and calculating the annual taxes is a pain for any employee. And it is an even bigger headache for the contract workers due to a higher degree of the complications involved.

Blockchain can make life easier for everyone. The smart contracts would work as fair accounting systems that would calculate the taxes for individuals, which can be easily audited by everyone on the blockchain network like employees, tax departments, etc.

Employee's salary, savings, donations, exemptions, investments, and other sources of income can be recorded on the shared ledger *(Fig 71-2)*. As a result, and based on this available information, his tax amount will be calculated and deducted at a predefined time without the need for any manual intervention.

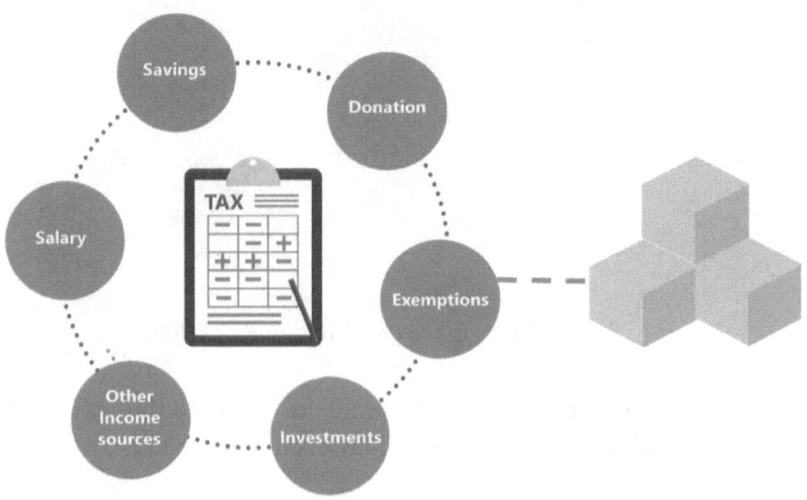

Fig 71-2: Tax information of employees on Blockchain

71.4. Blockchain in replacement of work contracts

Even today, the majority of organizations have all of their employee agreements on a piece of paper, and the HR department is required to validate and maintain these agreements. But with smart contracts, everything can be made seamless. All the agreement conditions can be predefined in a smart contract, and when the decided conditions are fulfilled smart contract gets executed automatically. For instance, if an employee's promotion or bonus conditions are fulfilled, the smart contract will get executed and an automatic bonus amount or promotion orders will be released to the respective employee *(Fig 71-3)*.

If an organization is required to hire a person on a contract basis, the work conditions and payment terms can be predefined in a smart contract, and when the predefined conditions are met, the smart contract will get executed, and an automatic payment will be released to the contractual resource.

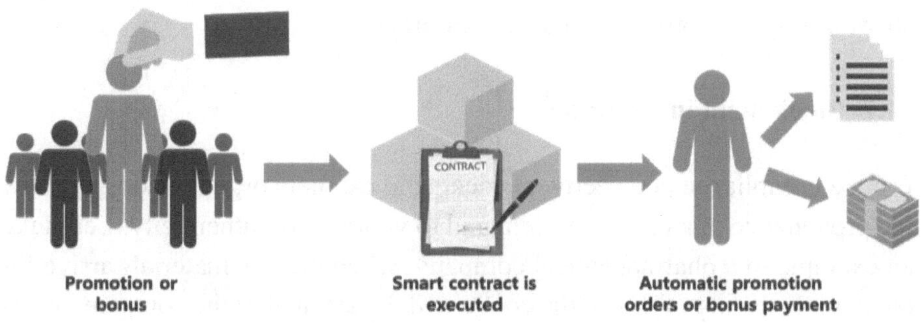

Fig 71-3: Promotion or bonus payment through Blockchain

71.5. Blockchain in attendance and wages of employees

Blockchain technology can be used to store biometric data of employees, such as fingerprint or iris scans. The attendance of employees can be stored and tracked on the shared ledger. Expenses done by employees for their official work can also be recorded on the Blockchain. Having a transparent and immutable record will make it much easier for the employees to get quick approvals and claim their expenses from the concerned department.

Today, if an employee has to claim for the official expenses, he has to go through a series of stakeholders to get the required approvals. This, in turn, becomes a frustrating and tedious task for an employee and also affects his work efficiency as a lot of time is wasted in getting these approvals. Claims can readily be settled as chances of fake claims will be negligible owing to the transparent and immutable characteristic of the Blockchain. This would decrease the unnecessary hassle for an employee, and he can devote his precious time in productive project work.

71.6. Blockchain in payroll

An essential and significant task of the Finance and Human resource department is to release employees' salaries on time after verifying their attendance and other perks that they receive. If all payroll conditions are defined on the smart contracts, salaries will be automatically released to the employees at the end of the month or week as predetermined. Thus, streamlining the complex management process.

71.7. Blockchain in Auditing

From a compliance perspective, Blockchain can help organizations to know the provenance of a particular item and to validate its authenticity. Let's take an example of a pharmaceutical company; when the raw materials arrive for the manufacturing of drugs, the concerned department of the company needs to verify the authenticity of the raw materials received. Through Blockchain technology, it will become easier for them to validate if the supplier has sent the authenticated raw materials.

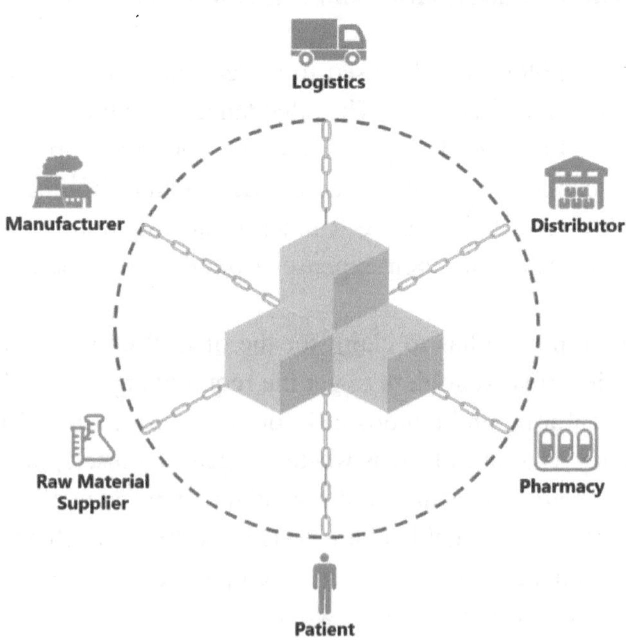

Fig 71-4: Real-time tracking of a product on Blockchain

Furthermore, after the drugs get manufactured, they need to arrange and keep a track of the logistics, product delivery, etc., which requires a lot of manual work, phone calls, emails, etc. But through Blockchain, they can keep a real-time track of the product's journey, thus simplifying their task *(Fig 71-4)*.

71.8. Blockchain in rating employer and organization

Every individual who applies for a job in a new organization wishes to know about the work ethics, culture, and reputation of that organization. He also wants to know if there are any challenges that he may face after joining the organization, like getting delayed salaries, work-life balance, working weekends, etc.

In another scenario, if an employee is not satisfied with his organization and finds some practices unethical, he should have a platform to rate his company and raise this concern without revealing his identity. But at the same time, the anonymous rating doesn't give the required credibility to any rating or review as many times these are also fake.

Blockchain offers a platform where an employee who has worked or is working can rate that organization without revealing his identity. Through Blockchain it can be verified that the reviewer has worked or is working with the company, but his identity won't be revealed. With such a platform in place, it would be much easier for a potential applicant to know the true picture of the organization and make a better-informed decision before joining any employer.

Chapter 72: Blockchain in Hotel Industry

72.1. Identity Management

Before checking in at any hotel, the person has to show his ID, passport, and various other documents to prove his authenticity. Thus leading to an increased check-in time. Through Blockchain technology, all the documents can be recorded on the Blockchain. When a person checks in at the hotel, the verification can be done using biometrics, either by face scanning or by thumbprint, to ensure that he is the same person for which the booking has been made. This will eliminate the need to carry proof documents and will thus also eliminate the chance of losing these precious documents.

A smart contract can be generated between the hotel and the customer. Once the customer books the room at a hotel that meets his needs, the smart contract will get executed, money will be deducted from the customer's digital account, and a digital room key will be provided to the customer. Upon arrival at the hotel, the customer can access his room through this digital key available on his phone. In such a scenario, minimal confirmations from the main desk will be required, thus reducing the waiting time.

72.2. Redemption of Loyalty points

The next application of Blockchain in the hotel industry can be better redemption of loyalty points. When you complete your stay at a hotel, in many cases, the hotel provides you with loyalty points as a reward. But in most instances, these loyalty points go unutilized due to their limited applications. In today's scenario, the loyalty points can only be used with that particular chain of hotels that own that loyalty program. Integrating these hotel loyalty points with a different chain of hotels or some other business is very challenging.

Through Blockchain technology, the loyalty points or tokens will be stored on the Blockchain. The interoperability nature of shared ledger technology will allow you to freely redeem, sell or exchange the loyalty token with

others. It will also empower you with the provision to use your hotel tokens across other industries.
You can use your hotel loyalty tokens to buy your meal, book an air ticket or buy a coffee, etc.

72.3. Transparency in Hotel Reviews

Another challenge that a customer faces while booking hotels is the fake or moderated online reviews that can sometimes even be misleading. On these online review platforms, anyone can write a hotel review without having the requirement to confirm that he or she even stayed there. Therefore it becomes difficult for consumers to know about the authenticity and accuracy of these online reviews.

Blockchain technology can address this issue by verifying the people giving reviews. Through the integration of Blockchain in the hotel industry, it can easily be verified if the people reviewing that hotel actually stayed in that particular hotel, thus, bringing transparency and reliability to online hotel reviews.

72.4. Reduced wait time

Waiting at hotels for check-in after a long journey can be frustrating. Wait time can be due to many reasons. For example, the room you booked is still not checked out, and cleaning has to be done, or it could be because of the time spent in the verification of the documents. But with Blockchain, this wait time can be minimized.

Imagine a scenario where hotels are able to track their guests and know the exact time of their arrival at the hotel. The availability of this real-time information will decrease the wait time during check-in and in turn, will increase guest satisfaction. Tracking guests' movements might be considered an invasion of privacy, but Blockchain provides a solution for this. With Blockchain, you can determine and authorize the hotels to a certain degree of required information without compromising your privacy.

72.5. Dispute Resolution

In the current scenario, if guests arrive at a hotel and find that the room they have booked is not what was advertised, they have little means of grievance redressal, especially if they have prepaid for their reservation.

Similarly, the ability of hotels to recoup losses for the damages caused by unruly guests is limited. Through Blockchain technology, smart contracts can be issued where all rules and conditions are pre-determined. In case of any dispute, the contracts will get executed, and appropriate compensation will be initiated for the sufferer.

72.6. Fraud Prevention

In 2021, around 2.8 million customers became victims of false hotel bookings through fraud websites resulting in a total fraud of around 5 billion USD. But with Blockchain technology, such incidents can be curbed easily. Blockchain can be leveraged to help customers validate if the booking is made with an authentic hotel.

72.7. Blockchain in the restaurant industry

(i) Cases of food fraud are on the rise these days. Imagine the level of satisfaction that you will get if you know the origin of the raw materials that a restaurant uses to prepare your food. The food you consume in restaurants is a part of the food supply chain. Raw materials like vegetables, fruits, etc., are produced by the farmers, passed through wholesalers and distributors, and received by restaurants where they are used for cooking those delicious dishes for you.

Through Blockchain technology, you will be able to track the origin of the food and the route it has taken. The technology will also ensure better quality control and food safety in restaurants.

(ii) Some restaurants differentiate themselves from the rest because of their specialized ingredients, e.g., gluten-free food, etc. Currently, there is no way for them to prove their genuineness, and at the same time, there is no way for a consumer to verify their claims. The restaurants can add proofs and sources of their ingredients on the Blockchain, establishing more trust in the customers about them.

(iii) Similarly, Blockchain technology will help you track and verify whether the online reviews about the restaurant are real and authentic.

72.8. Scalability concerns

(i) Blockchain used will be permissioned Blockchain. Storing the entire data about the reviews, identity documents, list of hotels and restaurants, etc., on Blockchain is very challenging as it is very costly and will significantly slow down the processing on Blockchain. Thus, distributed file storage IPFS can provide low-cost off-chain decentralized storage to store data. IPFS has been explained in detail in Chapter 15.

(ii) To make the Blockchain scalable, layer 1 (discussed in Chapter 12) and layer 2 (discussed in Chapter 13) scaling solutions will be required to be implemented.

Chapter 73: Blockchain solution to gun control

The United States of America is certainly an exceptional country when it comes to guns. It's one of the few nations where the right to bear arms is constitutionally protected. Among developed nations, the US is by far the most homicidal — largely due to the easy access many Americans have to firearms. In the US, firearm-related deaths have reached epidemic levels. In 2020, 45,222 people died from gun-related injuries in the U.S, out of which 54% of all gun-related deaths were suicides (24,292), while 43% were murdered (19,384). People in the United States are 25 times more likely to die from gun homicide than those in other industrialized nations.

In fact, the impact of fatal firearm injuries is three times greater than the impact of diabetes and almost four times greater than brain disease. Thus, firearm homicides and suicides are a continuing public health concern in the United States.

In a country where it is easier to be a gun owner than a car driver, it is clear that the current laws are not enough to ensure the safety of its citizens from potential murderers.

Enter Blockchain. Blockchain can be a solution that can solve this gun control problem in the US and other relevant countries.

73.1. Blockchain in performing background checks

The first application of Blockchain in gun control is while performing background checks. Background checks are required for obtaining guns, and these background checks are performed by querying the National Instant Criminal Background Check System (NICS). The NICS is a series of databases maintained by the Federal Bureau of Investigation (FBI).

Under the law, criminals or people suffering from mental health are not eligible to obtain guns. NICS is designed to be an instantaneous process and the vast majority of gun background checks take just minutes, and if the query turns up negative, then the gun transfer is also approved within minutes.

However, there are cases where the FBI takes more time to investigate. A normal scenario for this can be if the buyer happens to have a name same as that of a criminal, then his gun background check may take much longer. Besides, in certain cases, the buyers are mistakenly denied the purchase of a firearm as well. According to the FBI's own records, every year about 3,000 people officially pass the NICS background check required to receive a license to carry a gun, despite actually being prohibited from purchasing one under the state law.

To minimize these system errors, a Blockchain-based registry system can be put in place for performing these background checks more efficiently. The information about the person, such as any prior history of mental health issues and past crimes will be stored on the distributed ledger. People who pass the background check may own a gun, and on the other hand, those who don't will be prohibited from doing so. Also, as Blockchain is decentralized, it is significantly less vulnerable to hacking. Thus Blockchain technology can minimize risk and mitigate failures in the current system of gun ownership in the US.

73.2. Blockchain in the tracking of guns

The second application of Blockchain is in the tracking of guns. From manufacturing to the sale of a firearm, knowing where it is at any given point of time is important to ensure that it doesn't fall into the wrong hands. Implementation of a Blockchain-based system can solve this challenge of tracking guns throughout its complete journey. In this proposed system, the individuals currently owning a gun or purchasing a gun would get an electronic gun safe, similar to a cryptocurrency wallet. The electronic gun safe would be linked to an individual's biometric data, such as a retina scan or fingerprints.

Whenever a gun is manufactured, purchased, or sold, the transaction from one electronic gun safe to another would be recorded on the Blockchain in an immutable, time-stamped manner.

Additionally, prior to the transaction, the buyer of the gun would have to pass a background check. The transfer of guns in this Blockchain-based system, will be mediated through smart contracts. If an individual passes the background check, smart contract will initiate the gun transfer, and if not, the transfer will be denied and the gun will still be recorded against the seller's electronic gun safe.

Furthermore, the buyers of guns would be required to upload their electronic medical records and electronic criminal records on this platform. And whenever a medical event occurs, such as depression or a suicide attempt by the buyer, the platform would spit out this information to the state law enforcement for the protection of that individual and others around him.

Moreover, when the criminal record changes of a gun holder, then also local law enforcement will be notified.

And if in case the gun of a person gets stolen, that information will also be recorded on the Blockchain because crimes from stolen guns are a very common occurrence.

Thus, using Blockchain technology to monitor firearms could definitely help to reduce mass shootings by making it more difficult to obtain guns illegally and to purchase or possess a gun without passing a mental health background check.

73.3. Blockchain and smart guns

"Smart guns," also known as "personalized" firearms, are meant to prevent unauthorized persons from accessing and using firearms. Currently, there are two kinds of existing technologies in smart guns capable of reliably identifying authorized users.

- The first type is Radio frequency identification (RFID) tokens that can activate a firearm when they are in close proximity to it. These tokens can be integrated into watches, bracelets, rings, or other wearable devices. Entering a PIN on the wearable device activates or deactivates the weapon, which automatically shuts off after a certain interval or if the gun moves more than 15 inches from the wearable device.

- The second type is biometric recognition which activates a firearm after identifying biological features like a palm print, fingerprint, or grip.

These technologies are designed to prevent shootings that occur when unauthorized users like children—gain access to unsecured guns. Household guns are the most common weapons used by youth in violence against themselves or others. Between 70 to 90% of guns used in unintentional shootings among children, school shootings and youth suicides are obtained by shooters under the age of 18 from their home or the homes of their relatives or friends.

Smart guns also render them useless to criminals who steal them. A survey data suggests that approximately 380,000 guns are stolen from individual gun owners every year.

Blocksafe network is the first Blockchain-based system that manages smart gun functionality on the Blockchain and provides improved security and privacy. When a gun fires, the Blocksafe "shotspot" technology senses and logs details on the distributed ledger. If an unauthorized user tries to use a smart gun, then the Blockchain network notifies the owner of the gun via a smartphone.

The potential risk that smart guns face is security because the **IoT devices** on smart guns are susceptible to hacking. But the implementation of Blockchain technology can provide security and safety to smart guns and make them resistant to hacking.

73.4. Challenges in implementing Blockchain for gun control

(i) Blockchain would need to gain widespread acceptance. One or two states implementing Blockchain can't control gun violence since anyone with a federal firearms license can buy or sell a gun across state lines in the U.S. The system would need to roll out nationally, and it would cost money to implement.

(ii) There is also the issue of all the guns already in circulation. Registering all the nation's gun owners on the Blockchain system is challenging.

73.5. Scalability concerns

(i) Blockchain used will be permissioned Blockchain. Storing the entire data about the gun supply chain, personal data of individuals, background check verification, IoT data etc., on Blockchain is very challenging as it is very costly and will significantly slow down the processing on Blockchain. Thus, distributed file storage IPFS can provide low-cost off-chain decentralized storage to store data. IPFS has been explained in detail in Chapter 15.

(ii) To make the Blockchain scalable, layer 1 (discussed in Chapter 12) and layer 2 (discussed in Chapter 13) scaling solutions will be required to be implemented.

Chapter 74: Blockchain in the defense sector

The defense sector is a very critical and crucial sector for every country in this world. This sector is generally considered a resource-intensive sector, with many countries spending a substantial share of their GDP on this sector. The defense sector has always been a frontrunner in implementing the state of art technology solutions, and Blockchain is no different.

74.1. Blockchain as a communication platform

Blockchain, with its innate characteristics of security, auditability, accuracy, transparency, and data immutability, proves to be an excellent match for the defense industry, which involves a lot of complex processes, multiple stakeholders and requires the highest level of security for its data and communication channels.

The first and most basic requirement of the defense sector is to have a robust and secure communication platform. A platform that can help the agencies and defense officials to maintain the secrecy of the information shared and transmitted as per the protocols laid down. Blockchain can be a perfect solution for these requirements as it can provide a platform for secure and resilient communications in a highly contested environment. Effective information tracking and data source authentication are very crucial requirements of the defense sector. Military officials use this information to make important, sometimes even life-and-death decisions. With the implementation of Blockchain, they can make these decisions more confidently as it ensures data authenticity and data integrity. Time Stamped messages with their immutable audit trail, including the original source, makes them more trustworthy and reliable.

Further, Blockchain enables data inputs to be appended to a single, distributed ledger, thus reducing the risk of errors and simultaneously improving data reliability. US Military has partnered with a technology firm ITAMCO to develop a Blockchain-based secure messaging app. The app's goal would be to provide a robust, efficient, and much more secure platform for the Department of Defence Communications. This secure messaging platform has several use cases inside the defense services, for example, for communication between the troops on the ground and the Headquarters or sending information between intelligence officials and the Pentagon.

74.2. Blockchain in defense supply chain

Complex supply chain is the next big challenge that bothers this industry consistently. The defense supply chain, like any other supply chain, requires transparency and traceability for its robustness. Blockchain, with its feature of immutability, provides an immutable trail of the products and goods moving through the supply chain. This is a great feature for this sector, as defense officials can now track and trace all the supply chain transactions across various departments and supplier partners. This in turn, saves a lot of time and makes the whole system more efficient.

74.3. Blockchain in Cyberdefense

Cyber defense is one of the most promising solutions that Blockchain can provide for this sector. The defense industry has constantly been trying to find a solution for the issue of Cyber attacks. Threats of data manipulation and hacking always keep the defense sector on its toes as these activities can lead to a breach of the critical data, which in turn, can leave the defense services of the whole country vulnerable. The security protocols and databases currently used by the defense sector need to be upgraded to fend off global cyber threats.

Blockchain technology provides a perfect solution for these requirements of the defense sector. In traditional systems, a complete network becomes vulnerable even if one data center is hacked into or disabled by the enemy. But with Blockchain and its decentralized ledger system, there is no single point of failure, and the enemy needs to take down all data centers and devices to disable the complete network.

74.4. Blockchain in Military Drone Operations

One more application of Blockchain technology is in Military Drone Operations. AI and Blockchain, coupled with drone technology, can be used for various applications in defense services. These drones powered by AI can fly independently without requiring any intervention from a human.

Further, Blockchain technology can be used to record data collected by these drones in real-time and in an immutable ledger. Sometimes it becomes very difficult for humans to understand the data points used by AI systems to reach a particular decision. In such cases, Blockchain really helps to understand the decision made by the AI as the complete trail of the decision process will be recorded on the Blockchain.

For a better understanding, you can refer to the lecture on the Application of Blockchain in Artificial Intelligence (AI).

So extending this concept to our AI-powered drones, Blockchain technology can be used to record the actions and flight decisions taken by the drone during its whole journey. Of course, the drone may get destroyed or attacked by the enemy, but the information it captured and recorded will still be available on the Blockchain.

Hence it won't be incorrect if we assume that Blockchain technology is a natural match for the defense sector. The peculiar characteristics of immutability, transparency, and security that Blockchain provides have made it a perfect solution for solving many of the issues of the Defence industry.

74.5. Scalability concerns

(i) Blockchain used will be permissioned Blockchain. However, storing the entire data about the supply chain, AI, military drones, intelligence, etc., on Blockchain is very challenging as it is costly and will significantly slow down the processing on Blockchain. Thus, distributed file storage IPFS can provide low-cost off-chain decentralized storage to store data. IPFS has been explained in detail in Chapter 15.

(ii) To make the Blockchain scalable, layer 1 (discussed in Chapter 12) and layer 2 (discussed in Chapter 13) scaling solutions will be required to be implemented.

References

Paul, P., Aithal, P. S., & Saavedra, R. (2021). Blockchain Technology and its Types—A Short Review. *International Journal of Applied Science and Engineering (IJASE)*, *9*(2), 189-200.

Madavi, D. (2019). A comprehensive study on blockchain technology. *International Research Journal of Engineering and Technology*, *6*(1), 1765-1770.

Aggarwal, S. (2018). Blockchain technology: the next age of Internet. *International Journal of Research and Analytical Reviews*, *5*(3), 1920-1924.

Singh, S., Sharma, A., & Jain, P. (2018). A Detailed Study of Blockchain: Changing the World. *International Journal of Applied Engineering Research*, *13*(14), 11532-11539.

Sabry, S. S., Kaittan, N. M., & Majeed, I. (2019). The road to the blockchain technology: Concept and types. *Periodicals of Engineering and Natural Sciences (PEN)*, *7*(4), 1821-1832.

Kaur, A., Nayyar, A., & Singh, P. (2020). Blockchain: A path to the future. *Cryptocurrencies and Blockchain technology applications*, 25-42.

Sheth, H., & Dattani, J. (2019). Overview of blockchain technology. *Asian Journal For Convergence In Technology (AJCT) ISSN-2350-1146.*

Papadopoulos, K. (2019). Using Smart Contracts in Smart Energy Grid Applications. In *Sinteza 2019-International Scientific Conference on Information Technology and Data Related Research* (pp. 597-602). Singidunum University.

Nakamoto, S. (2008). Bitcoin: A peer-to-peer electronic cash system. *Decentralized Business Review*, 21260.

Back, A., Corallo, M., Dashjr, L., Friedenbach, M., Maxwell, G., Miller, A., ... & Wuille, P. (2014). Enabling blockchain innovations with pegged sidechains. *URL: http://www. opensciencereview. com/papers/123/enablingblockchain-innovations-with-pegged-sidechains*, *72*, 201-224.

Kuo, T. T., Kim, H. E., & Ohno-Machado, L. (2017). Blockchain distributed ledger technologies for biomedical and health care applications. *Journal of the American Medical Informatics Association*, *24*(6), 1211-1220.

Lashkari, B., & Musilek, P. (2021). A comprehensive review of blockchain consensus mechanisms. *IEEE Access*, *9*, 43620-43652.

ul Abadin, Z., & Syed, M. (2021, July). A Pattern for Proof of Work Consensus Algorithm in Blockchain. In *26th European Conference on Pattern Languages of Programs* (pp. 1-6).

Szalachowski, P., Reijsbergen, D., Homoliak, I., & Sun, S. (2019). {StrongChain}: Transparent and Collaborative {Proof-of-Work} Consensus. In *28th USENIX Security Symposium (USENIX Security 19)* (pp. 819-836).

Nguyen, C. T., Hoang, D. T., Nguyen, D. N., Niyato, D., Nguyen, H. T., & Dutkiewicz, E. (2019). Proof-of-stake consensus mechanisms for future blockchain networks: fundamentals, applications and opportunities. *IEEE Access*, *7*, 85727-85745.

Hu, Q., Yan, B., Han, Y., & Yu, J. (2021). An improved delegated proof of stake consensus algorithm. *Procedia Computer Science*, *187*, 341-346.

Snider, M., Samani, K., & Jain, T. (2018). Delegated proof of stake: features & tradeoffs. *Multicoin Cap*, *19*.

Majumdar, M. A., Monim, M., & Shahriyer, M. M. (2020, June). Blockchain based land registry with delegated proof of stake (DPoS) consensus in Bangladesh. In *2020 IEEE Region 10 Symposium (TENSYMP)* (pp. 1756-1759). IEEE.

Hakak, S., Khan, W. Z., Gilkar, G. A., Imran, M., & Guizani, N. (2020). Securing smart cities through blockchain technology: Architecture, requirements, and challenges. *IEEE Network*, *34*(1), 8-14.

Alyaseen, I. F. T. (2019). Consensus algorithms blockchain: A comparative study. *International Journal on Perceptive and Cognitive Computing*, *5*(2), 66-71.

Salimitari, M., & Chatterjee, M. (2018). An overview of blockchain and consensus protocols for IoT networks. *arXiv preprint arXiv:1809.05613*, 1-12.

Singh, P. K., Singh, R., Nandi, S. K., & Nandi, S. (2019, June). Managing smart home appliances with proof of authority and blockchain. In *International conference on innovations for community services* (pp. 221-232). Springer, Cham.

Al Asad, N., Elahi, M. T., Al Hasan, A., & Yousuf, M. A. (2020, November). Permission-based blockchain with proof of authority for secured healthcare data sharing. In *2020 2nd International Conference on Advanced Information and Communication Technology (ICAICT)* (pp. 35-40). IEEE.

Manolache, M. A., Manolache, S., & Tapus, N. (2022). Decision Making using the Blockchain Proof of Authority Consensus. *Procedia Computer Science*, *199*, 580-588.

Huang, H. S., Chang, T. S., & Wu, J. Y. (2020, July). A secure file sharing system based on IPFS and blockchain. In *Proceedings of the 2020 2nd International Electronics Communication Conference* (pp. 96-100).

Li, W., Zhou, Z., Fan, W., & Gao, J. (2022). Design of Data Sharing Platform Based on Blockchain and IPFS Technology. *Wireless Communications and Mobile Computing*, *2022*.

Trautwein, D., Raman, A., Tyson, G., Castro, I., Scott, W., Schubotz, M., ... & Psaras, Y. (2022, August). Design and evaluation of IPFS: a storage layer for the decentralized web. In *Proceedings of the ACM SIGCOMM 2022 Conference* (pp. 739-752).

Chen, Y., Li, H., Li, K., & Zhang, J. (2017, December). An improved P2P file system scheme based on IPFS and Blockchain. In *2017 IEEE International Conference on Big Data (Big Data)* (pp. 2652-2657). IEEE.

Cong, L. W., & He, Z. (2019). Blockchain disruption and smart contracts. *The Review of Financial Studies*, *32*(5), 1754-1797.

Turjo, M. D., Khan, M. M., Kaur, M., & Zaguia, A. (2021). Smart supply chain management using the blockchain and smart contract. *Scientific programming*, *2021*.

Wu, Y., Li, J., Zhou, J., Luo, S., & Song, L. (2022). Evolution Process and Supply Chain Adaptation of Smart Contracts in Blockchain. *Journal of Mathematics*, *2022*.

Khan, S., Amin, M. B., Azar, A. T., & Aslam, S. (2021). Towards interoperable blockchains: A survey on the role of smart contracts in blockchain interoperability. *IEEE Access*, *9*, 116672-116691.

Khan, S. N., Loukil, F., Ghedira-Guegan, C., Benkhelifa, E., & Bani-Hani, A. (2021). Blockchain smart contracts: Applications, challenges, and future trends. *Peer-to-peer Networking and Applications*, *14*(5), 2901-2925.

Gangwal, A., Gangavalli, H. R., & Thirupathi, A. (2022). A Survey of Layer-Two Blockchain Protocols. *arXiv preprint arXiv:2204.08032*.

Hafid, A., Hafid, A. S., & Samih, M. (2020). Scaling blockchains: A comprehensive survey. *IEEE Access*, *8*, 125244-125262.

Hong, Z., Guo, S., & Li, P. (2022). Scaling Blockchain via Layered Sharding. *IEEE Journal on Selected Areas in Communications.*

Qin, K., & Gervais, A. (2018). An overview of blockchain scalability, interoperability and sustainability. *Hochschule Luzern Imperial College London Liquidity Network.*

Schaffner, T. (2021). Scaling Public Blockchains. *A comprehensive analysis of optimistic and zero-knowledge rollups. University of Basel.*

Liu, Y., Liu, J., Salles, M. A. V., Zhang, Z., Li, T., Hu, B., ... & Lu, R. (2022). Building blocks of sharding blockchain systems: Concepts, approaches, and open problems. *Computer Science Review*, *46*, 100513.

Xi, J., Zou, S., Xu, G., Guo, Y., Lu, Y., Xu, J., & Zhang, X. (2021). A Comprehensive Survey on Sharding in Blockchains. *Mobile Information Systems, 2021.*

Yu, G., Wang, X., Yu, K., Ni, W., Zhang, J. A., & Liu, R. P. (2020). Scaling-out blockchains with sharding: an extensive survey.

Sguanci, C., Spatafora, R., & Vergani, A. M. (2021). Layer 2 blockchain scaling: A survey. *arXiv preprint arXiv:2107.10881.*

Gangwal, A., Gangavalli, H. R., & Thirupathi, A. (2022). A survey of Layer-two blockchain protocols. *Journal of Network and Computer Applications*, 103539.
Minoli, D., & Occhiogrosso, B. (2018). Blockchain mechanisms for IoT security. *Internet of Things*, *1*, 1-13.

Singh, A., Click, K., Parizi, R. M., Zhang, Q., Dehghantanha, A., & Choo, K. K. R. (2020). Sidechain technologies in blockchain networks: An examination and state-of-the-art review. *Journal of Network and Computer Applications*, *149*, 102471.

Thibault, L. T., Sarry, T., & Hafid, A. S. (2022). Blockchain Scaling using Rollups: A Comprehensive Survey. *IEEE Access.*

Yu, T., Luo, F., Pu, C., Zhao, Z., & Ranzi, G. (2022). Dual-blockchain-based P2P energy trading system with an improved optimistic rollup mechanism. *IET Smart Grid.*

Metcalfe, W. (2020). Ethereum, smart contracts, DApps. *Blockchain and Crypt Currency*, 77.

Besançon, L., Da Silva, C. F., Ghodous, P., & Gelas, J. P. (2022). A Blockchain Ontology for DApps Development. *IEEE Access*, *10*, 49905-49933.

Gray, G. R. (2021). Distributed Applications (dApps). In *Blockchain Technology for Managers* (pp. 89-97). Springer, Cham.

Chen, Y., Li, H., Li, K., & Zhang, J. (2017, December). An improved P2P file system scheme based on IPFS and Blockchain. In *2017 IEEE International Conference on Big Data (Big Data)* (pp. 2652-2657). IEEE.

Zheng, Q., Li, Y., Chen, P., & Dong, X. (2018, December). An innovative IPFS-based storage model for blockchain. In *2018 IEEE/WIC/ACM international conference on web intelligence (WI)* (pp. 704-708). IEEE.

Ali, M. S., Dolui, K., & Antonelli, F. (2017, October). IoT data privacy via blockchains and IPFS. In *Proceedings of the seventh international conference on the internet of things* (pp. 1-7).

Kumar, S., Bharti, A. K., & Amin, R. (2021). Decentralized secure storage of medical records using Blockchain and IPFS: A comparative analysis with future directions. *Security and Privacy*, *4*(5), e162.

Sun, J., Yao, X., Wang, S., & Wu, Y. (2020). Blockchain-based secure storage and access scheme for electronic medical records in IPFS. *IEEE Access*, *8*, 59389-59401.

Bhatia, R. (2020, October). Interoperability solutions for blockchain. In *2020 international conference on smart technologies in computing, electrical and electronics (ICSTCEE)* (pp. 381-385). IEEE.

Xiong, A., Liu, G., Zhu, Q., Jing, A., & Loke, S. W. (2022). A notary group-based cross-chain mechanism. *Digital Communications and Networks*.

Mohanty, D., Anand, D., Aljahdali, H. M., & Villar, S. G. (2022). Blockchain Interoperability: Towards a Sustainable Payment System. *Sustainability*, *14*(2), 913.

Lys, L., Micoulet, A., & Potop-Butucaru, M. (2020, September). Atomic cross chain swaps via relays and adapters. In *Proceedings of the 3rd Workshop on Cryptocurrencies and Blockchains for Distributed Systems* (pp. 59-64).

Ou, W., Huang, S., Zheng, J., Zhang, Q., Zeng, G., & Han, W. (2022). An Overview on Cross-chain: Mechanism, Platforms, Challenges and Advances. *Computer Networks*, 109378.

Hardjono, T. (2021). Blockchain gateways, bridges and delegated hash-locks. *arXiv preprint arXiv:2102.03933*.

Kapsoulis, N., Psychas, A., Palaiokrassas, G., Marinakis, A., Litke, A., & Varvarigou, T. (2020). Know your customer (KYC) implementation with smart contracts on a privacy-oriented decentralized architecture. *Future Internet*, *12*(2), 41.

Kumar, M., & Nikhil, P. A. (2020). A blockchain based approach for an efficient secure KYC process with data sovereignty. *Int J Sci Technol Res*, *9*, 3403-3407.

Rankhambe, B. P., & Khanuja, H. K. (2021). Hassle-Free and Secure e-KYC System Using Distributed Ledger Technology. *International Journal of Next-Generation Computing*, *12*(2).

Yadav, A. K., & Bajpai, R. K. (2020). KYC optimization using blockchain smart contract technology. *Int J Innov Res Appl Sci Eng (IJIRASE)*, *4*(3), 669-674.

Kulkarni, V., & Singh, A. P. (2017). Sustainable KYC through Blockchain Technology in Global Banks. *technology*, *6*, 18.

Alrebdi, N., Alabdulatif, A., Iwendi, C., & Lian, Z. (2022). SVBE: searchable and verifiable blockchain-based electronic medical records system. *Scientific Reports*, *12*(1), 1-11.

Elhadad, A. (2020). Data sharing using proxy re-encryption based on DNA computing. *Soft Computing*, *24*(3), 2101-2108.

Hang, L., Choi, E., & Kim, D. H. (2019). A novel EMR integrity management based on a medical blockchain platform in hospital. *Electronics*, *8*(4), 467.
Kumar, S., Bharti, A. K., & Amin, R. (2021). Decentralized secure storage of medical records using Blockchain and IPFS: A comparative analysis with future directions. *Security and Privacy*, *4*(5), e162.

Tanwar, S., Parekh, K., & Evans, R. (2020). Blockchain-based electronic healthcare record system for healthcare 4.0 applications. *Journal of Information Security and Applications*, *50*, 102407.

Uddin, M., Memon, M. S., Memon, I., Ali, I., Memon, J., Abdelhaq, M., & Alsaqour, R. (2021). Hyperledger fabric blockchain: Secure and efficient solution for electronic health records. *Comput., Mater. Continua*, *68*(2), 2377-2397.

Zhuang, Y., Chen, Y. W., Shae, Z. Y., & Shyu, C. R. (2020). Generalizable layered blockchain architecture for health care applications: development, case studies, and evaluation. *Journal of Medical Internet Research*, *22*(7), e19029.

Ali, M. S., Dolui, K., & Antonelli, F. (2017, October). IoT data privacy via blockchains and IPFS. In *Proceedings of the seventh international conference on the internet of things* (pp. 1-7).

Hang, L., & Kim, D. H. (2019). Design and implementation of an integrated iot blockchain platform for sensing data integrity. *Sensors*, *19*(10), 2228.

Jiang, Y., Wang, C., Wang, Y., & Gao, L. (2019). A cross-chain solution to integrating multiple blockchains for IoT data management. *Sensors*, *19*(9), 2042.

Lee, J., Azamfar, M., & Singh, J. (2019). A blockchain enabled Cyber-Physical System architecture for Industry 4.0 manufacturing systems. *Manufacturing letters*, *20*, 34-39.

Ngubo, C. E., McBurney, P. J., & Dohler, M. (2019, March). Blockchain, IoT and sidechains. In *Proceedings of The International Multiconference of Engineers and Computer Scientists*.

Sigwart, M., Borkowski, M., Peise, M., Schulte, S., & Tai, S. (2020). A secure and extensible blockchain-based data provenance framework for the internet of things. *Personal and Ubiquitous Computing*, 1-15.

Sultan, A., Mushtaq, M. A., & Abubakar, M. (2019, March). IOT security issues via blockchain: a review paper. In *Proceedings of the 2019 International Conference on Blockchain Technology* (pp. 60-65).

Damianou, A., Angelopoulos, C. M., & Katos, V. (2019, May). An architecture for blockchain over edge-enabled IoT for smart circular cities. In *2019 15th International Conference on Distributed Computing in Sensor Systems (DCOSS)* (pp. 465-472). IEEE.

Hosono, K., Maki, A., Watanabe, Y., Takada, H., & Sato, K. (2022). Efficient Access Method for Multi-access Edge Servers in Dynamic Map Systems. *International Journal of Intelligent Transportation Systems Research*, 1-14.

Jiao, Y., Wang, P., Niyato, D., & Xiong, Z. (2018, May). Social welfare maximization auction in edge computing resource allocation for mobile blockchain. In *2018 IEEE international conference on communications (ICC)* (pp. 1-6). IEEE.

Nyamtiga, B. W., Sicato, J. C. S., Rathore, S., Sung, Y., & Park, J. H. (2019). Blockchain-based secure storage management with edge computing for IoT. *Electronics*, *8*(8), 828.

Wu, Y., Dai, H. N., & Wang, H. (2020). Convergence of blockchain and edge computing for secure and scalable IIoT critical infrastructures in industry 4.0. *IEEE Internet of Things Journal*, *8*(4), 2300-2317.

Anwar ul Hassan, C., Hammad, M., Iqbal, J., Hussain, S., Ullah, S. S., AlSalman, H., ... & Arif, M. (2022). A Liquid Democracy Enabled Blockchain-Based Electronic Voting System. *Scientific Programming*, *2022*.

Khan, K. M., Arshad, J., & Khan, M. M. (2020). Investigating performance constraints for blockchain based secure e-voting system. *Future Generation Computer Systems*, *105*, 13-26.

Abuidris, Y., Kumar, R., & Wenyong, W. (2019, December). A survey of blockchain based on e-voting systems. In *Proceedings of the 2019 2nd International Conference on Blockchain Technology and Applications* (pp. 99-104).

Yao, J., Wei, L., & Liu, T. (2020). Blockchain-Based Voting System. *Computer System Networking and Telecommunications*, *3*(1).

MV, M. K., HA, S., BS, P., Thomas, L., & Murthy YV, S. (2019). End-to-End Verifiable Electronic Voting System Using Delegated Proof of Stake On Blockchain.

Arif, S., Khan, M. A., Rehman, S. U., Kabir, M. A., & Imran, M. (2020). Investigating smart home security: Is blockchain the answer?. *IEEE Access*, *8*, 117802-117816.

Lee, Y., Rathore, S., Park, J. H., & Park, J. H. (2020). A blockchain-based smart home gateway architecture for preventing data forgery. *Human-centric Computing and Information Sciences*, *10*(1), 1-14.

Moniruzzaman, M., Khezr, S., Yassine, A., & Benlamri, R. (2020). Blockchain for smart homes: Review of current trends and research challenges. *Computers & Electrical Engineering*, *83*, 106585.

Choo, K. K. R., Yan, Z., & Meng, W. (2020). Blockchain in industrial IoT applications: Security and privacy advances, challenges, and opportunities. *IEEE Transactions on Industrial Informatics*, *16*(6), 4119-4121.

Mohanta, B. K., Jena, D., Ramasubbareddy, S., Daneshmand, M., & Gandomi, A. H. (2020). Addressing security and privacy issues of IoT using blockchain technology. *IEEE Internet of Things Journal*, *8*(2), 881-888.

Qashlan, A., Nanda, P., He, X., & Mohanty, M. (2021). Privacy-preserving mechanism in smart home using blockchain. *IEEE Access*, *9*, 103651-103669.

Baucas, M. J., Gadsden, S. A., & Spachos, P. (2021). IoT-based smart home device monitor using private blockchain technology and localization. *IEEE Networking Letters*, *3*(2), 52-55.

Tariq, N., Qamar, A., Asim, M., & Khan, F. A. (2020). Blockchain and smart healthcare security: a survey. *Procedia Computer Science*, *175*, 615-620.

Jeong, S., Shen, J. H., & Ahn, B. (2021). A study on smart healthcare monitoring using IoT based on blockchain. *Wireless Communications and Mobile Computing, 2021.*

Bhawiyuga, A., Wardhana, A., Amron, K., & Kirana, A. P. (2019, December). Platform for integrating internet of things based smart healthcare system and blockchain network. In *2019 6th NAFOSTED Conference on Information and Computer Science (NICS)* (pp. 55-60). IEEE.

Shukla, R. G., Agarwal, A., & Shukla, S. (2020). Blockchain-powered smart healthcare system. In *Handbook of research on Blockchain technology* (pp. 245-270). Academic Press.

Queiroz, M. M., Telles, R., & Bonilla, S. H. (2019). Blockchain and supply chain management integration: a systematic review of the literature. *Supply Chain Management: An International Journal.*

Azzi, R., Chamoun, R. K., & Sokhn, M. (2019). The power of a blockchain-based supply chain. *Computers & industrial engineering*, *135*, 582-592.

Banerjee, A. (2018). Blockchain technology: supply chain insights from ERP. In *Advances in computers* (Vol. 111, pp. 69-98). Elsevier.

Clauson, K. A., Breeden, E. A., Davidson, C., & Mackey, T. K. (2018). Leveraging Blockchain Technology to Enhance Supply Chain Management in Healthcare:: An exploration of challenges and opportunities in the health supply chain. *Blockchain in healthcare today.*

Sylim, P., Liu, F., Marcelo, A., & Fontelo, P. (2018). Blockchain technology for detecting falsified and substandard drugs in distribution: pharmaceutical supply chain intervention. *JMIR research protocols*, *7*(9), e10163.

Mattke, J., Hund, A., Maier, C., & Weitzel, T. (2019). How an Enterprise Blockchain Application in the US Pharmaceuticals Supply Chain is Saving Lives. *MIS Quarterly Executive*, *18*(4).

Ahmadi, V., Benjelloun, S., El Kik, M., Sharma, T., Chi, H., & Zhou, W. (2020, February). Drug governance: IoT-based blockchain implementation in the pharmaceutical supply chain. In *2020 Sixth International Conference on Mobile And Secure Services (MobiSecServ)* (pp. 1-8). IEEE.

Haq, I., & Esuka, O. M. (2018). Blockchain technology in pharmaceutical industry to prevent counterfeit drugs. *International Journal of Computer Applications*, *180*(25), 8-12.

Tan, B., Yan, J., Chen, S., & Liu, X. (2018, December). The impact of blockchain on food supply chain: The case of walmart. In *International Conference on Smart Blockchain* (pp. 167-177). Springer, Cham.

Caro, M. P., Ali, M. S., Vecchio, M., & Giaffreda, R. (2018, May). Blockchain-based traceability in Agri-Food supply chain management: A practical implementation. In *2018 IoT Vertical and Topical Summit on Agriculture-Tuscany (IOT Tuscany)* (pp. 1-4). IEEE.

Casino, F., Kanakaris, V., Dasaklis, T. K., Moschuris, S., Stachtiaris, S., Pagoni, M., & Rachaniotis, N. P. (2021). Blockchain-based food supply chain traceability: a case study in the dairy sector. *International Journal of Production Research*, *59*(19), 5758-5770.

Tse, D., Zhang, B., Yang, Y., Cheng, C., & Mu, H. (2017, December). Blockchain application in food supply information security. In *2017 IEEE international conference on industrial engineering and engineering management (IEEM)* (pp. 1357-1361). IEEE.

Pradana, I. G. M. T., Djatna, T., & Hermadi, I. (2020, October). Blockchain Modeling for Traceability Information System in Supply Chain of Coffee Agroindustry. In *2020 International Conference on Advanced Computer Science and Information Systems (ICACSIS)* (pp. 217-224). IEEE.

Trollman, H., Garcia-Garcia, G., Jagtap, S., & Trollman, F. (2022). Blockchain for Ecologically Embedded Coffee Supply Chains. *Logistics*, *6*(3), 43.

Shojaei, A. (2019). Exploring applications of blockchain technology in the construction industry. *Edited by Didem Ozevin, Hossein Ataei, Mehdi Modares, Asli Pelin Gurgun, Siamak Yazdani, and Amarjit Singh. Proceedings of International Structural Engineering and Construction, 6.*

Kim, K., Lee, G., & Kim, S. (2020). A study on the application of blockchain technology in the construction industry. *KSCE journal of civil engineering*, *24*(9), 2561-2571.

Yang, R., Wakefield, R., Lyu, S., Jayasuriya, S., Han, F., Yi, X., ... & Chen, S. (2020). Public and private blockchain in construction business process and information integration. *Automation in construction*, *118*, 103276.

Scott, D. J., Broyd, T., & Ma, L. (2021). Exploratory literature review of blockchain in the construction industry. *Automation in construction*, *132*, 103914.

Elghaish, F., Hosseini, M. R., Matarneh, S., Talebi, S., Wu, S., Martek, I., ... & Ghodrati, N. (2021). Blockchain and the 'Internet of Things' for the construction industry: research trends and opportunities. *Automation in construction*, *132*, 103942.

Huang, S., Wang, G., Yan, Y., & Fang, X. (2020). Blockchain-based data management for digital twin of product. *Journal of Manufacturing Systems*, *54*, 361-371.

Aditya, U. S., Singh, R., Singh, P. K., & Kalla, A. (2021). A Survey on Blockchain in Robotics: Issues, Opportunities, Challenges and Future Directions. *Journal of Network and Computer Applications*, *196*, 103245.

Lopes, V., & Alexandre, L. A. (2018). An overview of blockchain integration with robotics and artificial intelligence. *arXiv preprint arXiv:1810.00329*.

Malsa, N., Vyas, V., Gautam, J., Shaw, R. N., & Ghosh, A. (2021). Framework and Smart Contract for Blockchain Enabled Certificate Verification System Using Robotics. In *Machine Learning for Robotics Applications* (pp. 125-138). Springer, Singapore.

Ferrer, E. C., Jiménez, E., Lopez-Presa, J. L., & Martín-Rueda, J. (2021). Following leaders in byzantine multirobot systems by using blockchain technology. *IEEE Transactions on Robotics*, *38*(2), 1101-1117.

Liu, Z., & Li, Z. (2020). A blockchain-based framework of cross-border e-commerce supply chain. *International Journal of Information Management*, *52*, 102059.

Kumar, G., Saha, R., Buchanan, W. J., Geetha, G., Thomas, R., Rai, M. K., ... & Alazab, M. (2020). Decentralized accessibility of e-commerce products through blockchain technology. *Sustainable Cities and Society*, *62*, 102361.

Treiblmaier, H., & Sillaber, C. (2021). The impact of blockchain on e-commerce: a framework for salient research topics. *Electronic Commerce Research and Applications*, *48*, 101054.

Deepa, N., Pham, Q. V., Nguyen, D. C., Bhattacharya, S., Prabadevi, B., Gadekallu, T. R., ... & Pathirana, P. N. (2022). A survey on blockchain for big data: approaches, opportunities, and future directions. *Future Generation Computer Systems*.

Karafiloski, E., & Mishev, A. (2017, July). Blockchain solutions for big data challenges: A literature review. In *IEEE EUROCON 2017-17th International Conference on Smart Technologies* (pp. 763-768). IEEE.

Liu, P. T. S. (2016, November). Medical record system using blockchain, big data and tokenization. In *International conference on information and communications security* (pp. 254-261). Springer, Cham.

Ekramifard, A., Amintoosi, H., Seno, A. H., Dehghantanha, A., & Parizi, R. M. (2020). A systematic literature review of integration of blockchain and artificial intelligence. *Blockchain cybersecurity, trust and privacy*, 147-160.

Zheng, Z., Dai, H. N., & Wu, J. (2019). Blockchain intelligence: When blockchain meets artificial intelligence. *arXiv preprint arXiv:1912.06485*.

Sakız, B., & Gencer, A. H. (2021). Blockchain Beyond Cryptocurrency: Non-Fungible Tokens. *ON EURASIAN ECONOMIES 2021*, 144.

Rehman, W., e Zainab, H., Imran, J., & Bawany, N. Z. (2021, December). Nfts: Applications and challenges. In *2021 22nd International Arab Conference on Information Technology (ACIT)* (pp. 1-7). IEEE.

Raman, R., & Raj, B. E. (2021). The World of NFTs (Non-Fungible Tokens): The Future of Blockchain and Asset Ownership. In *Enabling Blockchain Technology for Secure Networking and Communications* (pp. 89-108). IGI Global.

Yeasmin, S., & Baig, A. (2019, November). Unblocking the potential of blockchain. In *2019 International Conference on Electrical and Computing Technologies and Applications (ICECTA)* (pp. 1-5). IEEE.

Kashevarova, N. A., & Starikova, I. S. (2022). Non-fungible token: a promising digital tool for business. *Вестник университета*, 45.

Sestino, A., Guido, G., & Peluso, A. M. (2022). Non-Fungible Tokens (NFTs). *Springer Books*.

Yilmaz, M., Hacaloğlu, T., & Clarke, P. (2022). Examining the use of non-fungible tokens (NFTs) as a trading mechanism for the metaverse. In *European Conference on Software Process Improvement* (pp. 18-28). Springer, Cham.

Colicev, A. (2022). How can non-fungible tokens bring value to brands. *International Journal of Research in Marketing*.

Joy, A., Zhu, Y., Peña, C., & Brouard, M. (2022). Digital future of luxury brands: Metaverse, digital fashion, and non-fungible tokens. *Strategic Change*, *31*(3), 337-343.

Fairfield, J. A. (2022). Tokenized: The law of non-fungible tokens and unique digital property. *Ind. LJ*, *97*, 1261.

Popescu, A. D. (2021). Non-Fungible Tokens (NFT)–Innovation beyond the craze. In *5th International Conference on Innovation in Business, Economics and Marketing Research.*
Chiacchio, F., D'Urso, D., Oliveri, L. M., Spitaleri, A., Spampinato, C., & Giordano, D. (2022). A Non-Fungible Token Solution for the Track and Trace of Pharmaceutical Supply Chain. *Applied Sciences*, *12*(8), 4019.

Onete, C. B., Năstase, I. A., Felea, M., & Dina, R. The Potential of Non-Fungible Tokens (NFTs) in Higher Education as Perceived by Romanian Students.

Fowler, A., & Pirker, J. (2021, October). Tokenfication-The potential of non-fungible tokens (NFT) for game development. In *Extended Abstracts of the 2021 Annual Symposium on Computer-Human Interaction in Play* (pp. 152-157).

Dowling, M. (2022). Fertile LAND: Pricing non-fungible tokens. *Finance Research Letters*, *44*, 102096.

Colicev, A. (2022). How can non-fungible tokens bring value to brands. *International Journal of Research in Marketing.*

Serrano, W. (2022, March). Real estate tokenisation via non fungible tokens. In *The 2022 4th International Conference on Blockchain Technology* (pp. 81-87).

Regner, F., Schweizer, A., & Urbach, N. (2022). Utilizing Non-fungible Tokens for an Event Ticketing System. In *Blockchains and the Token Economy* (pp. 315-343). Palgrave Macmillan, Cham.

Wang, A., Gao, Z., Lee, L. H., Braud, T., & Hui, P. (2022). Decentralized, not Dehumanized in the Metaverse: Bringing Utility to NFTs through Multimodal Interaction. *arXiv preprint arXiv:2206.03737.*

Park, A., Kietzmann, J., Pitt, L., & Dabirian, A. (2022). The evolution of nonfungible tokens: Complexity and novelty of NFT use-cases. *IT Professional*, *24*(1), 9-14.

Pfeiffer, A., Denk, N., Wernbacher, T., Bezzina, S., Vella, V., & Dingli, A. (2022, June). Two novel use-cases for non-fungible tokens (NFTs). In *European Conference on Cyber Warfare and Security* (Vol. 21, No. 1, pp. 214-221).

Kaczynski, S., & Kominers, S. D. (2021). How NFTs create value. *Harvard Business Review, 10.*

Christodoulou, K., Katelaris, L., Themistocleous, M., Christodoulou, P., & Iosif, E. (2022). NFTs and the metaverse revolution: research perspectives and open challenges. *Blockchains and the Token Economy*, 139-178.

Regner, F., Urbach, N., & Schweizer, A. (2019). NFTs in practice–non-fungible tokens as core component of a blockchain-based event ticketing application.

Uribe, D., & Waters, G. (2020). Privacy laws, genomic data and non-fungible tokens. *The Journal of The British Blockchain Association*, 13164.

Musamih, A., Salah, K., Jayaraman, R., Yaqoob, I., Puthal, D., & Ellahham, S. (2022). NFTs in healthcare: Vision, opportunities, and challenges. *IEEE Consumer Electronics Magazine.*

Jones, N. (2021). How scientists are embracing NFTs. *Nature*, *594*(7864), 481-482.

Musamih, A., Dirir, A., Yaqoob, I., Salah, K., Jayaraman, R., & Puthal, D. (2022). NFTs in Smart Cities: Vision, Applications, and Challenges. *IEEE Consumer Electronics Magazine.*

Sparkes, M. (2021). What is a metaverse.

Dionisio, J. D. N., III, W. G. B., & Gilbert, R. (2013). 3D virtual worlds and the metaverse: Current status and future possibilities. *ACM Computing Surveys (CSUR)*, *45*(3), 1-38.

Wang, Y., Su, Z., Zhang, N., Xing, R., Liu, D., Luan, T. H., & Shen, X. (2022). A survey on metaverse: Fundamentals, security, and privacy. *IEEE Communications Surveys & Tutorials.*

Dwivedi, Y. K., Hughes, L., Baabdullah, A. M., Ribeiro-Navarrete, S., Giannakis, M., Al-Debei, M. M., ... & Wamba, S. F. (2022). Metaverse beyond the hype: Multidisciplinary perspectives on emerging challenges, opportunities, and agenda for research, practice and policy. *International Journal of Information Management*, *66*, 102542.

Yang, Q., Zhao, Y., Huang, H., Xiong, Z., Kang, J., & Zheng, Z. (2022). Fusing blockchain and AI with metaverse: A survey. *IEEE Open Journal of the Computer Society*, *3*, 122-136.

Duan, H., Li, J., Fan, S., Lin, Z., Wu, X., & Cai, W. (2021, October). Metaverse for social good: A university campus prototype. In *Proceedings of the 29th ACM International Conference on Multimedia* (pp. 153-161).

Park, S. M., & Kim, Y. G. (2022). A Metaverse: Taxonomy, components, applications, and open challenges. *Ieee Access*, *10*, 4209-4251.

Ning, H., Wang, H., Lin, Y., Wang, W., Dhelim, S., Farha, F., ... & Daneshmand, M. (2021). A Survey on Metaverse: the State-of-the-art, Technologies, Applications, and Challenges. *arXiv preprint arXiv:2111.09673*.

Kye, B., Han, N., Kim, E., Park, Y., & Jo, S. (2021). Educational applications of metaverse: possibilities and limitations. *Journal of Educational Evaluation for Health Professions*, *18*.

Kraus, S., Kanbach, D. K., Krysta, P. M., Steinhoff, M. M., & Tomini, N. (2022). Facebook and the creation of the metaverse: radical business model innovation or incremental transformation?. *International Journal of Entrepreneurial Behavior & Research*.

Gadekallu, T. R., Huynh-The, T., Wang, W., Yenduri, G., Ranaweera, P., Pham, Q. V., ... & Liyanage, M. (2022). Blockchain for the Metaverse: A Review. *arXiv preprint arXiv:2203.09738*.

Belk, R., Humayun, M., & Brouard, M. (2022). Money, possessions, and ownership in the Metaverse: NFTs, cryptocurrencies, Web3 and Wild Markets. *Journal of Business Research*, *153*, 198-205.

Kliestik, T., Novak, A., & Lăzăroiu, G. (2022). Live Shopping in the Metaverse: Visual and Spatial Analytics, Cognitive Artificial Intelligence Techniques and Algorithms, and Immersive Digital Simulations. *Linguistic & Philosophical Investigations*.

Hollensen, S., Kotler, P., & Opresnik, M. O. (2022). Metaverse–the new marketing universe. *Journal of Business Strategy*.
Vidal-Tomás, D. (2022). The new crypto niche: NFTs, play-to-earn, and metaverse tokens. *Finance Research Letters*, 102742.

Kerdvibulvech, C. (2022). Exploring the Impacts of COVID-19 on Digital and Metaverse Games. In *International Conference on Human-Computer Interaction* (pp. 561-565). Springer, Cham.

Hollensen, S., Kotler, P., & Opresnik, M. O. (2022). Metaverse–the new marketing universe. *Journal of Business Strategy*.

Al Sadawi, A., Madani, B., Saboor, S., Ndiaye, M., & Abu-Lebdeh, G. (2021). A comprehensive hierarchical blockchain system for carbon emission trading utilizing blockchain of things and smart contract. *Technological Forecasting and Social Change*, *173*, 121124.

Patel, D., Britto, B., Sharma, S., Gaikwad, K., Dusing, Y., & Gupta, M. (2020, February). Carbon credits on blockchain. In *2020 International Conference on Innovative Trends in Information Technology (ICITIIT)* (pp. 1-5). IEEE.

Wang, M., Wang, B., & Abareshi, A. (2020). Blockchain technology and its role in enhancing supply chain integration capability and reducing carbon emission: A conceptual framework. *Sustainability*, *12*(24), 10550.

Al-Saqaf, W., & Seidler, N. (2017). Blockchain technology for social impact: opportunities and challenges ahead. *Journal of Cyber Policy*, *2*(3), 338-354.

Szakonyi, A., Chellasamy, H., Vassilakos, A., & Dawson, M. (2021). Using Technologies to Uncover Patterns in Human Trafficking. In *ITNG 2021 18th International Conference on Information Technology-New Generations* (pp. 497-502). Springer, Cham.

Montasari, R., & Jahankhani, H. (2021). The Application of Technology in Combating Human Trafficking. In *Cybersecurity, Privacy and Freedom Protection in the Connected World* (pp. 149-156). Springer, Cham.

Ferrag, M. A., Shu, L., Yang, X., Derhab, A., & Maglaras, L. (2020). Security and privacy for green IoT-based agriculture: Review, blockchain solutions, and challenges. *IEEE access*, *8*, 32031-32053.

Lin, J., Shen, Z., Zhang, A., & Chai, Y. (2018, July). Blockchain and IoT based food traceability for smart agriculture. In *Proceedings of the 3rd international conference on crowd science and engineering* (pp. 1-6).

Torky, M., & Hassanein, A. E. (2020). Integrating blockchain and the internet of things in precision agriculture: Analysis, opportunities, and challenges. *Computers and Electronics in Agriculture*, *178*, 105476.

Holland, M., Stjepandić, J., & Nigischer, C. (2018, June). Intellectual property protection of 3D print supply chain with blockchain technology. In *2018 IEEE International conference on engineering, technology and innovation (ICE/ITMC)* (pp. 1-8). IEEE.

Engelmann, F., Holland, M., Nigischer, C., & Stjepandić, J. (2018). Intellectual property protection and licensing of 3d print with blockchain technology. *Transdisciplinary Engineering Methods for Social Innovation of Industry*, *4*(2), 103-112.

Wang, J., Wang, S., Guo, J., Du, Y., Cheng, S., & Li, X. (2019). A summary of research on blockchain in the field of intellectual property. *Procedia computer science*, *147*, 191-197.

Yu, S. (2021). Application of blockchain-based sports health data collection system in the development of sports industry. *Mobile Information Systems*, *2021*.

Lv, C., Wang, Y., & Jin, C. (2022). The possibility of sports industry business model innovation based on blockchain technology: Evaluation of the innovation efficiency of listed sports companies. *PloS one*, *17*(1), e0262035.

Shan, Y., & Mai, Y. (2020). Research on sports fitness management based on blockchain and Internet of Things. *EURASIP Journal on Wireless Communications and Networking*, *2020*(1), 1-13.

Abeyratne, R. (2020). Blockchain and aviation. In *Aviation in the Digital Age* (pp. 109-120). Springer, Cham.

Bouffault, O., Burchardi, K., Bender, J. P., Gopalakrishna, D., Gauche, V., & Paboudjian, C. (2019). WHAT COULD BLOCK-CHAIN DO FOR AIRLINES?. *BCG Analysis*.

Yadav, J. K., Verma, D. C., Jangirala, S., Srivastava, S. K., & Aman, M. N. (2022). Blockchain for aviation industry: Applications and used cases. In *ICT Analysis and Applications* (pp. 475-486). Springer, Singapore.

Salah, D., Ahmed, M. H., & Eldahshan, K. (2020). Blockchain applications in human resources management: Opportunities and challenges. *Proceedings of the Evaluation and Assessment in Software Engineering*, 383-389.

Yi, C. S. S., Yung, E., Fong, C., & Tripathi, S. (2020). Benefits and use of blockchain technology to human resources management: a critical review. *International Journal of Human Resource Studies*, *10*(2), 131140-131140.

Flecha-Barrio, M. D., Palomo, J., Figueroa-Domecq, C., & Segovia-Perez, M. (2020). Blockchain implementation in hotel management. In *Information and Communication Technologies in Tourism 2020* (pp. 255-266). Springer, Cham.

Dogru, T., Mody, M., & Leonardi, C. (2018). Blockchain technology & its implications for the hospitality industry. *Boston University*.

Lokre, S. S., Naman, V., Priya, S., & Panda, S. K. (2021). Gun tracking system using blockchain technology. In *Blockchain Technology: Applications and Challenges* (pp. 285-300). Springer, Cham.

Klein, R. (2020). CAN BLOCKCHAIN HELP WITH GUN REGISTRIES?.

Ahmad, R. W., Hasan, H., Yaqoob, I., Salah, K., Jayaraman, R., & Omar, M. (2021). Blockchain for aerospace and defense: Opportunities and open research challenges. *Computers & Industrial Engineering*, *151*, 106982.

Kuzmin, A., & Znak, E. (2018, July). Blockchain-base structures for a secure and operate network of semi-autonomous unmanned aerial vehicles. In *2018 IEEE International conference on service operations and logistics, and informatics (SOLI)* (pp. 32-37). IEEE.

Ossamah, A. (2020, June). Blockchain as a solution to drone cybersecurity. In *2020 IEEE 6th World Forum on Internet of Things (WF-IoT)* (pp. 1-9). IEEE.

Kumar, M. S., Vimal, S., Jhanjhi, N. Z., Dhanabalan, S. S., & Alhumyani, H. A. (2021). Blockchain based peer to peer communication in autonomous drone operation. *Energy Reports*, *7*, 7925-7939.

Krishnapriya, S., & Sarath, G. (2020). Securing land registration using blockchain. *Procedia Computer Science*, *171*, 1708-1715.

Khalid, M. I., Iqbal, J., Alturki, A., Hussain, S., Alabrah, A., & Ullah, S. S. (2022). Blockchain-Based Land Registration System: A Conceptual Framework. *Applied Bionics and Biomechanics*, *2022*.

Thakur, V., Doja, M. N., Dwivedi, Y. K., Ahmad, T., & Khadanga, G. (2020). Land records on blockchain for implementation of land titling in India. *International Journal of Information Management*, *52*, 101940.

Labrador, M., & Hou, W. (2019, August). Implementing blockchain technology in the internet of vehicle (IoV). In *2019 International Conference on Intelligent Computing and its Emerging Applications (ICEA)* (pp. 5-10). IEEE.

Konashevych, O. (2020). General concept of real estate tokenization on blockchain. *European Property Law Journal*, *9*(1), 21-66.

Gupta, A., Rathod, J., Patel, D., Bothra, J., Shanbhag, S., & Bhalerao, T. (2020, October). Tokenization of Real Estate Using Blockchain Technology. In

International Conference on Applied Cryptography and Network Security (pp. 77-90). Springer, Cham.

Tian, Y., Zhang, Y., Minchin, R. E., Asutosh, A., & Kan, C. (2020, November). An innovative infrastructure financing instrument: Blockchain-based tokenization. In *Construction Research Congress* (pp. 731-740).

Saari, A., Vimpari, J., & Junnila, S. (2022). Blockchain in real estate: Recent developments and empirical applications. *Land Use Policy*, *121*, 106334.

Bogucharskov, A. V., Pokamestov, I. E., Adamova, K. R., & Tropina, Z. N. (2018). Adoption of blockchain technology in trade finance process. *Journal of Reviews on Global Economics*, *7*, 510-515.

Nurmukhametov, R. K., Stepanov, P. D., & Novikova, T. R. (2018). Blockchain technology and its application in trade finance. *Financial analytics: problems and solutions*, *11*(2), 179-190.

Gupta, V. C., Agarwal, M., & Mishra, A. (2019). When trade finance meets Blockchain technology. *International Journal of Innovative Science and Research Technology*, *4*(10), 342-346.

Raikwar, M., Mazumdar, S., Ruj, S., Gupta, S. S., Chattopadhyay, A., & Lam, K. Y. (2018, February). A blockchain framework for insurance processes. In *2018 9th IFIP International Conference on New Technologies, Mobility and Security (NTMS)* (pp. 1-4). IEEE.

Tarr, J. A. (2018). Distributed ledger technology, blockchain and insurance: Opportunities, risks and challenges. *Insurance Law Journal*, *29*(3), 254-268.

Kalsgonda, V. P., & Kulkarni, R. V. (2020). Applications of blockchain in insurance industry: a review. *PIMT Journal of Res*, *12*(4), 1-3.

Sharma, P., & Chandra, R. (2022). Significance of Blockchain in Banking and Insurance. In *Applications, Challenges, and Opportunities of Blockchain Technology in Banking and Insurance* (pp. 99-127). IGI Global.

Okazaki, Y. (2018). Unveiling the potential of blockchain for customs. *WCO Research Paper*, *45*, 1-24.

McDaniel, C. A., & Norberg, H. C. (2019). Can blockchain technology facilitate international trade?. *Mercatus Research Paper*.

Harris, C. G. (2022). Towards a Blockchain Solution for Customs Duty-Related Fraud. In *International Conference on Database Systems for Advanced Applications* (pp. 120-134). Springer, Cham.

Liu, Z., & Li, Z. (2020). A blockchain-based framework of cross-border e-commerce supply chain. *International Journal of Information Management, 52*, 102059.

Treiblmaier, H., & Sillaber, C. (2021). The impact of blockchain on e-commerce: a framework for salient research topics. *Electronic Commerce Research and Applications*, *48*, 101054.

Kumar, G., Saha, R., Buchanan, W. J., Geetha, G., Thomas, R., Rai, M. K., ... & Alazab, M. (2020). Decentralized accessibility of e-commerce products through blockchain technology. *Sustainable Cities and Society*, *62*, 102361.

Jiang, J., & Chen, J. (2021). Framework of blockchain-supported e-commerce platform for small and medium enterprises. *Sustainability*, *13*(15), 8158.

Du, Y., Cao, J., Yin, J., & Song, S. (2020). An overview of blockchain-based swarm robotics system. *Artificial Intelligence in China*, 353-360.

Strobel, V., Castelló Ferrer, E., & Dorigo, M. (2018). Managing byzantine robots via blockchain technology in a swarm robotics collective decision making scenario.

Singh, P. K., Singh, R., Nandi, S. K., Ghafoor, K. Z., Rawat, D. B., & Nandi, S. (2020). An efficient blockchain-based approach for cooperative decision making in swarm robotics. *Internet Technology Letters*, *3*(1), e140.

Melnik, E. V., Klimenko, A. B., & Ivanov, D. Y. (2019, October). A blockchain-based technique for making swarm robots distributed decision. In *Journal of Physics: Conference Series* (Vol. 1333, No. 5, p. 052013). IOP Publishing.

Maslove, D. M., Klein, J., Brohman, K., & Martin, P. (2018). Using blockchain technology to manage clinical trials data: a proof-of-concept study. *JMIR medical informatics*, *6*(4), e11949.

Omar, I. A., Jayaraman, R., Salah, K., Yaqoob, I., & Ellahham, S. (2021). Applications of blockchain technology in clinical trials: review and open challenges. *Arabian Journal for Science and Engineering*, *46*(4), 3001-3015.

Nugent, T., Upton, D., & Cimpoesu, M. (2016). Improving data transparency in clinical trials using blockchain smart contracts. *F1000Research*, *5*.

Wong, D. R., Bhattacharya, S., & Butte, A. J. (2019). Prototype of running clinical trials in an untrustworthy environment using blockchain. *Nature communications*, *10*(1), 1-8.

Sadri, S., Shahzad, A., & Zhang, K. (2021, February). Blockchain traceability in healthcare: Blood donation supply chain. In *2021 23rd International Conference on Advanced Communication Technology (ICACT)* (pp. 119-126). IEEE.

Lakshminarayanan, S., Kumar, P. N., & Dhanya, N. M. (2020, February). Implementation of blockchain-based blood donation framework. In *International Conference on Computational Intelligence in Data Science* (pp. 276-290). Springer, Cham.

Çağlıyangil, M., Erdem, S., & Özdağoğlu, G. (2020). A blockchain based framework for blood distribution. In *Digital Business Strategies in Blockchain Ecosystems* (pp. 63-82). Springer, Cham.

Henriquez, R., Bittan, N., & Tulbassiyev, K. (2019). Blockchain and business model innovation: Designing a P2P mortgage lending system. *Netanel and Tulbassiyev, Kanat, Blockchain and Business Model Innovation: Designing a P2P Mortgage Lending System (April 14, 2019).*

Schepman, S. (2020). a review of use cases for blockchain in the mortgage and real estate industries.

Zhang, Q., Zhu, J., & Wang, Y. (2020, August). Trustworthy dynamic target detection and automatic monitor scheme for mortgage loan with blockchain-based smart contract. In *International Conference on Blockchain and Trustworthy Systems* (pp. 415-427). Springer, Singapore.

Kishor Singh, K. (2022). Application of Blockchain Smart Contracts in E-Commerce and Government. *arXiv e-prints*, arXiv-2208.

Zeng, X., Hao, N., Zheng, J., & Xu, X. (2019). A consortium blockchain paradigm on hyperledger-based peer-to-peer lending system. *China Communications*, *16*(8), 38-50.

Manda, V. K., & Yamijala, S. P. (2019). Peer-to-peer lending using blockchain. *International Journal Of Advance Research And Innovative Ideas In Education*, *6*, 61-66.

Miah, M. (2020). Blockchain technology in peer-to-peer elearning: Opportunities and challenges. In *Proceedings of the EDSIG Conference ISSN* (Vol. 2473, p. 4901).

Ulieru, M. (2016). Blockchain 2.0 and beyond: Adhocracies. In *Banking beyond banks and money* (pp. 297-303). Springer, Cham.

Arora, N., & Kaur, P. D. (2021, September). Blockchain Empowered Framework for Peer to Peer Lending. In *2021 9th International Conference on Reliability, Infocom Technologies and Optimization (Trends and Future Directions)(ICRITO)* (pp. 1-5). IEEE.

Ante, L., Sandner, P., & Fiedler, I. (2018). Blockchain-based ICOs: Pure hype or the dawn of a new era of startup financing?. *Journal of Risk and Financial Management*, *11*(4), 80.

Martino, P., Bellavitis, C., & DaSilva, C. M. (2019). Blockchain and initial coin offerings (ICOs): A new way of crowdfunding. *Available at SSRN 3414238.*

Arnold, L., Brennecke, M., Camus, P., Fridgen, G., Guggenberger, T., Radszuwill, S., ... & Urbach, N. (2019). Blockchain and initial coin offerings: blockchain's implications for crowdfunding. In *Business transformation through blockchain* (pp. 233-272). Palgrave Macmillan, Cham.

Joo, M. H., Nishikawa, Y., & Dandapani, K. (2019). ICOs, the next generation of IPOs. *Managerial Finance.*

Hartmann, F., Grottolo, G., Wang, X., & Lunesu, M. I. (2019, February). Alternative fundraising: success factors for blockchain-based vs. conventional crowdfunding. In *2019 IEEE international workshop on blockchain oriented software engineering (IWBOSE)* (pp. 38-43). IEEE.

Baber, H. (2020). Blockchain-based crowdfunding. In *Blockchain Technology for Industry 4.0* (pp. 117-130). Springer, Singapore.

Muneeza, A., Arshad, N. A., & Arifin, A. T. (2018). The application of blockchain technology in crowdfunding: towards financial inclusion via technology. *International journal of management and applied research*, *5*(2), 82-98.

Campino, J., Brochado, A., & Rosa, Á. (2022). Initial coin offerings (ICOs): Why do they succeed?. *Financial Innovation*, *8*(1), 1-35.

Collomb, A., De Filippi, P., & Sok, K. (2018). From IPOs to ICOs: the impact of blockchain technology on financial regulation. *Available at SSRN 3185347.*

Made in United States
Troutdale, OR
[illegible]

Made in United States
Troutdale, OR
01/26/2025